Consuming Glory

Consuming Glory

A Classical Defense of Divine–Human Relationality Against Open Theism

GANNON MURPHY

Wipf & Stock
PUBLISHERS
Eugene, Oregon

CONSUMING GLORY
A Classical Defense of Divine-Human Relationality Against Open Theism

Copyright © 2006 Gannon Murphy. All rights reserved. Except for brief quotations in critical publications or reviews, no part of this book may be reproduced in any manner without prior written permission from the publisher. Write: Permissions, Wipf & Stock Publishers, 199 W. 8th Ave., Suite 3, Eugene, OR 97401.

ISBN: 1-59752-843-9

Cataloging-in-Publication Data:

Murphy, Gannon
  Consuming glory : a classical defense of divine-human relationality against open theism / Gannon Murphy

xiv + 252p.; 20 cm.

Includes bibliography

ISBN: 1-59752-843-9

1. Open theism. 2. God—Biblical teaching. I. Title.
BT131 .M87 2006

Manufactured in the U.S.A.

All rights reserved
Printed in the United States of America

05 06 07 08 09 5 4 3 2 1

Unless otherwise indicated, Scripture quotations are taken from the New American Standard Bible®, Copyright © 1960, 1962, 1963, 1968, 1971, 1972, 1973, 1975, 1977, 1995 by The Lockman Foundation.

To Amy,
May God perpetually delight in Himself,
in you.

Contents

Foreword / ix

Preface / xi

Acknowledgments / xiii

1. Introduction / 1
2. Clark H. Pinnock: A Brief Biography / 24
3. Pinnock's Argument / 46
4. Hellenization, Libertarianism, and the Metaphysics of Love / 84
5. Classicalism, Compatibilism, and Trinitarian Glory / 139
6. Toward a Reformed Reconstruction of Divine-Human Relationality / 194
7. Summary and Conclusion / 236

Bibliography / 241

Foreword

THE READER has in her hands a well written and researched volume that expresses appreciation for my work in theology while, at the same time, defending some different conclusions. I do not think that the book will create new open theists—it was not written for that purpose. More likely, it will confirm the opinion of those who already consider it unsound. Why then am I writing the foreword of such a book which critiques me heavily? One reason is that Gannon Murphy lays out the evidence of what I have written in detail and in accuracy such that it will help to keep certain important debates alive. He supplies an exposition of my work which will introduce it to students and enable them to make progress in understanding with the help that he supplies.

A second reason for my writing this foreword is that I like the way in which Gannon practices the dialogical virtues. For example, he shows honesty and fairness, sympathy and friendliness, respect and a willingness to learn. It is a pleasure to run into such a person even if he plays for "the other team." Gannon does not go all out to win the debate—he also cares about how such discussions are best carried on. He is not mean-spirited, he does not impute guilt by association, and he does not practice name calling. Where he sees a strength in my position, he rejoices in it and where he detects weakness, he points it out kindly. He does not go in for the kill when he detects vulnerability. He also honors me by taking me seriously as a scholar. The issues which we are discussing are (we think) important ones and we want to help others get up to speed concerning them. Neither one of us thinks that he has "the whole truth and nothing but the truth." Both of us are aware that rhetorical weapons can be turned back on ourselves. I appreciate Gannon's observance of an admirable code of conduct. Thinking back to the crisis in the Evangelical Theological Society in 2003, which he describes in detail, the thing that saved the day regarding the challenge to my membership in the society was the unexpected appearance of grace that descended out of nowhere and sucked the poison from the atmosphere. It ended with many hugs between Roger [Nicole] and me.

It is not my place in a foreword to go after weaknesses, real or imagined, in the book (though I think that Gannon might have allowed it, but that it would not be right.) What might be appropriate and right, however, and might be constructive would be if I raised a single point concerning the love of God, a topic which surfaces at the very end of the book. Gannon is hesitant to grant priority to love as the crown jewel in our thinking about God. He thinks that no attribute, not even love, is central. He wants to safeguard God's right to love or not to love. He reads the Bible to be saying that God is free to save or to damn, to show love or not to show love, as he chooses, even if (it seems) arbitrary or whimsical. It is clear that this idea bothers him and I think it should bother him. St. John says that "God is love, and those who abide in love abide in God, and God abides in them" (John 4:16). This sounds as if love belongs to the essence of God and is more than an attribute that God possesses. The truth of theōsis and our future participation in the triune glory—is it not participation in everlasting love? We worship, do we not, the triune God, a community of three persons, who is essentially a God of self-giving love. Love is not just an attribute of God's but God's very nature and we should understand every attribute of God in light of his love. Omnipotence is the power of love. Immutability is the steadfastness of love. Omniscience is the personal knowing of love. Omnipresence is the ever presence of God to heal. Holiness is love as a purgative fire which does not yield to evil. Wisdom includes the foolishness of the cross. I wonder if [Gannon's] systematic vision quite captures the truth which the gospel holds out to us.

Clark H. Pinnock
Professor Emeritus of Theology
McMaster Divinity College
June 30, 2006

Preface

This book is a revision of my doctoral thesis presented at the University of Wales, Lampeter on March 21, 2006. The original title was, "A Critical Analysis of the Openness Theology of Clark H. Pinnock Toward a Reformed Reconstruction of Divine-Human Relationality."

I am pleased at the opportunity afforded me by Wipf and Stock to present the thesis in book form to a larger reading audience. My sincere hope is that God might use this work as one small primordial brick in a larger wall to be built by contemporary classical and Reformed theologians in a revived attempt to better explore the rich theological terrain of Divine-human relationality.

Though I am fundamentally Reformed in my theological commitments, the reader will quickly see—especially from chapters four and forward—that I am not averse to appropriating concepts from other Christian theological traditions in formulating both my doctrines of God and man. However, in so doing, I maintain throughout this work that these various appropriations are nevertheless consistent with the Reformed (and classical) tradition.

Perhaps the most controversial element in these appropriations is my use of Eastern theotic soteriology in chapter six which forms much of the basis for my formulation of Divine-human relationality. *Theōsis* is not a popular concept in classical Western theology, much less in Reformed. This is not surprising, of course, considering the somewhat well known problem of works-righteousness ecclesiology and spiritual praxis that has often attended theōsis throughout church history; not to mention the dangers of adopting an ill-formed deification concept that glorifies and exults in the powers of man rather than God. I ask the reader, however, especially those of a Reformed persuasion, to be patient and discerning in this section and to pay careful attention to the manner in which I both define and adopt the theotic concept. I modify the doctrine somewhat to make it consistent with classical Western theology and, ultimately, even argue that it is actually better suited in the Western Reformed context than it is in that originally forged by its Eastern forebears.

Preface

I recognize, of course, that this endeavor will be found equally incommodious among some Eastern Orthodox as it will Reformed or classical folks. Please know, however, that my intention is to not *destruct*, but to *construct*; to build up, not to tear down. In the end, what we must all seek is the Truth of God, not our own traditions and we must not cut ourselves off from the theological pearls offered by Christian brothers and sisters in differing traditions. We are each to be a stalwart *verum peto* as we strive to better understand the marvelous gift of our union with Christ.

Nevertheless, if I am wrong in my formulations, or in any part, I submit myself to the correction of my peers and ask God's wisdom and humility to change fittingly. I welcome the input of the reader.

Soli Deo Gloria
Gannon Murphy
Minneapolis, Minnesota
June 19, 2006

Acknowledgements

THE TIME and effort poured into this work over the course of several years would have been manifestly fruitless were it not for the tremendous help, encouragement, and support of numerous people to whom I am inestimably grateful. Such support has enabled me to sense the love and grace of God in a tangible way.

My thanks and love to mom and dad who not only originally funded this research as part of my doctoral work, but always encouraged me throughout. Your kinds words, feedback on my work, and interest in my studies has greatly blessed me.

To Dr. Simon Oliver of the University of Wales, Lampeter, I owe an especial debt of gratitude for a solid year of intense, constructive attention to my research. Several revisions and periods of revisiting various issues following Dr. Oliver's comments have made this work not only stronger, but significantly more satisfying and engaging. I could not have hoped for a better doctoral supervisor.

I am also especially grateful to Dr. Pinnock who gave liberally of his time to me in both several personal meetings, as well as in a continued written correspondence through which he provided feedback on this work and encouraged me to deal with the very difficult issues that inevitably attach to my own theological model. Dr. Pinnock's work, attention, and kindness have shaped both my theology and life for the better.

My thanks to Dr. Eryl Davies of the Evangelical Theological College of Wales who both helped me to hone in on this particular subject for study and then provided careful analyses of the early stages of the work to ensure that I was off on the right track. Thanks also to Drs. Kathy Ehrensperger and William Campbell at the University of Wales, Lampeter for helpful comments on several of the initial draft chapters.

Dr. Stephen Holmes of the University of St. Andrews, and Dr. Mark Cartledge of the University of Wales, Lampeter, my doctoral examiners, also provided much important feedback, which led to more important revisions and additions—especially as it relates to the centrality of *glory* in my doctrine of God.

Acknowledgements

    Lastly, and most importantly, my love and appreciation to Amy, my beautiful wife whom God set apart from eternity that we may share this life together, growing in our love for our mutual Savior, one another, and the three beautiful children He has blessed us with. You are more than I ever could have dreamed for. May God forever delight Himself, *in you.*

1

Introduction

THE EVENTS of Friday evening, November 21, 2002, will undoubtedly remain indelibly etched in the minds of hundreds of North American Evangelical scholars for decades to come. The fifty-fourth annual meeting of the Evangelical Theology Society (ETS) was underway in Toronto, Canada when a special plenary session was convened to address a twin set of "charges" laid against two long-standing members of the society. One of the members is widely renowned as one of North America's most preeminent Evangelical thinkers—Canadian theologian, Dr. Clark Harold Pinnock.[1]

Founded in 1949, the Evangelical Theological Society is considered by most North American Evangelicals to be the primary forum in which they "foster conservative biblical scholarship by providing a medium for the oral exchange and written expression of thought and research in the general field of the theological disciplines as centered in the Scriptures."[2] Membership in the Society is considered vital by many Evangelical scholars and each year hundreds of them attend the ETS conference which has tended to prove itself a bellwether of future theological trajectories for Evangelical Christianity.

Bringing charges against Pinnock was no small matter. He has been recognized by the ETS for his theological work since the 1960's when he published two influential books defending the inerrancy and inspiration of the Bible—one of the central beliefs binding the Evangelical world. Since then, he has been a prolific author, writing numerous articles, scholarly essays, and well over a dozen books covering such diverse topics as apologetics, hermeneutics, soteriology, pneumatology, and the doctrine of God. He has come to be known for his perspicuous, even-shocking pedagogical style combined with a willingness to push the theological envelope, ever

---

[1] The other ETS theologian against whom charges were brought was Dr. John Sanders of Huntington College in Huntington, Indiana.

[2] Evangelical Theological Society, "Purpose Statement"; http://www.etsjets.org (April 20, 2003).

testing the boundaries of the conventional delimitations of "orthodoxy." He has been both extolled and reviled by leaders in the Evangelical world—some calling him one of their finest, most progressive and insightful apologists; others calling him a dangerous rebel and heretic.[3] One prominent Evangelical refers to him as, "perhaps the most significant Evangelical theologian of the last half of the twentieth century."[4] Another says of him,

> No twentieth-century Evangelical thinker has been more controversial than Clark Pinnock. He has been lauded as an inspiring theological pilgrim by his admirers and condemned as a dangerous renegade by his foes. Yet no story of Evangelical theology in the twentieth century is complete without the inclusion of his fascinating intellectual journey . . .[5]

The charges, which meant the possible dismissal of Pinnock from the ETS, were brought forth by Swiss Reformed theologian, Dr. Roger Nicole—a charter member and past president of the Society (1956). Nicole's charges laid an axe at the root of what it means to be a member of the ETS, namely, an unwavering commitment to the doctrine of biblical inerrancy.[6] Indeed, the doctrinal requirements for membership in the ETS are simple. Members of the society (in addition to meeting certain academic requirements such as holding an advanced degree) must affirm the following two-part statement: "The Bible alone, and the Bible in its entirety, is the Word of God written and is therefore inerrant in the autographs. God is a Trinity, Father, Son, and Holy Spirit, each an uncreated person, one in essence, equal in power and glory."[7]

The essence of Nicole's charges were equally straightforward: Pinnock, in his advocacy of "open theism," has "violated the inerrancy clause" of

---

[3] Reformed theologian, R. C. Sproul, for example, is quoted as publicly calling Pinnock a "heretic" in Johan Tangelder, "The Teaching of Clark Pinnock," in *The Banner of Truth*; http://www.banneroftruth.co.uk/articles/2001/11/teaching.htm (August 10, 2003).

[4] Henry H. Knight, III in Barry Callen, *Journey Toward Renewal* (Nappanee, Ind.: Evangel, 2000) back cover.

[5] Stanley Grenz, editorial review of Barry L. Callen, *Clark H. Pinnock: Journey Toward Renewal: An Intellectual Biography* (Nappanee, Ind.: Evangel, 2000) front-inside cover.

[6] In fact, it is this very affirmation—controversial as it is in the theological world—that fundamentally contradistinguishes the ETS from the many other scholarly religious societies such as the American Academy of Religion and the Society of Biblical Literature which both offer a much more diverse body of biblical exegetes and a more "liberal" approach to hermeneutics and exegetics in general.

[7] Evangelical Theological Society, "Doctrinal Basis;" http://www.etsjets.org (April 21, 2003).

the ETS doctrinal statement.[8] Open theism, said Nicole, implicitly denies biblical inerrancy by attributing false statements to God, that is, episodes of Divine "ignorance" in which God thought (or hoped for) one thing concerning the future, when quite the opposite came to pass. At the start of the session, Nicole lamented saying, "I present this motion with a heavy heart"[9] and then delineated the charges in a statement presented to the Society.

Following the Constitution and Bylaws of the ETS, the session was convened to address the charges, to open up a discussion among the members of the Society, and to take a vote that would decide whether the matter should be referred to the Executive Committee for further review.[10] Such a review meant one year of rigorous examination of the teachings and writings of the accused, an opportunity for them to defend themselves, face their accuser, and for the Executive Committee to formulate a recommendation and present it to a second plenary session of the Society at the next year's annual meeting. The 2002 session was packed, with some seven hundred members and non-voting participants present.

Calling the atmosphere in Toronto *polemical* would be putting it mildly. During the preliminary period of open discussion, participants took turns speaking into a microphone sharing their perspectives. One ETS member described the situation as "pernicious"[11] saying the Society was "choking debate, substituting a judicial attack mechanism when [it] can't persuade the other[s] to change [their] mind."[12] Another well known member described it as "dangerous" because "it sends a message to our young scholars saying 'do not make a mistake.'"[13] Pinnock himself, a year earlier, had remarked that those who opposed him in the ETS were like "Evangelical mullahs" issuing a "fatwa" against him.[14] Professor John Sanders, the sec-

---

[8] From the official charges brought by Roger Nicole against Drs. Pinnock and John Sanders presented on November 21, 2002 at the fifty-fourth annual ETS meeting. A copy is included as Exhibit A.

[9] Doug Koop, "Evangelical Theological Society Moves Against Open Theists," in *Christianity Today* (November 22, 2002); http://www.christianitytoday.com/ct/2002/145/54.0.html (April 21, 2003).

[10] The Executive Committee consists of nine longstanding members of the ETS.

[11] Terence Paige, Associate Professor of NT at Houghton College; quoted personally during my attendance at the ETS special session, November 21, 2002.

[12] Quoted in Doug Koop, "Open Theists Called To Account" in *Christian Week*. December 17, 2002, Vol 16, Issue 19 (Winnipeg, Canada, 2002); http://www.christianweek.org/stories/vol16/no19/story1.html (April 25, 2003).

[13] Grant Osborne, professor of NT at Trinity Evangelical Divinity School in Deerfield, Ill.; quoted personally during my attendance at the ETS special session, November 21, 2002.

[14] Quoted in David Neff, "Foreknowledge Debate Clouded by 'Political Agenda'" in *Christianity Today*, November 19, 2001; http://www.christianitytoday.com/ct/2001/147/

ond accused member, offered similar remarks referring to the proceedings as an "Evangelical Taliban," attempting to foist its own idea of doctrinal orthodoxy on the rest of the Society.[15]

Yet those on the opposite side of the issue were equally as vehement and passionate. Noted apologist and past ETS president, Norman Geisler, stated that these were "important charges" and that "all the living founders [of the ETS] opposed the view."[16] Bruce Ware, who authored a book critiquing open theism had earlier contended that, "By its denying of God's foreknowledge of future free creaturely choices and actions, open theism is vulnerable to the charge of commending as God one whom the true God declares is false and worthless."[17] Finally, in a heated debate that ensued after an unidentified member of the Society contended that the proceedings were destroying academic freedom, Wayne Grudem, author of one of the newest and most widely used Evangelical systematic theologies, stated flatly that the question at hand was "not about squelching dialogue in the ETS, but is about whether the open theistic God is the God of the Bible."[18] Criticisms of one's colleagues do not come in more stern a fashion than this.

After the open discussion, a vote was taken. The results were 171 to 131 *in favor* of referral to the Executive Committee to consider the charges.[19] After the vote, Pinnock said, "It was a dramatic moment. I wasn't surprised with the result. I'm concerned that it will divide the Society, whatever happens to me. I just hope that this process will work, and that

---

13.0.html (April 20, 2003).

[15] Quoted in Eric Gorski, "Theological Society Debates 'Open Theism' Teaching," in *The Baptist Standard*, December 3, 2001; http://www.baptiststandard.com/2001/12_3/pages/open_theism.html (April 15, 2003).

[16] Norman Geisler, President of Southern Evangelical Seminary in Charlotte, NC and former ETS President; quoted personally during my attendance at the ETS special session. November 21, 2002.

[17] Russell D. Moore, "Evangelical Theological Society Rejects 'Open Theism,' Affirms God's Foreknowledge" in *Southern Baptist Theological Seminary News*, November 20, 2001. http://www.bpnews.net/bpnews.asp?ID=12210 (December 15, 2002).

[18] Wayne Grudem, former ETS President; quoted personally during my attendance at the ETS special session, November 21, 2002.

[19] Also in favor of referral was a vote of one hundred sixty-six to one hundred forty-three against John Sanders.

next year it won't pass. I'm hopeful."[20] Despite pressures from Nicole and numerous others to do so, Pinnock added, "I don't intend to resign."[21]

Purpose and Aim

The foregoing discussion should make evident the enormity of the current debate within Evangelicalism over openness theology along with the critical role played by Clark Pinnock. Pinnock argues both that exhaustive divine foreknowledge of future events destroys human freedom, and that *only* his proposal for open theism (which denies such foreknowledge) can provide an adequate footing upon which Divine-human relationality can be grounded.[22] The fundamental purpose and aim of this book is to examine and critique open theism, using Pinnock's version of it as representative, and to then offer a Reformed reconstruction of Divine-human relationality which preserves total Divine foreknowledge.

In so doing, this book picks upon a *part* of the debate over openness theology by examining the strictly *theological* implications of the proposal. I stress the word *theological* to underscore that this is a work in systematic and philosophical theology. Though numerous Scriptural texts are used by both Pinnock and myself in an attempt to make our respective cases, they are used in the form which John Hayes and Carl Holladay call "canonical criticism"[23] as they function from *within* the Evangelical tradition. When approaching the biblical text, this form of criticism carries with it certain antecedent assumptions of a religious nature. Understanding this approach is vital to the scope of this work. While other forms of criticism (for example, *form, redaction, historical, structural,* etc.) may be valuable at times, the scope and aim of this book does not allow a real consideration of these aspects as the subject deals with a controversy firmly situated within the Evangelical context and its shared context of beliefs. Canonical criticism approaches the biblical text as a theological whole and . . .

---

[20] Doug Koop, "Evangelical Theological Society Moves Against Open Theists" in *Christianity Today*. November 22, 2002; http://www.christianitytoday.com/ct/2002/ 145/54.0.html (April 21, 2003).

[21] Quoted in Doug Koop, "Open Theists Called To Account" in *Christian Week*. December 17, 2002, Vol 16, Issue 19 (Winnipeg, Canada, 2002); http://www.christianweek.org/stories/vol16/no19/story1.html (April 25, 2003).

[22] See especially, Pinnock, *Most Moved Mover* (Grand Rapids: Baker, 2001) 154–57. Pinnock says, for example, regarding Divine-human dynamism, that, "Convential theism in its various forms undermines this in one way or another. It suffers from the conditional of existential self-contradiction." [Ibid., 155].

[23] John Hayes and Carl Holladay, *Biblical Exegesis*, rev. ed. (Atlanta: John Knox, 1987) 122.

> . . . avoids the atomization and thus the isolated interpretation of texts. A text is to be read as part of the Bible in its entirety, not as an independent, single unit. Each passage is read as part of a biblical book, and the biblical book is seen as part of an even larger entity—the canon as a whole. The whole is thus greater and more authoritative than any of its parts. Thus even a biblical book has only penultimate authority since it is the Bible as a whole that possesses final canonical authority . . . the Bible is read in the context of a believing, interpretive community whose faith and beliefs provide the lens for interpreting the Scriptures.[24]

Pinnock and I have a mutual commitment to the Evangelical tradition which includes an acknowledgment of the Bible as the inspired word of God and, thus, its primacy in constructing theology. Our respective canonical criticisms approach the Scriptures in this manner, yet they yield radically different theological structures within our shared context.

Using the Bible as the fundamental theological resource for a new theology within Evangelicalism, openness theology raises a host of issues concerning both the doctrine of God and theological anthropology. Chief among these are the notions that classical formulations of God's exhaustive foreknowledge of future events ultimately destroys genuine relationality between the Divine and human, calls God's moral character into question, and, overall, descends into fatalism. This book examines Pinnock's arguments, provides a critical analysis, and then reconstructs Divine-human relationality in a specifically Reformed context which concomitantly avoids both the denial of exhaustive divine foreknowledge as well as, so I will argue, Pinnock's charge of fatalism.

Open Theism, Arminianism, Calvinism, and Molinism

Throughout this discussion, four key terms bear significantly on the controversy and require definitional precision. Other terms throughout this work will be defined in their native context. The first of such terms is *open theism* itself, especially according to the rendering manifest in Pinnock's proposal. The others are *Calvinism*, *Arminianism*, and *Molinism*. Special attention will be given to the latter three terms to address their specific application to the controversy over divine foreknowledge and human freedom.

---

[24] Ibid., 125.

Introduction

Openness Theology

The theological construct now commonly referred to in Evangelical circles as *openness theology* or, perhaps more frequently, *open theism*,[25] carries with it numerous other appellations as well including: "the open view,"[26] "relational theism" (one of Pinnock's favorite terms), the "relational model,"[27] "creative love theism,"[28] and sometimes "consistent Arminianism"[29] (a term often used derisively by detractors of open theism).[30] *Open theism, openness theology*, or the *openness model* are the preferred terms in this work. Other terms will be used on occasion, especially when specifically used by Pinnock himself to illustrate a particular theological or philosophical nuance that attaches to them.

Though certain isolated sprouts of open theistic *sounding* constructs have popped up from time to time throughout church history (for example, Faustus Socinus and the Socinian movement)[31], the first distinctly *Evangelical* work defending open theism was the collaborative effort of Drs. Clark Pinnock, Richard Rice, John Sanders, William Hasker, and David Basinger. The authors titled the book, *The Openness of God: A Biblical Challenge to the Traditional Understand of God* (1994). Though each author

---

[25] This term appears to be the most widely used by the open theists themselves. See, for example, Gregory Boyd, et al. "What is Open Theism?" Online. http://www.opentheism.org (June 5, 2002).

[26] See Gregory Boyd, *God of the Possible: A Biblical Introduction to the Open View of God* (Grand Rapids: Baker, 2000) 21.

[27] Pinnock, personal interview, Evangelical Theological Society. Toronto, Canada, November 20, 2002.

[28] Ibid.

[29] Amos Yong, *Time and Eternity, Divine Foreknowledge and Creaturely Freedom: Historical and Contemporary Issues* (St. Paul, Minn.: Bethel Theological Seminary, 2002) 22.

[30] Richard Rice, an open theist, appears comfortable with this term as evidenced in his, "Divine Foreknowledge and Free-will Theism," *The Grace of God and the Will of Man: A Case for Arminianism*. ed. Pinnock (Grand Rapids: Zondervan, 1989) 123.

[31] Charles Hodge observes that "Socinus argue[d] that the knowledge of God embraces all that is knowable. Future free actions being uncertain, are not the objects of knowledge, and therefore it is no impeachment of the divine omniscience to say that they cannot be known" [Charles Hodge, *Systematic Theology*, I.9.2 (Grand Rapids: Christian Classics Ethereal Library, 2005) 407. This is the same exact reasoning followed by most open theists including Pinnock. Other open theistic sounding writings throughout history include: W. Norris Clarke, *God, Knowable and Unknowable* (New York: Fordham, 1973); Roy Elseth, *Did God Know? A Study of the Nature of God* (St. Paul, Minn.: Calvary United Church, 1977); Lorenzo D. McCabe, *Divine Nescience of Future Contingencies a Necessity* (New York: Phillips and Hunt, 1882); Richard Swinburne, T*he Coherence of Theism*, rev. ed. (New York: Oxford University Press, 1993); John Polkinghorne, editor, *The Work of Love* (Grand Rapids: Eerdmans, 2001).

offers his own distinctive version of the openness model, they agree in the book's preface on the following basic rudiments:

> [Open theism] presents an understanding of God's nature and relationship with his creatures, which we call the openness of God. In broad strokes, it takes the following form. God, in grace, grants humans significant freedom to cooperate with or work against God's will for their lives, and he enters into dynamic, give and take relationships with us. The Christian life involves genuine interaction between God and human beings. We respond to God's gracious initiatives and God responds to our responses . . . and on it goes. God takes risks in this give-and-take relationship, yet he is endlessly resourceful and competent in working toward his ultimate goals. Sometimes God alone decides how to accomplish these goals. On other occasions, God works with human decisions, adapting his own plans to fit the changing situation. God does not control everything that happens. Rather, he is open to receiving input from his creatures. In loving dialogue, God invites us to participate with him to bring the future into being.[32]

Pinnock, in his own book, *Most Moved Mover: A Theology of God's Openness*, which is devoted entirely to explicating and defending open theism, expands on this, adding special attention to the issue of Divine-human relationality:

> According to the open view, God freely decided to be, in some respects, affected and conditioned by creatures and he established things in such a way that some things he desires may not happen. For example, God may want everyone to receive his love but apparently not all do so. God does not control everything that happens but sovereignly decided to make a world in which creatures could respond to God and where he would make himself available for such relationships. Creation, then, is an open project with which God has decided to be open himself . . . This is a God who creates a world that is not just a mechanical expression of his own purpose but an environment for other free, though finite, agents to exist with a degree of autonomy and a measure of real freedom.[33]

The most notable (and controversial) feature inherent in the open theistic model, however, is the fundamental denial of the classical Christian affirmation of God's exhaustive definite foreknowledge (EDF). According to

---

[32] Pinnock, et al, *The Openness of God: A Biblical Challenge to the Traditional Understand of God* (Downer's Grove, Ill.: InterVarsity, 1994) Preface.

[33] Pinnock, *Most Moved Mover*, 5.

open theists (and, ironically, Calvinists, contra Arminians, Molinists, and others), the reason for this is simple: if God infallibly foreknows everything that will come to pass, it follows logically that whatever is done in the present *had to occur according to that foreknowledge*. For example, if God has infallibly known from all eternity that Jane will decide next week to major in biology instead of mathematics, then next week's choice of biology over the latter is a sort of "foregone conclusion" in the divine mind. In a manner of speaking, it has "already happened" for God, though not for Jane. If God possesses EDF of future—and presumably volitive—human actions, in what sense can we speak of our decisions as meaningfully and significantly free? If EDF is granted, it appears unavoidable that our concept of anthropic volitional power must be altered or even abandoned in order to preserve a logical context in which to understand it.

Such is the classical Reformed or Calvinistic approach in dealing with this tension in which it is maintained that whatever is divinely foreknown must therefore be *predestined*. Or, as the influential Protestant scholastic, Francis Turretin (1623–1687), put it, "all things are foreseen by an infallible foreknowledge, so they must necessarily happen infallibly."[34] Herein lies the root of the Reformed tradition's understanding of human freedom in which the choices we make are considered to be a constituent part of God's immutable and eternal plan.

The problem, however, is that such a modification militates against the seemingly nonnegotiable open theistic (and Arminian and Molinist) postulate that human beings possess what they consider to be an autonomous, "libertarian" capacity for exercising free will (that is, a faculty of freewill which remains free of causal constraint). Indeed, this very capacity is precisely what undergirds their advocacy of "dynamic, give and take relationships" with God in which valid choices are made—and then responded to—by both parties in an ongoing reciprocity. Thus, Pinnock has written that the "logical force" of exhaustive definite foreknowledge implies "the fixity of all things from eternity past"[35] and must be discarded in order to preserve genuine anthropic freedom and vital relations between the human and the Divine.

Pinnock and other open theists insist that this is the only logical move available to theologians who wish to reconcile human freedom with the existence of God. The controversy emerges, then, from the simple fact that

---

[34] Francis Turretin, *Institutes of Elenctic Theology* (1688–90), James T. Dennison, editor (Phillipsburg, N. J.: Presbyterian & Reformed, 1992) 320.

[35] Pinnock, "From Augustine to Arminius: A Pilgrimage in Theology," in *The Grace of God and the Will of Man*, (Minneapolis: Bethany, 1989) 25.

the logical extrapolations of EDF have never before impelled Evangelical thinkers to take the extreme of simply denying it. There has been a near univocity among Evangelicals concerning EDF and it has always been maintained even by those who affirm a libertarian understanding of human freedom (especially Arminians and Molinists). This is the theological root cause of the fissure now dividing so many Evangelical scholars (there are also some political causes which are not the concern of this research). Throughout the history of Western Evangelicalism, EDF has been part of the warp and woof of nearly every theologian's doctrine of God. So ingrained and unquestioned was this affirmation that C. S. Lewis, ostensively an Arminian, once remarked that, "Everyone who believes in God at all believes that He knows what you and I are going to do tomorrow."[36] Renowned biblical exegete, Arthur Pink (1886–1952), stated that, "to deny God's foreknowledge is to deny His omniscience, and this is to repudiate one of the fundamental attributes of Deity."[37]

The doctrine of predestination notwithstanding, the Protestant Reformers held divine foreknowledge alone to be a requisite component of Christian theology and even went so far as to say that it was absolutely *foundational* to the lifeblood of the religion. Martin Luther (1483–1546) considered divine foreknowledge so axiomatic to Christian belief and practice that he said it is "essentially necessary and wholesome for Christians to know: That God foreknows nothing by contingency, but that He foresees, purposes, and does all things according to His immutable, eternal, and infallible will." [38] He adds that, "If, therefore, we are taught, and if we believe, that we ought not to know the necessary prescience of God, and the necessity of the things that are to take place, Christian faith is *utterly destroyed*, and the promises of God and the whole Gospel entirely fall to the ground"[39] [emphasis added]. John Calvin (1509–1564) describes God as the one "to whom all things are known from the beginning."[40] Italian Reformer, Jerome Zanchius (1516–1590), also drew a direct correlation between foreknowledge and the nature of deity saying that,

---

[36] C. S. Lewis, *Mere Christianity* (New York: MacMillan, 1960) 148.

[37] Arthur W. Pink, *The Sovereignty Of God* (Grand Rapids: Baker, 1984) 247.

[38] Martin Luther, On the Bondage of the Will, Sec. 9, Para. 1; trans. Henry Cole. http://www.truecovenanter.com/truelutheran/luther_bow.html#cpref (April 10, 2003).

[39] Ibid.

[40] John Calvin, *The Institutes of the Christian Religion*, 1.18.1, trans. Henry Beveridge (Grand Rapids: Eerdmans, 1989) 199.

[The] foreknowledge of God is not conjectural and uncertain (for then it would not be foreknowledge), but most sure and infallible, so that whatever He foreknows to be future shall necessarily and undoubtedly come to pass. For His knowledge can no more be frustrated, or His wisdom be deceived, *than He can cease to be God*. Nay, could either of these be the case, He actually would *cease to be God*, all mistake and disappointment being absolutely incompatible with the Divine nature"[41] [emphasis added].

Scottish Reformer, John Knox (1505–1572), said bluntly, "Whosoever goes about to remove from God, either yet to call in doubt his wisdom and foreknowledge . . . goes about, so far as in them is, to destroy and call in doubt his whole Godhead."[42] Given such statements, the importance of divine foreknowledge and its relationship to the very deity of the Godhead was naturally reflected in many of the earliest doctrinal codifications of the Protestant Reformation such as the *Formula of Concord* (1577) which said that, "the foreknowledge of God is nothing else than that God knows all things before they happen."[43] Later, the Westminster Divines formulated their connection between divine foreknowledge and providence in their confessional statement (1647) saying, "God the great Creator of all things doth uphold, direct, dispose, and govern all creatures, actions, and things, from the greatest even to the least, by his most wise and holy providence, *according to his infallible foreknowledge*"[44] [emphasis added].

Going further back in church history, we also observe nearly all of the major patristical writings, both early and late, tending to simply *assume* EDF. My own research discovered both explicit and implicit affirmations of EDF in Clement of Rome, Barnabas, Justin Martyr, Irenaeus, Tertullian, Athenagoras, Tatian, Clement of Alexandria, Basil, Cyril, Jerome, Gregory of Nyssa, Origen, Theophilus of Antioch, and Augustine.[45] Usually, little

---

[41] Jerome Zanchius, *Absolute Predestination*, Chapter 1, Postion 3; http://www.straitgate.com/books/zanchius/zanchius.htm (April 1, 2003).

[42] John Knox, "Letters to His Brethren and the Lords Professing the Truth in Scotland 1557" in *Selected Writings of John Knox* (Dallas: Presbyterian Heritage Publications, 1995) http://www.swrb.com/newslett/actualNLs/ltrbreth.htm (April 26, 2003).

[43] *The Lutheran Book of Concord*, Art. XI, 3; trans. and ed., Theodore G. Tappert, et al. (Philadelphia: Fortress, 1959) 616.

[44] Westminster Confession of Faith (1646), 5.1. Online. http://www.creeds.net/Westminster/c05.htm (April 20, 2003).

[45] See Clement of Rome, *First Epistle to the Corinthians*, 44.; Barnabas, *Epistle of Barnabas*, 3; Justin Martyr, *First Apology*, chapters 12, 28, 44–45 and *Dialogue of Justin the Philosopher and Martyr With Trypho the Jew*, chapters 23, 42, 70, 92, 118, 140–41; Irenaeus, *Against Heresies*, 4.29, 4.32, 4.38, 4.39, 5.1, 5.28, 5.36; Tertullian, *Against Marcion*, 2.5, 2.7, 2.9; Athenagoras, *On The Resurrection Of The Dead*, 2.; Tatian, *Address of Tatian to the Greeks*, chapter 29; Clement of Alexandria, *Paedagogus*, 1.8. and *The Stromata*, 1.17, 2.12, 2.13;

was done in these writings to try and reconcile EDF with human freedom. Rather, the writers tended to simply grant, without defense, that Divine foreknowledge is a constituent part of Christian theology. There were occasions, however, where God's foreknowledge was forcefully defended. Justin Martyr (c. 100–c165), wrote that, "God [is] slandered as having no foreknowledge."[46] Jerome (c. 340–420) argued that "in stripping Him of foreknowledge you also take away His divinity."[47] Augustine (354–430) declared that, "They are far more tolerable who assert the fatal influence of the stars than they who deny the foreknowledge of future events. For, to confess that God exists, and at the same time to deny that He has foreknowledge of future things, is the most manifest folly."[48]

Most of the medieval theologians were of similar accord though considerably more philosophical in their discourse. Boethius (c. 475–525) wrote, ". . . let our aim be to prove that, whatever be the shape which [the] series of causes takes, the fulfillment of God's foreknowledge is necessary, even if this knowledge may not seem to induce the necessity for the occurrence of future events"[49] Peter Lombard (c. 1100–1160) affirmed EDF saying, "the knowledge and foreknowledge of God is of things good and evil."[50] Thomas Aquinas (1225–1274) wrote, "That God knows future contingencies is shown also by the authority of Holy Scripture,"[51] such that, "the divine mind . . . knows future contingencies with infallible knowledge."[52] Aquinas adds further clarification in his *Shorter Summa* by appealing to foreknowledge as an integral part of the natural complexion of God in which, "God's

---

Basil, *De Spiritu Sancto*, 9.23, 16.38; Cyril, *On the Ten Points of Doctrine*, 1.5; Jerome, *Against the Pelagians*, 3.6; Gregory of Nyssa, *The Great Catechism*, 7; Origen, *de Principiis*, 1.2.2, 3.1.13, 3.1.17, 3.1.20; Theophilus of Antioch, *Theophilus to Autolycus*, 2.15; Augustine, *The City of God*, 9.2.

[46] Justin Martyr, "Dialogue with Trypho" 92, in *The Apostolic Fathers with Justin Martyr and Irenaeus*; ed. Philip Schaff (Grand Rapids: Christian Classics Ethereal Library, 2002) 345.

[47] St. Jerome, *Against the Pelagians*, Book III, Sec. 6; *The Principal Works of St. Jerome*. Trans. W. H. Fremantle (Grand Rapids: Christian Classics Ethereal Library, 1999) 747.

[48] Augustine, *The City of God*, IX.2., Trans. Marcus Dods (Grand Rapids: Christian Classics Ethereal Library, 2001) 138.

[49] Boethius, *The Consolation of Philosophy*, 5.5. Trans. W.V. Cooper and J.M. Dent; ed.: Israel Golancz (London: Temple Classics, 1902) 146.

[50] Peter Lombard, *The Sentences*, 1.6. Trans. Opera Omnia S. Bonaventurae (1882) 124. *Franciscan Archive*: http://www.franciscan-archive.org/lombardus/opera/ls1-06.html (April 11, 2003).

[51] Thomas Aquinas, *Summa Contra Gentiles*, I.67.8. Trans. Joseph Rickaby (London: Burns and Oates, 1905). Jacques Maritain Center at the University of Notre Dame: http://www.nd.edu/Departments/Maritain/etext/gc.htm (April 2, 2003).

[52] Ibid., I.64.

infallible foreknowledge embraces even contingent futures, inasmuch as God beholds *in His eternity* future events as actually existing"[53] [emphasis added]. Countless other examples exist in the Medieval theologians which evince general agreement on the matter—even if opinions varied concerning the precise nature of human freedom or even the dynamics of Divine foreknowledge itself.

This strong heritage of affirming EDF has not gone unnoticed in the contemporary Evangelical world and is often cited by its theologians as further reason to jettison the openness model. Pinnock, however, laments the fact that so much attention is given only to his denial of foreknowledge when his real aim is to preserve genuine relationality and to fend off what he feels are the unavoidable fatalistic implications of maintaining EDF. Instead of seeing a model that presents "a God with whom people can relate because he upholds their own creaturely significance," his opponents concentrate on the "charge that it is heretical [or] . . . the suspicion that it has gone too far."[54] He sees the constant emphasis on EDF to be a reductionistic and myopic view of the model's attempt to disinter a more relational theism which he views as ineluctably stilted in classical models. He views this negative attention as somewhat of a rigid doctrinal prejudice which misses the inner court of his theology for the vagaries of the entrance hall. Pinnock draws on the perennial tension between two rival theological factions within the Evangelical camp to explain why some are so reluctant to allow a place for open theism:

> Part of it is Wesleyan Arminianism versus Calvinism. Presumably no Calvinist would ever embrace it—so its more natural for Methodists and Arminians to ask whether they should . . . because they're already relational theists and therefore already hold to ninety percent of it. And that's why [the issue] becomes foreknowledge for them . . . the one they stick at—and almost nothing else. So if Christians are already relational theists then open theism is a more coherent form of it . . . In other words, we take it a little farther and make it a little better.[55]

In the longstanding debate over Divine foreknowledge and human freedom, Pinnock contends that open theism simply "makes the choices even sharper and

---

[53] Thomas Aquinas, *Shorter Summa*, trans. Cyril Vollert (Manchester, N. H.: Sophia, 1993) 157.

[54] Pinnock, *Most Moved Mover*, 24.

[55] Pinnock, personal interview, November 20, 2002.

clearer, being itself a more coherent alternative to Calvinism than Arminians have presented before."[56]

In short, the fundamental tenets of open theism include the following points:

1. Human beings possess autonomous libertarian freedom (that is, we make our decisions out of an unbridled free will, a freedom without causal constraint, that is, a freedom which allows the power of contrary choice). This is also known as "contra-causal freedom," "indeterministic freedom" or the "liberty of indifference." As open theist, William Hasker, puts it, this sort of freedom is such that, "An agent is free with respect to a given action at a given time if at that time it is within the agent's power to perform the action and also in the agent's power to refrain from the action."[57] This is to be contrasted with "compatibilistic freedom" (or the "liberty of spontaneity") as advocated by most Reformed thinkers in which humans make choices at each moment in accord with their desires and nature which, in turn, are within the architectonic providence of God.

2. Such freedom is incompatible with exhaustive Divine foreknowledge. Importantly, this is a point on which both open theists and Calvinists fundamentally agree, thereby contradistinguishing themselves from Arminians and Molinists (or any other school of thought which attempts to reconcile total foreknowledge with libertarian freedom such as Occamism, Frankfurtianism and others[58]). Both open theists and Calvinists maintain that Arminians and Molinists are logically inconsistent on this point. Thus, in the tension between God's omniscience and human freedom, open theism's response is to modify God's omniscience by saying it cannot include the future free acts of humans. The Augustinian-Calvinist response is to modify our understanding of human freedom so that it is compatible with total Divine foreknowledge, hence the term "compatibilistic freedom" or "compatibilism" which is a frequent term in the Reformed vocabulary.

---

[56] Pinnock, *Most Moved Mover*, xii.

[57] William Hasker, "A Philosophical Perspective," in *The Openness of God: A Biblical Challenge to the Traditional Understanding of God* (Downers Grove, Ill.: InterVarsity, 1994) 136–37.

[58] The scope and purpose of this work does not necessitate an excursus of the mechanics of all these views which, in my view, amount essentially to more fine-tuned philosophical subspecies of the broader Arminian philosophical genus.

3. Human beings can influence God and His decisions and lead Him to change His mind and alter His plans.
4. God does not know the future in its entirety. He cannot, because then creatures do not possess libertarian freewill and therefore the entire program of open theism in which God's sole purpose is Divine-human love relationships falls apart.
5. God must be *in time*. Otherwise, he would exist above it knowing it in its entirety. Pinnock says, for example, "As regards time, God's relation is temporal and not totally different from ours. He too operates from within time."[59] Open theism, then, with its stress on a temporally-bound Divine relationality is—in a quite literal way—a sort of *sic et nunc* theology proper.

Arminianism

Traditionally, the Arminian view holds that God possesses "simple foreknowledge" of human affairs but does not construe this knowledge to be in any way *causal* of the events which actually take place in space-time. This knowledge is complete and infallible, but not determinative. In dealing with the soteriological implications of this view, Jacobus Arminius (1560–1609) affirmed:

> ... if God resolve to use an irresistible power in the execution of his decree, or if he determine to employ such a quantum of power as nothing can resist or can hinder it from completing his purpose, it will follow that the thing will necessarily be brought into existence. Thus, "wicked men who persevere in their sins, will necessarily perish," for God will by an irresistible force, cast them down into the depths of hell. But if he resolve to use a force that is not irresistible, but that can be resisted by the creature, then that thing is said to be done, not necessarily but contingently, *although its actual occurrence was certainly foreknown by God, according to the infinity of his understanding, by which he knows all results whatever, that will arise from certain causes which are laid down, and whether those causes produce a thing necessarily or contingently.*[60] [emphasis added]

The fundamental purpose of the view was to escape the theological consequences of Calvin's *decretum horribile* in which the "double predestina-

---

[59] Pinnock, *Most Moved Mover*, 32.

[60] Jacobus Arminius, Article 5, *The Works of Jacobus Arminius*, vol. 1 (Grand Rapids: Christian Classics Ethereal Library, 2002) 151.

tion" of both the elect and the reprobate were considered to be according to nothing less than the unmitigated foreknowledge and *foreordination* of God. For Arminians, then, the eternal salvation or damnation of each human being are infallibly *known* by God, but not *caused* by God. It is thus an *incompatibilistic* view in that God's foreordination and human freedom are thought to be mutually annihilating concepts.

Traditionally, no attempt is made by Arminians to logically and philosophically square the juxtaposition of foreknowledge and freedom, the latter of which they insist is autonomous and libertarian. Rather, they are simply considered to be jointly veracious propositions—both taught in Scripture—but beyond the ability of human reason to justify. It is a clear dealing of the theological "mystery card" which, most Arminians argue, must inevitably be the case with *every* Christian doctrine and thus becomes a matter of where one draws the line. For them, the line is drawn almost from the start of the inquiry. In contradistinction to other positions—open theism included—Arminians do not make specific attempts to explain this mystery in detail, preferring to remain silent. Modern proponent of Arminian simple foreknowledge, David Hunt, explains the position thusly,

> The fact is that I'm not at all sure how God knows the future, and I do not want my defense of [foreknowledge] to be hostage to or dependent on a particular view on this subject. So my "official" position on the mechanism of divine foreknowledge will be agnostic. What I am committed to defending…is the view that God simply knows the future (leaving open the question of how he does it). By "simple" foreknowledge, then, I shall mean the view that the simple affirmation of [foreknowledge]—uncomplicated by exceptions, additions, qualifications et cetera—is by itself wholly compatible with human freedom, divine agency and enhanced providential control.[61]

Calvinism

In marked contradistinction to Arminianism, Calvinism draws an immediate connection between God's foreknowledge of events, and his causal agency behind them. For Calvinists, the two are mutually inseparable as the former logically *flows out from the latter*. Perhaps the most distinguishing feature of Calvinism, however, is that, while *all* the other views affirm something along the lines of libertarian human freedom, the Calvinist view

---

[61] David Hunt, "The Simple-Foreknowledge View," in *Divine Foreknowledge: Four Views*, ed. James Beilby and Paul Eddy (Downers Grove, Ill.: InterVarsity, 2001) 67.

denies humans this ability in view of the seemingly inextricable presence of the antecedent causality of *every* space-time event. Human freedom still exists, the Calvinist maintains, but it must be dramatically redefined. One attempt in this regard is to consider all human actions as free provided they spring forth from an agent's *desire* to commit that action. Calvinist, John Feinberg, for example, maintains that "an action is free, although causally determined, if it is done in accord with the agent's wishes."[62] This idea is reflected in the Calvinistic system of doctrine delineated in the classic Westminster Confession of Faith which affirms: "God from all eternity, did, by the most wise and holy counsel of His own will, freely, and unchangeably ordain whatsoever comes to pass; yet so, as thereby neither is God the author of sin, *nor is violence offered to the will of the creatures; nor is the liberty or contingency of second causes taken away, but rather established.*"[63]

Molinism

This view, named after its most notable historical defender, the Jesuit theologian, Luis de Molina (1535–1600), maintains along with the simple foreknowledge view the incompatibility of Divine foreordination and human freedom, but the compatibility of Divine foreknowledge and human freedom. It also presupposes libertarian human freedom.

The Molinist view has gained increasing currency with numerous contemporary Evangelical scholars. In short, it posits God's exhaustive knowledge of *counterfactuals*. One philosopher defines counterfactuals (or "counterfactuals of freedom") as God's knowledge of the "conditionals which specify how creatures will freely act in any possible situation, and that God knows these conditionals pre-volitionally, that is, before performing any act of will."[64] In other words, God has total knowledge of what every particular person *would* do in any given set of circumstances. If person (A), was in situation (X), she would inexorably do (C); if she were in situation (Y) she should would inexorably do (B), and so on, *ad infinitum*.

While Molina's opponents contended that any such counterfactual knowledge—if it even exists—should be placed *subsequent* to God's initial creation decree, Molina argued for the inverse, that it logically occurs *prior* to the decree, in-between or in the "middle" of God's natural knowledge

---

[62] John Feinberg, *No One Like Him: The Doctrine of God* (Wheaton, Ill.: Crossway, 2001) 741.

[63] Westminster Confession of Faith (1646) III.1.; http://www.creeds.net/reformed/Westminster/c05.htm (April 20, 2003).

[64] Bruce Dutra, "A New Criticism of Molina's Theory of Middle Knowledge" Presented at the *Midsouth Philosophy Conference* (University of Memphis, February 21, 2003) 1.

and his contingent knowledge. Hence, the position is often referred to as "middle knowledge."

Perhaps the most vocal Evangelical proponent of the middle knowledge view is William Lane Craig who elucidates the supposed advantage of the view:

> Not only does the Molinist view make room for human freedom, but it affords God a means of choosing which world of free creatures to create. For by knowing how persons would freely choose in whatever circumstances they might be in, God can—by decreeing to place just those persons in just those circumstances—bring about his ultimate purposes through free creaturely decisions. Thus, by employing his counterfactual knowledge, God can plan a world down to the last detail and yet do so without annihilating creaturely [libertarian] freedom, since what people would freely do under various circumstances is already factored into the equation by God.[65]

Therefore, God's EDF is ultimately the *product* of his middle knowledge coupled with his decrees thereby making EDF noncausal.

Pinnock, and open theists in general, reject *all* of these views as either logically incoherent (Arminianism and Molinism) or as unbiblical and theologically deleterious (Calvinism) and offer what they believe to be a more consistent, biblical alternative. For Pinnock, libertarian human freedom is a non-negotiable supposition and must therefore be made compatible *theologically*.

A Personal Note

I first became familiar with Pinnock's work in the context of Christian apologetics. Indeed, few students of apologetics, especially of the Evangelical variety, are unaware of his work in this area. Still today, when teaching apologetics, I frequently draw from his work, especially in the area of biblical historiography. His earliest apologetics book, *Set Forth Your Case*, was one of the first Christian apologetics books I read as a young Christian. In an age hallmarked by personal subjectivism over reason and intellectual reflection, I was enticed, even thrilled, by Pinnock's willingness to preserve a place for the *mind* in examining Christian claims. In the book, Pinnock writes,

> The aim of apologetics is not to trick a person into becoming a Christian against his will. It strives rather at laying the evidence for

---

[65] William Lane Craig, "The Middle-Knowledge View," in *Divine Foreknowledge: Four Views*, ed. James Beilby and Paul Eddy (Downers Grove, Ill.: InterVarsity, 2001) 122.

the Christian gospel before men in an intelligent fashion, so that they can make a meaningful commitment under the convincing power of the Holy Spirit. The heart cannot delight in what the mind rejects as false.[66]

Set Forth Your Case contains a wellspring of helpful apologetical resources employing a hypothesis-verification method to help establish such things as the historicity of the New Testament (NT), the resurrection, and other articles of the Christian faith. Having grown up in a tradition somewhat discouraging of the use of the mind in matters of faith, I delighted in the new intellectual vistas opened up for me in Pinnock's and other's works.

In early 1999, however, my perspective of the panoply of Pinnock's work began to change after controversy broke out at Bethel Theological Seminary (where I was then a seminarian) over the open theistic teachings of theology professor, Gregory Boyd. I had been unaware of Pinnock's involvement in the controversy up to that point and the crucial part he was playing in it. Much to my surprise, I soon learned that he was actually one the principle architects of the new view.

At roughly the same time that Pinnock and four other scholars published *The Openness of God*, Gregory Boyd had come out with a Christian apologetic work entitled, *Letters From a Skeptic*, in which he rather perspicuously denies the doctrine of Divine foreknowledge.[67] This book was written at a popular level and, thus, garnered a great deal of attention from both scholars and laypersons. Lesser known, however, were similar statements Boyd made much earlier in his doctoral dissertation at Princeton University entitled, *Trinity and Process: A Critical Evaluation and Reconstruction of Hartshorne's Di-Polar Theism Towards a Trinitarian Metaphysics*. The dissertation drew upon much thought from process theology while trying to integrate it with more classical Christian formulations.[68] I soon discovered that Pinnock also had sympathies with processianism which would become much more obvious in 2000 when he co-edited a book with process theologian, John Cobb, entitled, *Searching for an Adequate God: A Dialogue Between Process and Free Will Theists* (2000). In it, he states unambiguously that "The fact is that process and openness theists share important convictions."[69]

---

[66] Pinnock, *Set Forth Your Case* (Nutley, N. J.: Craig, 1968) 3.

[67] Gregory Boyd, *Letters from a Skeptic* (Colorado Springs, Col.: Chariot Victor, 1994) 30.

[68] See Gregory Boyd, *Trinity and Process: A Critical Evaluation and Reconstruction of Hartshorne's Di-Polar Theism Towards a Trinitarian Metaphysics* (New York: Lang, 1992).

[69] Pinnock, et al, ed., *Searching for an Adequate God: A Dialogue Between Process and Free Will Theists* (Grand Rapids: Eerdmans, 2000) ix.

Having followed Pinnock's rather "conservative" apologetical work, I was very surprised to find him defending the new view. Importantly, it is also rather unlikely that open theism would have gained as much ground as it has within Evangelicalism were Pinnock not a proponent. His renown and stature within the Evangelical camp has provided a kind of *de facto* imprimatur to the view which, in my estimation, would likely have fizzled out already were he not at the forefront of disseminating its teachings. Pinnock wields considerable influence in the Evangelical world. Ordinary Christians that have been around for a while know his name and, when see him endorsing a book or a view, may assume that the teaching therein is of a trustworthy nature. Thus, his support for the openness model has made him a worthy subject for study.

There are two more reasons for my interest in making Pinnock's open theism the primary focus of critique in this research. First, Pinnock's life as a theologian presents us with a fascinating, albeit enigmatic, intellectual and spiritual journey from—as one scholar puts it—"quintessential Evangelical apologist to anti-Augustinian theological reformist."[70] His theology has, over the past forty years, become quite nearly the diametrical inverse of what it was in the 1960's when he adhered to a fairly strict program of Calvinistic theology. In his own words, he "adopted Calvinist thinking in [his] student years in the sixties" but has now become a "progressive Wesleyan" who believes the God of Augustine, Anselm, Aquinas, Calvin, and Luther, "is not a highly loving God."[71] Indeed, such a God, Pinnock says, is more like an "oriental despot" than a loving, relational being.[72]

In this vein, Pinnock has gone on to challenge a number of other typically staple Evangelical doctrines besides the doctrine of foreknowledge. Among those are biblical inerrancy itself (*not* so much inspiration or authority), Hell, soteriological exclusivism (advocating instead a modified "modal" pluralism), and a new model of the atonement which denies the traditional concept of substitutionary or propitiatory atonement. These are theological areas which have remained virtually unquestioned (though not unexplored) in the history of Evangelicalism, enough so that many Evangelical scholars contend that the denial of any *one* of them constitutes a serious move away from the faith altogether. Pinnock, however, firmly maintains his Evangelical commitment and does not intend to depart from its heritage (which he undoubtedly values—especially in terms of the cen-

---

[70] Stanley Grenz, editorial review of Barry L. Callen, *Clark H. Pinnock: Journey Toward Renewal: An Intellectual Biography* (Nappanee, Ind.: Evangel, 2000). Back cover.

[71] Pinnock, personal interview, November 20, 2002.

[72] Pinnock, *The Grace of God and the Will of Man*, x.

trality of Scripture, Christ-centered salvation, and the importance of personal conversion). Rather, he advocates dialogue with the more "liberal" theological circles and is intent on promoting a campaign of dialectical reform that would bring greater sociocultural relevance to Evangelicalism as it enters the twenty-first century. Many of his works in the last fifteen years have therefore been an attempt to "update" Evangelicalism in order to rescue it from what he considers an antiquated obsolescence in which holdover, classical commitments have lead it astray.

Another reason for my interest in studying Pinnock's brand of open theism is that, while a rather significant number of scholarly and popular writings have been issued in the last five years or so concerning open theism in general, none of them have been specifically focused on Pinnock's unique rendering of it, nor—and more importantly—with reconstructing Divine-human *relationality* on a Reformed footing. Thus, there is a gap in scholarly research on this matter considering that a thorough treatment of open theism's most notable defender has not been conducted, nor has it been used as a inspirative cue to provide a contemporary reformulation of relationality in a manner consistent with classical theism. Pinnock has a unique brand of open theism to offer. Unlike the other, lesser-known open theists who tend to operate more in the areas of philosophy[73] and exegesis,[74] Pinnock is a thoroughgoing systematician who draws from a multiplicity of areas. Thus, in addition to being the most influential Evangelical proponent of the openness model, Pinnock is easily the premier openness *theologian*. In this sense, a thorough treatment of his version of open theism is timely.

Scope of this Work

This work unfolds in five phases. The first is a theological biography of Clark Pinnock which chronicles his metamorphosis from committed Augustinian-Calvinist, to classical Wesleyan Arminianism, and then finally to open theist and *anti*-Augustinian. The second chapter seeks to plot a course of theological trajectory for Pinnock to better understand his intellectual journey and the triggers which helped lead him to openness theology.

---

[73] John Sanders, William Hasker, and David Basinger are all professional philosophers and, thus, not only tend to approach the matter in this way but appear to me *to have arrived* at it thusly.

[74] Gregory Boyd is perhaps the most exegetical of the open theists as even a cursory review of his, *God of the Possible*, will demonstrate especially when compared to the other open theists.

The third chapter is primarily descriptive, covering Pinnock's arguments in favor of the openness view which include his defense from Scripture, theological systematization, philosophy, and influences. This chapter also includes an assessment of his arguments against classical theology, chief among them being that classical theology has been seriously and negatively influenced by Grecian metaphysics.

Chapter four provides a critical analysis of Pinnock's central premises in defense of openness theology. Here, I also detail what I perceive to be the strengths and weakness of Pinnock's system including whether or not it is internally consistent (that is, logically coherent) and externally consistent, that is, whether it is consistent within the doctrinal framework of his other Evangelical commitments. This especially concerns theology proper, theological anthropology, and Divine-human relationality. I further argue in the chapter for a soteriology that begin with monergistic regeneration, grounded in the purposes of God, rather than in the libertarian freedom of humans.

Chapter five furthers my critical analysis by replacing Pinnock's central premises with an alternative set that maintains both exhaustive Divine foreknowledge as well as a model of "meticulous providence." The chapter begins with arguments in favor of exhaustive Divine foreknowledge, coupled with a compatibilistic understanding of human freedom. A subsequent discussion of the relationship between God and time follows.

In the same chapter, the issue of human cognition and reflection on God's nature is taken up where I defend analogical predication and Reformed accommodationism against Pinnock's implicit ontic-epistemic univocity. Next, an application of the issues of foreknowledge, compatibilism, time, and religious language are made to our understanding of history, with special emphasis on the problem of evil. Lastly, I argue for a different creational teleology than Pinnock—fundamentally a God-centered, glory-focused universe. Each of these elements lay the groundwork for what the next chapter brings together as the final step in reconstructing Divine-human relationality.

Chapter six provides an alternative relational model to open theism which attempts to preserve the basic mechanics of a historic Reformed view, but reconstructs the issue of Divine-human relationality from a contemporary and multidisciplinary (that is, *systematic*) perspective. Here, I argue that the basic postulates of Reformed theology, such as the foreordination of human history and *salvation* itself, do not destroy genuine relationality, but actually establish it. God's meticulous providence ironically provides the needed framework for a deeply rich, *relational* participation of humans

Introduction

with the Divine being as they are brought into adoptive communion with the Trinity.

2

Clark H. Pinnock: A Brief Biography

CLARK PINNOCK's theological journey is a fascinating, albeit enigmatic, one. He begins, in his own words, as an "ordinary, converted fundamentalist"[1] who in his earliest days in the 1960's as a biblical scholar issued staunchly Evangelical works defending biblical infallibility, inerrancy, plenary verbal inspiration, and the exclusivity of Christian salvation. In one of these, *A Defense of Biblical Infallibility*, Pinnock forcefully contends that the complete verbal inspiration of the Bible must be accepted in order to properly do theology:

> It is verbal inspiration which assures us that the truth we possess is valid, having been effectively communicated to us by God. In effect, the attack on verbal inspiration is an assault on the effective truth of the revelation of God, the citadel of Christianity . . . The foundation of theology is, therefore, only as secure as the Bible is trustworthy[2]

Evangelical sentiment over biblical infallibility does not come in more vehement a fashion than this. At the time, Pinnock was incensed by what he perceived to be the acids of "liberal" academic thought corroding the ecclesial milieu of his youth—complete with its theories of "higher criticism," demythologization, and anti-supernaturalism. He believed that these theories had undercut the power and efficacy of Scriptural vitality in the church which, in turn, led it to "[forget] both the truth and reality of God."[3] Moreover, Pinnock was a deeply committed Augustinian-Calvinist,

---

[1] Pinnock, personal interview, Evangelical Theological Society, Toronto, Canada, November 20, 2002.

[2] Pinnock, *A Defense of Biblical Infallibility* (Philadelphia: Presbyterian & Reformed, 1967) 17–18.

[3] Pinnock, "I Was A Teenager Fundamentalist," *The Wittenburg Door*, 70 (December 1982—January 1983) 18.

steeped in the Reformed-Baptist tradition believing that "Calvinism was just scriptural Evangelicalism in its purest expression."[4]

Yet as we fast forward into the 1990's and up to the present day, we witness a radical shift in Pinnock's trajectory where he begins publishing works in diametrical variance with his earlier views. Works bearing thunderous testimony to this shift include his *Theological Crossfire: An Evangelical/Liberal Dialogue* (1990), in which he tries to build dialogical bridges with a "liberal" theologian to develop a more dialectical theology; *Searching for an Adequate God: A Dialogue Between Process and Free Will Theists* in which Pinnock celebrates the common emphasis of these two theologies on the centrality of Divine *dynamism* rather than a supposed metaphysical stasis in the classical models.

Finally, and though there is a gradual progression of works leading up to it,[5] Pinnock severed the Gordian knot with the theological affinities of his earlier days when he issued *The Openness of God: A Biblical Challenge to the Traditional Understanding of God* (1994, co-editor and contributor); then his recent solo work, *Most Moved Mover: A Theology of God's Openness* (2001). Both of these works sternly repudiate the Augustinian-Calvinist tradition and move far beyond even the theology of Arminianism into Pinnock's relational and creative-love theism complete with the postulate of Divine nescience of future events.[6] In fact, so far would Pinnock's shift be from his earlier years boldly defending the integrity and absolute *requisite* of classical theism, that—in the latter of the aforementioned works—he goes to the unprecedented extent of referring to the classical doctrine of

---

[4] Pinnock, "From Augustine to Arminius: A Pilgrimage in Theology," in *The Grace of God and the Will of Man: A Case for Arminianism* (Grand Rapids: Zondervan, 1989) 17.

[5] Most notably in *Grace Unlimited* (Minneapolis: Bethany Fellowship, 1975) a defense of Arminianism in which Pinnock concentrates more on the issue of libertarian human freedom and "decision theology" than on the implications for Divine foreknowledge.

[6] Despite his forceful contention that "The doctrine of this predestination is injurious to the glory of God, which does not consist of a declaration of liberty . . ." [James Arminius, "On Predestination," 1.3, in *The Works of James Arminius*, Vol 1 (Grand Rapids: Christian Classics Ethereal Library, 2002) 116] it is important to remember that Arminius nevertheless maintained the doctrine of complete, Divine foreknowledge concerning salvation and reprobation saying, "this decree has its foundation in the foreknowledge of God, by which he knew from all eternity those individuals who would, through his preventing grace, believe, and, through his subsequent grace would persevere . . . and, by which foreknowledge, he likewise knew those who would not believe and persevere." [James Arminius, Declaration 5.4, *The Works of James Arminius*, vol. 1 (Grand Rapids: Christian Classics Ethereal Library, 2002) 127] This, of course, is precisely what Pinnock's creative-love theism denies.

God (especially as modeled in Augustine, Aquinas, Luther, and Calvin) as issuing from "a pagan inheritance" which must be overturned.[7]

Other theological reversals also emerge along the way in which Pinnock radically departs from other relatively unquestioned Evangelical doctrines, many of which he had earlier spent prodigious energies defending. Such doctrines include biblical inerrancy, Hell, soteriological exclusivism, and significantly, the atemporality and even *noncorporeality* of God. All of this thought coalesces and culminates in a robustly love-centered theology for which the openness model supplies the needed architectonic.

Naturally, a central question emerges: To what do we owe Pinnock's radical theological metamorphosis from committed Evangelical apologist and Calvinist, to Arminian and theological reformist, and finally, vociferous open theist and *anti-*classicalist? The following sections attempt to trace this progression.

Clark Harold Pinnock was born in Canada to Christian parents in 1937. Biographer, Barry Callen, makes some important observations about his formative years and the ecclesiastical traditions that Pinnock found himself heir to which would undoubtedly play an important part in sculpting his early career:

> [Pinnock's] paternal grandparents were Samuel and Madora Pinnock from the British Midlands. In the early 1890's, these pious Methodist people went to Nigeria as British Methodist missionaries. They became Baptist by conviction while in Nigeria (change of view on baptism) and joined the U.S. Southern Baptist mission. Samuel soon was seeking Africanization of the leadership of this mission, a philosophy well ahead of its time and not surprisingly resisted by the mission leaders. Here was a hint of the progressive spirit of Samuel's yet-unborn grandson, Clark . . . The heritage they passed on to [him] would include a keen interest in international mission, genuine Christian piety, an appreciation for scholarship and writing, British roots, Canadian identity, and Baptist affiliation.[8]

Pinnock recalls that it was primarily through the evangelistic zeal and "witness" of his grandmother that he was initially converted to fundamentalist Christianity and subsequently "introduced in a natural way during the

---

[7] Pinnock, *Most Moved Mover: A Theology of God's Openness* (Grand Rapids: Baker, 2001) 65.

[8] Barry L. Callen, *Clark H. Pinnock: Journey Toward Renewal* (Nappanee, Ind.: Evangel, 2000) 16–17.

1950's to the institutions of what is inexactly called 'Evangelicalism.'"[9] In his teens and twenties, Pinnock became active in numerous Evangelical organizations such as InterVarsity Christian Fellowship and regularly attended a Canadian Baptist church which, however, he would later characterize as having been sorely affected by the inroads of liberalism.[10]

Pinnock recalls that the theological landscape of North American Evangelicalism in the 1950's postwar era was heavily dominated by Reformed theological models adding somewhat pejoratively that "critics have not exaggerated much when they have wanted to call [the era] 'neo-Calvinism.'"[11] Pinnock offers this picture of his early theological inculcation and development:

> Certainly most of the authors I was introduced to in those early days as theologically 'sound' were staunchly Calvinistic: John Murray, Martyn Lloyd-Jones, Cornelius Van Til, Carl Henry, James Packer, Paul Jewett. Theirs were the books that were sold in the Inter-Varsity bookroom I frequented. They were the ones I was told to listen to; sound theology was what they would teach me. A simple fact, which I did not think much about at the time, was that Calvinian theology enjoyed an elitist position of dominance within postwar Evangelicalism on both sides of the Atlantic. This was due in part to the fact that it was and is also a scholarly and historic system of Evangelical theology. Therefore, it is no surprise that I began my theological life as a Calvinist who regarded alternate Evangelical interpretations as suspect and at least mildly heretical.[12]

He further explains that he "adopted Calvinist thinking in [his] student years"[13] almost by a process of osmosis and apparent lack of options since Reformed theology seemed to enjoy a veritable hegemony over Evangelical academics. Nevertheless, despite some silent misgivings about the Reformed models in which he was groomed, he pressed on with the goal in mind of becoming a missionary or Christian scholar.

Perhaps wishing to follow in the footsteps of his grandfather—a linguist, translator, and missionary—Pinnock entered into the University of Toronto to study the Bible and Semitics. This lead to a B.A. degree in ancient Near-Eastern studies which he received with honors in 1960. He was recognized at the University for his academic achievements and garnered

---

[9] Pinnock, *The Grace of God and the Will of Man*, 16.
[10] Callen, *Journey Toward Renewal*, 17.
[11] Pinnock, *The Grace of God and the Will of Man*, 17.
[12] Ibid.
[13] Pinnock, personal interview, November 20, 2002.

a British Commonwealth Scholarship which he could use to study at the British university of his choice.[14] He settled on the University of Manchester where the internationally known Bible scholar and Christian apologist, F. F. Bruce (1910–1990), was then Rylands Professor of Biblical Criticism and Exegesis. Bruce became Pinnock's doctoral supervisor overseeing his dissertation entitled, *The Concept of the Spirit in the Epistles of Paul*.[15]

In 1965, Pinnock began teaching New Testament studies, and later systematic theology, at New Orleans Baptist Seminary (NOBS) where he gained a reputation as a fiery defender of strict Biblicism and Evangelical orthodoxy. Indeed, it was while teaching in New Orleans that he issued his most vigorous works in defense of the traditional Evangelical views of theology proper, biblical inerrancy, and the facticity and historical reliability of Christendom's seminal redemptive acts such as the literal, bodily resurrection of Christ, miracles, and the Virgin Birth. These works included: *A Defense of Biblical Infallibility*, and a similar work, *Biblical Revelation— The Foundation of Christian Theology* in which Pinnock summed up his epistemological basis at the time for doing theology declaring that an unswerving commitment to biblical inerrancy is nothing less than "urgent for Protestants because the *sola Scriptura* principle cannot be maintained without it. An erring authority cannot serve as the only source and judge of Christian theology."[16] He also contended that,

> The result of denying inerrancy, as skeptics well know, is the loss of a trustworthy Bible. Limited inerrancy is a slope, not a platform. Although we are repeatedly assured that minor errors in unimportant matters would not greatly affect the substance of the Christian faith nor the authority of Scripture, this admission has the effect of leaving us with a Bible which is a compound of truth and error, with no one to tell us which is which.[17]

Calvinist theologian, J. I. Packer, whom Pinnock had widely read and greatly admired in his early days with InterVarsity Fellowship wrote the

---

[14] Callen, *Journey Toward Renewal*, 26.

[15] Though Pinnock's interest in pneumatology was clearly evident in this early work, his scholarly attention to this particular area of systematics seems to have gone nearly dormant until much later in his career—after his major doctrinal changes against Augustinian-Calvinism—when, as one of Pinnock's admirers puts it, it resurfaced and "flowered powerfully" in his 1996 book, *Flame of Love: A Theology of the Holy Spirit*, in which Pinnock celebrates having "caught the fire [of the Spirit] again" [Pinnock, *Flame of Love: A Theology of the Holy Spirit* (Downers Grove, Ill.: InterVarsity, 1996) 248].

[16] Pinnock, *Biblical Revelation—The Foundation of Christian Theology* (Chicago: Moody, 1971) 80.

[17] Ibid.

forward for the book in which he hailed it as "a major triumph"[18] against the influx of liberal higher criticism. He described Pinnock as a veritable voice in the wilderness who deftly "vindicates the historic Protestant view of Scripture as the given Word, true and trustworthy, of the self-announcing God, against the cognitive, relativist, existentialist, and ultimately nihilist idea of revelation which in a thousand forms has flooded our churches."[19]

Pinnock also wrote during this period, *Set Forth Your Case: An Examination of Christianity's Credentials*, which remains a noted Evangelical work in the "evidential school" of Christian apologetics and is still one of the most frequently quoted works on the subject by Evangelicals who are more favorably disposed toward "the early Pinnock." In it, he argues indefatigably for Evangelical orthodoxy and the literal, historico-grammatical hermeneutical principle. He contends that the Bible is trustworthy and true and that the denial of this principle goes immediately against the grain of the abundance of available evidence, thus betraying an unbridled "skepticism . . . and irrational bias"[20] on the part of liberal scholars. The purpose of the work was summed up with the distinctly classical sounding admonition to place our religious and epistemological stock totally in the hands of "the sovereign and triune God . . . infinite and personal."[21]

In 1969, Pinnock left his teaching post at NOBS to begin teaching at Trinity Evangelical Divinity School (TEDS) in Deerfield, Illinois. Though usually not considered "liberal" by any means, TEDS was nevertheless markedly different from the more fundamentalist environment that Pinnock had become accustomed to in New Orleans. Since its founding in the early 1900's, TEDS had quickly gained a reputation as a place of scholarly achievement and forward thinking with professors carrying degrees from many of the world's finest institutions including Cambridge, Oxford, Harvard, and Yale. TEDS was not an environment in which a young scholar could simply pound the dogmatic pulpit without sufficiently marshalling a solid intellectual and defensible basis for doing so.

This was a wonderful career advancement for Pinnock. Yet what he never could have known at the time was the manner in which this new environment would lead him to question much of the theology he had hitherto taken for granted. His entire theological foundation was about to be challenged and ultimately torn asunder, reigning in a tumultuous and,

---

[18] J. I. Packer, "Forward," Pinnock, *Biblical Revelation—The Foundation of Christian Theology* (Chicago: Moody, 1971) 5.

[19] Ibid.

[20] Pinnock, *Set Forth Your Case* (Nutley, N. J.: Craig, 1968) 58.

[21] Ibid., 107.

to date, seemingly interminable course of constant theological reformulation.

Pinnock himself describes the period as the one which created for him the first "hole in the dike"[22] of classical theology. Curiously, though, unlike many theologians who experience a terrible cognitive dissonance, or come to a place of plaguing doubt about their earlier doctrinal convictions, Pinnock reports that this experience was one of "considerable relief."[23] He welcomed the opportunity to close the door on the Evangelical stronghold of Augustine and Calvin and felt that he had finally become "free from hyper-transcendence."[24]

Where Pinnock would, however, find a common, almost archetypical strain with other theologians who have broken ties with earlier convictions (Pinnock compares himself with Karl Barth in this regard)[25] was the manner in which the break was precipitated, that is, with a single link in the theological chain being broken. For Barth, it was a philosophical concern over the God of classicalism who he thought came to resemble an "imperious potentate"[26] who micromanages the world without consideration of human volitional agency. For Pinnock, the chain link was similar. He reached a point of violent objection to the classical Reformed doctrine of the perseverance of the saints after engaging in a study of the book of Hebrews. This doctrine, which Pinnock had firmly held to earlier in his career, is embodied in the Westminster assertion that,

> They, whom God has accepted in His Beloved, effectually called, and sanctified by His Spirit, can neither totally nor finally fall away from the state of grace, but shall certainly persevere therein to the end, and be eternally saved. This perseverance of the saints depends not upon their own free will, but upon the immutability of the decree of election, flowing from the free and unchangeable love of God the Father; upon the efficacy of the merit and intercession of Jesus Christ, the abiding of the Spirit, and of the seed of God within them, and the nature of the covenant of grace: from all which arises also the certainty and infallibility thereof.[27]

---

[22] Pinnock, *The Grace of God and the Will of Man*, 17.

[23] Ibid., 18.

[24] Pinnock, "How My Mind Has Changed," in Callen, *Journey Toward Renewal*, 243.

[25] Pinnock, *The Grace of God and the Will of Man*, 15.

[26] Ronald Goetz, "The Karl Barth Centennial: An Appreciative Critique," *The Christian Century* (May 7, 1986) 458. Reprinted in *Religion Online*: http://www.religion-online.org/showarticle.asp?title=1037 (April 15, 2003).

[27] Westminster Confession of Faith (1646) 17, 1–2; http://www.creeds.net/Westminster/c05.htm (April 20, 2003).

This doctrine seemed exegetically unwarranted to Pinnock and he felt it was deleterious to maintaining a sound soteriology. He describes the breaking of this first link:

> I was teaching at Trinity Evangelical Divinity School at the time and attending to the doctrine [of perseverance] particularly in the book of Hebrews. If in fact believers enjoy the kind of absolute security Calvinism had taught me they do, I found I could not make very good sense of the vigorous exhortations to persevere (for example, 3:12) or the awesome warnings not to fall away from Christ (for example, 10:26), which the book addresses to Christians. It began to dawn on me that my security in God was linked to my faith-union with Christ and that God is teaching us here the extreme importance of maintaining and not forsaking this relationship. The exhortations and the warnings could only signify that continuing in the grace of God was something that depended at least in part on the human partner. And once I saw that, the logic of Calvinism was broken in principle, and it was only a matter of time before the larger implications of its breaking would dawn on me. The thread was pulled, and the garment must begin to unravel, as indeed it did.[28]

Pinnock later refers to the doctrine of perseverance as "likely the weakest link in Calvinian logic, scripturally speaking."[29] As far as he was concerned, not only does the Bible countermand it, but our own experience and observation of human behavior in the church belie the gross inaccuracy of the Westminster contention. Many professing Christians most certainly *do* fall away and they *do* repudiate their faith. We must therefore be constantly on our guard against the guiles and trappings of evil which militate against Christian belief and lure us away from the fold. It is up to *us*. We must not become complacent, placing our stock in a presupposed and faulty sense of security that God will somehow unilaterally ensure our prolongation in the faith and that through the sanctificatory process we will become impervious to a genuine fall from grace—even a permanent one.

Yet, it is doubtful that it was only exegetical concerns that led Pinnock in this newfound direction. Countless numbers of biblical exegetes and theologians have read the same biblical passage which Pinnock cites against perseverance but have been unaltered by it (or even further emboldened

---

[28] Pinnock, *The Grace of God and the Will of Man*, 17.
[29] Ibid.

in their own position) and have opted instead to understand it in light of other scriptural revelation which seems to support the perseverance doctrine. Thus Pinnock's acquiescence to the more Arminian interpretation of this passage must at least in some way evince a prior philosophical and experiential sympathy toward that interpretation coupled with some prior misgivings toward the Reformed model.

This is at least intimated in Pinnock's more recent reflection that "what had dawned on me was what I had known experientially *all along* in my walk with the Lord, that there is a profound mutability in our dealings with God. What happens between us is not simply the product of a set of premundane divine decrees that, written on an everlasting and unchangeable scroll, determine all that takes place in the world"[30] [emphasis added]. Heeding this experiential impulse, Pinnock would later contend in his first official work defending Arminianism (not yet full-bodied open theism), that a relational mutability and our ability to *determine our own course* in life and in our relationship with God through libertarian human freedom is "one of the deepest of all human intuitions" and a "fundamental self-perception."[31] Far from humans being the resultant product of a timeless "all-determining fatalistic blueprint,"[32] we are "free creatures able to accept or reject [God's] purposes for us."[33] Calvinistic determinism is deeply flawed since "universal man almost without exception talks and feels as if he were free."[34] He attempts to further drive the point home adding that "when a theory comes along, whether philosophical, theological, or psychological, which endeavors to deny this intuition of freedom, it is up against a basic self-perception that will eventually overwhelm it."[35]

This "all-determining fatalistic blueprint" is a theme that Pinnock has returned to time and again since his conversion to the Arminian (and then open theistic) view. In his 1975 work, *Grace Unlimited*, he contrasts the Calvinistic "blueprint" with the relationality made possible in a world in which God and humans work *together*. Thus, the "predestination" spoken of in Scripture refers more to . . .

> . . . God's setting goals for people rather than forcing them to enact preprogrammed decrees. God predestines us to be conformed to the image of his Son (Rom 8:29). That is his plan for us whether or

---

[30] Ibid., 18.

[31] Pinnock, *Grace Unlimited*, 95.

[32] Pinnock, *The Grace of God and the Will of Man*, 18.

[33] Ibid.

[34] Pinnock, *Grace Unlimited*, 95.

[35] Ibid., 96.

not we choose to go down that path. God's plan for the world and for ourselves does not suppress but rather sustains and includes the spontaneity of significant human decisions. We are co-workers with God, participating with him in what shall be hereafter. The future is not stored up on heavenly videotape, but is the realm of possibilities, many of which have yet to be decided and actualized.[36]

Though citing mainly exegetical concerns toward the beginning of his newfound views, Pinnock has progressively become more reflective and lucid in sharing the elements which led up to his change of mind and even finally admits that, early on, he harbored personal difficulties with Augustinianism/Calvinism. This concession from his own experience is crucial, indeed the *sine qua non*, as we shall see, in properly understanding Pinnock's theological methodology, one which he adopted during this experience and continued to carry with him today. He writes that,

> As a Calvinist . . . I had professed to believe in a kind of human freedom, a compatibilist kind that claims our actions can be both free and determined at the same time. Sometimes I would try to explain it, other times I would give up and call it an antimony, *but deep down I knew there was something amiss*. I was faintly aware that an action forever predetermined to be what it will be, however necessitated, whether by external factors or internal motives, did not deserve to be called a "free" action. Now, given my new discovery, I was able to move away from that construction and see the biblical view of human freedom in a different way. God made us "responsible" beings able to respond freely to his word and call. Of the essence of this creature that bears God's own image, marking it off from all the others in this world, is this wonderful capacity to relate or decline to relate to God, to love or not love him. It was not open to me to regard people not as the product of timeless decrees but as God's covenant partners and real players in the flow and the tapestry of history[37] [emphasis added].

Despite these weighty concessions, Pinnock has insisted that the driving force behind his doctrinal vacillations have been fueled by a fresh reading of scripture, not from any hidden set of *a priori* philosophical suppositions or a wooden rationalism which he says some people "might unkindly suggest."[38] Pinnock maintains firmly that he is rendering a more faithful theological witness to the portrait of Scripture and a system that

---

[36] Ibid., 20.
[37] Pinnock, *The Grace of God and the Will of Man*, 18.
[38] Ibid.

remains in greater fidelity to its doctrinal currents concerning the Creator-creature relationship. For him, his system brings the two closer together in a dynamic relationship while the classical models fix an unbridgeable chasm through the Creator-creature distinction making the concept of relationality unintelligible.

This newfound system did, of course, come at some cost to Pinnock and he admits having to rigorously rethink (as he seems to continue to do) nearly every major area of Christian theology to make it consistent with his new model. He observes that "Just as one cannot change the pitch of a single string on a violin without adjusting the others, so one cannot introduce *a major new insight* into a coherent system like Calvinian theology without having to reconsider many other issues"[39] [emphasis added].

Since the 1970's, Pinnock's theology has had many strings getting retuned. He left TEDS in 1974 for Regent College in Vancouver, Canada before transferring just three years later to McMaster Divinity College in Hamilton, Ontario where he remained for twenty-seven years, teaching systematic theology until his retirement in 2002. Pinnock's time at McMaster led him to rethink nearly every major aspect of Christian theology including biblical inerrancy which he had previously so ardently defended. In fact, in 1984 Pinnock issued, *The Scripture Principle*, a work devoted to demonstrating the *erroneousness* of maintaining too strict a doctrine of inerrancy. Far from his earlier contention that "An erring authority cannot serve as the only source and judge of Christian," Pinnock now thought that strict inerrancy and infallibility is simply too rationalistic and that "Naive rhetoric about biblical infallibility could easily lead to a tragic Judaizing of the Christian faith."[40] He has not sought to completely renounce the doctrine of inerrancy,[41] but to update and improve it in his effort to combat this perceived Evangelical naiveté. Inerrancy must be defined "in relation to the *purpose* of the Bible," not in *textual* accuracy.[42] Pinnock firmly contends that inerrancy and infallibility should stop being defined so technically and should simply represent the idea that Christians trust, follow, and believe what Scripture says. Submission to biblical authority is thus demonstrated in hearing and obeying, but not in affirming a wooden textual perfection. When specifically asked if he repudiated any of his earlier works concerning the doctrine of inerrancy Pinnock said,

---

[39] Ibid.

[40] Pinnock, *The Scripture Principle* (San Francisco: Harper & Row, 1984) 62.

[41] Pinnock continues to annually sign the Evangelical Theological Society's doctrinal statement which includes the inerrancy clause.

[42] Pinnock, *The Scripture Principle*, 225.

Well, I suppose. I think the first book I wrote on that, *Biblical Revelation*, was too rationalistic . . . *The Scripture Principle* is kind of a softer version of that . . . I don't think inerrancy is important because I think its so confusing . . . I think it means "I believe the Bible" and, if so, I do. But its got so many qualifications as to what that means. I hold it . . . but its not very clear.[43]

This rethinking of the traditional view has not been well received by many Evangelical thinkers. Wayne Grudem, a major player in the openness theology debate, remarked at the 2002 ETS meeting that he has been using *The Scripture Principle* in his classes for years as an example of a theologian who does not merely redefine the doctrine of inerrancy, but who flatly *denies* it. Grudem mentioned this during the formal processes leading up to the vote in favor of referring Pinnock to the executive committee for review to help underscore the manner in which Pinnock has, since the 1970s, made a habit of coming at perpendicular angles to what most of the members of the Society unquestionably affirm. In fact, as early as 1977 this became publicly evident when a coalition of Evangelical scholars met in Chicago to form the *International Council on Biblical Inerrancy* in an effort to combat the growing tide of hermeneutical liberalism coursing through most of the theological schools in the West. Pinnock categorically denounced the coalition saying that it missed the mark and that Evangelicals should only be fighting the extremely overt liberal scholars (for example, those opposing miracles, revelation, etc.) instead of those who simply question Evangelicalism's inerrancy formula.[44] This was one of the first public indications of "the new Pinnock" which obviously came as a shock to many within the Evangelical community who had lauded his earlier works in which he defended precisely what he now branded a hyper-rationalistic distraction. Two years later, Evangelicals began publicly commenting on Pinnock's vacillatory track record to the extent that the well known Christian commentator, Harold Lindsell, former editor of *Christianity Today*, remarked that "his uneven track record leaves some of

---

[43] Pinnock, personal interview, November 20, 2002.

[44] Pinnock later officially denounced the ICBI in writing saying, ". . . there are a large number of Evangelicals in North America appearing to defend the total inerrancy of the Bible. The language they use seems absolute and uncompromising: 'The authority of Scripture is inescapably impaired if this total divine inerrancy is in any way limited or disregarded, or made relative to a view of truth contrary to the Bible's own (Chicago Statement, preamble). It sounds as if the slightest slip or flaw would bring down the whole house of authority. It seems as though we ought to defend the errorlessness of the Bible down to the last jot and tittle in order for it to be a viable religious authority (Pinnock, *The Scripture Principle*, 127).

us with an uneasy thought that additional damaging concessions may be on the way."[45]

Given Pinnock's changing views on biblical inerrancy and the doctrine of perseverance, it seems somewhat natural that his next focus would be directed on the area of soteriology. Having already abandoned the doctrine of perseverance, Pinnock came to believe that God's purpose and will can indeed be frustrated by human decisions. He thus concluded that for a Christian to continue in saving grace depends, at least in part, on the human partner. Following this, it was also natural that he would reject other doctrinal "chain links" like Divine election, total depravity, and the particularity of the atonement. In the midst of this, in 1974, he was quoted as saying, "I have become increasingly skeptical of the value and truthfulness of Calvinist theology. I am concerned that it threatens the integrity of the gospel which is offered in the New Testament without reservation to all sinners, and not to an arbitrarily selected number."[46] His books which followed such as *Grace Unlimited* (1975) and *The Grace of God and the Will of Man: A Case for Arminianism* (1989) were designed to support this new contention.

During this time, Pinnock also rekindled an earlier affinity with the charismatic movement which began after what he reports as "a charismatic experience in a prayer meeting." Even so, he remained in a "mainline church"[47] while attending various charismatic meetings. Pinnock recalls that much of this was brought out in him through "The new Vineyard music [which] has been very influential in churches that do not consider themselves to be charismatic."[48] Norman Geisler, a longtime critic of Pinnock's theology reports that Pinnock has often been observed to display (during prayer meetings and the like) many of the more emotional and demonstrative aspects of worship endemic to the charismatic movement—especially at the Toronto Airport Christian Fellowship (a Vineyard church) dubbed by charismatics, "The Toronto Blessing." Internationally known is the wild handclapping, near-convulsive shaking, jerking and so on that take place there. It is a "Word of Faith" church that has fallen under heavy doctrinal, theological, and practical scrutiny by such organizations as the *Christian Research Institute* a California-based, Evangelical counter-cult and apolo-

---

[45] Harold Lindsell, *The Bible in the Balance* (Grand Rapids: Zondervan, 1979) 43.
[46] Ibid.
[47] Quoted in Maxwell Ryan, "Pinnock's Uneasy Journey" in *Christianweek*, vol. 14 No. 5, May 30, 2000; http://www.christianweek.org/stories/vol14/no05/story4.htm (July 15, 2003).
[48] Ibid.

getics ministry.⁴⁹ Pinnock also claims to have received "a word of prophecy" on several occasions and to have "received healing from a serious macular degeneracy" in his only functioning eye after a prayer meeting in 1982.⁵⁰

Most important at this point in Pinnock's theologizing, however, is the fundamental place of prominence he begins to assign to Divine love. Without reservation, Pinnock would come to affirm, as he does today, that love forms the apical feature of his theology. When asked about this, especially as it relates to the formulation of his doctrine of God, Pinnock responds that love is central to the very *constitutive nature* of the Divine being "in the Trinity as a tri-unity of love . . . the Holy One is love . . . God is love. This is a Wesleyan theology . . . the universal love of God."⁵¹ When asked if this formulation of God's love was to be conceived in stark contrast to the God of classical models in which the Divine being would be conceived of as "unloving," Pinnock responded in the affirmative saying that "the Augustinian God who damns on purpose . . . That's not a loving God. It raises doubts as to a loving God and puts some question on the goodness of God, yes."⁵²

Three important theological corollaries have resulted, in turn, from Pinnock's repudiation of God's meticulous sovereignty (with the magnification of Divine glory as forming the locus of theology proper as in Calvinism) and with his replacement of an unyielding desire to make love the apex of his doctrine of God. These include his *annihilationism, soteriological pluralism*, and finally, his *open theism*—complete with a radical rethinking not only of exhaustive foreknowledge but Divine atemporality and even corporeality. We begin with a brief look at the first two before finally arriving at Pinnock's open theism. Taking a look at these issues will aid in our understanding of the overall manner in which Pinnock's revisions begin to form a constitutive whole.

Pinnock's annihilationism, or as he prefers, "conditional immortality" is lucidly and forcefully explicated in his 1992 essay "The Conditional View" in the book *Four Views on Hell*. In it, Pinnock declares his passionate refusal to believe in a God who sends people to Hell and takes "pleasure to torture the wicked everlastingly" while the saints in heaven look on in appreciation like "watching a cat trapped in a microwave squirm in agony

---

⁴⁹ See, for example, Hank Hanegraaff, *The Counterfeit Revival* (Nashville: Word, 2001) 41–56.

⁵⁰ Johan Tangelder, "The Teaching of Clark Pinnock" in *The Banner of Truth*; http://www.banneroftruth.co.uk/articles/2001/11/teaching.htm (August 10, 2003).

⁵¹ Pinnock, personal interview, November 20, 2002.

⁵² Ibid.

while taking delight in it."⁵³ This Hell-sending God who "control[s] everything like an oriental despot"⁵⁴ and is "virtually incapable of responsiveness"⁵⁵ is for Pinnock, "easier to associate with Satan than God, measured by ordinary moral standards and/or by the gospel . . . The traditional view of Hell is a very disturbing concept that needs reconsideration."⁵⁶ Pinnock reasserts this contention adding these startling words in another article dealing with the conditional immortality view in *The Criswell Theological Review*: "How can Christians possibly project a deity of such cruelty and vindictiveness whose ways include inflicting everlasting torture upon his creatures, however sinful they may have been? Surely a God who would do such a thing is more nearly like Satan than like God . . ."⁵⁷

One quickly observes that Pinnock has no qualms whatsoever about stating exactly how he thinks and feels about the issues involved in his theology. This is a feature of Pinnock's style that some Evangelicals have found both endearing and ghastly, some even blasphemous. In *Four Views on Hell*, he writes, "Everlasting torment is intolerable from a moral point of view because it makes God into a bloodthirsty monster who maintains an everlasting Auschwitz for victims whom he does not even allow to die. How can one love a God like that?"⁵⁸ Millard Erickson, responds to these statements by Pinnock and likely reflects a sentiment shared by many Evangelicals when theological issues are discussed in such a fashion:

> If . . . one is going to describe sending persons to endless punishment as "cruelty and vindictiveness," and a God who would do so as "more nearly like Satan than God," and "a bloodthirsty monster who maintains an everlasting Auschwitz," . . . he had better be very certain he is correct. For if he is wrong, he is guilty of blasphemy. A wiser course of action would be restraint in one's statements, just in case he might be wrong.⁵⁹

This sort of tempering of one's theological musings, however, has never been Pinnock's *modus operandi* and will likely continue to be one of the characteristic hallmarks of his methodology. Pinnock feels that such "pur-

---

⁵³ Pinnock, "The Conditional View," in *Four Views on Hell;* ed. William Crocket (Grand Rapids: Zondervan, 1996) 140.

⁵⁴ Pinnock, *The Grace of God and the Will of Man*, x.

⁵⁵ Ibid., 24.

⁵⁶ Pinnock, *Four Views on Hell*, 140.

⁵⁷ Pinnock, "The Destruction of the Finally Impenitent," *Criswell Theological Review* (Issue 4, Spring 1990) 246–47.

⁵⁸ Pinnock, *Four Views on Hell*, 149.

⁵⁹ Millard Erickson, *The Evangelical Heart and Mind* (Grand Rapids: Baker, 1993) 152.

ple prose"⁶⁰ is actually quite necessary at times in order to drive home his points, in this case, that for God to be a loving God, Hell simply cannot be punitive or eternal. Nor can it even be the softer view of *non-punitive separationism* as some such as C. S. Lewis may have suggested.⁶¹ For if it is, God is the consummate monster. In order to maintain Divine love as the center of his theology, the doctrine of Hell must therefore be reworked and thought of, as he puts it in his article *Fire, Then Nothing*, that the unrepentant will face "extinction, which is the second death."⁶² In a more recent work, Pinnock sheds a retrospective light on his adoption of the annihilationist viewpoint:

> I was led to question the traditional belief in everlasting conscious torment because of moral revulsion and broader theological considerations, not first of all on scriptural grounds. It just does not make any sense to say that a God of love will torture people forever for sins done in the context of a finite life . . . It's time for Evangelicals to come out and say that the biblical and morally appropriate doctrine of hell is annihilation, not everlasting torment.⁶³

For Pinnock, this is the *only* moral alternative to the classical view. It should be noted that this is another excellent example of the dichotomic theological methodology common in his work in which one of two extremes are isolated and then singularly posited as our only option. This is a theme which recurs mightily in Pinnock's teachings on open theism. God, for example, is said to be either "a loving parent"⁶⁴ and a "dynamic" partner in a loving "give-and-take relationship"⁶⁵ with humans (as in open theism), or, an "all-controlling despot"⁶⁶ and immobile "solitary monad"⁶⁷ (as in classicalism). This polar extremism, of course, has not gone unnoticed and

---

⁶⁰ Pinnock, personal interview, November 20, 2002.

⁶¹ C. S. Lewis seems to have advocated this idea in such writings as *The Problem of Pain* and *The Screwtape Letters*, namely, that those in Hell are not actively punished but are merely in the abyss of the absence, or separation, from of God. See Brian J. Lee, "Lewis's Reflections of Hell," *Modern Reformation*, vol. 11, No. 3 (May / June, 2002) 25.

⁶² Pinnock, "Fire, Then Nothing," *Christianity Today* (March 20, 1987) 40–41.

⁶³ Pinnock and Delwin Brown, *Theological Crossfire: An Evangelical/Liberal Dialogue* (Grand Rapids: Zondervan, 1990) 226–27.

⁶⁴ Pinnock and Robert Brow, *Unbounded Love* (Downers Grove, Ill.: InterVarsity, 1994) 31.

⁶⁵ Pinnock, et al, *The Openness of God: A Biblical Challenge to the Traditional Understand of God* (Downer's Grove, Ill.: InterVarsity, 1994) Preface.

⁶⁶ Pinnock, *Most Moved Mover*, 4.

⁶⁷ Ibid., 6.

has been roundly criticized by several theologians as a tactic that is both unconstructive and only serves to cloud objectivity and clarity.[68]

If the traditional doctrine of Hell is not compatible with Pinnock's understanding of the love of God (the starting point of his theology) then the same is true in equal or even greater measure with regard to his soteriological pluralism or "inclusivism" as he prefers. In his essay defending the inclusivistic view in the recent book, *Four Views on Salvation in a Pluralistic World*, Pinnock writes, "Inclusivism believes that, because God is present in the whole world, God's grace is also at work in some way among all people, possibly even in the sphere of religious life."[69] In another work dealing with soteriology, *A Wideness in God's Mercy*, Pinnock says "it is surely valid to infer that divine grace is prevenient everywhere. God's ever-gracious Spirit is not confined to the walls of the church."[70] He goes on to say, "When Jews and Muslims, for example, praise God as the Creator of the world, it is *obvious* that they are referring to the same being"[71] [emphasis added]. This is a clear departure from the traditional Evangelical view and demonstrates clearly why Pinnock has amassed so many detractors within the very camp he consistently proclaims as his own (itself a curiosity, leading some to wonder why Pinnock insists on continuing to consider himself an Evangelical instead of something more "mainline"). Evangelical writer, Alan Howe, comments that "Clark Pinnock is representative of a growing number of theologians who claim the name 'Evangelical,' but who have so subverted it that they are in reality engaged in the construction of a different theological edifice altogether."[72]

Pinnock boldly contends that, with terrible future consequences, St. Augustine reinterpreted "vocational election into a soteriological category"[73] and that the Protestant Reformers haplessly adopted this hyper-

---

[68] See, for example, Michael Horton, "Hellenistic or Hebrew? Open Theism and Reformed Theological Method," *Beyond the Bounds*, ed. John Piper et al. (Wheaton, Ill.: Crossway, 2003) 210–15; John Frame, *No Other God* (Phillipsburg, N. J.: Presbyterian & Reformed, 2001) 15–24; and, though not directed toward Pinnock himself, but rather those from whose thought he often draws from, Thomas Weinandy, *Does God Suffer?* (Notre Dame, Ind.: University of Notre Dame Press, 2000) 1–11.

[69] Pinnock, "An Inclusivistic View," *Four Views on Salvation in a Pluralistic World*, ed. Dennis Okholm and Timothy Phillips (Grand Rapids: Zondervan, 1996) 98.

[70] Pinnock, *A Wideness in God's Mercy: The Finality of Jesus Christ in a World of Religions* (Grand Rapids: Zondervan, 1992) 105.

[71] Ibid.

[72] Alan Howe, "The Evangelical Megashift & the Theology of Clark Pinnock," *The Christian Research Network*; http://web.ukonline.co.uk/crn/page15.html (August 10, 2003).

[73] Pinnock, *A Wideness in God's Mercy*, 25

predestinarian theology. The result has been to cast "a deep shadow over the character of God," and has even resulted in "pride, arrogance, superiority, and intolerance" among classical Evangelical theologians.[74] Pinnock calls for an end to exclusivistic language common in Evangelicalism and to begin emphasizing instead "a wideness in God's mercy and a boundlessness in his generosity towards humanity as a whole."[75] This, again, stems from putting the love of God at the top of his theology. He writes that his "optimism of salvation" is "grounded in the love of God for all humanity."[76] He further refers to this as "modal" or "cautious" inclusivism in which "God may use religion as a way of gracing people's lives and that it is one of God's options for evoking faith and communicating grace . . . Modal inclusivism then holds that grace operates outside the church and may be encountered in the context of other religions."[77]

Howe offers this stern criticism of the manner in which he feels Pinnock has departed from the core soteriological beliefs of Evangelicals:

> The starting point of *A Wideness in God's Mercy* is the suggestion that it is time that Evangelicals rethought the matter of the eternal destiny of the unevangelised. Although he rejects the universalism of the liberal Bishop John Robinson . . . the pluralism of John Hick . . . and the inclusivism of the Roman Catholic Karl Rahner, his insistence that salvation is through Jesus Christ alone does not represent the traditional Evangelical understanding. Instead, Pinnock sees general revelation and the illumination of Christ the Logos as offering the *possibility* of salvation by the light which they afford. In plain terms, Pinnock advocates the notion of "pagan saints" . . . [the notion] that some will be saved without hearing the gospel, and that others will receive a post-mortem opportunity to receive salvation. By widening the scope of God's saving activity beyond what Scripture allows, Pinnock abandons Evangelical exclusivism with regard to salvation, that is the biblical understanding that only those who respond to the gospel within the covenant dealings of God with His people are saved. So we must ask how different in reality Pinnock's view is from the "anonymous Christianity" of Rahner and Vatican II. In Pinnock, the Christian may not know he is such and may never have heard the saving truth of the gospel. At a stroke the missionary enterprise is rendered unnecessary and the door is left wide open for the inclusion of non-Christians

---

[74] Ibid.
[75] Ibid., 18.
[76] Ibid., 13.
[77] Pinnock, *Four Views on Salvation in a Pluralistic World,* 100.

in the believing community. Pinnock, the theologian of the new Evangelicalism, merely pays lip-service to the preaching of the gospel of Jesus Christ: he has re-made the scope of salvation in the image of Roman Catholic inclusivism. He has succeeded in building one more bridge back to Rome.[78]

Howe's observation of Pinnock's similarities to and affinities with Roman Catholic theology, especially that of Vatican II and John Paul II, is a keen and important one. Pinnock himself, in a bold theological exodus away from the typical Evangelical practice of regularly critiquing the Roman Magisterium's theological teaching, has expressed his profound *indebtedness* to Rome for helping shape his soteriology. He writes, "I have always appreciated the Roman Catholic theology of Vatican II when it comes to matters of religious pluralism, and have felt that this approach offers some good leads."[79] Indeed, at the 1992 meeting of the Evangelical Theology Group at the American Academy of Religion convention in San Francisco, Pinnock declared, "I am appealing to Evangelicals to make the shift to a more inclusive outlook, much the way the Catholics did at Vatican II."[80]

This should really come as little surprise considering Pinnock's overtly ecumenical efforts made evident in such works as *Theological Crossfire*. Pinnock is very concerned with the manner in which Evangelical Christianity is conceived by those outside the Evangelical camp and desires a higher level of sophistication in theological and dialogical efforts. For him, Evangelicalism must come of age and dislodge itself from the mire of ecclesial tribalism. He contends that many of the traditional arguments appealed to by Evangelicals today are too retrogressive and anachronistic and "may have worked in the Middle Ages, but . . . not as arguments today."[81]

In contrast to the ostensive close-mindedness of so many Evangelical theologians, Pinnock lauded John Paul II as one "committed to dialogue because he respects the gifts of God in people and looks for signs of Christ's presence and the working of the Holy Spirit."[82] Pinnock further commend-

---

[78] Alan Howe, "The Evangelical Megashift & the Theology of Clark Pinnock," *The Christian Research Network*; http://web.ukonline.co.uk/crn/page15.html (August 10, 2003).

[79] Pinnock, "Religious Pluralism: A Turn to the Holy Spirit," *The McMaster Journal of Theology and Ministry*. November 2002; http://www.mcmaster.ca/mjtm/5–4.htm (July 8, 2003) 1.

[80] Cited in Stafford North, "Church and Culture," *Oklahoma Christian University Faculty Websites*: http://www.oc.edu/faculty/stafford.north/culture.html (August 5, 2003).

[81] Pinnock, *Four Views on Hell*, 149. This statement is made specifically with regard to the idea of an infinite Hell as in traditional models but reflects Pinnock's overall disdain for a retrogressive theology.

[82] Pinnock, *The McMaster Journal of Theology and Ministry*, 2.

ed the Pope for reaching out and apologizing to other faiths for past abuses in his effort to build dialogical bridges, adding this soteriological insight undergirded by what he feels is a more robust *Roman* pneumatology:

> Although it is true that Vatican II had [attempted to apologize and reach out to other peoples] (for example, *Gaudium et Spes,* paragraph twenty-two; *Lumen Gentium,* paragraph sixteen), the difference is that such references by the council to the universal activity of the Spirit, offering grace to every person, were occasional rather than sustained, as with John Paul. With this pope, it has become a principal theme in practically every context in which he has spoken of the non-Christian world. And, whereas the conciliar text spoke only of the working of the Spirit in individuals, this pope is prepared to speak of the activity of the Spirit in non-Christian religions and by so doing he has left a mark on the development of these ideas . . . he does not say that the non-Christian religions constitute an ordinary means of salvation nor (as far as I know) has he ever recognised them even as extra-ordinary means of salvation. He has never suggested that we understand non-Christian religions as mediations of salvation.[83]

However,

> For John Paul, the reason why there are spiritual treasures in the religions of the world, why there is a sense of kinship, and why dialogue is promising, is the reality of the Holy Spirit, who is alive and active in world history, both before and after Christ, and who inspires the searchings of humankind. He believes that, while there are many religions in the world, *there is one Spirit seeking to bear fruit in them all.*[84]

Pinnock continues by illustrating the lives of two prominent Roman Catholic theologians, Gavin D'Costa and Jacques Dupuis, and the manner in which both followed the lead of John Paul II and made the Holy Spirit the key factor in their theologizing. He also quotes Jürgen Moltmann in support of his attraction to Roman pneumatology and soteriology who says,

> In both Protestant and Catholic theology, there is a tendency to view the Holy Spirit solely as the Spirit of redemption. Its place is in the church and it gives men and women the assurance of eternal blessedness. Thus the redemptive Spirit is cut off both from bodily life and the life of nature. It makes people turn away from this

---

[83] Ibid., 3.
[84] Ibid.

world and hope for a better world beyond. They then seek and experience in the Spirit a power that is different from the divine energy of life which according to the Old Testament interpenetrates all the living.[85]

It is interesting and important to note here that while Pinnock is comfortable quoting the Pope, catholic theologians, Moltmann, and others in support of soteriological inclusivism, most of the quotations he marshals on the part of Evangelicals are cited either negatively or even derogatorily. In his more recent works, pejorative terms such as "settlers," "paleo-orthodox," and "traditionalists,"[86] are often used to describe those who embrace classical Evangelical models, especially Calvinism. Such people Pinnock characterizes as those who are afraid to change and instead pitch permanent tents and raise suspicions toward anyone questioning their long-held beliefs. On the other hand, Pinnock considers himself "More like a pilgrim than a settler, I tread the path of discovery and do my theology en route."[87] Adding further emphasis to this "en route" approach, Pinnock considers himself a "reformist" who approaches theology "in a spirit of adventure, being always curious about what I may find":

> For me, theology is like a rich feast, with many dishes to enjoy and delicacies to taste. It is like a centuries-old conversation that I am privileged to take part in, a conversation replete with innumerable voices to listen to . . . I also do theology contextually, recognizing that theology will reflect the culture in which it emerges. Everything I write is not only about something but is addressed to someone. I may have been unwise in introducing too many of my discoveries in too short a time since I have fallen under a cloud of suspicion on account of it. I know perfectly well that Evangelicals are leery of innovation in theology (because it reminds them of liberalism), and that they expect their theologians to defend tradition, not challenge it. I have only myself to blame for calling too many things into question too quickly.[88]

This continues Pinnock's enigmatic legacy of strenuously maintaining his commitment to Evangelicalism while nevertheless challenging and

---

[85] Jürgen Moltmann, *The Spirit of Life: A Universal Affirmation* (Minneapolis: Fortress, 1992) 8. Quoted in Pinnock, "Religious Pluralism: A Turn to the Holy Spirit," *The McMaster Journal of Theology and Ministry.* November 2002; http://www.mcmaster.ca/mjtm/5–4.htm (July 8, 2003).

[86] Pinnock, "A Pilgrim on the Way," *Christianity Today* (February 9, 1998, vol. 42, No 2) 43.

[87] Ibid., 43.

[88] Ibid.

criticizing many of its major doctrinal distinctives. The derogatory quoting of Evangelical theologians, coupled with the laudatory citing of *non-*Evangelicals is an element manifested in many of Pinnock's recent works defending open theism.

Today, following his retirement from McMaster Divinity College, Pinnock continues to write, lecture, discuss, and defend his openness theology. Ultimately, whatever else Evangelicals may fault him for, they certainly cannot accuse him of being *practically* inconsistent with his new teachings, especially as it concerns Divine foreknowledge. Toward the end of a recent interview, Pinnock was asked, "So, what's next for Clark Pinnock?" He responded, "I am talking to God about it. Neither of us knows yet."[89]

---

[89] Pinnock. Interview, *Ship of Fools Theology*. Online. (August 4, 2003).

3

Pinnock's Argument

LIKE OTHER Evangelicals, Pinnock, both early on and now, affirms biblical authority and its indispensability in doing theology.[1] In his book, *The Scripture Principle*, Pinnock affirms that the Bible provides us with

> ... a locus of the Word of God in a humanly accessible form available to us. It means that the Bible is regarded as a creaturely text that is at the same time God's own written Word, and that we can consult his Word, which reveals his mind, and seek to know his will in it. It means that God has communicated authoritatively to us on those subjects about which Scripture teaches, whether doctrinal, ethical, or spiritual, and that we believers willingly subject ourselves to this rule of faith.[2]

In another important work concerning his use of Scripture in doing systematic theology, Pinnock affirms that "I take Scripture to be, on what I think to be good and sufficient evidence, the prescriptive norm and paradigm tradition, the canon and rule of faith and practice."[3] Indeed, he declares, "belief in the infallibility of the Scriptures is the pillar which supports theology—without it the edifice would surely crumble."[4] Pinnock affirms that his adherence to the Bible inexorably requires acquiescence to *all* of its teachings despite the fact that the majority report in modern scholarship may consider him intellectually primitive. He immediately senses

---

[1] Well-known Evangelical, E. J. Carnell, defined Evangelicalism as "that branch of Christendom which limits the ground of religious authority to the Bible" [E. J. Carnell, *The Case for Orthodox Theology* (Philadelphia: Westminster, 1959) 13]. B. B. Warfield wrote, "The simple adjunction in this solemn and decisive manner of a written authority, carries with it the implication that the appeal is made to the indefectible authority of the Scriptures of God, which in all their parts and in every one of their declarations are clothed with the authority of God Himself." [Benjamin B. Warfield, *The Inspiration and Authority of the Bible* (Phillipsburg, N. J.: Presbyterian and Reformed, 1948) 240]

[2] Pinnock, *The Scripture Principle* (San Francisco: Harper & Row, 1984) 62.

[3] Pinnock, "How I Use the Bible in Doing Theology," *Religion Online*, Article No. 18; http://www.religion-online.org/cgi-bin/relsearchd.dll (June 10, 2003).

[4] Ibid.

the gravity of his conviction against the backdrop of theologies that are more open to giving science and reason an equal or even greater footing with Scripture:

> The significance of [this] conviction . . . stands as a granite boulder squarely in the path of liberal revision and therefore attracts a good deal of anger and contempt. It is a serious impediment to theological experimentation and by itself practically rules out most of the precious convictions liberals hold fast to, that is, the validity of other religions, a purely functional christology, situational ethics, and the like. A high doctrine of Scripture and theological novelty do not go well together as everyone ought to be aware by now. *Sachkritik* is simply ruled out and this is all very frustrating to theological freethinkers.[5]

Pinnock thus repudiates the Bultmannian method of "content criticism" wherein we critique the content of some parts of Scripture for not conveying the "real intention"[6] of the text. We are not at liberty to "spiritually translate" the Bible to form an idea of what the text *should* mean verses what it actually says.

At the same time, however, it has been Pinnock's stated aim to "update" the church in conformity with modern scholarship and to rid Evangelicalism of arguments that "may have worked in the Middle Ages"[7] but not in a postmodern age of scholarly enlightenment. Against what he perceives to be the paleo-constructive exegetical methods employed by many Evangelical scholars today, Pinnock argues for the need to modernize:

> Every generation reads the Bible in dialogue with its own vision and cultural presuppositions and has to come to terms with the worldview of its day. Augustine did this when he sought to interpret the biblical symbols in terms of Hellenistic culture and became the first predestinarian in Christian theology. The church fathers before him had denied fatalism, but Augustine out of his experience and intellect devised the system I have been struggling with. Today, like Augustine, we are reading the Bible afresh but in the twentieth century context and finding new insights we had not noticed before. Just as Augustine came to terms with ancient Greek thinking, so we are making peace with the culture of modernity. Influenced by

---

[5] Ibid.
[6] Rudolph Bultmann, *Theology of the New Testament* (London: Scribner, 1951) 181.
[7] Pinnock, "The Conditional View" in *Four Views on Hell,* ed. William Crocket (Grand Rapids: Zondervan, 1996) 149.

modern culture, we are experiencing reality as something dynamic and historical and are consequently seeing things in the Bible we never saw before. The time is past when we can be naïve realists in hermeneutics; who we are influences what we see.[8]

Pinnock appears considerably discontent with the notion that conservative systematicians have not been as creative in building their theologies out of their ostensive respect and allegiance to the so-called "divine side of Scripture." In other words, the *human* element of the Bible appears to him grossly eclipsed behind an over-preoccupation with the *theopneustos* principle. This is not merely due, Pinnock says, to Evangelical time being monopolized by forging an apologetic for infallibility and fending off attacks against their *sola Scriptura* conviction, but to a more regrettable *revelational* complacency:

> . . . how is it that those who take a high view of the Scriptures are known to produce less by way of creative biblical interpretation than those who either bracket the question or treat the text as a human document? One might think that presupposing infallibility would stimulate relatively more productivity rather than less. It might be that the time of the conservatives is taken up in defending the Bible, not leaving them time to expound it. But that does not seem to be true, quite apart from the inelegance of such a situation in itself—the results in the area of methodology are not full and impressive enough to support this explanation. I suspect the answer is to be found in a less complimentary direction. I think that our preoccupation with the divine side of the Bible has resulted in our neglecting the human side of it and misled us into thinking that we have already grasped (and appropriated in our Evangelical traditions) the revelational freight which it delivers. We have tended to opt out of critical study of the Bible and left it to others in a spirit of complacency as though the meaning of the Bible were exhausted already. If so, we are guilty of an impiety and will live to see the transfer of exegetical wealth from our side to the other.[9]

For Pinnock, this is a clarion call to begin looking at Scriptural teachings afresh, free of the hermeneutical shackles of what he understands to be an obsolete and bygone era of Evangelical hyper-simplicity. This liberation from hermeneutical complacency has, Pinnock contends, lead him to find the new insights of openness theology that had earlier been missed

---

[8] Pinnock, "From Augustine to Arminius: A Pilgrimage in Theology," *The Grace of God and the Will of Man: A Case for Arminianism* (Grand Rapids: Zondervan, 1989) 27.

[9] Pinnock, "How I Use the Bible in Doing Theology," *Religion Online*, Article 18; http://www.religion-online.org/cgi-bin/relsearchd.dll/ showarticle?item_id=9 (June 10, 2003).

by the classicalists. Once faulty classical presuppositions are jettisoned, the general ring of Scripture should lead us to the openness model if we will only listen.

Pinnock's thinking here somewhat resembles Barth's *sachexegese* principle wherein Scripture should be interpreted in light of its central idea, or *sache* which—Pinnock's believes—has been sorely missed on the part of the classicalists. Barth wrote that, "The universal rule of interpretation is that a text can be read and understood and expounded only with reference to and in light of its theme."[10] Following the Bible's "theme" or central idea means that the underlying message contained within it may be something that God's spirit inculcates in us, *apart* from the *exact* words of the text. Indeed, Pinnock writes that "Barth was right to speak about a distance between the Word of God and the text of the Bible."[11] He sums his view up saying that, "inerrancy is relative to the *intention* of the text"[12] and that, "inerrancy is a metaphor for the determination to trust God's Word completely."[13]

Following this new approach, Pinnock believes that he and his fellow open theists "are seeing things in the Bible we never saw before."[14] It certainly is not the case, however, that Pinnock claims for himself some sort of unbridled exegetical objectivity or special ability upon which he has then built his openness theology. This is at least intimated in *Most Moved Mover* where he writes, "It was proper . . . for early theologians to engage Hellenistic thought, even though they sometimes did so naively. Similarly, it is proper for us to engage modern ideas, even though we too run the risk of making mistakes."[15] This modern engagement of new ideas means, for Pinnock, "a philosophy which values change and can imagine God, not as distant from the world and immobile, but as intimately involved with the world and dynamic."[16]

Nathan MacDonald has observed that this more dynamic philosophical understanding of Divine activity has formed for Pinnock what Terence Fretheim has called "controlling metaphors."[17] These metaphors, which act

---

[10] Karl Barth, *Church Dogmatics*, I.2, trans. G. W. Bromiley (Edinburgh: T. & T. Clark, 1957) 493.

[11] Pinnock, *The Scripture Principle*, 99.

[12] Ibid., 78.

[13] Ibid., 225.

[14] Pinnock, *The Grace of God and the Will of Man*, 27.

[15] Pinnock, *Most Moved Mover: A Theology of God's Openness* (Grand Rapids: Baker, 2001) 114.

[16] Ibid.

[17] See Nathan MacDonald, "From Augustine to Arminius, and Beyond," *Reconstructing*

as a kind of exegetical eyepiece for the interpreter, are vital for discovering "the kind of God" to which the world is related. Fretheim has also called attention to the "variety of [biblical] texts which point to a divine limitation with respect to God's knowledge of the future."[18] He further contends that biblical exegetes and theologians must find a renewed recognition of those metaphors which have been hitherto neglected.[19] Pinnock's familiarity with Fretheim's work is manifestly clear from around 1989 onward. Earlier, when he contributed to the book, *Predestination and Free Will* (1986), his arguments included very little biblical support. Yet with the publication of *The Grace of God and the Will of Man* in 1989, Pinnock draws upon Scripture more often and, at the same time, Fretheim's influence becomes plain. This is carried over into *The Openness of God* in 1994 and certainly *Most Moved Mover* in 2001 where several of Fretheim's works are quoted. *The Suffering of God*, Fretheim's defense of the importance of making a place for Divine suffering, is quoted in *all* of them. What Pinnock adds, however, is the even sharper idea of "root metaphor." As MacDonald observes,

> Pinnock argues that people have a "root metaphor" of what God is like, [in *Theological Crossfire: An Evangelical/Liberal Dialogue*, Pinnock says,] "Root metaphors for God are very influential. These are the basic portrayals of God which affect how we view and relate to him." The root metaphor many Evangelicals have is one of God as monarch or judge, and Pinnock believes that a more biblical model is that of God as loving parent.[20]

This "root metaphor" of God as a loving parent has no doubt become for Pinnock his controlling exegetical lens. He even carries this interpretive lens over to those passages which speak of Divine wrath which he understands "more along the lines of spurned love"[21] as opposed to justly and condignly deserved punishment or judgment. The root metaphor controls how *all* of Scripture is seen, systematized, and integrated into an organic unity. As Pinnock writes in his 1994 book, *Unbounded Love* with Robert Brow:

Theology: A Critical Assessment of the Theology of Clark Pinnock, ed. Tony Gray and Christopher Sinkinson (Carlisle, Cumbria, UK: Paternoster, 2000) 24; Terence E. Fretheim, *The Suffering of God: An Old Testament Perspective* (Minneapolis: Fortress, 1984) 11.

[18] Fretheim, *The Suffering of God*, 45; quoted in MacDonald, *Reconstructing Theology*, 23.

[19] Murray Joseph Haar, "Book Review: The Suffering of God: An Old Testament Perspective," *Theology Today*, vol. 42, Issue 1 (Princeton Theological Seminary, April 1985) 141.

[20] MacDonald, *Reconstructing Theology*, 24.

[21] Pinnock. Personal interview. Evangelical Theological Society (Atlanta, Georgia, November 19, 2003).

> God's fatherhood is the root metaphor of creative love theism. The metaphor was already in use in the Old Testament. The intent was not to identify God as a male, since God is beyond gender. This is confirmed by the fact that God is also pictured in female images: as mother who protects her children like a hen, nurtures them from her breast and never forgets how much she loves them. Isaiah pictures God as a pregnant woman crying out in labor (42:14). God, who is not a sexual being, needs both human genders to represent himself. The point of such gender-specific metaphors is that God is like a loving parent, continually working to provide an environment designed to free people for the joy of loving . . . God has decided to exclude no one—exclusion can happen only as a result of the human decision to love darkness rather than light.[22]

Pinnock maintains that it is he and other openness theologians who, when looking at the biblical data, have unearthed the true picture of God, unlike the classicalists, and are "comfortable with terms such as love, patience, wisdom, and repentance" (as concerns the nature of God), whereas "traditional theologians prefer abstract philosophical terms like aseity, simplicity, immutability, and impassibility."[23] He further contends that, "the open view of God takes seriously the fact that God is personal. God is not a metaphysical iceberg but a loving God who interacts with us in a dynamic fashion."[24] And,

> Augustinian and Thomistic traditionalists face a future which is wholly settled and whatever will be will be. The open view on the other hand has God asking us as partners to shape the future with him in our prayers and actions. Vital Christians believe this and operate on the basis of the open model, even if they do not admit to holding it.[25]

The importance of paying close attention to Pinnock's use of highly descriptive words to characterize his view over and against the classical view cannot be understated. A certain understanding and accompanying revulsion of Augustinian-Calvinism is made abundantly evident as Pinnock argues for his new theological system. Unlike the God of classicalism, Pinnock advocates,

---

[22] Pinnock and Brow, *Unbounded Love*, 31.

[23] Pinnock, *Most Moved Mover*, 26.

[24] Pinnock. Interview in *Ship of Fools Theology*; http://ship-of-fools.com/Shop/Theology/2001_11/PinnockInterview.html (August 4, 2003).

[25] Ibid.

> ... a God who creates a world that is not just a mechanical expression of his own purposes but an environment for other free, though finite, agents to exist with a degree of autonomy and a measure of real freedom. This is a God who loves being in covenant partnership with the creature and longs to draw us into a community of love, both with God and among ourselves. God's perfection is not to be all-controlling or to exist in majestic solitude or to be infinitely egocentric. On the contrary, God's fair beauty according to Scripture is his own relationality as a triune community. It is God's gracious interactivity, not his hyper-transcendence and/or immobility, which makes him so glorious. According to the gospel, God is free and self-communicating love, not a solitary monad.[26]

The radicality of these statements should be clear—especially in light of Pinnock's largely Evangelical audience. In this single paragraph, we find the classical deity referred to as a "majestic solitude," "infinitely egocentric," and as a "solitary monad," characterized by "hyper-transcendence and/or immobility"; one who is "all-controlling"; everything beneath him as "just a mechanical expression of his own purposes." His deity as conceived in open theism, however, is one of "fair beauty," who loves us and is "free and self-communicating." It is time now, Pinnock believes, to exegetically and theologically disinter immanence and give it an equal (or greater) standing with transcendence.

In doing so, despite earlier contentions that "in systematic theology we reach for the whole of the scriptural witness,"[27] Pinnock now somewhat strangely admits that "In terms of biblical interpretation, I give *particular weight to narrative* and to the *language of personal relationships* in it . . . [the Bible] describes genuine personal interactions, not manipulation"[28] [emphasis added]. No doubt, for an Evangelical, this is a non-conventional hermeneutical principle and, perhaps to some, questionable territory since most Evangelical scholars have typically advocated the hermeneutical practice of interpreting passages of the *narrative* form in light of the *didactic*,

---

[26] Pinnock, *Most Moved Mover*, 5–6.

[27] Pinnock, "How I Use the Bible in Doing Theology," Online.

[28] Pinnock, *Most Moved Mover*, 20. We may note that, while I have not found any direct references to Hans Frei by Pinnock, this position bears some similarly to those expressed in Frei's, *The Eclipse of Biblical Narrative*, where he advocates closer attention to narrative readings of the biblical text and the folly of literalistic or overly-prepositional approaches. Frei claims that, "a realistic or history-like (though not necessarily history) element is a feature, as obvious as it is important, of many of the biblical narratives that went into the making of Christian belief." Hans Frei, *The Eclipse of Biblical Narrative* (New Haven: Yale University Press, 1974) 10.

not the reverse.[29] For Pinnock, we note that such narrative texts are then further interpreted under the eyepiece of the loving-parent metaphor.

Apart from his hermeneutical methods, another important feature of Pinnock's methodology is his rigorous use of the logical truth-finding principle of non-contradiction in which the axiomatic corollary of the "law of excluded middle" is consistently applied. Something is said to be *either* this or that, true or false, never an amalgamation or admixture of propositions in which the two seemingly opposing premises can perhaps be made to ultimately cohere. For Pinnock, there is rarely a *tertium quid* when dealing with doctrinal tensions. So rigorous in fact is Pinnock's use of the law of non-contradiction that Reformed theologian, Robert Reymond, in a stern critique of Pinnock's openness proposal calling it "quasi-deistic," nevertheless lauds him for his effective and consistent use of it.[30] For Reymond, even Pinnock's rendition of open theism is more sensible and logically coherent than classical Arminianism, though it is *less Scriptural*.[31]

In his presentation of the openness view at the University of Calgary, Pinnock offers a summation of open theism along with the very *logical* contention that a relational dynamism cannot be maintained between Creator and creature without abandoning exhaustive Divine foreknowledge. The situation that faces us is *either* full-bodied Augustinian-Calvinism complete with Divine foreknowledge and predestination, *or*, it must resistlessly be the God of open theism:

> Open theism is . . . a relational and Trinitarian doctrine with an emphasis on God as personal and interactive, both in his immanent triune nature and in the economic relationships which he enjoys with creatures. Call it "Evangelical personalism" if you like. As a version of free will theism, it holds that God could control the world if he wished to but that he chooses not to—for the sake of loving relationships . . . God voluntarily self-limits so that freely chosen loving relations would be possible. In giving us genuine, that is, libertarian, freedom, God gave up complete control over the decisions that are made and chose to create a world in which

---

[29] See, for example, Millard Erickson, *God the Father Almighty: A Contemporary Exploration of the Divine Attributes* (Grand Rapids: Baker, 1998) 237. There, Erickson writes, "There are two basic types of Scripture: narrative and didactic. We can choose to rely primarily on the narrative passages and conform the didactic or explanatory passages to them . . . On the other hand, we can interpret the narrative passages in light of the teaching of didactic passages. This is usually the preferred hermeneutical principle, since teachings are generally less susceptible to ambiguity and consequent interpretation than are actions."

[30] Robert Reymond, *A New Systematic Theology* (Nashville: Thomas Nelson, 1998) 350–52.

[31] Ibid.

humans have significant powers of "say so." It means that creatures can do things that God does not want them to do.[32]

In contrast,

> ... high Calvinists believe that whatever occurs is willed by God (not merely permitted) and the world now is now exactly as it should be. Even terrible atrocities occur (it is said) for some higher and somehow greater good. Free will theists, however, believe that this would make God the author of evil. In our view, history is full of things that God did not want to happen. We acknowledge that God could dominate the world but chooses not to. By an act of self-limitation, God restrains his power for the sake of the creature such that, at this moment, God's will is not being done on earth as in heaven. It means that God took risks in creating a truly significant world. It means that, although God has goals, he makes use of open routes ... Open theism does however add a new feature to standard free will theism. It has a "twist" which makes it different, namely, its understanding of divine omniscience as "current omniscience" or "present knowledge."[33]

Pinnock expands on the logical implications of the two opposing views saying, "If you start with exhaustive foreknowledge, you go straight to predestination and impassibility, but if you start with God's suffering love, you go straight to the open view of God as a real person."[34]

A Three-Pronged Argument

Following his root exegetical metaphor of parental love, three main arguments form the backbone of Pinnock's defense of openness theology: the negative influence of Greek philosophy on classical Western theology, *love* as the central metaphysical attribute of deity, and libertarian human freedom.

The Negative Influence of Greek Philosophy

Pinnock considers his theology, and the movement of open theism in general, akin to a *new* reformation comparable even with that of sixteenth century.[35] He declares that "Open theism calls for theological change. We

---

[32] Pinnock, "Open Theism: "What is this? A new teaching? And with authority!", 1.

[33] Ibid.

[34] Pinnock, *Most Moved Mover*, 184.

[35] Pinnock, "Open Theism: What is this? A new teaching? And with authority!" presented at the University of Calgary, February 3, 2003, page 5; http://www.ucal-

want to carry 'reformation' farther."[36] One reviewer of Pinnock's jointly-authored book, *The Openness of God*, agrees viewing the openness model as even heralding a kind of "second reformation":

> Almost five centuries ago, Christians thrilled at the recovery of the truth of salvation by grace that had been hijacked from them for a millennium of church history. [Open theism] throbs today with the same excitement at the rediscovery of a God infinitely greater and freer than the cold abstractions of medievally minded reductionist theologians make him to be.[37]

One of the central arguments behind heralding open theism as a new reformation is the notion that Western theology has been negatively impacted by pagan-Greek philosophy. Classical theology, Pinnock believes, suffers from the perennial problem of falling into a "God of the philosophers" instead of the personal, relational, revelational God portrayed in Scripture which modern theologians of his ken are now discovering. "The God of the gospel," he says,

> ... is not the god of philosophy, at least not Hellenic philosophy. The God and Father of Jesus Christ is compassionate, suffering, and victorious love. The god of philosophy is immutable, timeless, and apathetic. We must speak boldly for the sake of the gospel: Augustine was wrong to have said that God does not grieve over the suffering of the world; Anselm was wrong to have said that God does not experience compassion; Calvin was wrong to have said that biblical figures that convey such things are mere accommodations to finite understanding. For too long pagan assumptions about God's nature have influenced theological reflection.[38]

It has been said that nearly all of Western philosophy is a footnote on Plato. In theological reflection, the same contention might well be applied to Augustine. Not that every Christian theologian agrees with the great bishop of Hippo, but simply that he was really the first theologian to write on nearly every major area of systematic theology that theologians still grapple with today. Augustine is the *sine qua non* starting point for doing Christian theology (at least *Western* theology). But for Pinnock, Augustine as a starting point presents a serious problem and disastrous con-

---

gary.ca/UofC/faculties/HUM/RELS/chairs/cchair/crsrc/Pinnock.OpenTheism.pdf (April 12, 2003).

[36] Pinnock, "Open Theism: "What is this? ... ," 5.

[37] Gilbert Bilezikian, *The Openness of God: A Biblical Challenge to the Traditional Understanding of God* (Downer's Grove, Ill.: InterVarsity, 1994) back cover.

[38] Ibid., 27.

sequences for theology because "the pagan neo-Platonic influence was alive [in Augustine's work] from first to last."[39] Augustinian theology, Pinnock contends, "put God in a kind of box" preferring Neoplatonic immutability and impassibility over dynamism and self-suffering love.[40] Pinnock acknowledges his indebtedness here to Emil Brunner's work *The Christian Doctrine of God* in which Brunner takes pains to unpack the notion of an overtly Grecian heritage in classical theology.[41]

For Pinnock, the gravity of this "pagan inheritance" cannot be understated. It is an infectious virus that has poisoned the church's doctrine of God for at least the last 1600 years—especially during the High Middle Ages in which foundations were laid for Enlightenment and Modern theologies—and has created a disunity between practical church life and theological formulations, the latter of which remain too abstract and foreign to the biblical witness:

> These inharmonious elements are the result of the coupling of biblical ideas about God with notions of the divine nature drawn from Greek thought. The inevitable encounter between biblical and classical thought in the early church generated many significant insights and helped Christianity evangelize pagan thought and culture. Along with the good, however, came a certain theological virus that infected the Christian doctrine of God, making it ill and creating the [practical/abstract disunity]. The virus so permeates Christian theology that some have come to take the illness for granted, attributing it to divine mystery, while others remain unaware of the infection altogether.[42]

Openness theology is intended to provide "a needed antibiotic to aid the healing process, bringing about a healthier doctrine of God."[43]

Jesus, Pinnock reminds us, spoke Aramaic, not Greek, and the Bible was written in Jerusalem, not Athens.[44] The point here, is to draw on the

---

[39] Ibid., 65, footnote 1.

[40] Ibid., 69.

[41] See Emil Brunner, *The Christian Doctrine of God* (Cambridge: James Clarke, 2002) 152–56.

[42] Pinnock, et al, *The Openness of God: A Biblical Challenge to the Traditional Understand of God* (Downer's Grove, Ill.: InterVarsity, 1994) 8–9.

[43] Ibid.

[44] Pinnock, *Most Moved Mover,* 68. This particular argument is apparently meant to underscore the fact that Platonism was not a major driving influence on Jesus. While this is almost certainly true (that is, that Jesus' worldview was decidedly Judaistic, not Grecian), it does seem a rather odd point to make since the New Testament was, nevertheless, written in Greek.

rhetorical spirit of Tertullian's famous question, "What has Athens to do with Jerusalem? What concord is there between the Academy and the Church?"[45] Such sentiments are meant to safeguard Christian thinkers from adopting foreign concepts of God which could lead to idolatry. In fact, Pinnock cites the Christian historian, Justo Gonzalez, as flatly contending that classical theology oftentimes actually *does* commit a form of idolatry.[46] An example of such idolatrous mistakes is taken from Aquinas' *Summa Theologica* in which we read the Angelic Doctor's statement that, "Since God is outside the whole order of creation and all creatures are ordered to him and not conversely, it is manifest that creatures are really related to God himself, whereas *in God there is no real relation to creatures, but a relation only in idea*, inasmuch as creatures are referred to him" [emphasis in original].[47] Pinnock is quite obviously incensed that such a thing be considered the "orthodox" view. Aquinas' appropriation of Aristotelian paradigms is infuriating to him and he asks whether biblical Christians "really want to assume that God is an 'unmoved mover' or something approximating it?"[48]

Pinnock also militates against building a doctrine of God on an Anselmian notion of "perfect-being theology"[49] which only seems to make God more remote and intangible.[50] As far as he's concerned, such thinking requires a stilted methodology of deducing Divine attributes from the starting point of some supposed conception of *Logos* perfection which forces the true *Semitic* God into a Procrustean bed that strips the deity of any vestige of relationality. Pinnock views this as a continuation of the very type of

---

[45] Tertullian, *The Prescription Against Heretics*, VII, in Ante-Nicene Fathers, vol. III. Trans., and ed. Alexander Roberts and James Donaldson (Grand Rapids: Christian Classics Ethereal Library, 1999) http://www.ccel.org/fathers2/ANF-03/anf03-24.htm#P3125_1133921.

[46] Justin Gonzalez, *Manna: Christian Theology from a Hispanic Perspective* (Nashville: Abingdon Press, 1990) chapter 6; referenced in Pinnock, *Most Moved Mover*, 69, footnote 13.

[47] Thomas Aquinas, *Summa Theologica* I, 1a, 13.7; cited in Pinnock, *Most Moved Mover*, 69

[48] Pinnock, *Most Moved Mover*, 70.

[49] "Perfect-being theology" is the popular term given especially those ideas developed in Anselm's *Proslogium* where God is defined as "that than which nothing greater can be conceived" [Anselm, *Proslogium*, 2.3, trans. Sidney N. Deane (Grand Rapids: Christian Classical Ethereal Library, 2000) 27.]. As such, "this Being is said to exist always; since, for it, it is the same to exist and to live, no better sense can be attached to this statement, than that it exists or lives eternally, that is, it possesses interminable life, as a perfect whole at once. For its eternity apparently is an interminable life, existing at once as a perfect whole. [Anselm, *Proslogium*, 24.2, Trans. Sidney N. Deane (Grand Rapids: Christian Classical Ethereal Library, 2000) 69.]

[50] Pinnock, *Most Moved Mover*, 70.

human speculation that has led classical theologians astray. Thus, using the theologies of Augustine and Aquinas (especially) as a foil, Pinnock concludes that,

> . . . there has been a Christianization of Greek, and a Hellenization of Christian thought. There was a tension between the ideals of an immutable perfection beyond the world and a creative sovereignty over and in the world. As a result, pressure was exerted on theology toward a monopolarity and one-sidedness, toward conceiving Reality in every respect absolute and whose relations to the word are nominal and external.[51]

For Pinnock, the syncretic influx of Hellenism has placed God so far beyond the mundane world of humans that it has lead us to formulate a one-sidedly transcendent deity. Building a doctrine of God on this perennial notion of God's extreme otherness has paid a terrible toll "at the expense of divine relatedness"[52] and has left us existentially isolated. How can we dare invite people into a loving, saving relationship with Christ when we espouse a deity that more resembles a Platonic demiurge or Leibnizian monad as opposed to a dynamic, triune God of relational love?

Love as the Apical Feature of Deity

Against classicalism, Pinnock states that God is not a "supreme monad that exists in eternal solitude"[53] or "a cosmic stuffed shirt."[54] Rather, He is a "creator who is not remote but closely integrated, by choice, with the world."[55] Further, "The world is dependent on God but God has also, voluntarily, *made himself dependent on it* in some important aspects"[56] [emphasis added]. Very simply—and quite unlike the classical conception of God's purpose for creating the world[57]—God "chose to create in order to share love."[58] God's original creative desire is the "multiplication of loving

---

[51] Ibid., 71.

[52] Ibid., 72.

[53] Ibid., 28.

[54] Ibid., 42.

[55] Ibid., 31.

[56] Ibid.

[57] Classical Evangelical theology has predominantly affirmed God's purpose for creation being the magnification of his glory. For contemporary expositions of this classical doctrine, see, for example, Wayne Grudem, *Systematic Theology*, 271-72; Robert Reymond, *A New Systematic Theology of the Christian Faith*, 396-98; Millard Erickson, *Christian Theology*, 399.

[58] Pinnock, *Most Moved Mover*, 28.

relationships."[59] Love and the multiplication of love relationships through dynamic interchanges with His creatures is God's "natural purpose."[60] It is a purposivity that flows naturally from the fundamental metaphysical nature of God "whose very being is self-giving love."[61] Pinnock sums up the view by saying that God "is a lover who wants people to love him freely in return."[62]

Pinnock takes the Scriptural text of 1 John 4:16b, "God is love" (cf. 1 John 4:8),[63] to be as close as one gets to gleaning a core metaphysical definition of the Divine ontology. As he puts it, God's *"very being* is self-giving love"[64] [emphasis added]. In his *Flame of Love*, he also writes, "Let us begin with the doctrine of God and focus on the liveliness of the Trinity and the identity of the Spirit within a loving relationality . . . Almost everything else I will have occasion to say will spring from this ontology."[65] Pinnock expands in *Unbounded Love* in order to better understand the constituent roles of the persons of the Triune Godhead and how these roles interplay with human volitionality:

> The Father is the loving source of our being. The Son beams forth the light of God and comes alongside us to befriend us. The Spirit works from within to inspire, guide and free us to love. Because God is love, we can be sure that no one will be excluded from knowing God by ignorance or lack of opportunity. Only those who deliberately reject God's love will be excluded, and they will really have excluded themselves. God has decided to exclude no one—exclusion can happen only as a result of the human decision to love darkness rather than light (John 3:19-21).[66]

The centrality of "the metaphysics of love"[67] in defining God and its corollary effect on all of Pinnock's theology cannot be understated. It is the

---

[59] Pinnock, personal interview, November 19, 2003.

[60] Ibid.

[61] Pinnock, *Most Moved Mover*, 27.

[62] Pinnock, "An Interview With Clark Pinnock," *Modern Reformation Magazine*, June 1998; http://www.modernreformation.org/mr98/novdec/mr9806freespace.html (November 16, 2003).

[63] All Scripture quotations are from the *New American Standard* (1971) version unless otherwise noted.

[64] Pinnock, *Most Moved Mover*, 27.

[65] Pinnock, *Flame of Love: A Theology of the Holy Spirit* (Downers Grove, Ill.: InterVarsity, 1996) 21.

[66] Pinnock and Brow, *Unbounded Love*, 32.

[67] Pinnock, *Most Moved Mover*, 113.

looking glass through which every other Christian doctrine is interpreted and unified (covenantally as *parental* love). For example, Pinnock defines sin as "the decision of the creature not to welcome love,"[68] Hell as "spurned love,"[69] and salvation as "freeing love"[70] in which we enter into "a new relationship in the family of God"[71] (contra the classical forensic models seen, for example, in Augustine, Anselm, and Calvin.). He even adds to this the idea that salvation itself is a kind of Buberian form of *I-Thou* dynamism.[72]

Pinnock is intent on bringing God down to earth rather than positioning Him in the supposed Neoplatonic netherworld of classicalism. He marshals biblical support for God's intimate, participative nature in history citing passages such as Jeremiah 23:24: "Do I not fill the heavens and earth?" and Revelation 21:3-4, "Behold, the tabernacle of God is among men, and He will dwell among them, and they shall be His people, and God Himself will be among them." Pinnock admonishes us to "not tilt overly to transcendence lest we miss the truth that God is with us in space."[73] He quotes Fretheim:

> The Old Testament witnesses to a God who shares in our human history as past, present, and future, and in such a way that we may even speak of a history of God. God has so bound himself in relationship to the world that we move through time and space together. Though God is the uncreated member of the community, he too can cry out: "How long?" (Jer 4:14; 13:27; Hos 8:5).[74]

Herein is where the classical models, owing to their pagan-Greek embryology, have totally undercut the fundamental metaphysics of love which Pinnock so passionately feels is taught in Scripture and provides the root metaphor of parental love. The substance of true divine love and "orthodox," perfect-being theology are concepts just as mutually annihilating as exhaustive divine foreknowledge and human freedom. Pinnock cannot grasp how an "absolutely perfect and pure actuality . . . not subject to any deficiency"[75] can possibly be involved in human affairs on any meaningful or intelligible level. Rather than being a dynamic God of love who *is* love

---

[68] Pinnock and Brow, *Unbounded Love*, 30.

[69] Pinnock. Personal interview. Evangelical Theological Society; Atlanta, Georgia, November 19, 2003.

[70] Pinnock and Brow, *Unbounded Love*, 111.

[71] Ibid., 27.

[72] Ibid., 24.

[73] Ibid., 32.

[74] Fretheim, *The Suffering of God*, 44; quoted in Pinnock, *Most Moved Mover*, 33.

[75] Pinnock, *Most Moved Mover*, 117.

itself, God becomes a static, metaphysical principle incapable of real relationships. In a particularly perspicuous passage—one rich with metaphysical claims and proposed deductions from the classical view—Pinnock gets to the heart of where he believes classical theology ultimately leads us:

> [Classicalism] entails God's immutability and simplicity and means that, in relation to time, God is timeless and does not realize his essence in successive moments. God's eternity means simultaneity not everlastingness. It means that God is always in full possession of the perfection of his being. God does not owe his being to any other; he exists by himself as completely unconditioned. Pure actuality means there is no becoming in God. God cannot change because change would presuppose a transition from potency to act and require change either for the better or the worse. This affects God's relationship with the world. God cannot have real relationships with a changeable world because that would involve give and take. God can impact us, but we cannot impact him in any mutual way otherwise he would change. But God never changes and cannot change in relation to the world—only the world can change in relation to God. There cannot be reciprocity of relations between God and the world because then the world would be unable to affect God. God must also be apathetic, unaffected by our joys or sorrows. We are in the presence of an immobility package of attributes shaped by philosophy not Scripture, that is, immutability requires timelessness requires impassibility requires omniscience.[76]

With such deductions, it is easy to see why Pinnock is so forcefully opposed to "orthodox" theology. This passage comes very close to summarizing Pinnock's entire view of the God of classicalism, built on the heritage of the so-called "Vincentian Rule."[77] A distillation of such theology renders a God who is totally *a se esse* and is perfect, pure, non-deficient, lacking

---

[76] Ibid.

[77] This term will be used again, so a definition is called for. Evangelical classicalists have traditionally stressed the need for abiding by the so-called "Vincentian Rule" whereby the putative orthodoxy of any new teaching is distinguished from heterodoxy first by means of Holy Writ, but then, if a seemingly intractable disagreement persists, by weighing the teaching against what Vincent of Lerins (c. 400–450) called "that faith which has been believed everywhere, always, [and] by all." [Vincent of Lerins, "A Commonitory for the Antiquity and Universality of the Catholic Faith Against the Profane Novelties of all Heresies," C. A. Heurtley (Translator), *The Fathers of the Church*, chapter 2, paragraph 6; http://www.newadvent.org/fathers/3506.htm (December 8, 2004)]. Thus, should some new doctrine arise that cuts across earlier thinking on the matter, adherence should be rendered toward the historic position of the church universal (that which has been believed everywhere . . .) and the teaching dispatched as heresy or aberration. Where Scripture is silent or apparently unclear, *catholicity* must play a part.

potential (that is, is pure actuality), unconditioned, immutable, simple, timeless, and omniscient. But, according to Pinnock, *as such*, this God is also non-relational, non-reciprocal, apathetic, distant, impassionate, unaffectionate, and immobile.[78]

For Pinnock, it remains "obvious," that a person cannot truly enjoin a relationship with a God who is any of the items in the second set, which are precisely where he thinks the items in the first set ineluctably lead us. Timelessness and lack of potentiality (a corollary of immutability), for example, reduce to unrelatedness, disaffection, estrangement and so forth.

Pinnock also delineates a "double problem" we are faced with when contemplating a God that is described in term of the items in the first set. The first is a rehashing of his contention that such attributes are unbiblical and counter Hebraic (the latter of which should instead ground our hermeneutic). Pinnock argues that the Bible uses personal not "absolutist" language.[79] Greek categories do not permit a living God with a personal nature. Rather, they render God as a philosophical abstraction which does great damage to the Bible's revelatory disclosure of His closeness and personal interaction with the world. Secondly, the classical view is fundamentally unintelligible and leads to a crisis of faith. An unchangeable, impassible God is literally "irrelevant" to human creatures and it makes "little difference whether we love him or not, or even exist."[80] Pinnock has both an intellectual and existential revulsion here. It is intellectually contradictory to think of a timeless being entering into time and interacting with temporal beings; it is existentially ineffectual to try and *relate* to a timeless being. Similarly, it is rationally antithetical to maintain God's meticulous providence of world events and also hold to human freedom; and it is existentially repugnant to disaffirm the human intuition of autonomous freewill. We sense our freedom as autonomously free, it must therefore be so. In sum, the salient point is that the classical understanding of the incommunicable attributes of God has got to be wrong if theologians are to salvage any of the so-called *communicable* attributes, the rubric under which the logical opposite of the items in the second set would fall (that is, relatedness, reciprocity, concern, passion, affection, mobility, and so on). Pinnock writes that:

> Two models of God in particular are the most influential that people commonly carry around in their minds. We may think of God primarily as an aloof monarch, removed from the contingencies of the

---

[78] The list is my own distillation.

[79] Pinnock, *Most Moved Mover*, 117.

[80] Ibid., 118.

world, unchangeable in every aspect of being, as an all-determining and irresistible power, aware of everything that will ever happen and never taking risks. Or we may understand God as a caring parent with qualities of love and responsiveness, generosity and sensitivity, openness and vulnerability, a person (rather than a metaphysical principle) who experiences the world, responds to what happens, relates to us and interacts dynamically with humans.[81]

The language here is strong and, again, pits chiefly noncommunicable attributes against communicable ones. But does this mean that classical theologians, while affirming the former set of attributes, conclude that God is therefore uncaring, unresponsive, ungenerous, and insensitive? During our interviews, Pinnock acknowledged that many classical theologians have spoken to *some* degree of God's love. His charge, however, is that they are, again, living on the borrowed capital of openness thought. It is an irreconcilable cognitive dissonance that the classical theologian must inevitably suffer from when touting God's total sovereignty on one hand but His concomitant love on the other, since it is meaningless and contradictory to speak of a God that can both foreknow an action—much less *ordain* it—and then emotionally decry or disapprove of the event *post hoc*. More importantly, the metaphysics of love simply do not allow this. God himself does not want it. God wants to take risks for the sake of loving relationships that might occur as the very fruit of risk. This cannot logically be brought about through meticulous providence which inescapably annihilates the concept of risk or openness.

Apologetics has played an important role in Pinnock's thinking on these matters. He has always had somewhat of an apologetic intent in shaping his views and making them palatable to the cultural milieu. It is little surprise, then, to find him commenting on traditional theism with the complaint that,

> No wonder people are abandoning "God," if they think that is who God is. Can anyone blame them? How can one love a remote God, indifferent to what happens, and unable to suffer or respond? A good deal of atheism is a child of traditional theism that cuts God off from human life and undercuts the very meaning and value of life.[82]

Following this line of apologetical reasoning, Pinnock worries that the integrity of Christian theology is at stake with the continuing hegemony of

---

[81] Pinnock, *The Openness of God: A Biblical Challenge to the Traditional Understand of God* (Downer's Grove, Ill.: InterVarsity, 1994) 103.
[82] Ibid.

classical formulations still holding sway. Not only does it suffer from insuperable contradictions which facilely smuggle themselves into our thinking as "mysteries," but it lacks existential appeal. It is an existential and illogical behemoth which propounds that, "God is timeless yet acts in time; that God's knowledge is exhaustive yet freedom is real; that God's power is all-controlling yet things happen contrary to his will; that God is unchangeable and yet knows and relates to a changing world."[83]

This line of thinking and dissatisfaction with the classical models which, to Pinnock, seem more intent on weaving their own dogmas than learning from Scripture, led him in 1990 to call for a new "postmodern orthodoxy" saying that "Academic theology has gone wrong in the past . . . by pretty much ignoring the narrative form of revelation. It has looked for truth in doctrine rather than in narrative."[84] In another place dealing with the implications of these issues on soteriology, Pinnock again focuses on the problem of Evangelicalism's theological inheritance from Medieval and Reformed Scholasticism which had led it away from Divine love: "The conjunction of cultural change with an uneasiness regarding certain inherited traditions has pressured theologians today to develop a better model for handling the doctrine of salvation as it pertains to the multitudes who have lived their lives outside the church and apart from the gospel. The willingness of Christians to *tolerate equivocation* about God's salvific will has diminished, and more and more it is being taken for granted that God's boundless mercy is a primary truth that cannot be compromised"[85] [emphasis added].

When we understand that the biblical God is distinct in His very being from the "god" of the Hellenistic philosophers, we will move beyond thinking of Him as "a metaphysical iceberg and a solitary being suffering from his own completeness."[86] Pinnock desires that Evangelical theologians stop wallowing in the past and get on board with the modern philosophical turn to relationality being advocated by a growing cache of contemporary theologians.[87] This is a worldview which focuses more on the dynamic cat-

---

[83] Ibid.

[84] Pinnock, *Tracking the Maze: Finding our Way Through Modern Theology from an Evangelical Perspective* (San Francisco: Harper & Row, 1990) 182.

[85] Pinnock, "An Inclusivistic View," *Four Views on Salvation in a Pluralistic World*, Dennis Okholm and Timothy Phillips, editors (Grand Rapids: Zondervan, 1996) 97.

[86] Pinnock, *Most Moved Mover*, 118.

[87] A recent vocal representation and helpful summary of the postmodern shift to relational theologies and anthropologies is seen in, F. Leron Shults, *Reforming Theological Anthropology: After the Philosophical Turn to Relationality* (Grand Rapids: Eerdmans, 2003). Shults himself also argues against classical theology from the viewpoint of an unbiblical Grecian

egories of interrelatedness as opposed to the sort of static "substantialist" or dualist categories of Grecian metaphysics. Openness theology, Pinnock contends, is in a much better sociocultural position to communicate the gospel to the new world. "Conventional theism" he states flatly and somewhat immodestly, "tends to be unbiblical and unintelligible, whereas the open view is both scriptural and timely."[88] Pinnock appears confident that, over the next few decades, the Hellenistic categories of thought that have dominated critical reflection on the nature of God will eventually taper off, dying not with a bang but a whimper. Our postmodern categories of dynamism are rescuing us from a theological heritage held captive by ancient Aristotelian and modern Newtonian notions of "black and whites." Pinnock quotes fellow openness theologian, Gregory Boyd:

> Throughout this century, and especially in the last several decades, we have been stepping out of the Newtonian worldview into a worldview which is thoroughly dynamic, relativistic, and relational. Such classical concepts as substance, absolute time and space, and thing in itself, are losing their viability among modern people. Such concepts as process, force, energy, and relationally defined essence, are gradually taking their place.[89]

This fresh emphasis paves the way for a new era of apologetics and outreach to those who might think of Christianity as hopelessly contradictory and unintelligible.

A key example of this is Pinnock's dealings with the thorny issue of theodicy which poses unique problems for classical theologians (that is, relating meticulous providence with "accidents," moral evil, inequality, and so on). Pinnock, like most of his fellow open theists, finds a window out of these problems with openness theology by which it yields what he calls a "logic of love theodicy."[90] The theodicy is sketched along these lines:

1. God created for the sake of loving relationships.

2. This required giving real freedom to the creature that it not be a robot.

3. Freedom, however, entails risk in the event that love is not reciprocated.

---

metaphysical intrusion (esp. 163–75; 189–210).

[88] Ibid., 119.

[89] Gregory Boyd, *Trinity and Process: A Critical Evaluation and Reconstruction of Hartshorne's Di-Polar Theism Towards a Trinitarian Metaphysics* (New York: Lang, 1992) 1–11, as quoted in Pinnock, *Most Moved Mover*, 121.

[90] Pinnock, *Most Moved Mover*, 131.

4. Herein lies the possibility of moral and certain natural evils—those which appear irredeemably malicious and demonic.

5. God does not abandon the world but pledges a victory over the powers of darkness. In such a theodicy, God does not will evil but wills love and therefore, freedom that opens the door to things going right or wrong.

6. Though God does not protect us from ourselves, God is there redeeming every situation, though exactly how, we may not yet always know.[91]

Not only is this an excellent example of how the dynamics of open theism seem to provide Pinnock with a way of understanding God, evil, and human volition, but it illustrates, again, how his metaphysics of love—as the apical theological feature—trickles down to every minutia.

All of this is contrasted with classicalism's ostensive "blueprint model of divine providence" in which evil serves a greater good purposed from eternity and in which "every gruesome detail contributes" to God's purpose and "makes the problem of evil insoluble."[92] Pinnock laments that Augustine later abandoned his "free will theodicy" in favor of a meticulous sovereignty view which must inevitably conclude that God is the author of sin and evil. Diametrically opposing this, he declares that when he sees "nature red in tooth and claw—tornados, typhoid and plagues that savagely kill the innocent—that this did not come from the hand of God."[93] Rather, God is genuinely aggrieved by these things and did not want them to happen.

Considering the question of whether or not it was even *worth* it for God to go through all the trouble of creating such a world as ours—rife with evil and suffering as it is—Pinnock appeals again to the primary locus of the metaphysics of love in attempting an answer:

> . . . [God created] because God is a serious lover who wants these relationships of love most deeply. It is a desire in God we humans can easily identify with because we know how precious they are. By creating such a word, high-level values became possible. In spite of evils, how many would conclude that creation was not worth it? What a spectacle the world is! It is an emergent, evolving system, which moves from elementary particles to complex personal life. How can one not be impressed by what appears to be the self-

---

[91] Ibid., 132.

[92] Ibid., 133.

[93] Ibid., 134.

expression of divine purpose, limited as it is by certain metaphysical constraints yet moving toward something marvelous—a community of persons living in a freely chosen relationship with God![94]

Libertarian Free Will

Central to the preceding doctrine of God and, for example, the related theodicy, is the notion of libertarian free will. Pinnock does not do much by way of specifically defending his libertarian anthropology. Rather, he makes an *existential* appeal to the reality of autonomous libertarian freedom by saying it is simply "one of the deepest of all human intuitions" and a "fundamental self-perception."[95] During our interviews, Pinnock even acknowledged that a specific defense of libertarianism is lacking[96] and that it has simply been an *a priori* supposition of open theists. The basic argument, however, is simply that true Divine-human love and relationality cannot take place if either determinism or complete Divine foreknowledge are a reality. The future must be boundless and open.

With capital-L, *Love* as the apical feature of his theology, this in turn requires a suffering, vulnerable God who is personally affected, even altered, based upon what human beings choose to do with their autonomous libertarian freedom. It, coupled with an unknown future, is a necessary mechanic for the operation of genuine, reciprocal love. As Pinnock states:

> God sovereignly grants human beings significant freedom, because he wants relationships of love with them. In such relationships, at least in the human realm, either party may welcome or refuse them. We may choose to cooperate with God or work against his will for our lives. God has chosen to enter into dynamic give-and-take relationships with us which allow God to affect us and also let us affect God. As co-laborers with God, we are invited to bring the future into being together along with him.[97]

Pinnock repudiates the notion that some Reformed theologians have resorted to that various *antinomies* can stand side-by-side and be held in theological tension. J. I. Packer is a well-known exponent of this notion:

---

[94] Pinnock, *Most Moved Mover*, 140.

[95] Pinnock, *Grace Unlimited*, 95.

[96] Pinnock, personal interview, November 20, 2002.

[97] Pinnock, "An Interview With Clark Pinnock," *Modern Reformation Magazine*, June 1998; http://www.modernreformation.org/mr98/novdec/mr9806freespace.html (November 16, 2003).

> An antinomy exists when a pair of principles stand side by side, seemingly irreconcilable, yet both undeniable. There are cogent reasons for believing each of them; each rests on clear solid evidence; but it is a mystery to you how they can be squared with each other. You see that each must be true on its own, but you do not see how they both can be true together.[98]

For Pinnock, the tension of which Packer speaks is exegetically and theologically lacking:

> There is no antinomy here. God rules the world in such a way as to allow for creaturely input. There are not two sets of texts—one affirming exhaustive sovereignty and the other affirming human freedom. That would create a contradiction. We are not asked to believe that God exercises all-controlling sovereignty and still holds human beings morally responsible. The Bible is coherent and the contradiction is imaginary. All-controlling sovereignty is not taught in Scripture. There may be mysteries that go beyond human intelligence but this is not one of them. One can hold both to divine sovereignty and human freedom because sovereignty is not all-controlling. The Bible, not rationalism, leads to this solution.[99]

Genuine human freedom must allow for the possibility of mishaps and things not going according to a fixed plan. The future, therefore, cannot be settled as it implies "the fixity of all things from eternity past"[100] and that, philosophically speaking, "it makes sense to think about the future as partly settled and partly unsettled, otherwise it would be the realm of settled actualities and not open possibilities."[101] Pinnock settles for no middle ground on what the implications of such a thing would be for our understanding of the world. Indeed, it would "undercut meaningful human life."[102] Both the metaphysics of love and genuine freedom are destroyed on a closed view of the future. For Pinnock, such a view robs both humans *and* God of the ability to make meaningful contributions to history as real, dynamic, and versatile. Existential resignation would be the only fitting disposition if such a philosophical scheme were true. The world would be a frozen plane of wooden, non-emotive, non-volitional actualities, bereft of interchangeable love. At best, our experience of love and relationships would be

---

[98] J. I. Packer, *Evangelism and the Sovereignty of God* (Leicester: InterVarsity, 1961) 18–19.

[99] Pinnock, *Most Moved Mover*, 55.

[100] Pinnock, "From Augustine to Arminius: A Pilgrimage in Theology" in *The Grace of God and the Will of Man* (Minneapolis: Bethany, 1989) 25.

[101] Pinnock, *Most Moved Mover*, 137.

[102] Ibid.

illusory as we are meticulously controlled by God as flesh-costumed puppets. A sense of responsibility and veridical culpability also dissolves as one would be inexorably led to look at life and simply declare, "Que sera, sera." Since motives and actions do not change the settled future anyway, why do anything? Exhaustive definite foreknowledge implies necessitarianism and fatalism, this destroys libertarian freedom (which is non-negotiable), so foreknowledge is jettisoned.

Thus, on the open view, an open future paves the way for meaningful life in which human beings can contribute to realities using each of their God-given constitutive faculties—reason, volition, emotion, and so on. In *Most Moved Mover*, Pinnock brings Boyd into the discussion once again at this point and approvingly quotes his assertion that,

> Knowing that what transpires in the future is not a foregone conclusion but is significantly up to us to decide, we will be more inclined to assume responsibility for the future. We will be more inclined to pursue what could be rather than resign ourselves to what will be. Life is life indeed when there when there are possibilities not just certainties.[103]

Pinnock also follows some of his fellow open theists in appealing to modern quantum physical science in support of the notion that the future is a realm of at least partly unsettled possibilities. Newtonianism and the implied mechanistic determinism of causes and effects is, to Pinnock, an outmoded and now defunct scientific worldview. Classicalists who still think in such terms are stuck just as much in the anachronisms of seventeenth and eighteenth century scientific thought as they are in patristical Neoplatonism. Quantum mechanics, Pinnock supposes, lends scientific credence to open theism in its implications for human freedom and the behavior of the universe at its most elementary level which now appears to be fundamentally non-deterministic and noncausal. New discoveries in physics under such luminaries as Bohr, Planck, and Heisenberg appear to violate the earlier principles of classical physics—principles which have long been an integral part of the warp and woof of occidental thinking. For Pinnock, this is an obvious appeal to the so-called "Copenhagen Interpretation" of quantum mechanics wherein quantum activity is thought to be *essentially* noncausal. Causality is thought to bear upon our environment macroscopically, but not necessarily microscopically. Heisenberg's "Indeterminacy Principle" suggests that reality, at its most basic level, is not the product of

---

[103] Greg Boyd, *God of the Possible* (Grand Rapids: Baker, 2000) 94; quoted in Pinnock, *Most Moved Mover*, 137.

antecedent cause and effect but is literally uncaused phenomenon. This is an added proof for Pinnock that open theism is correct:

> The passing of mechanistic theory, signaled by the rise of quantum physics and chaos theory, yields a vision of the universe which is open to both divine and human agency. It reveals a supple and subtle world of true becoming and whose future is open. We did not need science to tell us this but neither do we decline its witness. The future is not yet formed—in significant ways it is being made as we go along.[104]

Of course, the primary force of such arguments are meant to be theological, not scientific. But, for Pinnock, the very mechanics of the universe show that God is open to change and has created the world in such a way that the future is unsettled, thereby paving the way for meaningful relationships with His creatures.

This constant stress upon the future as a series of potentialities as opposed to "foregone" actualities points back to Pinnock's doctrine of God as *Love*. As theologian John Frame has observed, open theists have a vested interest in conceiving of God as fundamentally *vulnerable*.[105] God must not only be sensitive and responsive, but must take risks and be vulnerable to disappointment as, for example, when His love or gracious offer of soteriological mercy is "spurned." In order for the sundry biblical narratives communicating God's "sorrow" or "sadness" over a certain temporal situation to be genuine (even when such terms are considered anthropomorphic), they must issue from His vulnerability which is built, in part, on His temporality and nescience of future contingencies. God has high hopes for all humans, but they make facultative choices which touch upon the vulnerability of God and evoke emotive responses in Him, even regret and repentance. The alternative to allowing such things to be true of God are too onerous for Pinnock to integrate into his theological systematization. Indeed his typical characterizations of the classical model and the openness model are highly polarized, and rarely offer a *via media* for synthesization. There is no room for a loving God or free human beings in classical models.

---

[104] Pinnock, "Open Theism: "What is this? A new teaching? And with authority!" presented at the University of Calgary, February 3, 2003, 8; http://www.ucalgary.ca/ UofC/faculties/HUM/RELS/chairs/cchair/crsrc/Pinnock.OpenTheism.pdf (April 12, 2003).

[105] See John Frame, *No Other God* (Phillipsburg, N. J.: P&R, 2001) 55.

Against Impassibility

Not surprisingly, Pinnock challenges the classical theological notion of Divine impassibility, the doctrine that God is incapable of or impervious to being acted upon or *affected* by anything in the created order.[106] Impassibility and genuine human freedom are simply incompatible. Here again, Pinnock paints a picture of a God who is intimately involved in the world, far from the disinterested, "aloof monarch"[107] of classicalism. He envisions a God that does not rule the world unilaterally, but is moved and affected by the vicissitudes of free human history. "It is clear to me," Pinnock writes, "both from Scripture and from experience that, although God's purposes remain constant, his particular actions are always fitted gracefully into the demands of specific historical situations."[108] Temporal events invoke God's *passions*. The actions of God's creatures arouse in Him spontaneous sorrow, joy, pleasure, or even jealously. The things we do aggrieve or gladden Him. Pinnock proclaims that in Scripture "[God's] nature is not characterized merely by intelligence but is also characterized by *pathos*"[109] [emphasis added]. Objecting again to the influence of Grecian metaphysics in classical models, Pinnock quotes Abraham Heschel: "The God of the [Greek] philosophers is unknown and indifferent to man; he thinks but does not speak; he is conscious of himself but oblivious of the world; while the God of Israel is a God who loves, a God who is known to man and concerned with man."[110]

By contrast, Pinnock contends that traditional theology destroys this portrayal of God whereas the openness model celebrates God's dynamic interactivity. God's purpose of love in creating the world requires mutuality; a dynamic give-and-take interchange unavailable in classical theology which prefers to think of God as an "all-controlling despot."[111] This sentiment is seen in nearly all of Pinnock's writings after his period of theological vacillation at Trinity Evangelical Divinity School away from Calvinism

---

[106] G. R. Lewis, "Impassibility of God," in *The Evangelical Dictionary of Theology* (Grand Rapids: Baker, 1984) 553.

[107] Pinnock, "Systematic Theology," in *The Openness of God: A Biblical Challenge to the Traditional Understand of God* (Downer's Grove, Ill.: InterVarsity, 1994) 103.

[108] Pinnock, "There Is Room For Us: A Reply To Bruce Ware," *Journal of the Evangelical Theological Society* (vol. 45, No. 2, June 2002) 215.

[109] Pinnock, *Most Moved Mover*, 55.

[110] Abraham J. Heschel, *The Prophets* (New York: Harper & Row, 1955) 224, quoted in Pinnock, *Most Moved Mover*, 56.

[111] Pinnock, *Most Moved Mover*, 4.

to a more open model of the future and human freedom. In *Unbounded Love*, he writes,

> Creative love theism celebrates a different set of theological categories from those of the forensic model. Even when the images overlap (both models see God as Judge, for example), the meaning is somewhat different. When it thinks of God as Judge, creative love theism does not think of him as a law-court judge, but as a judge of the biblical type (recall how judges in the Old Testament cared about liberating oppressed people and putting things right). Both models may speak of God as a king, but with different views of the meaning of sovereignty. When creative love theists think of monarchy, we do not picture an all-determining power but a Davidic king who protects and shepherds his flock and delegates power to others. Jesus' metaphor of the Father who loves us unconditionally is the central image in creative love theism rather than Judge or Sovereign, and it controls the meaning of these other metaphors.[112]

For Pinnock, God first unilaterally created the world *ex nihilo*, but then "bound" Himself to it. This involved a "self-limitation" on God's part and a willing act of "self-sacrifice." Creation, then, "marked the beginning of the passion of God who decided to relate to the world intensely and let himself be affected by it. God wants to share in our history and participate in our life. He wants to communicate with us in as personal a way as possible, even if need be, as a suffering God."[113] Drawing support from numerous Old Testament narratives,[114] Pinnock concludes that 1) God suffers *because* of his people, 2) God suffers *with* his people, and 3) God suffers *for* his people.[115] This suffering finally culminates in the New Testament—primarily in the incarnation—in which God changes for the sake of humanity as an outpouring of his unsurpassable love and purpose for the world. God has "created us to love and be loved, and he is burdened by every interference with the freedom to love caused by the system of sin that grips us."[116] In the incarnation, we therefore behold a God who enters into the suffering of humanity. This suffering is not restricted to the Son, however, but is an *economic* suffering within the Trinity. Father, Son, and Spirit conjoin in mutual suffering, though each person experiences it in different ways. For

---

[112] Pinnock and Brow, *Unbounded Love*, 29.

[113] Pinnock, *Most Moved Mover*, 56.

[114] For example, Hosea 11:1-8; Deut 1:31; Jer 2:2-5; Is 5:5; 42:14; 49:15; 54:7-8; Ex 3:7-8; 4:22; Amos 5:1-2.

[115] Ibid., 56–57.

[116] Pinnock and Brow, *Unbounded Love*, 85.

example, the Father suffers through the death of His Son, while the Spirit grieves both the Father's pain and the Son's subservient self-surrender. Here again, Pinnock lauds the openness model and its allowance for Divine suffering-passion, over and against the proposed static God of classicalism:

> A God who cannot suffer, as tradition has had it [in its doctrine of impassibility], is less than man and far from the God of the gospel. The Hellenes thought that change was a mark of an inferior being, whereas the gospel presents us with perfection of a very different kind. It presents a God who is perfect in his changing and perfect in his relating to the world. This is a God who gives himself sacrificially to us and does not remain in splendid isolation. It is in this act of becoming that Jesus is most, not least, like God. What a contrast to the metaphysical absolute that has difficulty being personal, much less incarnate.[117]

The cross is God's ultimate expression of God's "wooing" fallen humanity back into covenant partnership with him. We see the "weakness" of God by which he saves people.[118] It is important to Pinnock to stress that God does not "overpower" his people, but *invites* them into participation with his Divine love and glory. He draws upon kenotic theology here describing God as "most present when he shared the experience of absence with Jesus . . . he humbled himself and became a slave, but this self-emptying was what he had seen his kenotic Father do."[119] Pinnock does not deal with any of the major implications of kenotic theology such as the credibility of the concept of an assumed Divine limitation or the problem of Christ's complete incarnational Deity, but is content to draw upon it only to the extent that it portrays God's suffering and sacrificial love.

Divine Nescience

Pinnock has long appealed to what he has called a "wideness in God's mercy."[120] It shows us that, "Instead of using his power to enforce compliance (which destroys true [libertarian] freedom), God travels the path of vulnerable love. He only takes steps to redeem the world when it goes wrong and makes himself vulnerable, because he cares so much."[121] The Bible should

---

[117] Pinnock, *Most Moved Mover*, 58.
[118] Ibid.
[119] Ibid.
[120] Pinnock, *A Wideness in God's Mercy: The Finality of Jesus Christ in a World of Religions* (Grand Rapids: Zondervan, 1992) 20–25.
[121] Pinnock, *Most Moved Mover*, 58.

leave us with the impression not that God is an immovable force that cannot be contended with, but is a sensitive, caring parent who is loving and responsive. This is a God that relates to the world not in static terms, as with the Greeks, but in dynamic terms. Contra the Westminster Divines, "God's will is not the sole explanation for everything that happens . . . History is the combined result of what God and creatures do."[122] This dynamism must, therefore, preclude the possibility of total Divine foreknowledge.

Against the charge that his theology limits God's knowledge, Pinnock's insists that his view of God's knowledge actually *is* exhaustive:

> . . . its just that the future can't totally be known. Its like with omnipotence. God cannot do the contradictory. There are things he can't do and there's things he can't know. So, I really do not see it as limiting anything. Its all the omniscience one could have. Where in the creeds does it say you can't hold that view?"[123]

Pinnock therefore feels confident in maintaining a doctrine of complete omniscience since, logically, God's *scientia* can only be built upon "proper" objects of knowledge. One cannot have knowledge of things *which are not there to be known*. Therefore, God is still omniscient—even though He is ignorant of the future—because the future is not a properly logical object of knowledge. It has not yet occurred and is therefore not real. God cannot create square circles, make a better God than Himself, make rocks so big He cannot lift them, and He cannot know the future. Divine nescience of future contingencies is not a metaphysical flaw, but a natural outworking of the consistency of God's being which is altogether rational and coherent.[124]

For Pinnock, classicalism (which reduces to fatalism) cannot have it both ways. Classicalists cannot speak of a God of love and dynamism who interacts with history and His creatures *unless they assume an open theistic model*. He recognizes that classical, even Calvinistic, theologians are trying to meet the demand of working Divine dynamism into their systematic

---

[122] Pinnock, *The Openness of God* (Downers Grove, Ill.: InterVarsity, 1994) 15.

[123] Ibid.

[124] While the complex philosophical dimensions of time and its interplay with theism are not the focus of this work, we note here that Pinnock evinces an implicit preference for the so-called "Tensed" or "A-theory" of time wherein only the present truly exists. Historical antecedents pass out of existence and do not exist (any longer), and the future likewise has no being. The opposite view, the "Tenseless" or "B-theory" of time, understands all successively ordered events to have the same ontological status—they exist without becoming and, thus, the past and future are just as real—and therefore *knowable*—as the present. Finite beings merely *experience* historical events as indexical or tensed realities.

theologies. But, in his calculus, they are hopelessly dependent upon the borrowed capital of openness theology:

> Of special interest is the way in which conservative Calvinist authors now want to say that God responds to us and is unhappy when things go badly. They are trying to work such themes into their work. They know that Evangelicals believe these truths *and try to co-opt them*, even though divine changeableness is incompatible with theological determinism. Many are taking advantage of the rhetoric of the open view of God, which Bible readers find compelling, and are trying to work it into their own language.[125] [emphasis added]

Underlying these statements is the important commonality between Calvinists and open theists which fundamentally separates them from Arminians and Molinists. Namely, that autonomous libertarian human freedom is, by resistless logic, incompatible with exhaustive Divine foreknowledge. Calvinists and open theists usually agree that their positions are the most logical ones (though most Calvinists do find libertarian freedom itself to be logically and philosophically untenable).[126] Calvinists, therefore, typically see their position as biblical and logical, Arminian and Molinist positions as somewhat biblical but illogical, and open theists as more reasonably logical than the former, but terribly unbiblical.

The openness response in order to solve the logical dilemma is to simply vanquish God's foreknowledge, while the Reformed response is to radically alter our conception of the facultative powers of human freedom. To wit, human freedom is compatibilistic, not libertarian. Pinnock himself views this dichotomy clearly and would likely be the first to say that one must choose between the two. Open theism, as he puts it, "makes the choices even sharper and clearer, being itself a more coherent alternative,"[127] adding elsewhere that "a theologian is not obliged to be logically consistent, but there is a price to pay for exempting oneself from the laws of rationality, it is intelligibility."[128]

Pinnock would, of course, sternly contest the notion that his position is unbiblical at all. Indeed, for him, logic is only the forecourt to the inner sanctum of open theism's newly-discovered biblicism. It is Calvinists that

---

[125] Pinnock, *Most Moved Mover*, 75.

[126] See my discussion of the problems associated with libertarian free will from a Calvinistic perspective on pages 128–37 of this volume.

[127] Pinnock. Personal Interview. Evangelical Theological Society. Toronto, Canada, November 20, 2002.

[128] Pinnock, *Most Moved Mover*, 76.

are logical but unbiblical, not open theists. Open theism advocates Divine *personality* over Divine *substance* or essence as found in classical formulations which concern themselves with explicating God's glory and power over parental love. For Pinnock, his theological work "Is not a question of diminishing the glory of God, which is so well captured in traditional thinking, but a recapturing God's true beauty so often obscured by it."[129] Herein is where the pagan influence must be expurgated. Complete foreknowledge is something that is eisegetically read into the biblical text when the theologian begins with the pagan-Greek eyepiece. Against his critics in the Evangelical Theological Society, Pinnock reviles the notion that Scripture manifestly teaches complete Divine prescience. In a particularly bold response to the ETS's 2001 annual meeting concerning open theists in its ranks, Pinnock wrote that,

> Contrary to the resolution of the ETS in 2001 that the Bible "clearly" teaches exhaustive definite foreknowledge, the fact is that Scripture often indicates that the future is partly settled and partly not settled. God does not know everything in advance, because he does not want to know everything in advance. God awaits the responses of his creatures and keeps the future open. You can only get around these facts by dismissing the inconvenient evidence. One has to accept one set of texts that are interpreted in a deterministic fashion and put aside another set that are inconvenient. It surprises me when critics say with one breath that they defend the inerrancy of the Bible and with the next breath explain why they cannot possibly accept a whole block of material which is plainly relevant. One has the impression that texts are not considered inerrant unless they fit the system.[130]

The assimilation of pagan metaphysics into the "system" requires classicalists to simply negate God's give-and-take relationships with humanity which are central to biblical revelation and have been hitherto buried beneath a supposed Vincentian orthodoxy. Vincentianism has very nearly *killed* the proper formulation of theology proper. "The implications of [its] views are frankly fatalistic," Pinnock says, and "they eliminate human freedom and take away human responsibility; they make God the author of sin and discourage motives toward exertion; they make God unjustly partial and make nonsense of petitionary prayer."[131]

---

[129] Ibid., 79.

[130] Pinnock, "There Is Room For Us: A Reply To Bruce Ware," *Journal of the Evangelical Theological Society* (vol. 45., No. 2. June 2002) 217.

[131] Pinnock, "There Is Room For Us," 218.

Things like response to prayer, reciprocity, and other actions that form the backbone of Christian praxis must assume a Divine person, not a substance or metaphysical principle as Neoplatonic patristicalism supposedly does. Pinnock acknowledges that the patristic theologians and classicalists certainly did argue for a personal and triune God, but seems to think that their efforts amount to little more than semantics in service to towing the line of settled orthodoxy. He contends that,

> . . . the various forms of conventional theism argue that God is personal but leave the impression of absolutism . . . As absolute monarch, God is the author of a story in which he is really the sole performer and we are but names in the script. All this renders so many biblical metaphors almost meaningless."[132]

Divine Temporality

The preceding arguments, *of necessity*, lead Pinnock to adopt a *temporal* view of the Divine nature. He refers to God as a "temporal agent" who is only above time in the sense that "he is above finite experience and measurement of time but he is not beyond 'before and after' or beyond sequence of events. Scripture presents God as temporally everlasting, not timelessly eternal."[133] Pinnock quotes Yale philosopher Nicolas Wolterstorff as an added defense of Divine temporality:

> If God were eternal [as in classicalism], he could not be aware, concerning any temporal event, whether it was occurring, not aware that it will be occurring, nor could he remember that it had occurred, nor could he plan to bring it about. But all of such actions are presupposed by and are essential to, the biblical presentation of God as a redeeming God. Hence God as presented by the biblical writers is fundamentally in time.[134]

Though the relationship between God and time has always been a much debated topic within all theological traditions, it has rarely been denied within Evangelicalism. It is axiomatic to open theism, however, since God would—of inescapable necessity—need to be *in time* for it to work. For, if God were fundamentally outside of time, time would be relative and essentially non-indexical, that is, there would be no Divine past, present, or future (as Wolterstorff observes) and, therefore, God would perceive all

---

[132] Pinnock, *Most Moved Mover*, 80.
[133] Ibid., 96.
[134] Nicolas Wolterstorff as quoted in Pinnock, *Most Moved Mover*, 97.

space-time events at once—what Paul Tillich and C. S. Lewis called "the eternal now."[135] Certainly, since at least Augustine and Boethius, classical theologians have almost universally affirmed Divine timelessness, not in an overly abstract or Platonic way, but as part of His implicative nature as sovereign Creator.[136] Timelessness has usually been conceived of as part and parcel of God's *aseity*, His attribute of *self-existent* eternal power.

Pinnock's open theism vehemently opposes the notion of God beholding the events of the world from the vantage point of timeless eternity. God does not "look forth from the high watchtower of His Providence,"[137] as Boethius put it, but rather "knows events as they take place and takes note of what transpires."[138] God's counsel is not timeless and fixed. History is being fashioned according to the *general* plan of God's counsel, but the question is, Pinnock asks, "what will *we* do with his counsel?"[139] Far from the immutable, forensic assurance offered in the classical models, this fresh reading of Scripture—unshackled by Grecian metaphysics and the controlling metaphors of classicalism—should spurn us to ask what part humans play in shaping redemptive history.

---

[135] See for example, Paul Tillich, *The Eternal Now* (New York: Scribner, 1963) 138, where Tillich says,

> [When God says] "I am the beginning and the end" . . . This is said to us who live in the bondage of time, who have to face the end, who cannot escape the past, who need a present to stand upon. Each of the modes of time has its peculiar mystery, each of them carries its peculiar anxiety. Each of them drives us to an ultimate question. There is one answer to these questions—the eternal. There is one power that surpasses the all-consuming power of time—the eternal: He Who was and is and is to come, the beginning and the end. He gives us forgiveness for what has passed. He gives us courage for what is to come. He gives us rest in His eternal Presence.

[136] Timelessness has usually been conceived of as part and parcel of God's aseity, His attribute of self-existent eternal power. Charles Hodge speaks for most Evangelicals when he says, "God is without beginning of years or end of days. He is, and always has been, and always will be . . . to Him there is neither past nor future; that the past and the future are always and equally present to Him." Thus, Pinnock's departure from this largely unchallenged Evangelical axiom further underscores his departure from many of his own tradition's beliefs [Charles Hodge, *Systematic Theology*, I.V.6. (Grand Rapids: Christian Classics Ethereal Library, 2005) 295].

[137] Boethius, *The Consolation of Philosophy*, Trans. W. V. Cooper; ed. Israel Golancz (London: Temple Classics, 1902) 130.

[138] Pinnock, *Most Moved Mover*, 59.

[139] Ibid.

Divine Corporeality

Pinnock's proposal for Divine temporality does not end there, however. He adds to this the possibility that God may also share with humans a *physical* body. Just as atemporality presents a difficulty for Pinnock in terms of his understanding of Divine-human relationality, so too does the idea that God is perfectly formless and non-corporeal:

> God is a relational being who thinks and acts, loves and knows . . . Being in someway embodied is not as foreign to Scripture as it is to tradition, which prefers spirit to flesh. The fact is that Scripture does not insist on God being formless . . . The only *personal* agents we know about are embodied agents. It might help us to imagine divine agency of God were somehow, mysteriously, embodied. It might also explain the divine passibility and even divine omniscience if God could access feelings of ours and his own. It would also overcome the spirit-matter dualism that so impoverished our sense of God's sacramental presence in the church. I would venture to say that corporeality is a subject that ought to be on the modern agenda and which has been neglected hitherto. We need to consider more carefully what form of corporeality would be appropriate to ascribe to God.[140]

Pinnock does not elaborate on the rather odd phrase "form of corporeality."[141] But the motive here is plain: "The only persons we encounter are embodied persons and, if God is not embodied, it may prove difficult to understand how God is a person."[142]

The suggestion of Divine corporeality has come as nothing less than a shock to most Evangelicals for whom God's ontological nature as *spirit* is simply categorically unquestionable. Jesus Himself, says, "God is spirit, and those who worship Him must worship in spirit and truth" (John 4:24). Charles Hodge observes that all of the Reformers were united on this front saying, "They generally taught, in the first place, that the unity and simplicity of the divine essence precludes not only all physical composition of constituent elements, or of matter and form, or of subject and accidents; but also all metaphysical distinction as of act and power, essence and exis-

---

[140] Ibid., 80–81.

[141] Something either enjoins corporeality or it does not. Thus, by "form of corporeality" Pinnock can only mean speculation over shape and dimension, something which he does not offer.

[142] Pinnock, *Most Moved Mover*, 34.

tence, nature and personality; and even of logical difference, as genus and specific difference."[143]

This might be seen as a natural step in Pinnock's progression toward trying to make God more understandable as a loving, caring parent. It is certainly the most recent addition in his progression from Augustinianism to Arminianism and beyond. In his earlier work, *Unbounded Love*, for example, the language against the classical formulation is strong, but it stops short of ever making God out to be corporeal. Rather, the aim is less aggressive, namely, to abandon the idea of God as some kind of sovereign, male egoist:

> Creative love theism is a composite model with the following basic features. First it celebrates the grace of God that abounds for all humanity. It embraces a wideness in God's mercy and rejects the idea that God excludes any persons arbitrarily from saving help. Second, it celebrates Jesus' category of father to express God's openness and relationality with us. God seeks to restore relationships with estranged people and cannot be thought of primarily as a Judge seeking legal settlement . . . Third it envisions God as a mutual and interrelating Trinity, not as an all-determining and manipulative transcendent (male) ego.[144]

Pinnock's arguing against the idea of classical theology—proposing a God with an over-inflated male ego—certainly gained some criticism at the time, but nowhere near the firestorm that his latest progression has stimulated. Norman Geisler, a longtime friend and colleague of Pinnock's, publicly declared his teachings to be heretical on a nationally-syndicated radio show and expressed frustration over Pinnock's continual speculative meanderings.[145] With corporeality now being a possible next step for Pinnock, it is rather easy to see why many Evangelicals have shared—over the last twenty-five years— Dr. Harold Lindsell's concern that, as his theology continues to progress, "additional damaging concessions may be on the way."[146] This is the fear shared by many within the ETS who view Pinnock as having a corrosive effect on the metal of Evangelical theological scholarship (that is, built on Vincentianism).

---

[143] Hodge, Systematic Theology, I.V.2, 283.

[144] Pinnock and Brow, *Unbounded Love*, 8.

[145] Norman Geisler interviewed by Hank Hanegraeff on "The Bible Answer Man" Broadcast, Fall 2003.

[146] Harold Lindsell, *The Bible in the Balance* (Grand Rapids: Zondervan, 1979) 43.

Relationship to Process Theology

Pinnock acknowledges his indebtedness to such process theologian-philosophers as Brightman, Chardin, Hartshorne, and Whitehead because "they make room in their thinking for ideas like change, incarnation and divine suffering, ideas which are central to the gospel but awkward for conventional theology influenced by ancient metaphysics."[147] This indebtedness to the writings of process thinkers is made even more clear in Pinnock's contributory article, "Between Classical and Process Theism" in the book *Process Theology* in which he explains some of the commonalities and disparities between open theism, processianism, and classicalism. In it he declares that, "God has used process thinkers to compel me to change certain ideas which I had and bring them up to Scriptural standards."[148] Pinnock's contributory piece to *The Openness of God*, dealing with the implications of open theism for doing systematic theology, also makes this statement bearing an obvious affinity with process thought:

> Experiencing temporal passage, God confronts a future that is open. The distinction between what is possible and what is actual is valid for God as well as for us. The past is actual, the present is becoming, and the future is possible. The everlasting One is active and dynamic through all of this flow, envisaging future possibilities and working to realize them. Transcendent to temporal passage, God is in the process without being involuntarily subject to it.[149]

Such statements sound almost as though they were taken right from the pages of Hartshorne or Whitehead themselves with the sole exception of God not being *involuntarily* subject to creation. Pinnock has taken pains to point out this distinction between open theism and processianian: "We do not think that God is ontologically limited as in process theology but that God voluntarily self-limits so that freely chosen loving relations would be possible."[150] This is an important distinction to Pinnock both in maintaining a Trinitarian theology as well as a Creator-creature distinction. Apart from this, however, the bifurcation of actual and possible (or concrete and abstract) is vintage Hartshorne who declared that, "The infinity of possibilities in God's nature is inexhaustible in actuality even by divine power, or

---

[147] Ibid., 142.

[148] Pinnock, "Between Classical and Process Theism," *Process Theology*, ed. Ronald Nash (Grand Rapids: Baker, 1987) 317.

[149] Pinnock "Systematic Theology," *The Openness of God: A Biblical Challenge to the Traditional Understanding of God* (Downer's Grove, Ill.: InterVarsity, 1994) 120.

[150] Pinnock, "Open Theism: What is this? A new teaching? And with authority!" 1.

any conceivable power. For each creative synthesis furnishes materials for a novel and richer synthesis."[151] In another place, Hartshorne says,

> God orders the universe . . . by taking into his own life all the currents of feeling in existence. . . . In the depths of their hearts all creatures (even those able to "rebel" against him) defer to God because they sense him as the one who alone is adequately moved by what moves them. He alone not only knows but feels (the only adequate knowledge, where feeling is concerned) how they feel, and he finds his own joy in sharing their lives, lived according to their own free decisions, not fully anticipated by any detailed plan of his own. Yet the extent to which they can be permitted to work out their own plan depends on the extent to which they can echo or imitate on their own level the divine sensitiveness to the needs and precious freedom of all, in this vision of a deity who is not a supreme autocrat, but a universal agent of "persuasion," whose "power is the worship he inspires" (Whitehead), that is, flows from the intrinsic appeal of his infinitely sensitive and tolerant relativity, by which all things are kept moving in orderly togetherness . . .[152]

In *Most Moved Mover*, Pinnock refers readers to Hartshorne's well known book, *Omnipotence and Other Theological Mistakes* in order to glean a better understanding of how models of the doctrine of God are philosophically constructed. He also delineates his basic points of agreement with Hartshorne and Whitehead which includes:

- The love of God as priority.
- Libertarian human freedom.
- Criticalness of conventional theism.
- A more dynamic model of God.
- God has real, and not merely rational, relationships with the world.
- God is genuinely affected by what happens in the world.
- God knows whatever *can* be known, which excludes exhaustive foreknowledge.
- The value of philosophy in shaping theological convictions.
- A positive connection with Wesleyan/Arminian traditions.[153]

---

[151] Charles Hartshorne, "The Dipolar Conception of Deity," *The Review of Metaphysics* (Vol 21, December 1967) 285.

[152] Charles Hartshorne, *The Divine Relativity: A Social Conception of God* (New Haven: Yale University Press, 1948) xvii.

[153] Pinnock, *Most Moved Mover*, 142–43.

Chapter Summary

Thus we have the primary tenets of Pinnock's open theism. It is a view that wishes to make peace with postmodernity, attempts to show classical Western theology as having derived from a pagan-Greek inheritance, strives to explicate for us the fundamental metaphysic of God as Love, and positions autonomous libertarian freewill to be axiomatic. The result is a view in which Divine-relationality relies upon a God who exercises neither omnicausal sovereignty nor possesses exhaustive foreknowledge. Such are incompatible with genuine human freedom *and* Divine love—the building blocks of relationality and the very purpose of creation itself.

4

Hellenization, Libertarianism, and the Metaphysics of Love

THE TITLE of this chapter reflects Pinnock's primary theological premises from which his openness theology flows and which I now critique. In the last chapter, we surveyed Pinnock's arguments for openness theology: his insistence that classicalism is deleterious to the vitality of the faith, having suffered from a Greek-pagan inheritance; His focus upon love as the central attribute of Deity; and his contention that anthropological libertarianism is "one of the deepest of all human intuitions" and a "fundamental self-perception,"[1] the denial of which is fatal to Divine-human relationality. Pinnock builds upon these axioms an alternative model for the complexion of God in his own version of openness theology which reasons that Divine nescience is an axiomatic corollary of God's purpose for creation, that is, the uncoerced, contra-causal reciprocality of Divine-human love relationships—stemming from the fundamental being of God as Love. This model is billed as a new, fresher theological package—akin even to a modern reformation—which seeks to disinter the immanence of God hitherto buried by classicalism's ostensive hyper-concentration on theological transcendentalism.

Immanence and Transcendence

We must observe at the very start of this analysis that much of the history of the doctrine of God has been a tussle between immanentist and transcendental schools. Contemporary theologians Stanley Grenz and Roger Olson go to the extent of calling the chronic undulation between these two poles "the *central* theological concern" dominating Western theology for much of its history and certainly for the last one hundred years[2] [emphasis added]. I am inclined to agree with this assessment.

---

[1] Pinnock, *Grace Unlimited* (Minneapolis: Bethany Fellowship, 1975) 95.
[2] Stanley Grenz and Roger Olson, *20th Century Theology: God & the World in a Transitional Age* (Downers Grove, Ill.: InterVarsity, 1992) 10.

Hellenization, Libertarianism, and the Metaphysics of Love

Augustine had a lasting influence for a time, having seemed to have found a reasonably comfortable symmetry between the two. For Augustine (and, though some differences apply, Anselm and Aquinas, after him), immanence and transcendence were not two mutually exclusive realities vying in competition with one another. Rather, they are more like two sides of the same coin, yet wherein the one, immanence, *issues* from the other, transcendence. Far from functioning as an impediment, transcendence *supplies* immanence.³ God is not an "aloof monarch" at all, but is present in every detail of redemptive history complete with its human machinations. As Thomas Weinandy has put it, "For the early Fathers the act of creation which manifests and establishes the complete otherness of God, and thus his eternal, all-powerful and unchanging nature, is the very same act which relates him to the created order and so founds his loving and salvific relation to it."⁴ More will be said of this later when I consider Pinnock's treatment of the classical tradition.

The Augustinian position enjoyed a dominant period, but it did not last.⁵ Though the issue would continue to be grappled with during the Middle Ages and well into the Reformation, it reached a critical stage during the period of Enlightenment rationalism which fixed a major chasm between the natural and the Divine. Whatever concentration of immanentistic thinking there was after the Reformers (for example, Luther's theology of the cross, Calvin's robust doctrine of prayer, etc.) it suffered a series of terrific blows during this time as many thinkers opted for more deistic paradigms in their quest for epistemic harmony between science and reason and the doxastic realm of religion and metaphysics. God's place in the world suddenly became much smaller and the prospect of special revelation

---

³ For Augustine, God's transcendent otherness was always balanced with an affirmation of His thoroughgoing immanence. God is *wholly other* but, *because* of this (rather than in opposition to it), is *wholly present* in his being and power at all times and in all places within the created universe—sustaining the multifarious events in their indexical passage. Only the sovereign God, transcending space-time can do this. For, the eternal God, "did not begin to work only after countless ages of time had elapsed, because no age of time, past of still to come, could either come or go if it were not that you abide for ever and cause time to come and go" [Augustine, *Confessions*, 7.15; trans. R. F. Pine-Coffin (London: Penguin, 1961) 150]. Further, God "condescends *to inhabit each individually* and the whole harmonious body, being no greater in all than in each, since He is neither expanded nor divided" [emphasis added]. Augustine, *City of God*, 10.3; ed. Phillip Schaff (Grand Rapids: Christian Classics Ethereal Library, 2001) 263.

⁴ Thomas Weinandy, *Does God Suffer?* (Notre Dame, Ind.: University of Notre Dame Press, 2000) 113.

⁵ A nice summary of the Augustinian position and influence, and then later challenges to the view, is found in Grenz and Olson, *20th Century Theology*, 16–23.

was severely crippled. The almost inevitable Christian theological reaction to this was to bank more heavily on transcendence. Søren Kierkegaard's works are a fine example of this in which reason and revelation began to separate making the Danish philosopher an important precursor to modern fideism with his advocation of the existential "leap" and his stress upon "truth as subjectivity."[6]

Classical theology, however, was in the process of picking itself up by the bootstraps and beginning a reconstruction of its understanding of the tension between immanence and transcendence. Notable figures in the classical stream during the Enlightenment and Modern period included Joseph Butler with his *Analogy of Religion*; Thomas Reid with his *Essays on the Intellectual Powers of Man*; William Paley with *A View of the Evidences of Christianity*; and Charles Hodge's *Systematic Theology* and *Princeton Sermons*. Indeed, the latter of these, Hodge, would set the tone for much of the future of the classical *Evangelical* doctrine of God which Clark Pinnock would at first inherit gladly, but later vehemently eschew.

At the same time, however, were the later reactionary philosophies of Enlightenment thinkers Kant, Hegel, Schleiermacher, and Ritschl.[7]

---

[6] Søren Kierkegaard, *Concluding Unscientific Postscript*, trans. David Swenson, et al., from *A Kierkegaard Anthology*, ed. Robert Bretall (Princeton, N. J.: Princeton University Press, 1946) 195–226.

[7] Grenz and Olson, *20th Century Theology*, 25–61.

Reacting to classical Protestant and Catholic transcendental understandings of God, modern "liberal theology" was born. Kant[8] and Hegel[9], in particular, placed the human mind at the center of truth (and its knowability) and tended to relativize tradition. It is an understatement that the waning classical establishment at the time was not altogether pleased with the efforts of these men to revive immanence and reserve a place for it in the church. Their attempts were distasteful to creedal orthodoxy as, in the process of resurrecting some concept of Divine-human involvement, these

---

[8] Put simply, Kant has an autonomous view of human knowledge in which intuition and concepts constitute all that is known. He does, however, elucidate upon knowledge as deriving from two principle sources:

> Our knowledge springs from two fundamental sources of the mind; the first is the capacity of receiving representations (receptivity for impressions), the second is the power of knowing an object through these representations (spontaneity [in the production] of concepts). Through the first an object is given to us, through the second the object is thought in relation to that [given] representation (which is a mere determination of the mind). Intuition and concepts constitute, therefore, the elements of all our knowledge, so that neither concepts without an intuition in some way corresponding to them, nor intuition without concepts, can yield knowledge. Both may be either pure or empirical. When they contain sensation (which presupposes the actual presence of the object), they are empirical. When there is no mingling of sensation with the representation, they are pure. Sensation may be entitled the material of sensible knowledge. Pure intuition, therefore, contains only the form under which something is intuited; the pure concept only the form of the thought of an object in general. Pure intuitions or pure concepts alone are possible a priori, empirical intuitions and empirical concepts only a posteriori.

[Immanuel Kant, *Critique of Pure Reason*, trans. Norman Kemp Smith (New York: Macmillan, 1929) 92]. Kant later classifies the idea of God as a "pure [concept] . . . extended further than experience can follow" [Kant, *Critique of Pure Reason*, 130].

[9] The distinctiveness of Hegel's view is the idea that God, or the "Absolute Spirit," is manifested only through the knowing minds of its creatures, who function as its vehicle. In this sense, human consciousness is an act of the finite conducing infinity. Put another way, the Absolute Spirit is made real through cognitive, conscious experience. Says Hegel:

> Self-consciousness exists in itself and for itself, in that, and by the fact that it exists for another self-consciousness; that is to say, it is only by being acknowledged or "recognized." The conception of this, its unity in its duplication, of infinitude realizing itself in self-consciousness, has many sides to it and encloses within it elements of varied significance. Thus its moments must on the one hand be strictly kept apart in detailed distinctiveness, and, on the other, in this distinction must, at the same time, also be taken as not distinguished, or must always be accepted and understood in their opposite sense. This double meaning of what is distinguished lies in the nature of self-consciousness: of its being infinite.

G. W. F. Hegel, *The Phenomenology of Mind*, trans. J. B. Baillie (New York: Harper, 1967) 229.

thinkers tended to abscond themselves from many of the cardinal tenets of historic Christendom. Moreover, the immanence that was proffered by them was largely subjective and esoteric, ungrounded in the objectivity of biblical revelation as upheld in classicalism. Kant, for example, with his transcendental idealism advocated a sort of deep, visceral awareness of God that emerges through piety and feeling, but at the same time, propounded an unbridgeable *noetic* gulf between the noumenal and phenomenal hemispheres which inescapably has the effect of attenuating religious language and the ability to systematize.[10] Kant's position was to "deny knowledge, in order to make room for faith."[11] Schleiermacher's solution was not altogether different but placed more emphasis on *feeling* the Divine as opposed to articulating an architectonical metaphysic. "The sum total of religion," Schleiermacher wrote, "is to feel that, in its highest unity, all that moves us in feeling is one; to feel that aught single and particular is only possible by means of this unity; to feel, that is to say, that our being and living is a being and living in and through God."[12] Church doctrine thus becomes a more "scientific expression of the pious feelings [of] the believer."[13] Ritschl was heavily influenced by Kant and Schleiermacher, the former by linking the Christian faith with ethics and expunging metaphysics from theology, the latter by stressing the centrality of subjective experience. Religion cannot be known through the rational faculty, but through religious experience. In turn, this experience is related through a social *community*. Indeed, the Kingdom of God itself is "the corporate product of community."[14] For each of Kant, Hegel, Schleiermacher, and Ritschl, is an emphasis on Divine immanence somehow manifested, coupled with a tendency to see an deep ontological, though subjective, bond between the human and divine spirit.

---

[10] For some helpful discussions, see R. C. Sproul, John Gerstner, Arthur Lindsley, *Classical Apologetics* (Grand Rapids: Zondervan, 1984) 29–32; D. W. Hamlyn, *History of Western Philosophy* (London: Penguin, 1987) 215–42; Philip Rossi, "Kant's Philosophy of Religion," *The Stanford Encyclopedia of Philosophy* (Stanford: Stanford University, 2005) Online. http://plato.stanford.edu/entries/kant-religion.

[11] Kant, *Critique of Pure Reason*, 29.

[12] Friedrich Schleiermacher, "On Religion: Speeches to its Cultured Despisers" (1799) in *A History of Christianity*, ed. Clyde Manschreck (Grand Rapids: Baker, 1981) 338.

[13] Louis Berkhof, *Systematic Theology* (Grand Rapids: Eerdmans, 1996) 59.

[14] Albrecht Ritschl, *The Christian Doctrine of Justification and Reconciliation*, trans. H. R. Mackintosh and A. B. Macaulay (Edinburgh: T. & T. Clark, 1900) 12. Ritschl further adds that, "Those who believe in Christ . . . constitute the Kingdom of God in so far as, forgetting distinctions of sex, rank, or nationality, they act reciprocally from love, and thus call into existence that fellowship of moral disposition and moral blessings which extends, through all possible gradations, to the limits of the human race." Ritschl, *The Christian Doctrine of Justification*, 285.

Later, in the twentieth century, the Neoorthodox movement, headed by Barth, Brunner, Bultmann, and Niebuhr[15], would react militantly against what they perceived as the decidedly anthropocentric locus of the nineteenth-century apologists for immanence and attempted to swing the pendulum back over to transcendence. The Neoorthodox theologians stressed that God was "wholly other" (*totaliter aliter*) from the world and human beings. A cache of subsequent theologians, some ostensively Evangelical, such as T. F. Torrance, Donald Bloesch, Herman Dooyeweerd, Cornelius Van Til, and Al Wolters would assume some of this thinking into their own theologies but would try to make it consistent with their belief in the reliability and centrality of biblical revelation.[16] But the manner in which they spoke of God as "wholly other" was also unacceptable to some Evangelicals as it seemed to make God so utterly removed and detached from the world that it was difficult to imagine how He could be involved in our lives at all. This was especially true concerning the resultant theological anthropology that descended from the overstress on Divine transcendence. Barth and Brunner, for example, came to reject the classical understanding of the *imago Dei* as an analogy of being (*analogia entis*) as advocated by Aquinas and the Reformers and opted instead to advance their idea of an "analogy of relationship" (*analogia relationis*) in which the image of God is not something *in* humans, but is rather a part of their relationship to God or even other humans.[17]

The Neoorthodox view also came to see the application of human logic toward God (and therefore an *analogia entis* entailing such things as rationality and will) as a fool's errand. Talking about God in a systematic way, these theologians conjectured, seems to lead to so much semantical banter. Systematization is stilted as the constitutive human faculties are thought to be inalterably "restricted to this side of the ontological boundary between God and the created order."[18]

As far as many classical theologians were concerned, however, the theological fallout of this attempt to rescue transcendence back from the immanentists was, quite simply, *fatal* to Christianity in no less a fashion than the religious philosophy to which they were reacting. For, if human beings are so utterly dissimilar from God, there seems to be no possible nexus or

---

[15] See Berkhof, *Systematic Theology*, 60–111, for a nice summation from a Calvinist perspective.

[16] R. C. Sproul, et al., *Classical Apologetics*, 75.

[17] Millard Erickson, *Christian Theology* (Grand Rapids: Baker, 1998) 524.

[18] Ronald Nash, *The Word of God and the Mind of Man* (Grand Rapids: Zondervan, 1982) 95; Cited in John Gerster et al., *Classical Apologetics* (Grand Rapids: Zondervan, 1984) 75.

reference point by which meaningful or intelligible interchange and reciprocality can take place between them. Moreover, it seemed as though nothing whatsoever could be concretely articulated about God. Calling God "good" or "righteous" may be acceptable pietistically or doxastically, but does not necessarily have a vertical metaphysical referent because, according to the Neoorthodox, these are limited, finite human concepts being foisted on a transcendent God who cannot possibly lend Himself to such ascriptions. Thus, the broad share of classicalists eschewed Neoorthodoxy on the supposition that the concept of *totaliter aliter*—though it answered Enlightenment criticism and preserved a form of Divine transcendence—nevertheless was self-referentially untenable, and led inexorably to a "pious agnosticism."[19] Further, it was fideistic since one was asked to simply *believe* while avoiding alethic statements or questions about the nature of God.

Herein begins the theological systematizing of post-Enlightenment classicalism which came to dominate Evangelical theology. The very hallmarks of twentieth-century Evangelicalism were constituted by theologies that attempted to remain biblically based while repudiating both Enlightenment rationalism as well as the fideistic backlash it seemed to spurn under the pens of the Neoorthodox who, at times, felt free to reinterpret and "demythologize" the Bible. Much of this new Evangelical theology emanated from the "Old Princeton School" with such theologians as Archibald Alexander, Charles Hodge, J. A. Alexander, B. B. Warfield and J. Gresham Machen. The later emergence of Westminster and Fuller seminaries would continue the Evangelical thread in American theology while the United Kingdom was also witnessing a resurgence of Evangelical classicalism in such places as London Bible College and London Theological Seminary.

By the time Clark Pinnock was entering the ministry in the 1960s, Western Evangelicalism had reached a fever pitch with its attempt to revive "true truth"[20] as Francis Schaeffer would call it. Pinnock rightly points out, however, that its theology was heavily dominated by the Reformed models and that "the authors [he] was introduced to . . . as theologically 'sound,' were staunchly Calvinistic: [such as] John Murray, Martyn Lloyd-Jones, Cornelius Van Til, Carl Henry, James Packer, [and] Paul Jewett."[21] Indeed, the systematic theologies most commonly used in Evangelical schools

---

[19] R. C. Sproul, et al. *Classical Apologetics*, 75.

[20] Francis Schaeffer, "Escape From Reason," in *Trilogy* (Wheaton, Ill.: Crossway, 1990) 218.

[21] Pinnock, "From Augustine to Arminius: A Pilgrimage in Theology," in *The Grace of God and the Will of Man: A Case for Arminianism* (Grand Rapids: Zondervan, 1989) 17.

throughout the twentieth century were almost entirely on a scale from moderately to thoroughly Calvinistic such as Louis Berkhof's *Systematic Theology* and Augustus Strong's *Systematic Theology* and, after the 1980's, Millard Erickson's *Christian Theology*, Robert Reymond's *A New Systematic Theology of the Christian Faith* and Wayne Grudem's *Systematic Theology*. All of these theologies are decidedly transcendental in their doctrines of God, but nevertheless remain committed to *sola Scriptura*, the historicity of Christ's incarnation, and the Holy Spirit's active role in human affairs and in salvation. Though there are a few notable exceptions, Arminian-Wesleyan theologies were few and far between as proponents of those schools appeared less inclined to systematize. The process theologians, who did indeed grapple significantly with immanence, nevertheless were largely ignored by Evangelicals who found them to be far too unorthodox. Thus, as far as Western Evangelicalism was concerned, Calvinism maintained a veritable hegemony over its academics and, even though many congregates may have been *practical* Arminians, Evangelical theologians were primarily Reformed. Today, however, this is rapidly changing.

The tension between immanence and transcendence has never been completely resolved in Reformed theology and its critics have remained. Given my brief survey of the perennial immanence-transcendence debate, I think it clear that Pinnock's writings function as an important contemporary voice for the historical corpus of immanence-dominated theologies that are now enjoying a vacillatory comeback in response to the Calvinistic stronghold on Evangelical theology. In short, Evangelical theology, like much of liberal theology before it, is moving away from transcendence toward immanence and Pinnock's theology is a clear indication of the radical extent to which this is taking place. His stress on human autonomy and libertarian free will is, in many ways, one of the few philosophical holdovers of modernism that has made its way into popular postmodern thinking, with the marked difference that—whereas the church of the Enlightenment tended to temper its understanding of these faculties against the popular societal grain which extolled the powers of human will—both society *and* the church of postmodernity often appear to take libertarian free will for granted. The latter also seems largely unmindful of the tradition of deterministic compatibilism that has been its theological heritage. Libertarianism seems to have been conduced, not so much by a process of intellectual examination, but through a kind of sociocultural osmosis. Indeed, far from being grounded on strictly biblical axioms (as Pinnock claims), Simon Oliver comments that Pinnock's constant stress upon human autonomy "has much more to do with Western liberal democracy (back to Locke and Kant) than Christian theology."[22]

Immanentistic theologies and philosophical libertarianism tend to be coupled together like rider and horse. The reason for this is not difficult to surmise. For many, the doctrine of transcendence in classical theology—especially in Reformed or Calvinistic schools—seems to be too highly emphasized at the expense of immanence. The result, it is thought, is such that creation becomes merely an afterthought of God, the byproduct of an architectonic, impregnable sovereignty. The universe becomes a kind of "prosthesis or puppet theater of God"[23] in which humans may have the *experience* of freedom and Divine-human relationality, but it is, in fact, illusory. The classical doctrine of transcendence is therefore thought to reduce to, as Pinnock puts it, an "all-determining fatalistic blueprint"[24] which blots out the possibility of free movements in creation which, in turn, is the basis for moral accountability and relationality—both human-to-human, and human-to-Divine. The rejection of classical transcendence is not the starting point, but the deductive product of reasoning backwards first from human experience and secondly from a philosophical commitment to preserving libertarian autonomy. Our autonomous freewill is "one of the deepest of all human intuitions" and a "fundamental self-perception"[25] which becomes nonnegotiable.

I am very sympathetic to Pinnock's criticism that classical, especially Reformed, theologies have not done enough to unpack, much less emphasize, Divine immanence and its importance for an understanding of Divine-human relationality. Reformed theology has excelled in its explication of forensic theology, the relationship between law and gospel, covenant, and many of the Divine attributes considered within theology proper, but I believe it has indeed been lacking in its articulation of the nature of the reciprocality between God and His human creatures. It has not been *totally* lacking, of course, especially in its work with the biblical covenants—a study which is, by its very nature, concerned with God's relationship to man. This is usually corporate in nature, however, and does not concern itself to any great extent with the classic Evangelical emphasis on each person's "personal relationship with Christ." Reformed theologians, I believe,

---

[22] Simon Oliver, personal correspondence, March 1, 2005.

[23] William Dembski, "Transcendence," in *The New Dictionary of Christian Apologetics* (Downer's Grove, Ill.: InterVarsity, forthcoming); http://www.designinference.com/documents/ 2003.10.Transcendence_NDOCApol.pdf (March 10, 2004).

[24] Pinnock, *The Grace of God and the Will of Man*, 18.

[25] Pinnock, *Grace Unlimited*, 95.

have effectively observed the centrality of soteric corporatization and the "holy nation" principle of Israel in the OT and the church in the New (as the "New Israel"), but we must not miss the obvious fact that *nations* are comprised of *individuals*. The concerns which Pinnock raises pertain to how the individual relates to the broader soteric framework.

This is an area in which I find the greatest resonation with Pinnock's openness program and would affirm that his theology is a significant contribution to our understanding of immanence and relationality. For classicalists, such as myself, it forms a clarion call to respond, and to move into a phase of theological investigation centered on better understanding and exploring our dynamic (not merely forensic) relationality with God. This perceived deficiency on the part of Reformed theology in particular provides the basis of my work in chapter six in which I attempt to form a contemporary reconstruction of Divine-human relationality which is nevertheless firmly situated in the classical-Reformed paradigm.

A Three-Pronged Critique

We recall that one of the few, though not insignificant, methodological characteristics that has remained with Pinnock throughout his life as a theologian has been a rigorous commitment to the employment of logical reasoning. In building his case for open theism, Pinnock has said, "It is surely a *real* contradiction . . . to assert 1) that God determines all events, and 2) that man is free [in the libertarian sense] to accept or reject his will."[26] This use of the law of noncontradiction is another important point of concord between Pinnock and myself. I wholeheartedly agree that intelligible discourse about God ("God talk") is manifestly impossible if we rush to label as "mysteries" that which are, in fact, flatly contradictory propositions.

Throughout this critique, this methodological point of agreement for theological discourse is vitally important. Pinnock grants, as I do, that when we ponder and build our theologies, whatsoever the mind can *actually* conceive of is properly logical and therefore possible, though not necessarily actual. That is, the only things one can actually conceive of, are logically possible things. One cannot conceive of four-pointed triangles or one-ended sticks. Conceptualization of such postulates, much less discussion of them, is a fated enterprise. One can, however, conceive of alien beings, ghosts, or unicorns and, therefore, nothing *formally* precludes them from existing. Green aliens from Mars could logically exist. What would preclude their existence is nothing in formal logic but simply material reality itself.

---

[26] Pinnock, *Grace Unlimited*, 109.

But, in the reverse direction, this shows us, epistemically, that if one posits, for example, an *invisible* green alien, we cannot concede the possibility of such an existence. A claim can be formally valid, but materially false. But a claim *cannot* be formally false and materially actual. Thus, an inherently contradictory relationship between God and humans (as Calvinists and open theists *mutually* contend Arminians and Molinists have), can neither be imagined (that is, conceived) nor discussed with the slightest measure of intelligibility. I agree, then, with Pinnock that Arminians and Molinists posit a model of Divine-human relationality that is *formally* invalid.

Importantly, none of this is to be confused with having a mental conception of a mysterious but internally non-contradictory cognitive object or event. This is epistemically possible, but limited and admittedly prone to error. In this manner, "God talk" can be conducted such that it is cognitively apprehensible and not purely relative, but with the qualification that it is construed as provisional. *Finitum non capax infinitum*—"the finite cannot contain the infinite," while certainly true, must be tempered with the biblically implicit axiom that *finitum posse apprehensio infinitum*, "the finite can *apprehend* something of the infinite." Were this not true, theology would be pointless.

Given this discussion of the important place given to logic in theological discourse, I take Pinnock's reasoning from the suppositions of Hellenization, libertarianism, and the metaphysics of Love—to the *conclusion* of his openness theology—to be *formally* valid. The latter is the natural and logically inevitable outworking of a theology based on these premises. Libertarian freewill and exhaustive Divine foreknowledge are mutually annihilating propositions. Molinists posit an imaginative and creative solution to the problem by hypothesizing God's modal knowledge of counterfactuals and infinitely issuing possible worlds. They argue that God can see what a person *would* do with their libertarian freedom given certain possible-world situations and, based on this analysis, chose to actualize *this* world. What seems to me to be a glaring inconsistency in this reasoning, however, is that the Molinistic conception of human freedom is just like that of the open theists and Arminians—it is contra-causal and undetermined. Logically speaking, therefore, this has the effect of merely backing the problem up a step and reverting Molinism squarely back on the problems associated with the Arminian simple-foreknowledge view. Namely, if human freedom is genuinely contra-causal, how then can God infallibly know that in a particular counterfactual situation a libertarian free agent will choose X over Y as Molinists affirm? If, in situation S, person P has the *autonomous* ability to choose either X or Y, how does the possession of counterfactual knowledge of possible-world scenarios improve by any measure God's ability to know what a libertarian free agent will do in situation S? For, in order to infallibly know that P will always choose X in situation S, God must know not only all of the circumstances present in S but must know precisely the reasons (or causes) which inclined the libertarian agent's will to perform X. If God does not possess this modal knowledge of freewill actions, then He cannot know that X will always be chosen over Y even if situation S were rewound a thousand times. Molinists therefore seem to affirm in the midst of their argumentation the very thing they deny and, unlike Pinnock's view, I believe their position is formally invalid and therefore materially false. In my interviews with Pinnock, he acknowledged agreement on this point and shared with me an equal measure of bewilderment concerning how such a seemingly obvious (indeed *fatal*) difficulty seems to have escaped the attention of the Molinistic philosophers.[27]

Pinnock's own logical and theological conclusions depend, however, on the veracity of his three fundamental premises which I believe deserve a challenge. If there is reason to think that these premises should be revised or even abandoned, then this critique will serve to show the inviability of Pinnock's openness program. I will not argue against the logicality of creative love theism on the heels of granting his premises as, again, I hold Pinnock's deductions to be substantially correct. Indeed I find the logical incompatibility of libertarian free will and exhaustive Divine foreknowledge to be insuperable. I believe, with Pinnock, to be incorrect those who have been willing to label the juxtaposition of these two premises a "mystery" or a "paradox" when they are, in fact, simply logically incompatible. The remainder of this critique, therefore, will reach to the heart of Pinnock's theology by examining his three elemental premises.

The Negative Influence of Greek Philosophy

We have seen Pinnock's arguments favoring the notion that classical-orthodox theology has been poisoned by the metaphysics of Hellenism and its concomitant "perfect being" philosophy. I find there to be a rather startling and ironic situation that emerges in light of this assertion when we examine Pinnock's own exposition of his alternative to classicalism in the openness model. Despite his passionate objection toward the injection of Hellenistic thought into the history of Christian theological development,

---

[27] Dr. William Lane Craig is perhaps the most well known defender of the Molinistic view within Western Evangelicalism and is regarded by many, myself included, as an extremely capable philosopher. His major defense of Molinism appears in *The Only Wise God* (1987, reprinted, Eugene, Ore.: Wipf & Stock Publishers, 2000).

the description of his *own* theological system appears to me to emerge not only as a decidedly rational one, but a decidedly *Greek*-rational one. In many ways, this is to be expected from a theologian who cut his teeth and formed his views within the circles of classicalism. Pinnock's own methodology finds itself firmly situated in the Greek-rational approach. He decries the need to adopt a more Hebraic mindset when approaching exegesis yet is decidedly Plato-Aristotelian in his own theological systematization. Most of the so-called "biblical theology" criticisms against classical Western theology have pointed out that its philosophical categories tend to represent the more rational/syllogistic intellectual methodologies of Plato and Aristotle as opposed to the more deferential-doxastic-mystical approach of the ancient Hebrews (or those found in the East, Latin America, and so on). The Hebrews were not systematizers as the classicalists were (and are) and as Pinnock himself is. Pinnock's theological product, complete with Divine nescience of future contingencies and libertarian freewill, is in fact something to be expected almost exclusively from within a reflective Grecian-systematic tradition. The tools originally forged by the post-Socratic Greeks are the very tools Pinnock now uses to develop his creative love theism. It is unthinkable that ancient Hebrew thought, in contradistinction to Hellenism, would have articulated anything even remotely resembling the *deduction* from libertarianism to open theism's divine nescience (or, in fairness, reformed theories of atemporalism, double-predestination, etc.). The evidence of this is quite simply in the historical record itself which demonstrates an absence of this kind of thinking in Hebraic theology. This is not to say that the Greeks were *rational* and the Hebrews *irrational*. To say so would be a fine piece of chronological snobbery. Rather, it is to acknowledge one of the contributions of the biblical theology movement which called attention to what Brevard Childs refers to as the "Hebrew mentality" contrasted with "Greek thought patterns," the latter of which tend to be more "abstract, rationalistic, and theoretical."[28]

In the context of this discussion, my intention is not to defend all of the postulates of the biblical theology movement (which, indeed, I disagree with in terms of the extent to which it takes its arguments), but only to acknowledge what I think is a valuable insight, namely, that the Hebrew writers of the Old Testament were disinclined to systematize, in marked contradistinction to Western theology which most certainly tends to follow a more Greek methodological approach.

The Psalmist, for example, is content to affirm that God is "from everlasting to everlasting" (Ps 90:2) as opposed to proffering a system of Divine

---

[28] Brevard S. Childs, *Biblical Theology in Crisis* (Philadelphia: Westminster, 1970) 23.

temporality or atemporality; eternalism or sempiternalism. He is happy declaring that "Before a word is on my tongue, you know it completely, O Lord" (Ps 139:4), as opposed to contemplating whether or not this knowledge is formed as a nescient probability quotient or is infallibly foreknown from a position of atemporality, or whether this knowledge is the product of a deterministic pancausalism. The Talmudist is likewise pleased to discuss the need for *Yomah* without becoming exercised over whether its nature is forensic or exemplary and so on.[29] All of it is quite "matter of fact" and ever couched in reverence. In no way do I believe that this makes the reasoning of the Greeks invalid nor its appropriation by classical theologians improper. It is simply a matter of record that the Greek-rational approach was not the *modus operandi* of the Hebrews but has been in Western theology—*including* Pinnock's.

What was shared in common among the majority of classical philosophers after Aristotle is what we now commonly term as classical logic—the melding of Platonic and Aristotelian truth-finding mechanisms. Pinnock uses this methodology meticulously—his entire theological edifice is built on it—and he even chides those who do not employ it saying they suffer from unintelligibility.

Take away much of the prose, and I doubt that much of Pinnock's theology could not be formatted syllogistically. Platonic logic bases itself in the law of excluded middle wherein a proposition is either true or false—there is no *tertium quid* (we recall Pinnock calling exhaustive Divine foreknowledge and libertarian human freedom propositions that "create a contradiction"[30]). In Aristotle, we find the further development of the syllogism wherein we find such principles as the universal affirmative (every X is Y), the universal negative (no X is Y), the particular affirmative (some X is Y) and the particular negative (not every X is Y). This methodology has a strong vintage in classical theology and its common thread can be seen much earlier than Augustine (where Pinnock starts in his critique of classicalism) in such notable Christian apologists as Justin Martyr and Origen who were heavily Platonic, again, not in all their conclusions, but in their Greek-rational methodology. It is their methodology, and it is Pinnock's.

Several other interesting observations emerge from Pinnock's criticism of Hellenism's supposed infective properties on classical theology. The

---

[29] See, for example, the tract *Yomah*, chapter 1, *The Babylonian Talmud*, trans. Michael Rodkinson; http://www.sacred-texts.com/jud/t03/index.htm (April 8, 2005). The Talmudist is content merely quoting Levitical law, namely, that it pleases God that atonement should be made by those who honor Him.

[30] Pinnock, *Most Moved Mover*, 55.

first is that the notion of Divine nescience was originally suggested, not by Jewish or Christian scholars, but by Cicero—the great Greco-Roman orator and philosopher whom Augustine became immersed in during his days as a professor of rhetoric. Cicero arrived at this position in considering the implications for human freedom and in preserving himself from a notion of wooden fatalism—*precisely* as Pinnock does. And, like Pinnock, Cicero finds no *tertium quid*, either future contingencies are unknown in the Divine realm, or everything is in the hands of the Fates. Augustine writes, "all this he seems to do in order that he may not grant the doctrine of fate, and by so doing destroy free will. For he thinks that, the knowledge of future things being once conceded, fate follows as so necessary a consequence that it cannot be denied."[31] It is here that *Augustine*—far from adopting a "Greek" position—takes the position of biblical Christianity over the speculations of Greco-Roman philosophy and writes:

> [Cicero denies] that there is any knowledge of future things, and maintains with all his might that there is no such knowledge either in God or man, and that there is no prediction of events. Thus he both denies the foreknowledge of God, and attempts by vain arguments, and by opposing to himself certain oracles very easy to be refuted, to overthrow all prophecy, even such as is clearer than the light (though even these oracles are not refuted by him) . . . Nevertheless, they are far more tolerable who assert the fatal influence of the stars than they who deny the foreknowledge of future events. For, to confess that God exists, and at the same time to deny that He has foreknowledge of future things, is the most manifest folly.[32]

Yet, long before Cicero, it was Aristotle who surmised much the same consequent, arguing that no being can make—in the present—either positive or negative judgments about some event in the future as the future simply does not exist as a proper referent upon which true knowledge might be engendered. As an illustration, Aristotle writes,

> A sea-fight must either take place tomorrow or not, but it is not necessary that it should take place tomorrow, neither is it necessary that it should not take place, yet it is necessary that it either should or should not take place tomorrow. Since propositions correspond with facts, it is evident that when in future events there is a real alternative, and a potentiality in contrary directions, the correspond-

---

[31] Augustine, *The City of God*, V.IX., trans. Marcus Dods (Grand Rapids: Christian Classics Ethereal Library, 2001) 138.
[32] Ibid.

ing affirmation and denial have the same character . . . This is the case with regard to that which is not always existent or not always nonexistent. One of the two propositions in such instances must be true and the other false, but we cannot say determinately that this or that is false, but must leave the alternative undecided. One may indeed be more likely to be true than the other, but it *cannot be either actually true or actually false*. It is therefore plain that it is not necessary that of an affirmation and a denial one should be true and the other false. For in the case of that which exists potentially, but not actually, the rule which applies to that which exists actually does not hold good[33] [emphasis added].

Given this, Ronald Nash has commented that,

> What really troubles me about [the] allegation . . . that orthodox theology has been strongly influenced by Greek thought, is that in this particular case it is open theism that manifests the influence of Greek thinking. The idea of a finite God; that is the territory of Plato and Aristotle. If you're looking at least at the idea that a supreme being cannot know the future, that comes directly from Aristotle.[34]

In part, Cicero and Aristotle's speculation over a being's nescience of future propositions shows us that the Greek-rational approach to metaphysics has yielded results far from what Pinnock tends to characterize as univocal among classical theologians. Though he speaks of classicalism as being broadly infected with Grecian metaphysics that favors impassibility, immutability, and so on, it is not always clear precisely which Grecian metaphysical system Pinnock is referring to.[35] Paul Gavrilyuk comments that,

> The idea that there is a sharp distinction between the Hellenistic God who is apathetic and the biblical God who has emotions and is involved in human affairs to the point of suffering . . . misrepresents both the philosophers and the biblical authors. On the one hand, the diversity of conflicting accounts of divine nature, emotions, and intervention in the Hellenistic philosophies and the Hellenistic

---

[33] Aristotle, *On Interpretation*, I.9, trans. E. M. Edghill (Cambridge, Mass.: The Internet Classics Archive, Massachusetts Institute of Technology, 2005); http://classics.mit.edu/Aristotle/interpretation.1.1.html (June 22, 2006).

[34] Ronald Nash, "Open Theism: An Interview with Dr. Ronald Nash."; http://www.christkirk.org/stannespub/nash.shtml (June 22, 2006).

[35] Pinnock sometimes appears to use the terms "Greek," "Hellenistic" and cognate terms interchangeably with "Neoplatonism" and "Aristotelianism." Indeed these are key schools of thought in Greek philosophy, but I doubt they can simply be used a synonyms for all things "Greek."

> religions at large does not yield a picture of a single impassible philosophical deity, disinterested in the world. This picture is a scholarly caricature, and [a] convenient strawman . . .[36]

There simply is no such thing as a singular "Greek" metaphysical view of God. Greek philosophers ran the gamut from naturalists, agnostics, atheists, panentheists, and intimations of monotheism. There may be a somewhat common philosophical *methodology* among them since Plato, but their views are far from monolithic. This logical-rational methodology has been friendly to as many different philosophical systems as science has been to different cosmologies since Ptolemy.

Pinnock unfortunately also neglects the fact that, historically, even among the primary classical theologians he criticizes (Augustine and Aquinas), that their theologies contradicted, indeed *confuted*, far more of the Grecian metaphysics than they employed. Certain Greek ideas and methodologies were inarguably adapted[37] (often for apologetic reasons as much as systematic), but the ultimate referents or explanations that the Greek metaphysicians placed behind these referents were *always* and categorically jettisoned as inimical to Christian theism.

Plato, for example, had his non-personal Forms, or at best the non-omnipotent Demiurge (subservient to the non-personal "Good") that must persuade the recalcitrant "Receptacle"[38] to take on form thus creating the world as a product of "necessity and mind." As Plato writes in *Timaeus*: ". . . the creation is mixed, being made up of necessity and mind. Mind, the ruling power, persuaded necessity to bring the greater part of created things to perfection, and thus and after this manner in the beginning, when the influence of reason got the better of necessity, the universe was created."[39] Implicit in this is the eternality of nature and the impossibility of creation *ex nihilo*.[40] Plato also considered humans to be modeled after a plurality of gods,[41] advanced reincarnation,[42] negated the possibility of God's active

---

[36] Paul Gavrilyuk, *The Suffering of the Impassible God: The Dialectics of Patristic Thought* (Oxford: Oxford University Press, 2004) 15.

[37] See discussion on page 111.

[38] Plato, *Timaeus*, 96. Trans. Benjamin Jowett (Cambridge, Mass.: The Internet Classics Archive, Massachusetts Institute of Technology, 2005) http://classics.mit.edu/Plato/timaeus.html (April 8, 2005).

[39] Ibid., 71.

[40] Ibid., 59.

[41] Ibid., 82.

[42] Plato, *Meno*, 81, trans. Benjamin Jowett (Cambridge, Mass.: The Internet Classics Archive, Massachusetts Institute of Technology, 2005) http://classics.mit.edu/Plato/meno.html (April 12, 2005).

involvement in history and, at times, seems to have advanced a kind of deism.[43] Many other teachings at odds with historic Christianity could be noted, all of which were roundly disavowed by the classicalists.

Aristotle's metaphysics, though providing some of the investigative tools which Aquinas would later employ in his own understanding of the *scientia Divina*, nevertheless presents a worldview fundamentally perpendicular to the faith held and defended by him. Aristotle's discussion of the idea of a single God in his *Metaphysics* is remarkably short, even passive, and follows only on the heels of a lengthy discussion on the nature of substance after which he ultimately deduces that "it is necessary that there should be an eternal unmovable substance."[44] Only then does he give brief mention of what such substance might be. For Aristotle, there exists a purely formal being whose life consists of eternal, self-contemplative thought (*noesis noeseos*). Probably a better name for Aristotle's god would simply be "Thought." As he elucidates in the *Metaphysics*:

> . . . thought thinks on itself because it shares the nature of the object of thought; for it becomes an object of thought in coming into contact with and thinking its objects, so that thought and object of thought are the same. For that which is capable of receiving the object of thought, that is the essence, is thought. But it is active when it possesses this object. Therefore the possession rather than the receptivity is the divine element which thought seems to contain, and the act of contemplation is what is most pleasant and best. If, then, God is always in that good state in which we sometimes are, this compels our wonder; and if in a better this compels it yet more. And God is in a better state. And life also belongs to God; for the actuality of thought is life, and God is that actuality.[45]

This Thought is also First Cause, but never leaves the quiet eternal repose in which it subsists. It does not incur into space-time to interact with and care for human history. Much less does it have a plan which unfolds in our world. Whatever teleology there is, it is an unconscious teleology. As Frederick Copleston describes it:

---

[43] On Plato's deistic tendencies, see *Statesman*, 272–74. Trans. Benjamin Jowett (Cambridge, Mass.: The Internet Classics Archive, Massachusetts Institute of Technology, 2005) http://classics.mit.edu/Plato/stateman.html (April 12, 2005).

[44] Aristotle, *Metaphysics*, XII.6.1 Trans. W. D. Ross (Cambridge, Mass.: Massachusetts Institute if Technology, The Internet Classics Archive, 2005) http://classics.mit.edu/Aristotle/metaphysics.12.xii.html (April 8, 2005). On the subject matter of Book XII of Aristotle's *Metaphysics*, see Helen Lang, "The Structure and Subject of Metaphysics " in *Phronesis* 38 (1993) 257–80.

[45] Ibid., XII.7.3.

[Aristotle's] First Mover, being immaterial, cannot perform any bodily action. His action must be purely spiritual, and so intellectual. In other words, God's activity is one of thought. But what is the object of His thought? Knowledge is intellectual participation of the object: now, God's object must be the best of all possible objects, and in any case the knowledge enjoyed by God cannot be knowledge that involves change or sensation or novelty. God therefore knows himself in an eternal act of intuition or self-consciousness. Aristotle, then, defines God as "thought of thought." God is subsistent thought, which eternally thinks itself.[46]

There is no indication that Aristotle ever thought of his unmoved mover as either holy or as an object befitting worship "still less as a Being to Whom prayers might profitably be addressed."[47] And, as Copleston says, "Aristotle's God is entirely self-centered . . . [as such] it would be out of the question for men to attempt personal intercourse with Him"[48] as Augustine, Anselm, and Aquinas frequently and prayerfully did.

Plotinus and the Neoplatonists also denied Divine personality, advancing instead an emanationist pantheism. Plotinus held to a chain of emanations: the One, the Mind (*nous*), and the Soul as the basis for his cosmology. Reality flows outward from the One—from unity to multiplicity—the universe constituting that which is most multiform. "So from this," Plotinus muses, "the One Intellectual Principle, and the Reason-Form emanating from it, our Universe rises and develops part."[49] But this One is fundamentally unknowable. It cannot be "named or conceived"[50] though is it the very thing which makes naming and conceiving possible.

Numerous other examples of the diversity of views among the post-Socratic secular philosophers could be cited and there is no real need to catalogue them here. The salient point is that the traditional theologians whom Pinnock criticizes (especially Augustine and Aquinas) railed against the fundamental views of these philosophers in advancing an *ex nihilo* creation wrought by an omnipotent, personal, *Triune* God—thus securing a decidedly anti-"Greek" Creator-creature distinction. Indeed, I would argue that history favors the view that Christianity had a far greater impact on

---

[46] Frederick Copleston, *A History of Philosophy*, vol. I (Paramus, N. J.: Newman Press, 1950) 316.

[47] Ibid., 117.

[48] Ibid.

[49] Plotinus, *Enneads*, 3.2.2, trans. by Stephen Mackenna and B. S. Page (Philadelphia: University of Pennsylvania, 2005) http://ccat.sas.upenn.edu/jod/texts/plotinus. April 12, 2005.

[50] Ibid., 6.6.13

Hellenistic philosophy than the other way around. One theologian even suggests the "Christianization of Hellenistic terms and concepts"[51] at the pens of such early theologians as Justin Martyr, Origen, Athanasius, and Augustine (as seen in the previous example of Cicero).

Herein is where we must consider whether Pinnock has treated fairly the tradition passed on to us by these seminal thinkers by sweepingly characterizing it as "pagan," having relegated "God in a kind of box"[52], and allowing "neo-Platonic ideas to influence [its] interpretations."[53] We must ask: Was Augustine merely a Neoplatonist in bishop's garb? Was Aquinas merely the agent of Aristotle cloaked in Christian veneer? For Pinnock, the answer is obviously, *yes*.

Of course, few from a Reformed perspective would desire to defend *everything* that Augustine and Aquinas believed. Chad Owen Brand, for example, observes that Augustine held to an "ecclesiology [that] was clearly more Catholic then Protestant, and even in his soteriology there were elements that the Reformed tradition does not accept [such as baptismal regeneration and his lack of a perseverance doctrine]."[54] Much the same can be said of Aquinas with the weightier addition, however, of his decidedly non-Reformed, *synergistic* view of regeneration (something I specifically oppose later in this chapter).[55]

Nevertheless, I find it nothing less than egregious to charge that the theologies of these men were simply "pagan." It is also a rather puzzling accusation considering Pinnock's own admission that, "Just as Augustine came to terms with ancient Greek thinking, so we [open theists] are making peace with the culture of modernity"[56] and to then go on to happily

---

[51] Douglas F. Kelly, "Afraid of Infinitude," *Christianity Today* vol. 39 (Jan. 9, 1995) 33.

[52] Pinnock, *Most Moved Mover*, 69.

[53] Ibid.

[54] Chad Owen Brand, "Orthodoxy and Open Theism and Their Connections to Western Philosophical Traditions," in *Beyond the Bounds*, ed. John Piper et al. (Wheaton, Ill.: Crossway, 2003) 54.

[55] Aquinas says that "It is the part of man to prepare his soul, since he does this by his free-will. And yet he does not do this without the help of God moving him, and drawing him to Himself" [Thomas Aquinas, *Summa Theologica*, II.109.6; trans. the Fathers of the English Dominican Province (Grand Rapids: Christian Classics Ethereal Library, 1999) 1506]. Thus, for Aquinas (unlike Augustine, but also quite unlike Pelagianism), prevenient grace (what Aquinas calls "habitual grace" [Ibid. 1505] (a kind of *ongoing* prevenience)) is absolutely axiomatic to regeneration and saving faith. This grace, while necessary, is not, however, *sufficient*. Humans must volitionally acquiesce in tandem with "the help of God." See Aquinas' fuller discussion at ibid, II.109.5–6., 1499–1511.

[56] Pinnock, *The Grace of God and the Will of Man*, 27.

declare his indebtedness to Hegel, Chardin, and Whitehead.[57] Further still, Pinnock admits that the thought of modern culture has had the effect on him of "consequently seeing things in the Bible we never saw before."[58] How is it that when Augustine, Aquinas, and other classical theologians utilize some of their cultural and philosophical influences in their theologies, it is characterized by Pinnock as infective and pagan, but when he does the very same thing in his own work (merely with different sources) it is "fresh" and "exciting"?[59] Is not the real issue simply that Pinnock *disagrees* with them? Surely it is. But it is one thing to disagree with someone's theology, and another thing altogether to castigate it as *pagan*. Though I appreciate Pinnock's desire to rethink the doctrine of God as historically received by Evangelicals, I find the labeling unhelpful and more emotive and reactionary than fair and objective.

To be sure, few if any scholars disacknowledge that Augustine and Aquinas (not barring others), were well schooled in Greek thought and, to varying degrees, incorporated that thought within their theologies. Augustine demonstrably drew on Plotinian thought in such areas as defining evil as a privation of the good (*privatio bonum*),[60] in some of his views concerning the soul,[61] and in his quasi-eudaemonistic moral anthropology in relation to a maximal Good.[62] His doctrine of God including, among other things, incorporeality, invisibility, infinity, non-diffusiveness, immutability, and simplicity, was also *self*-confessedly influenced by some "books of the Platonists."[63]

However, we might first acknowledge that the secular philosophical views which Augustine appropriated never demonstrably contradicted Scripture. Indeed, Augustine labors to point out that such insights by the Neoplatonists only functioned as a transitive, yet incomplete, "schoolmaster" which drove him toward the *same* axioms *already taught* in Scriptural revelation.[64] Rather, Augustine used some Neoplatonic ideas to try and

---

[57] Pinnock, *Most Moved Mover*, 142.

[58] Pinnock, *The Grace of God and the Will of Man*, 27.

[59] Ibid., 27–28.

[60] See, for example, Augustine, *Confessions*, 3.7.12. 63; Plotinus, *Enneads*, 1.8.10.

[61] For a good overview of Augustine views on the soul, see Roland Teske, "Augustine's theory of soul," *The Cambridge Companion to Augustine*, ed. Eleonore Stump and Norman Kretzmann (Cambridge: Cambridge University Press, 2001) 116–22.

[62] A helpful overview of Augustine's flirtations with Neoplatonic eudaemonism is offered by Michael Mendelson, "Saint Augustine," *The Stanford Encyclopedia of Philosophy* (Stanford: Stanford University, 2005) http://plato.stanford.edu/entries/augustine/

[63] Augustine, *Confessions*, 7.20.1, 154.

[64] Ibid.

further unpack what was contained within Scriptural revelation. Further, wherever Neoplatonic thought *did* contradict Scripture, it rejected in light of it. Augustine believed that secular philosophy was to be used as a *tool* for doing theology, but only to the extent that it remained fecund. Indeed, whatever helpful insights there may be in non-Christian philosophy, Augustine (sounding much like Justin Martyr some three centuries earlier[65]) actually considered them the erroneously hijacked property that properly belongs only to Christians:

> ... if those who are called philosophers, and especially the Platonists, have said aught that is true and in harmony with our faith, we are not only not to shrink from it, but to claim it for our own use from those who have unlawful possession of it ... they contain also liberal instruction which is better adapted to the use of the truth, and some most excellent precepts of morality; and some truths in regard even to the worship of the One God are found among them. Now these are, so to speak, their gold and silver, which they did not create themselves, but dug out of the mines of God's providence which are everywhere scattered abroad, and are perversely and unlawfully prostituting to the worship of devils. These, therefore, the Christian, when he separates himself in spirit from the miserable fellowship of these men, ought to take away from them, and to devote to their proper use in preaching the gospel. Their garments, also—that is, human institutions such as are adapted to that intercourse with men which is indispensable in this life—we must take and turn to a Christian use.[66]

Secondly, Augustine explains that Platonist thought was grossly inadequate, being speculative by force of reason alone, while lacking what is ultimately and inevitably needed: *revelation*. Most important among these inadequacies was the fact that Augustine "did not read in [the Platonists] that the Word was made flesh and came to dwell among us."[67] Much less did he find a triune theology which was absolutely central to his mature theology. Indeed, much of Augustine's seminal work, *De Trinitate*, was

---

[65] Mentioning Plato, among others, Justin says, "Whatever things were rightly said among all men, are the property of us Christians ... For all the writers were able to see realities darkly through the sowing of the implanted word that was in them. For the seed and imitation impacted according to capacity is one thing, and quite another is the thing itself, of which there is the participation and imitation according to the grace which is from Him." [Justin Martyr, "Second Apology" XIII, *The Apostolic Fathers with Justin Martyr and Irenaeus*, Edited b y Philip Schaff (Grand Rapids: Christian Classics Ethereal Library, 2002) 52.

[66] Augustine, *On Christian Doctrine*, II.60. Trans. J. F. Shaw (Grand Rapids: Christian Classics Ethereal Library, 2005) 784.

[67] Ibid., 7.9.2.

designed to confute non-Christian, philosophical concepts of God. Mary Clark comments that *De Trinitate* had three main objectives:

> [Augustine] wished to demonstrate to critics of the Nicene creed that the divinity and co-equality of Father, Son, and Holy Spirit are rooted in Scripture. He intended to tell pagan philosophers the need for faith in a divine mediator so that divine self-revelation and redemption can occur. Finally, he wanted to convince his readers that salvation and spiritual growth are connected with knowing themselves as images of the Triune God, from whom they came and toward whom they go, with a dynamic tendency to union realized by likeness to God who is Love.[68]

Augustine's doctrine of God was rooted in the biblical revelation of the creative, relational Trinity, while his doctrine of man was consistently subsumed, or better, *consumed*, within that dynamic, sustaining framework. Augustine himself sums up the fourteenth chapter of *De Trinitate* as an explication of the biblical portrait of human beings being brought into communion with the Godhead, "by God's gift" being granted "the partaking of that very God Himself."[69] Augustine's doctrine of God certainly included transcendence and immutability,[70] but these concepts were an integral *part* of his understanding of the dynamics of *redemption* and "in God's involvement in the world, and in the supremacy of Scripture over all of the intellectual machinations of man"[71] as we seek to understand God's nature.

Thirdly, as Chad Owen Brand rightly observes, Augustine's doctrines of predestination and perseverance were chiefly the product of his exegesis of Paul and John.[72] As one reads his *Treatise on the Predestination of the Saints*, for example, noticeably absent is any positive mention of Platonism. Indeed, the treatise is heavily laden with Scripture references intermingled with exegesis[73] with Augustine mentioning secular philosophy only deri-

---

[68] Mary Clark, "De Trinitate," in *The Cambridge Companion to Augustine*, ed. Eleonore Stump and Norman Kretzmann (Cambridge: Cambridge University Press, 2001) 91.

[69] Augustine, *De Trinitate*, XIV.12.15, trans. Arthur W. Haddan (Grand Rapids: Christian Classical Ethereal Library, 2005) 283.

[70] Ibid, I.8.15. 29. Also, *Confessions*, VII.1, 10.; 133, 146.

[71] Chad Owen Brand, "Orthodoxy and Open Theism and Their Connections to Western Philosophical Traditions," in *Beyond the Bounds*, ed. John Piper et al. (Wheaton, Ill.: Crossway, 2003) 55.

[72] Ibid.

[73] See, Augustine, "Treatise on the Predestination of the Saints," II.34–35, *Saint Augustin's Anti-Pelagian Works*, trans. Peter Holmes and Robert Wallis, revised by B. B. Warfield (Grand Rapids: Christian Classical Ethereal Library, 2005) 864–65. Here, before defining predestination as, "the foreknowledge and the preparation of God's kindnesses, whereby they are

sively—including a reference to his criticisms of Porphyry whom he also characterized in *The City of God* as "the most learned of the philosophers, though the bitterest enemy of the Christians."[74] Thus, whatever Hellenizing tendencies are to be found in Augustine, there are also quite clearly *anti-*Hellenizing tendencies and a thorough desire to ground Christian doctrine in Scripture.

Aquinas' theology charts a similar methodological course as that of Augustine. Aquinas freely appropriates secular philosophy, chiefly that of Aristotle, and puts it into service theologically. The similarities and dissimilarities between Aquinas and Aristotle have been sufficiently catalogued elsewhere and there is no need to repeat them here.[75] The major point for our purposes is to acknowledge, as Joseph Owens points out, that the situation with Aquinas and Aristotle "points to a radical difference between [the two], despite Aquinas's use of the Aristotelian vocabulary. The philosophical phrasing employed by the two thinkers may to a large extent be the same, but the meanings attached to the same expressions can be very different for each of them."[76] Etienne Gilson succinctly states, "Aristotle's God, inaccessible as he was, was far less than the WHO IS of Thomas Aquinas."[77] Dovetailing Gilson, we might describe Aquinas's position as one in which the philosophical efforts of human reason may glean hazy clues concerning the "*What* Is" of God, but never the "*Who* Is" in the absence of the self-revelatory disclosure of God in Scripture, *by grace*. Aquinas says quite clearly: "to see the essence of God is possible to the created intellect by grace, and not by nature."[78] Gerald Bray writes,

---

most certainly delivered, whoever they are that are delivered" [II.35, 865], Augustine labors to demonstrate the doctrine as unwaveringly biblical, citing both John and Paul.

[74] Augustine, *The City of God*, XIX.22., 592.

[75] See especially, Etienne Gilson, *The Christian Philosophy of St. Thomas Aquinas* (Notre Dame, Ind.: University of Notre Dame Press, 1956, 2002) 7–25; Joseph Owens, "Aristotle and Aquinas" in *The Cambridge Companion to Aquinas* (Cambridge: Cambridge University Press, 1993) 38–57; and Mark Jordan, "The Alleged Aristotelianism of St. Thomas Aquinas," *The Etienne Gilson Series* 15 (Toronto, Canada: Pontifical Institute of Mediaeval Studies, 1990).

[76] Owens, *The Cambridge Companion to Aquinas*, 40.

[77] Gilson, *The Christian Philosophy of St. Thomas Aquinas*, 106.

[78] Thomas Aquinas, *Summa Theologica*, I.12.4. Trans. Fathers of the English Dominican Province (Grand Rapids: Christian Classics Ethereal Library, 1999) 68. By seeing the "essence" of God, Aquinas does not mean that we see God as He is *in Himself*, nor that we garner a full comprehension of God. Rather, the secret things of God remain secret, and our knowledge always remains partial (Ibid., I.12.8; 73–74). To see the essence of God is to be granted, by grace, a kind of *unitive* vision (Ibid., I.12.9; 74–75).

Thomas argued that there was another order of reality which Aristotle could not explain—the realm of grace. Grace could be understood only by revelation, which was mediated through the church and its sacraments. According to Thomas it did not contradict or destroy nature; rather, grace perfected it.[79]

Natural reason and grace are complementary to the extent that the theologian brings the former into service under the latter. Indeed, "there is no reason why those things which may be learned from philosophical science, so far as they can be known by natural reason, may not also be taught us by another science *so far as they fall within revelation*"[80] [emphasis added]. And further, ". . . it was necessary for the salvation of man that certain truths *which exceed human reason* should be made known to him by divine revelation. Even as regards those truths about God which human reason could have discovered, it was necessary that man should be taught by a divine revelation; because the truth about God such as reason could discover, would only be known by a few, and that after a long time, *and with the admixture of many errors*"[81] [emphasis added]. Here we see, not only that human reason is insufficient and prone to error, but it is fundamentally *non-salvific*. Only the condescension of God in grace can provide the means of salvation and, along with it, true knowledge of the Divine. Yet the two need not be thought of as mutually exclusive. Rather, as the Angelic Doctor eloquently put it, "those who use philosophical texts in sacred teaching, by subjugating them to faith, do not mix water with wine, but turn water into wine."[82]

Now, while I have acknowledged that I do have some misgivings concerning the extent to which Aquinas employed Aristotelian tools for exploring theology, I must nevertheless add to the discussion that I think Pinnock has either ignored or simply misunderstood the true thrust of his doctrine of God. An example of this is manifest in his [mis]quoting *Summa Theologica* 1.13.7: "Since God is outside the whole order of creation and all creatures are ordered to him and not conversely, it is manifest that creatures are really related to God himself, whereas *in God there is no real relation to creatures, but a relation only in idea*, inasmuch as creatures are referred to

---

[79] Gerald Bray, *The Doctrine of God* (Downer's Grove, Ill.: InterVarsity, 1993) 43.
[80] Aquinas, *Summa Theologica*, I.1.1.2; 3.
[81] Ibid., I.1.1; 3.
[82] Thomas Aquinas, *Expositio Super Librum Boethii De Trinitate*, 2.4, ad 5. Quoted in Mark Jordan, "Theology and Philosophy," in *The Cambridge Companion to Aquinas* (Cambridge: Cambridge University Press, 1993) 235.

him" [emphasis in original source].[83] Pinnock asks, "Is it not astonishing that this is what so many have the temerity to call the 'orthodox' view?"[84]

For one thing, this statement by Aquinas has hardly ever been officially declared "the orthodox view," at least by any Protestant theologian. Rather, what classical theologians have typically considered "orthodox" concerning the doctrine of God is any theology that preserves the Vincentian guidelines of certain Divine attributes or perfections such as eternality, omnipotence, omniscience (including foreknowledge), incorporeality, personhood, tri-unity, and so on—not any particular theory that remains within those guidelines (including Thomas' ideas concerning Divine-human relationality). Pinnock commits a category fallacy here in confusing the specific with the general and thus narrowly strawmans traditional "orthodoxy" as entailing a very specific subset.

Pinnock does not grant that, historically, classical theologians have actually been quite liberal in providing tremendous latitude to theologians who theologize *within* the broader delimitations of orthodoxy. In other words, one is free (that is, will remain orthodox) to build his or her theology as they wish, provided they stay within certain parameters, and not deny any of those perfections of God that have remained staples of Vincentianism.[85] Aquinas' theology has traditionally been considered orthodox not because *everything* he wrote is necessarily correct, much less obligatory on those who wish to be orthodox, but because he consistently operated within Vincentian guidelines. To think otherwise is to imply that being orthodox is the same thing as being a *Thomist*. This is *prima facie* absurd and it surprises me that Pinnock does not make this distinction.

Secondly, and more importantly, Pinnock commits a fallacy of equivocation by wholly mischaracterizing what Aquinas means by his statement that "in God there is no real relation to creatures, but a relation only in idea." Pinnock takes this as another indication of the God of classicalism being distant and aloof. But, as Thomas Weinandy astutely observes,

> At first sight, as Aquinas' critics are incessantly pointing out, this appears to mean that while creation is related to God, God is not related to the creature. If this interpretation were correct, it would not only disavow and exclude God's love for and care of creation,

---

[83] Aquinas, *Summa Theologica* Ia.13.7 cited in Pinnock, *Most Moved Mover*, 69.
[84] Pinnock, *Most Moved Mover*, 69, n.16.
[85] See my discussion of the "Vincentian Rule" on page 61.

but it would even more critically repudiate that God was actually the Creator. Such a position would be sheer nonsense and, moreover, one that Aquinas would hardly espouse.[86]

Aquinas is a complex philosophical theologian and, when reading him, it is incumbent upon the reader to pay close attention to terminology. For Aquinas, there are three types of relationality: mutual logical relations (or "unreal" relations), real relations, and mixed relations.[87] The first type describes a mental relationship in which the terms have awareness or knowledge of the other, but such that the relationship between the terms are not fundamentally altered. In the second instance, the terms interact with one another in such a way as to alter the various states or nature of the other. Importantly, this type of relationship is said to be modulated by some mediating factor between the two terms. For example, a husband and wife expresses themselves to one another through a kiss, a conversation, touch, and so on. The relationship is mediate. In the third instance, the relationship is "mixed." That is, one term of the relationship is logical while the other is real. This implies a relationship of terms in a different ontological order in which one is altered or changed by the relationship, while the other remains consistently the same. It is this relationship which Aquinas believed to exist between God and humans.[88]

The scenario may sound coldly logical and impersonal but this is far from what Aquinas espoused. His *Summas*, and the highly terminological methodology found therein, may seem rather pedantic and laborious by today's standard of theologizing, but we must not let such complexity throw of us off from what the Angelic Doctor wanted to describe. A mixed relation, possible only between a distinct Creator-creature relationship, is actually a deeply relational intimacy that surpasses anything possible in creature-creature relationships.

For God to be the logical term in the Creator-creator relationship does not imply a *lack* in God equating unrelatedness, nor does it mean that God's relationship with humans is "unreal" in the sense of being nonexistent. Quite the contrary. It rather means that God, as the logical term in the relationship, participates *as He is in Himself*—which is the very thing that establishes both the emergence and continued existence of the human subject. In turn, this creates a relatedness to the human subject *as he or she is*. This mixed relation is thus unlike any other relationship (for example,

---

[86] Thomas Weinandy, *Does God Suffer?* 130–31.

[87] Thomas Aquinas, *Summa Theologica*, I.13.7, trans. Fathers of the English Dominican Province (Grand Rapids: Christian Classics Ethereal Library, 1999) 88–89.

[88] Weinandy, *Does God Suffer?* 130.

human to human) in that God, as logical term, is related to humans in a most intimate manner as the relationship is *unmediated*.[89] As Weinandy explains,

> ... if God creates by no other act than the pure act that he is, and if the creature only is by being related to the pure act that God is, then God is actually related to and present in the creature by his very essence ... While the relationship between God and creatures is equally 'act' to 'act,' it is not mediated nor is it a partial expression of their being. The 'act' (the *esse*) by which the creature is a creature only is 'act' because it is related to the 'act' by which God is (*ipsum esse*). The Creator-creature relation is an unmediated relationship between the pure act of God as *ipsum esse* and the act, the *esse*, by which the creature is. The creature is totally defined as a creature in this relation for it establishes the creature as created. Moreover, unlike relations between human beings, the Creator-creature relation is perpetual and uninterrupted. Thus, this relation is absolutely immediate (no mediating action), supremely dynamic (pure act to created act), utterly intimate (a relation between God as he is in himself and the creature as it is in itself), and unbreakably enduring (it can never be severed).[90]

Aquinas' God is indeed immutable, but unlike the implications of full-bodied Aristotelianism, he is far from *immobile*. He is intimately and consistently involved with the world He created and with His creatures. Pinnock repeatedly confuses unchangeability with stasis.[91] The latter certainly is aloof and distant, but, thankfully, it was never the sort of God promulgated by Aquinas (or Augustine). Aquinas adopted some of the Aristotelian language, but he adapted it to the creative, purposive, personal Lord of all things. Simon Oliver helps unpack the manner in which Aquinas appropriated some positive elements of Aristotelianism, but baptized them with the fuller Christian understanding:

> Aquinas's initial contributions on the nature of God ... formulates a radical distinction between finite and infinite which can be expressed in terms of motion: on the one hand, God is simple and beyond all motion, lacking potency and in full actuality, while, on the other hand, created nature is "the distinctive form or quality of such things as have within themselves a principle of motion." How is this ontological difference traversed? [For Aquinas] ... God

---

[89] Ibid., 134.

[90] Ibid., 135–36.

[91] See, for example, Pinnock, "Systematic Theology," in *The Openness of God* (Downers Grove, Ill.: InterVarsity, 1994) 103.

is related to creation as the first unmoved mover, but . . . this understanding is further enhanced by Aquinas as motion is related through analogical participation to the immanent life of the divine . . . [creational motion has a] relation to the immanent life of God in the emanation of the persons of the Trinity, the principle of all motion . . . Aquinas' understanding of creation, understood as the 'motion' of the emanation of all things from God, is founded on a participation in the eternal Trinitarian life of God. God is not only the principle of motion, but also motion's term or *telos*. [There is an inherent] teleology within nature and the concomitant ends of all things . . . God [is] the prime mover of creation towards its proper end through the work of grace.[92]

Contra Pinnock *and Aristotle*, Oliver adds that,

> This is hardly a distant or impervious deity. But neither is this a deity who needs to 'experience' or 'suffer' in order to be, for example, compassionate. God could not be any more compassionate than he already is . . . For Aquinas, God 'envelops' motion and is the first unmoved mover by 'touch.' Motion is, in the end, the means of our participation in divine eternity and an analogical participation in the dynamic and eternal interchange of love in the Trinity.[93]

Those of the Reformed persuasion have echoed much the same in this regard. Berkhof, for example, comments that objections of Pinnock's kind are,

> . . . based to a certain extent on misunderstanding. The divine immutability should not be understood as implying immobility, as if there were no movement in God. It is even customary in theology to speak of God as *actus purus*, a God who is always in action . . . God enters into manifold relations with man and, as it were, lives their life with them.[94]

From the foregoing discussions, it is my conclusion that Pinnock's criticism of Hellenism's influence on Christian theology is wholly unhelpful. It is a faulty caricature of classical theology which fails to appreciate both the differences between Greek philosophy and the theology of the classicalists. It also commits a genetic fallacy[95] that draws negative conclusions based on

---

[92] Simon Oliver, *Philosophy, God and Motion* (London: Routledge, 2005) 166–67.

[93] Simon Oliver, written correspondence, March 1, 2005.

[94] Berkhof, *Systematic Theology*, 59.

[95] By this I mean the fallacy of argumentation in which the origin of a claim is taken as evidence that discredits the claim itself. For example, the argument that Hitler believed the world is round is not a good argument in favor of a flat earth.

the mere origin or incidental similarity of various views. This is a perilous tack for open theism to take since it owes such a tremendous debt to the process theology of Whitehead and Hartshorne,[96] a system which denies, among other things, God's independence, the deity of Christ, the Trinity, omnipotence, omnipresence, and other essential Christian beliefs which open theists affirm. Divine nescience of future contingencies was also the position of the sixteenth century Socinians who expressly denied exhaustive foreknowledge for the same reason that Cicero did: to preserve the libertarian understanding of human freewill. The Socinians further denied the Trinity, the sovereignty of God, the Divinity of Christ, the need for Christ's death as atonement, and several other things—again things that open theists affirm. Thus, again, it is altogether unhelpful to merely point out the vintage or origin of one's position. Just as classical theologians are not "pagan philosophers" simply because they adopt some Greek principles, Pinnock and his fellow open theists should not be characterized as Socinians, processians, or as those "poisoned by Grecian metaphysics." Both classical and open theistic models have some points in common with Greek metaphysics. But just because the Greeks agree with various items attached to either model, does not necessarily mean they are wrong. Nor is it valid to criticize the mere vintage of one's philosophical concepts without marshalling one's own philosophical case. As Wolfhart Pannenberg has wisely written (and yet himself a critic of Hellenism in Christian theology),

> [One may criticize] the "incomplete exorcism" of pagan elements in Hellenistic Christian theology, elements that have been influential throughout all subsequent Christian history. But criticism of such an "unbaptized God" does not dispense the theologian from arguing for the philosophical validity of the alternative he proposes. It is not enough to oppose philosophical concepts of timeless eternity by asserting the temporal character of God's action in history.[97]

Any theological system must be weighed in terms of its own philosophical commitments and defense. It is not enough to merely criticize the origin of one's position and then expect a proffered alternative to triumph *ex hypothesi*. Much of the remainder of this critique will attempt to show that Pinnock evinces at times not only a lack of positive argumentation for his views, but has apparently not always considered the implications of his openness alternative.

---

[96] See pages 82–88.

[97] Wolfhart Pannenberg, "A Trinitarian Synthesis" (Book Review of Robert W. Jenson's, *Systematic Theology*, in *First Things*, 103 (May 2000) 50.

Love as the Apical Feature of Deity

I now move to Pinnock's second premise—that immanentistic love stems from God's very metaphysical nature or essence which itself is love. Love is as close as we ever come in Scripture to gleaning a substantive definition of the precise and complete ontology of God. As we have seen, Pinnock holds God's very nature and concomitant purpose for creating the world summed up in the statement that God "is a lover who wants people to love him freely in return"[98] and that the biblical text of 1 John 4:16b, "God is love" (cf. 1 John 4:8), is as close as one gets to gleaning a core metaphysical definition of God's basic ontology.

I have earlier stated my sympathy with Pinnock's desire to unearth Divine love and relationality within the Evangelical world—perceiving, as he does, some measure of deficiency in a solid understanding of these biblical truths in relation to a study of the metaphysics of God especially as it relates to transcendence. Later, I discuss how these important aspects of theology and anthropology might be understood in a classical, indeed Reformed, context. But we pause here to first consider whether love as the apical feature of Pinnock's theology is the proper starting point.

As with libertarian human freedom (which I review next), I find it unfortunate that Pinnock begins with "love as the central attribute of God" with only an assertion and in the absence of a solid defense.[99] When Pinnock relays the Johannine statement that "God is love," it is not made clear why this assertion should form the locus of our understanding of God's constituent nature and essence. Following our shared *canonical critical* approach,[100] we might ask why *this* text is supremely privileged over other "God is" texts such as "God is the King" (Ps 47:7), "God is holy" (Ps 99:9), "God is a sun and shield" (Ps 84:11), "God is spirit" (John 4:24), "God is just" (2 Thes 1:6), "God is the builder" (Heb 3:4), "God is a consuming fire" (Heb 12:29), "[God is] Holy, Holy, Holy" (Is 6:3a), "the Lord of hosts" or "God is light" (1 John 1:5). God "is" many things in the *whole* of Scripture, not just love. A reason must be given why love should be made the primary "is" of God if the canonical critical approach demands that the

---

[98] Pinnock, "An Interview With Clark Pinnock," *Modern Reformation Magazine* (June 1998) Online: http://www.modernreformation.org/mr98/novdec/mr9806freespace.html (November 16, 2003).

[99] Pinnock, personal interview, Evangelical Theological Society. Atlanta, Georgia, November 19, 2003.

[100] I remind the reader that this work assumes, in part, a canonical critical approach in an attempt to systematize within the Evangelical tradition as opposed to employing other critical approaches such as *form*, *redaction*, or *structural* (see page 5).

Bible as a constitutive whole be read *analogia fide* (that is, in light of other texts).

There is another problem in using the 1 John 4:16 text as a definitive statement of the essence of God. As Old Testament scholar, Nathan MacDonald observes:

> . . . John's primary concern in 1 John 4 is not to define who God is, but to indicate what love is. John "spells out precisely the nature of love which is demanded by every believer." He does this by reference to God's actions. For John, our understanding of the nature of love is so poor it can only be explained with reference to God's love. Thus to explain God's nature by love, and not love by God's nature, is to seriously misunderstand what John is doing.[101]

To take "God is love" as an operational statement of God's very nature is not only at odds with the Johannine purpose in making the statement, but also twists the use of language and the Jewish idiom involved. R. C. Sproul, observes that,

> When the Bible says that God is love, that statement is not what we call an analytical statement whereby we can reverse the subject and predicate, and say that therefore love is God. That's not what the Bible means. Rather, what the Jewish form of expression says here is that God is so loving and His love so consistent, so profound, so deep, so transcendent, and such an integral part of His character that to express it in the maximum way possible, we say that he is love.[102]

Another way of saying this is simply that, whatever true *love* is, *God* is—but not the reverse. Love itself is defined by the very character and constituent nature of God. Indeed, there is no true love where God is not also present. But to make capital-L Love an exhaustive, connotative term for God's being itself is simply to curtail the fuller biblical portrait.

The question might be asked whether it is wise at all to declare anything the central or defining attribute of God. Reformed theologian John Frame comments that "Rather than making any single attribute central, classical theology teaches that all of God's defining attributes are ways of describing his simple essence. So God's attributes are not parts of divisions

---

[101] MacDonald, Nathan, "From Augustine to Arminius, and Beyond," in *Reconstructing Theology: A Critical Assessment of the Theology of Clark Pinnock*, ed. Tony Gray and Christopher Sinkinson (Carlisle, Cumbria, UK: Paternoster, 2000) 27.

[102] R. C. Sproul, *Now That's A Good Question* (Carol Stream, Ill.: Tyndale, 1996) 6.

within his nature, but each attribute is necessary to his being."[103] I agree with Frame in the main and see wisdom against the danger of restricting God to any *one* defining attribute or controlling feature. To do so is to pick a "part" of the Divine nature and confuse it for the whole. I do not entirely agree, however, that some level of understanding of the central purpose of God—and therefore, something of God's very nature—cannot be gleaned from Scripture and held as a controlling principle or even, as in Pinnock's system, a controlling metaphor.[104] Finding such a control point is, of course, not an easy exercise. For those committed to *sola Scriptura*, it must come directly from the Bible. Yet, it will also be a principle that will inevitably shape and guide his or her understanding of the Bible itself. Systematic theology is manifestly impossible without doing so. An integrating motif of sorts is needed in which to bind the major areas and sub-points of theology from the doctrine of God itself, to christology, pneumatology, anthropology, hamartiology, soteriology, ecclesiology, eschatology, and so on. This motif is a major theological concept under which all the other areas of theology are subsumed and contextualized. It is a unifying theme that binds doctrines together and makes them into a unified and systematic whole. Thus, I find the need for a controlling metaphor to be an unavoidable reality. Indeed, I take no issue with Pinnock's stress upon the need for a controlling metaphor but rather with what he has selected for it.

The pure-love theory of God fails to account for doctrines crucial to a full-orbed biblical understanding of God's nature and His activity in creation. D. A. Carson observes that,

> If the love of God is exclusively portrayed as an inviting, yearning, sinner-seeking, lovesick passion . . . the cost will be massive. There is some truth in this picture of God . . . Made absolute, however, it not only treats complementary texts as if they were not there, but it steals God's sovereignty from him and our security from us. It espouses a theology of grace rather different from Paul's theology of grace, and at its worst ends up with a God so insipid he can neither intervene to save us nor deploy his chastening rod against us. His love is too 'unconditional' for that. This is a world far removed from the pages of Scripture.[105]

---

[103] John Frame, *No Other God*, (Phillipsburg, N. J.: Presbyterian & Reformed, 2001) 51–52.

[104] I am not advancing this as Frame's position.

[105] D. A. Carson, *The Difficult Doctrine of the Love of God* (Wheaton, Ill.: Crossway, 2000) 22.

I fault no theologian for freely developing a theological system which he or she understands to be correct and good. But when they declare, as Pinnock does, to be totally committed to the *sola Scriptura* principle, parameters are placed upon the degree of latitude available in forging that theology. From this perspective, numerous doctrines become problematic on a pure-love system. The doctrine of an eternal Hell, for example, is a particularly troublesome doctrine for those who treat of God's nature in this manner (as evinced by Pinnock's denial of it and resultant eschatological position of "conditional immortality"). Or, on a broader level, the doctrine of creation and its purpose becomes necessarily tainted.

Divine Glory

The eschatological teleology one identifies in the doctrine of creation is vitally important to Christian theology because it cuts to the core of what God's purpose is in creating, thereby reflecting something of His own being. No question is more sublime to the Christian than *why* God created and Scripture is hardly silent on the matter. Though love is manifestly a constituent part of the broader purpose of creation, I take Scripture to teach *glory* not only as the primal creative teleology of creation, but also as an effective controlling metaphor for God. This is stated in both narrative and didactic texts (for example, Rev 4:11; Ps 19:1). This purpose extends in a particularly unique way to what Scripture portrays as God's people of whom the Lord says he creates and calls specifically "for [His] glory" and "for the display of His splendor" (Isa 43:7; 60:21, NIV). The Bible speaks of "a Royal Priesthood" that serves to magnify His glory in a unique way through their calling to "proclaim the excellencies of Him" (1 Pet 2:9). Yet the Bible portrays even the reprobate as being used of God for the purpose of glorifying Him in an outworking of His judgment on them (Rom 9:17; Exod 14:17; Ezek 28:22). Little is done in Scripture to justify these actions in the face of God's sovereignty over creation and the details of its history. They are merely declared to be inalterable truths that are accepted doxastically as opposed to rationally. Our thoughts are portrayed as incapable of taking it all in as only an omnipotent God can (for example, Isaiah 55:8).

The Scripture further portrays "The heavens" as "declar[ing] the glory of God" and "the skies proclaim[ing] the work of his hands." "Day after day they pour forth speech" and "night after night they display knowledge" (Ps 19:1-2, NIV). The earth, the sun, the moon, the stars, and all the wonders of the universe are exhibited as bearing thunderous testimony to the glory of an Almighty God. These are pictured as testifying to the truth of God not with an ambiguous whisper but as a cosmic shout such that all humans are accountable to God. Paul writes, "what may be known about God is plain to them, because God has made it plain to them. For since the creation of the world God's invisible qualities—his eternal power and divine nature—have been clearly seen, being understood from what has been made, so that men are without excuse . . ." (Rom 1:19-20). The Lord "has made His wonderful works to be remembered" (Ps 111:4, NKJV). Indeed, "all things" says Paul, "were created through Him and for Him" (Col 1:16). Not surprisingly, Calvin referred to all of creation summarily as the theater of God's glory.[106]

The Hebrew for "glory," *kabod*, connotes *weightiness*, *bulk*, or *density* (for example, 1 Sam 4:18, 1 Kgs 12:10, 2 Chr 10:10, Neh 5:18, Job 33:7, Ps 32:4, Prov 27:3, Isa 6:10, Lam 3:7)—even *burdensomeness* or a sense of being *laden* (for example, Exod 5:9, Isa 47:6, Isa 1:4). We may, in the modern West, be too often tempted to think of glory primarily in terms of a sort of ethereal "light" which, though implying radiance or brightness which are certainly a constituent part of the Biblical portrait of the countenance of the Lord (for example, Ps 18:12, Ezek 1:27-28), nevertheless do not carry with it the association of a sort of smothering, near-suffocative immensity that it would have undoubtedly conjured in the ancient mind.

To behold the "weightiness" of God in the OT was an occasion of terror upon those whom the Lord condescended to reveal Himself. When this happened, the weight of glory poured over them and would bear upon them with such devastating force and density that such encounters generically rendered the beneficiary speechless, deeply shaken, and indelibly changed.

Divine beauty itself is a Divine terror that engulfs the beneficiary and distresses him. Ezekiel describes a vision of the terrible beauty of the Lord surrounded by "living creatures" in a vast expanse, "sparking like ice, and awesome" (Ezek 1:22). The voice of the Almighty struck him as "the roar of rushing waters . . . the tumult of an army" (verse 24). The Lord appeared to him as "glowing metal . . . full of fire . . . like the appearance of a rainbow in the clouds on a rainy day, so was the radiance around Him" (verse 28a). The prophet says only that he summarily "fell facedown" (28). Archetypally, he rises only as the same Spirit that prostrates him, lifts him (28).

The prophet Isaiah describes his vision of the Lord seated on a throne, "high and exalted" while "the train of his robe filled the temple" (Isa 6:1). Surrounding the Lord are winged seraphs, covering their faces and feet, while they call to one another, "Holy, holy, holy is the LORD Almighty;

---

[106] John Calvin, *Institutes of the Christian Religion*, 1.6.2, trans. Henry Beveridge (Grand Rapids: Eerdmans, 1989) 51.

the whole earth is full of his glory" (verses 2-3). Isaiah was broken by this experience crying, "Woe to me! . . . I am ruined!" (verse 5). Yet, just as with Ezekiel, the Lord graces the prophet and lifts him up following the cleansing touch of a hot coal in the hand of a seraph (verses 6-7). Again, the Lord that strikes down, rises up.

In the New Testament, the Greek for "glory" is *doxa* which also has a relatively broad semantical range from "esteem" or "reputation" to "splendor," "brightness," or "majesty." *Doxa* is used some 150 times in the New Testament, commonly in reference to Jesus (see John 1:14, 12:41), or in Jesus' own descriptions of Himself (see Matt 24:30; John 17:24). Indeed, Jesus expresses the will of God in His High Priestly Prayer to be that the elect should ". . . be with me where I am, and to see my glory . . ." (John 17:24).

Scripture thus fittingly portrays God as demanding that He be worshipped in accord with His deserving greatness. We read that humans must "ascribe to the Lord the glory due his Name" and "Bring an offering and come before him" and "worship the Lord in the splendor of His holiness" (1 Chr 16:29, NIV). We are to, "Fear God and give him glory . . . Worship him who made the heavens, the earth, the sea and the springs of water" (Rev 14:7). God's elect are charged to "Tell of His glory among the nations, His wonderful deeds among all the peoples" (1 Chr 16:24) and to make disciples for Him (Matt 28:18).

Following the *sola Scriptura* principle, this seems a better starting point in which to frame an understanding of the other tenets of the Christian faith. It provides a motif or architectonic eyepiece through which all its components can be unified. Love can be understood as a constituent part of a glory teleology in which God is further glorified *through* love—but not through love exclusively. This glory theme will be further drawn upon later when, as a replacement motif for Pinnock's love orientation, I argue that it better suits New Testament soteriology. The purpose here has been to demonstrate the insufficiency of love alone as a controlling metaphor for a *sola Scriptura* theology. It is too restrictive and ignores other "God is" passages which might better inform our understanding of God's nature. For such a major controlling metaphor to be granted, it must be defended beyond a mere assertion and the citation of single biblical text.

Libertarian Free Will

Pinnock's third operating premise is that human beings posses autonomous libertarian freewill. It is the most vital faculty God bestows to humankind and is the hinge upon which their destinies turn. That this position forms that fundamental starting point for Pinnock's theological anthropology is clear. It is the basis upon which humans are unique as creatures, have relations with God, are held accountable, and—not least of all—procure individual salvation. What is rather startling, however, is that—as with Divine love as the apical feature of his doctrine of God—Pinnock devotes almost no time whatsoever to first defending the libertarian supposition. We are told only that 1) libertarian freedom is "one of the deepest of all human intuitions" and a "fundamental self-perception,"[107] 2) that its rejection simply leads to fatalism, reduces us to automatons, and makes God "the puppet master who pulls all the strings"[108] and 3) we find a few passing references to quantum physics which, in Pinnock's view, supports a philosophy of indeterminacy.[109]

None of these points, however, can really be construed as arguments in favor of the libertarian supposition. "Human intuitions," for example, are a notoriously poor litmus test for truth. Science tells us that we are made of very basic elements such as carbon atoms despite the fact that I may not "feel" that way. Indeed, on a biblical worldview, Christians are called to believe all manner of religious premises that our intuitions often seem to contradict. The Bible teaches, for example, that human beings are sinners. But this counters the intuition that many human beings have that they are basically good or meritorious. Numerous other examples could be given.

Or, if we take the issue of contrasting libertarianism only with fatalism, we find that Pinnock ignores other positions, most notably compatibilism, which argues for a basic human freedom which is also determined, not by the "Fates" or by pure mechanistic force as in fatalism, but by an all-sovereign *personal* God who is exacting purpose in every human thought and action.

A passing reference to quantum physics is also inadequate. Scientists are still undecided as to the true inner working of the sub-atomic realm. Only those who subscribe to the so-called "Copenhagen interpretation" are those who believe the advancements of Werner Heisenberg are proof of a

---

[107] Pinnock, *Grace Unlimited*, 95.

[108] Pinnock, "God Limits His Knowledge," in *Predestination and Free Will: Four Views of Divine Sovereignty and Human Freedom*, ed. David Basinger and Randall Basinger (Downer's Grove, Ill.: InterVarsity, 1986) 145.

[109] Pinnock, *Most Moved Mover*, 137. Pinnock quotes Greg Boyd, *God of the Possible* (Grand Rapids: Baker, 2000) 94; also Pinnock, "Open Theism: "What is this? A new teaching? And with authority!" presented at the University of Calgary, February 3, 2003. page 8; http://www.ucalgary.ca/ UofC/faculties/HUM/RELS/chairs/cchair/crsrc/Pinnock.Open Theism.pdf (April 12, 2003).

genuine, noncausal chaos. And these scientists are by no means an easy majority. But even if the Copenhagen interpretation is substantially correct, most philosophers now recognize that it would be wholly irrelevant to the issue of libertarianism and determinism. For example, Richard Popkin and Avrum Stroll, in a popular introduction to philosophy, observe that,

> . . . the Heisenberg principle is actually irrelevant to the main issues involved in the argument between the libertarians and the determinists. It may show that a certain number formulation of complete determinism is no longer adequate, or in keeping with present day physical theory. But this does not indicate in the slightest that because we may never be able to discover all the determining factors in the physical world, therefore human volitions [in the libertarian sense] are free. The Heisenberg principle has not led to any conclusion concerning the indeterminacy of our knowledge above the level of particle motions, which, in fact, are predictable in large numbers, but not in individual cases. Indeterminacy on the lowest level of physical action certainly does not show that free will is involved, or that any decisions have been made by the particles to act the way they do. Hence, no serious analogy between the results of modern physical science and the basis of human volition seems possible.[110]

It is difficult to imagine how the Copenhagen interpretation, if true, would help the libertarian case at all. Would it mean that the uncaused, arbitrary motion of a single, or a few, subatomic particles is what accounts for a particular decision? Could the decision to embrace the Christian faith be explained in this way? If so, then Pinnock has not proven freewill or moral responsibility in making decisions, but utter chaos. Far from establishing human accountability, it would reduce one's actions to uncaused phenomenon with no explanation whatsoever. Moral decisions become a freak of chance occurrences at the quantum level.

Pinnock appeals to freewill as the anthropological locus of his entire openness program but does not comment on how or why the "will" does what it does. The question is not whether someone's "will" chose something or not. Even most Reformed theologians do not argue this point. The question is why does the "will" choose what it chooses. It is not enough to simply say that someone chose something of his or her own "free will." For, we might back the question up a step and ask, why did that person's "will" incline one way and not the other?

---

[110] Richard Popkin and Avrum Stroll, *Philosophy Made Simple* (Oxford: Made Simple, 1993) 139.

Pinnock does not deal with these issues. The libertarian understanding of freewill is included as an operating principle but is not positively argued for. Nor is it defended against its flaws. Pinnock does not grapple with what many construe to be overwhelming problems with the libertarian position. Indeed, after surveying the arguments for and against libertarianism and determinacy, Popkin and Avrum conclude that "there is overwhelming evidence suggesting that human beings are completely determined."[111]

In my estimation, this lack of defense severely weakens Pinnock's theological system. If a theologian intends to rear a new position on a vitally important matter concerning the doctrine of God, it would seem prudent to make such a central motif thoroughly circumspect. It is not enough to simply assume the facticity of a major philosophical position when the issue itself has engendered great divergence among scholars for as long as philosophical speculation has been alive. It is true that the libertarian position, as seen earlier, has been tacitly adopted in much of Western Christendom. It is only a recent development in Evangelicalism, however, that such a position—at the technical level—should cause one to rethink the very constituent nature of God and the scope of His omniscience. If a single philosophical supposition causes one to rethink the majority opinion of two thousand years of historical Christian theology (that is, exhaustive Divine foreknowledge), it seems clear that pains should be taken to first establish that supposition.

For the purposes of this critique, we must begin, therefore, at an earlier point in the process by asking: *What is the will?* The answer to this is hardly obvious. The term "free will" is not found in Scripture. Ironically, considering that Pinnock deplores classical theology's reliance on Grecian metaphysics, the term finds its origin in the Stoics, translated from the Latin *liberum arbitrium*.[112] True, the Stoics also believed in a kind of predestination. But they nevertheless maintained that the human will retained a libertarian autonomy. It is up to humans entirely to determine their course in life, including with regard to their "salvation" which involves consciously willing "indifference" to the external world. In short, good or evil depends upon oneself and the inclinations they muster in the will. The Stoics commented little on the ostensible inconsistency between human autonomy and predestination and their silence perhaps stands as mute testimony of its intractability.

The term *free will* first made its way into Christian metaphysics through Tertullian who seems to have assumed a libertarian rendering of

---

[111] Ibid., 141.

[112] Alister McGrath, *Christian Theology* (Oxford: Blackwell, 2001) 444.

it.[113] Augustine, however, appears to be the first systematician to recognize the need for tempering its use in order to maintain a fully biblical metaphysic. This concern emerges early in Augustine's writings, especially with *De Libero Arbitrio* (386), where, though somewhat unclear concerning precisely what the powers of the will are (especially, contra-causal versus determined), he strongly affirms the doctrine of original and inherited sin[114] and describes the human faculty of willing as fraught with "ignorance" and "difficulty."[115] It is not entirely clear, however, the degree to which the human will is able, of its own accord, to overcome these obstacles. Indeed, both Book I and II of *De Libero Arbitrio* often seems to suggest a libertarian optimism in which it is up to the human will itself to turn toward the "true good"[116] and that moral responsibility hinges upon the power of "contrary choice."[117]

The "later Augustine," however, would abandon such an optimism of the will and come to categorically deny that the post-Adamic will is ever able to choose the good without effectual Divine intervention. *De Gratia et Libero Arbitrio* (c. 427) makes this abundantly clear in that "the hidden determinations of God" are such that people "in one and the same condition . . . derive their hereditary evil from Adam" and while "one is assisted so as to be baptized . . . another is not assisted, so that he dies in his very bondage."[118] Further, it is "the grace of God, without which we are not able to do any good thing."[119] For Augustine, the concept of indifference in the will was at odds with Divine revelation. He affirmed that humans posses it, but insisted that it is held captive by an inherited sin nature and, therefore, is in need of monergistic Divine liberation before it can freely choose salvation

---

[113] See, for example, Tertullian, *Against Marcion*, 2.5, trans. Peter Holmes. (Grand Rapids: Christian Classics Ethereal Library, 1999) http://www.ccel.org/ fathers2/ANF-03/anf03–29.htm#P4271_1391977 (April 10, 2003). Here, Tertullian firmly assigns foreknowledge to God, but with equal firmness declares autonomous freewill: ". . . we must first vindicate those attributes in the Creator which are called in question-namely, His goodness and foreknowledge . . . [But] that man was by God constituted free, master of his own will and power."

[114] Augustine, *On Free Choice of the Will*, III.19, trans. Thomas Williams (Indianapolis: Hackett, 1993) 107–08.

[115] Ibid., III.18; 107.

[116] Ibid., I.18; 19. See the fuller discussion at Ibid., I.18–19; 19–20.

[117] Ibid., II.1; 30.

[118] Augustine, "On Grace and Free Will," 45; *St. Augustin: Anti-Pelagian Writings*, ed. Phillip Schaff (Grand Rapids: Christian Classics Ethereal Library, 2005) 762.

[119] Ibid., 7, 732.

in Christ. Indeed, if humans are free at all, they are "freely in bondage."[120] One must be sovereignly freed from above in order to choose the things of God. Obviously, this precludes human autonomy.

But we still must inquire as to the ontology of the will itself. Pinnock does not appear to dispute the typical Christian notion that human beings are constituted as one being comprised of the physical and spiritual natures, or—mind, body, and spirit—in which the first of these is a collaborative project of the latter two. But where, then, is the seat of free will on Pinnock's account? Is it in the physical or spiritual component? Or perhaps an amalgamation of both? This he does not answer.

An alternative to the spirit-body dualism would be the view that the will is a kind of *tertium elementum*, somehow amorphously attached to the human person and which behaves independently—arbitrating one's decisions. The will is its own entity and operates apart from external factors thus maintaining the indifference principle so crucial to Pinnock's theology. The difficulty with this, of course, is that it only backs the problem up a step since we would be forced to asked whether this third element itself was physical, spiritual, or both. What other categories might the Christian theologian have? An Evangelical committed to *sola Scriptura* would also have the onus of locating this third element in the pages of Scripture.

Strangely, though innumerable classical theologians throughout history continually reference the faculty of free will in their writings, few have actually conjectured anything resembling a concise, concrete definition of it. Indeed, Calvin observes that "The thing meant by free will, though constantly occurring in all writers, few have defined."[121] Calvin does, however, glean some intimations:

> Origen . . . seems to have stated the common opinion when he said, 'It is a power of reason to discern between good and evil; of will, to choose the one or other.' Nor does Augustine differ from him when he says, 'It is a power of reason and will to choose the good, grace assisting—to choose the bad, grace desisting.' Bernard, while aiming at greater acuteness, speaks more obscurely, when he describes it as consent, in regard to the indestructible liberty of the wills and the inalienable judgment of reason. Anselm's definition is not very intelligible to ordinary understandings. He calls it a power of preserving rectitude on its own account. Peter Lombard, and the Schoolmen, preferred the definition of Augustine, both because it

---

[120] Augustine, The *Enchiridion*, 30; *The Fathers of the Church*. Trans. J. F. Shaw; http://www.newadvent.org/fathers/1302.htm (April 13, 2004).

[121] John Calvin, *Institutes of the Christian Religion*, 2.2.4, trans. Henry Beveridge (Grand Rapids: Eerdmans, 1989) 226.

was clearer, and did not exclude divine grace, without which they saw that the will was not sufficient of itself. They however add something of their own, because they deemed it either better or necessary for clearer explanation. First, they agree that the term will (arbitrium) has reference to reason, whose office it is to distinguish between good and evil, and that the epithet free properly belongs to the will, which may incline either way. Wherefore, since liberty properly belongs to the will, Thomas Aquinas says . . . that the most congruous definition is to call free will an elective power, combining intelligence and appetite, but inclining more to appetite.[122]

Most theologians of the patristic age seem to have assumed something vaguely resembling libertarian free will, a fact conceded by Calvin[123] and which must be similarly conceded by those of a Reformed persuasion.[124] When later theologians throughout the Middle Ages and the Reformational Period discussed free will, it was quite often, as Calvin suggests, rather obfuscatory and complex. For a faculty so crucial to Christian theology to have lacked a widely agreed upon definition for so long has caused no shortage of problems for the cogency and fecundity of discussions concerning Divine sovereignty and human freedom. Rudimentary axioms central to the building of systematic theologies, while perhaps mysterious and always worthy of further consideration, do well to be stated neatly and clearly in the interest of clarity. Many theologians seem to merely talk past one another when discussing this perennial issue because of terminological deficiencies. 1) They do not agree upon or even state what they believe the power of free will is, and 2) whenever words such as "will," "freedom," or "choice" are used there are presuppositional definitions being smuggled in that either resemble a more determinate or indeterminate conception. Unfortunately, I find much of this to be true in Pinnock's openness proposal. Not only is the "will" never clearly defined, but cognate terms such as "freedom" consistently assume an undefended libertarian philosophical framework and lack acknowledgement of alternative understandings of freedom, choice, and will. Much future progress, I believe, hinges upon doing the necessary preliminary work with terminology and the philosophical presuppositions so crucial to clear theological discourse.

---

[122] Ibid., 226–27

[123] Ibid 227.

[124] For example, the following patristical writings seem to assume libertarianism: Justin Martyr, *Dialogue with Trypho*, 88; Clement of Alexandria, *The Stromata*, 2.4; Hippolytus, *The Refutation of All Heresies*, 10.39; Origen, *De Principiis*, Preface 5. It must be added, however, that they also uniformly affirmed exhaustive Divine foreknowledge as seen in chapter 1, f. 44.

It was not until the eighteenth century writings of Puritan theologian, Jonathan Edwards, that some theologians began to have a possible working definition of the will while remaining consistent with biblical anthropology. Reformers such as Luther and Calvin certainly railed vigorously against the notion of human autonomy, the former in his classic response to Erasmus, *The Bondage of the Will* and Calvin in the *Institutes*. But neither proffered a simple definition of its faculty or nature. Indeed, Luther even referred to *free will* as "a mere empty term, whose reality is lost."[125] But their concern was less philosophical than evangelistic. The driving factor for the Reformers was that the human *spirit* is dead in trespass and sin. In turn, the noetic effects of this are total and nothing but the unmitigated mercy of God can liberate the mind toward salvation following the soul's unilateral regeneration by an act of God. The Reformers acknowledged that humans make choices. But their concern was not with arriving at a philosophical definition of the faculty of free will. Indeed, they were usually quite put off at philosophical attempts to contain the issue. Rather, it was pointing out the gravity of human fallenness and the need for redemption that drove their theologies. Whatever "will" humans may possess, they only said it was dead in sin and impotent in matters of salvation without a sovereign work of God.

Edwards, however, provided perhaps the most concise definition of the will ever proffered in the classical stream of Christian theology. In his classic, *Freedom of the Will*, he begins by defining the will simply as "the mind choosing" or "that by which the mind chooses any thing."[126] A further elucidation is provided in which Edwards states that "The faculty of the will, is that power, or principle of *mind*, by which it is capable of choosing: an act of the will is the same as an act of choosing or choice"[127] [emphasis added]. Edwards understood that what we call *free will* must fall within the basic constituent nature of human ontology. Edwards locates the seat of free will in the *mind*. But it is not as simple as the mind merely choosing among options for which it has no prior inclination. Rather, the mind chooses according to its *desires* which are housed both in the body and in the spirit. "A man never," says Edwards, "in *any* instance, wills anything contrary to his desires"[128] [emphasis added]. The "willful" person never acts

---

[125] Martin Luther, *On the Bondage of the Will*, Sec. 50, Para. 3, trans. Henry Cole; http://www.truecovenanter.com/truelutheran/luther_bow.html#cpref (April 10, 2003).

[126] Jonathan Edwards, *The Freedom of the Will*, I.1.2 (Grand Rapids: Christian Classics Ethereal Library, 2000) 2.

[127] Ibid.

[128] Ibid, I.2.5; 3.

Hellenization, Libertarianism, and the Metaphysics of Love

according to an unfettered *liberum arbitrium* without any reference to what drives the person's desires in the spiritual and moral realm. John Gerstner, an expert on Edwards, observes that the choosing person *always* make a choice according to what seems good to him as a whole person:

> . . . he is not weighing carefully what should seem good to him, in as detached and objective manner as he ought to do . . . he is allowing some rather frothy considerations to have undue weight . . . it's their weight as motives which determines his choice. Even when it is a foolish choice, it is still a choice based on motives. It may be the wrong kind of choice, but one thing it is not and cannot be (in a sane person) is a choice without any constraining motives or considerations. This normal person, good or bad, is always choosing according to what seems good to him. Maybe what seems good to him . . . ought not to seem good to him. There is a question about his very motives, but there is absolutely no doubt that the strongest motive triggers his will into motion. The will, even in that case, is not really, technically, willful or arbitrary, or acting independently of considerations. That type of thing can never happen in a rational human being. A rational human being never makes a choice of his mere, bare "free will."[129]

Thus, regardless of one's definition of free will, it is either something that is determined or undetermined; caused or uncaused. If it is uncaused (recall that one of libertarianism's alternate terms is *contra-causal freedom*), then there is no reference point in which to ground the choice as a morally responsible one. The choice becomes merely arbitrary without reference to any moral or spiritual motivational influences. How then was the choice made at all? This appears to me to be the Achilles' Heel of Pinnock's vision of human free will. Far from his insistence that libertarian free will is the *sine qua non* of moral responsibility, it actually seems to have the ironic effect of making free will an arbitrary freak of gross unpredictability. On the other hand, if choices are made based on the very moral and spiritual disposition of the agent, then at once we observe two things: 1) the choice was made according to what the choosing agent *wanted* to do and was therefore free because it pleased the choosing agent to do so; 2) the choice was also *determined* according the chooser's natural disposition. On a philosophical level, this seems to give compatibilism (as the position is traditionally called) the upper hand.

---

[129] John Gerstner, "A Primer of Free Will," in *Primitive Theology* (Morgan, Pa..: Soli Deo Gloria Publications, 1996) 230.

To be sure, Pinnock's ultimate motivation in asserting contra-causal freedom is soteriological. God must be chosen free of determinative factors that ultimately drive that decision. He adds that "the Bible seems to assume my view"[130] by including passages which call upon people to repent and believe. Soteriologically, the issue of making this decision to accept or reject the gospel's offer of salvation centers around the matter of regeneration. To wit, is the regenerating power of God installed in the believer's life *before* or *after* the decision is made to receive Christ as Savior? The former position, called the *monergistic* view of regeneration (or *irresistible grace*), is the classical position of Calvinists. According to this view, "the grace of God is the only efficient cause in beginning and effecting conversion."[131] Thus, proponents of monergism consider the *decision* itself to receive Christ as the natural and inevitable *fruit* of the Holy Spirit's unilateral work in regeneration. The decision to receive Christ is not an anthropological impetus that *invites* God's saving power, but a *response* rendered certain following the regenerative call of the Holy Spirit in those whom God has chosen beforehand. God quickens the fallen spirit of the elect, decisively and calculatedly, toward the outward call cast forth by the preaching of the gospel in order that it be *willingly* and gladly embraced. This view assumes compatibilistic freedom since monergistic regeneration is thought of as both free *and* determined on Reformed reasoning. It is a work done *inside* the creature—in the deepest recess of his or her being—and alters the soul's disposition such that the choice made by that person now reflects "a new creation" wrought by God. It is genuine not because the human chose it from a position of *liberum arbitrium*, but because it reflects an act of God's creative activity and liberating grace. Monergists do not dispute the fact that the Bible calls upon people to believe and to receive salvation. Rather, they juxtapose such texts with those that bear upon *whom* such people are and *why* it is they make that decision which is thought to be the fruit, not cause, of regeneration.

This view is, of course, distasteful to Pinnock as it makes the decision to receive the things of God solely determinative of God's activity in the human by which He "turns" their internal disposition toward Christ. It may be "given" but it is not "chosen" and, therefore, is not free on Pinnock's libertarian account. The alternate view, therefore, is *synergism* which is Pinnock's position (and also that of traditional Arminianism). On this view, the decision to receive Christ as one's Savior comes *prior* to regeneration and, indeed, is the inauguratory condition for such. Though perhaps

---

[130] Pinnock, personal correspondence, August 3, 2004.

[131] C. G. Fry, "Monergism," in *The Evangelical Dictionary of Theology* (Grand Rapids: Baker, 1984) 729.

aided by a prevening grace, regeneration follows one's personal decision to "accept" Christ as their Savior.

In the section that follows, I offer a defense of the monergistic view. This defense is intended to demonstrate that, contra Pinnock, the biblical data favors the monergistic position and, by implication, the compatibilistic understanding of human freedom especially as it relates to salvation. If this can be shown, then Pinnock would have good reason to jettison his denial of exhaustive Divine foreknowledge as an implicit compatibilism would dissolve the tension. For, on a monergistic rendering, foreknowledge is merely the byproduct of *foreordination*.

A Defense of Monergistic Regeneration

St. Paul seems to favor the monergistic position when he states in his epistle to the Roman church that, given God's sovereignty, Divine favor "does not, therefore, depend on man's desire or effort, but on God's mercy" and that "God has mercy on whom he wants to have mercy, and he hardens whom he wants to harden" (Rom 9:16, 18; NIV). In a classic diatribic literary form common to Paul, the apostle immediately anticipates the standard objection to this teaching saying, "One of you will say to me, 'then why does God still blame us? For who resists his will?'" (Rom 9:19, NIV). To this, Paul delivers a forceful rejoinder, perhaps indeed a rebuke, reminiscent of Job's famous interchange with God:

> But who are you, O man, to talk back to God? Shall what is formed say to him who formed it, "Why did you make me like this?" Does not the potter have the right to make out of the same lump of clay some pottery for noble purposes and some for common use? (Rom 9:19-21, NIV)

It appears to me resistless that Paul's answer to his objector in this passage would be vacant of meaning if he had at first been promulgating some form of open theistic soteriology where human choice *precedes* Divine favor. For, were Pinnock's schema true, Paul's response to why God "still blames us" would simply be that God is *reacting* to the results of our own free choice, that is, how we use our own intrinsic powers of moral agency and freewill. But we see Paul doing precisely the opposite. His focus has nothing whatsoever to do with humans and their powers of free will. Rather, he forcefully tears down such notions, stressing very clearly that *all* outcomes rest squarely with God and His intrinsic divine prerogative to exercise providence over His creatures. According to John's gospel, Jesus himself seems to support this saying, "the Son gives life to whom he is pleased to give it"

(John 5:21b, NIV). Robert Mounce sums up Romans 9 saying, "The point is that God's favors are not determined by anyone or anything outside of Himself. God's purpose in election rests not upon human will (*thelō*) or effort (*trechō*) but on divine mercy."[132] John Calvin, quoting Augustine, comments on Romans 9 saying, "When [God] is pleased to save, there is no free will in man to resist. Wherefore, it cannot be doubted that the will of God . . . cannot be resisted by the human will or prevented from doing what he pleases, since with the very wills of men he does so."[133]

C. E. B. Cranfield rejects this interpretation of Romans 9 saying it does "not suggest that this freedom of God's mercy is an absolute freedom either to be merciful or to be unmerciful. They give no encouragement at all to the notion that there is behind God's mercy a will of God that is different from His merciful will."[134] I cannot agree with Cranfield's assessment. It seems to me that Paul's reply (verses 19-21) makes no more sense against the backdrop of such an understanding than would the very objection posed by the imaginary interlocutor. If Cranfield's interpretation were correct, then Paul could have simply responded to the objection by appealing to God's justice in responding to the choice of man. Paul, however, appears to do precisely the opposite by appealing to God's "right" to do whatsoever he pleases with humans, and the inability of the latter to call it into question.[135]

For Pinnock, it is free will that saves by permitting God's grace to enter one's life. But for Paul, the fact that divine favor and one's salvation *depends* (Rom 9:16) entirely on the grace and mercy of God is at the heart

---

[132] Robert Mounce "Romans," *The New American Commentary* (Nashville: Broadman and Holman, 1995) 200.

[133] Calvin, *Institutes*, 3.23.14; 238.

[134] C. E. B. Cranfield, *The Epistle to the Romans*, International Critical Commentary (Edinburgh: T. & T. Clark, 1979) 483.

[135] Cranfield also contends that Romans 9 is not concerned with salvation but with the historical destiny of nations (ibid., 479). A full discussion of this theory is beyond the scope of this work. Suffice it to say here that I believe this theory to be mistaken. As Thomas Schreiner observes:

> [This theory] fails to account for both the specific context of Romans 9 and the wider context of Romans 9–11 . . . what concerns Paul in Romans 9–11 is not merely that Israel has lost temporal blessings, or that its historical destiny has not evolved the way he anticipated. Paul agonizes over the placve of Israel in Romans 9–11 because too many of his nation were not *saved*. (Thomas Schriener, "Does Romans 9 Teach Individual Election Unto Salvation?"; *The Grace of God, The Bondage of the Will*, ed. Thomas Schreiner and Bruce Ware (Grand Rapids: Baker, 1995) 91 [Schreiner develops this thesis in greater detail on pages 91–98].

of his message. This is the essence of the idea of monergistic regeneration—for something to depend entirely on something else is for the latter to be the complete and sufficient cause of the former, that is, salvation depends on God, not man. Monergism, then, upholds the proper biblical model of salvation, whereas synergism does not.

The biblical data supporting the notion that God's unilateral, salvific grace is the operative factor effecting salvation is strong. Now, this is not to say that human beings do not *participate* in their salvation. In fact, often misunderstood on a monergistic view of salvation is that the Divine monergism itself is precisely what makes human participation in salvation genuine. As the Spirit of regeneration quickens the deadened spirit of the human toward whom He so inclines, a new liberating life of the spirit is breathed into the human such that faith is the inevitable and joyous response. Importantly, this faith is not merely done *to* the person by God, but *through* the person as an existentially all-encompassing act. Nothing whatsoever is being done contrary to the will of the person in whom the Spirit moves effectually. Rather, the will too, in connection with a regenerated spirit, is spiritually inclined and given a new object for its affections. "The will" itself, Augustine observes, "is prepared by the Lord."[136] Monergistic regeneration is, in short, not a Divine *violation* of the human will, but a Divine *liberation*.

Such unilateral savings grace is seen in the gospel of John where the apostle speaks of those to whom Christ has given the power to become the children of God—they "were born, not of blood nor of the will of the flesh nor of the will of man, but of God" (John 1:13). Indeed, Christ Himself says to Nicodemus, "Flesh gives birth to flesh, but the Spirit gives birth to spirit" (John 3:6, NIV). And, "The wind blows where it wishes and you hear the sound of it, but do not know where it comes from and where it is going; so is everyone who is born of the Spirit" (John 3:8). And, as if anticipating the charge of a Divine nepotism of sorts, Jesus asks rhetorically, "Is it not lawful for me to do what I wish with what is my own?" (Matt 20:15).

This sovereign work of God in regeneration was portended in Old Testament prophecy where regeneration is portrayed as being solely the work of God. God promises a future time in which He would pour out His Spirit on a people of His choosing, bestowing upon them new life and creating in them new desires: "I will give you a new heart and put a new spirit within you; and I will remove the heart of stone from your flesh and give you a heart of flesh. I will put My Spirit within you and cause you to walk

---

[136] Augustine, *A Treatise On Grace and Free Will*, chapter 32, *St. Augustine: Anti-Pelagian Writings*, ed. Phillip Schaff (Grand Rapids: Christian Classics Ethereal Library, 2005) 750.

in My statutes, and you will be careful to observe My ordinances." (Ezek 36:26-27). These are the people, that is, God's elect, of whom Paul speaks in Romans 8 in what has come to known as *the Golden Chain of Salvation*: "For those whom He foreknew, He also predestined to become conformed to the image of His Son, so that He would be the firstborn among many brethren; and these whom He predestined, He also called; and these whom He called, He also justified; and these whom He justified, He also glorified" (Rom 8:29-30). This passage alone seems to present insuperable problems for Pinnock's theology on at lest three levels. First, it speaks unambiguously of God's foreknowledge of the elect. Secondly, it speaks clearly of the predestination that Pinnock wishes to avoid. Thirdly, it adds that God "calls" those whom He has foreknown. This calling is presented as the inauguratory condition of justification.

It is not just Paul, however, who seems to propound the doctrines of monergism. In the sixth and tenth chapters of John's Gospel, it is Jesus Himself who appears to teach this very thing saying, "All that the Father gives me will come to me, and whoever comes to me I will never drive away . . . And this is the will of him who sent me, that I shall lose none of all that he has given me, but raise them up at the last day . . . No one can come to me unless the Father who sent me draws him, and I will raise him up at the last day" (John 6:37, 39, 44). Jesus adds in verse 65 that ". . . no one can come to me unless the Father has enabled him." In this one passage alone, Jesus at once seems to affirm at least four of the so-called "five points of Calvinism" including *total depravity* ["no one can come" unless he is drawn (verse 44)], *unconditional election* [the Father *gives* believers to the Son, (verse 37)], *irresistible grace* ["*All* that the Father gives will come . . ." (verse 37)], and *perseverance of the saints* ["I shall lose *none* of all that he has given me (verse 39)].

Later, in chapter 10, Jesus engages in a very revealing dialogue with some unbelieving Pharisees and declares the nature of His relationship, as the Great Shepherd, with His "sheep":

> "I am the good shepherd; I know my sheep and my sheep know me—just as the Father knows me and I know the Father—and I lay down my life for the sheep. I have other sheep that are not of this sheep pen. I must bring them also. They too will listen to my voice, and there shall be one flock and one shepherd. The reason my Father loves me is that I lay down my life—only to take it up again. No one takes it from me, but I lay it down of my own accord. I have authority to lay it down and authority to take it up again. This command I received from my Father." At these words the Jews were

again divided. Many of them said, "He is demon-possessed and raving mad. Why listen to him?" But others said, "These are not the sayings of a man possessed by a demon. Can a demon open the eyes of the blind?" Then came the Feast of Dedication at Jerusalem. It was winter, and Jesus was in the temple area walking in Solomon's Colonnade. The Jews gathered around him, saying, "How long will you keep us in suspense? If you are the Christ, tell us plainly." Jesus answered, "I did tell you, but you do not believe. The miracles I do in my Father's name speak for me, but you do not believe *because you are not my sheep*. My sheep listen to my voice; I know them, and they follow me. I give them eternal life, and they shall never perish; no one can snatch them out of my hand. My Father, who has given them to me, is greater than all; no one can snatch them out of my Father's hand. I and the Father are one." (John 10:14-30)

Of critical importance here, is the order in which Jesus iterates His rebuke in verse 26. Why does Jesus say the Pharisees do not believe? His answer is that *they are not His sheep*. Pinnock's system reverses this order. In order for it to work, a person's not being numbered among the sheep must be due to their non-belief. But Jesus makes it clear here that in order to believe in the first place, one must be included among His sheep whom *the Father gives to Him* (verse 29). Again, from a position of *sola Scriptura*, this is indeed a "hard saying" but is impossible to ignore.

This order of things in how a believer comes to believe is restated in different ways throughout other parts in Scripture. Luke makes mention of it in Acts 13:48 where he records that upon hearing the gospel message, the Gentiles there "began rejoicing and glorifying the word of the Lord; and as many as *had been appointed to eternal life believed*" [emphasis added]. The belief of the Gentiles was the *result*, not cause, of the appointment to eternal life given to them by God. Other texts that seem to favor the monergistic position include the following:

- "For to you it has been granted for Christ's sake, not only to believe in Him, but also to suffer for His sake." (Phil 1:29)
- *"In the exercise of His will* He brought us forth by the word of truth, so that we would be a kind of first fruits among His creatures." (James 1:18)
- "You did not choose Me but I chose you, and appointed you that you would go and bear fruit and that your fruit would remain." (John 15:16)

- "A woman named Lydia, from the city of Thyatira, a seller of purple fabrics, a worshiper of God, was listening; and *the Lord opened her heart to respond* to the things spoken by Paul." (Acts 16:14)
- ". . . no one knows the Son except the Father; nor does anyone know the Father except the Son, and anyone to whom the Son wills to reveal Him." (Matt 11:27)
- "You gave Him authority over all flesh, that to all whom You have given Him, He may give eternal life." (John 17:2)
- "The Lord's bond-servant must not be quarrelsome, but be kind to all, able to teach, patient when wronged, with gentleness correcting those who are in opposition, if perhaps *God may grant them repentance leading to the knowledge of the truth*, . . ." (2 Tim 2:24-25)

Pinnock rightly points out, however, that there are numerous passages which seem to favor his view such as 1 Timothy 2:3-4: "This is good and acceptable in the sight of God our Savior, who desires all men to be saved and to come to the knowledge of the truth." St. Peter also says that "The Lord is not slow about His promise, as some count slowness, but is patient toward you, not wishing for any to perish but for all to come to repentance" (2 Pet 3:9). How, then, does this square with the idea that God must appoint people first to believe in the gospel message and, then, unilaterally regenerate them so that they are able to do so? Are not these passages a clear contradiction of the idea of monergism?

Three Modes (or Functions) of the Divine Will

The solution to this might be found in conjecturing different *types* of God's will. R. C. Sproul has articulated three types: God's *sovereign, efficacious (or decretive) will*, His *preceptive will*, and his *will of disposition*.[137] The first of these, God's *sovereign, efficacious will*, refers to that will of God which is both hidden and irresistible. It is with this will, for example, that God created the world and all its functioning elements like light. When He said, "Let there be light" (Gen 1:3), the light could not have "refused" to shine. It was God's sovereign, efficacious will that the light shine and so it was. Similarly, God has an eternal plan for mankind which falls under the rubric of this will. His plan in redemptive history *will* happen. The prophet Isaiah

---

[137] R. C. Sproul, *Chosen By God* (Wheaton, Ill.: Tyndale, 1986) 195–97.

says, "For the LORD Almighty has purposed, and who can thwart him? His hand is stretched out, and who can turn it back?" (Isa 14:27, NIV)

The second of the wills of God, His *preceptive will*, refers to that which God has *revealed* to us through His biblical *precepts*. God's preceptive will is not hidden from humans as with His decretive will. This includes such things as the Decalogue and Christ's command to "love the Lord your God with all your heart, and with all your soul, and with all your mind" (Matt 22:37). This is what the Lord wills *us* to do and we *can* and *do* refuse to do it at times. We are charged with abiding by the precepts of God's revealed will to us in Scripture. The rest is within the sole purview of God. That we can and do transgress God's preceptive will does not indicate that God's ultimate plans are somehow thwartable from a Scriptural vantage point. Indeed, even transgression *of* and want of conformity *to* God's precepts is pictured as fitting within His redemptive plan.

The third will of God, His *will of disposition*, describes simply that which brings *delight* to God. Sproul describes God's will of disposition in terms of "what is pleasing to him."[138] "God does not take delight in the death of the wicked. There is a sense in which the punishment of the wicked does not bring joy to God." However, "He chooses to do it because it is good to punish evil. He delights in the righteousness of his judgment but is 'sad' that such righteous judgment must be carried out."[139]

On this understanding, Peter and Paul communicate, in the passages cited earlier, something of God's will of disposition. As Grudem puts it, "these verses simply tell us that God invites and commands *every* person to repent and come to Christ for salvation, but they do not tell us anything about God's secret decrees regarding who will be saved."[140] Millard Erickson, compares 1 Tim 2:3-4 and 2 Pet 3:9 with the passage in Ezekiel where God proclaims, "I take no pleasure in the death of the wicked, but rather that they turn from their ways and live . . ." (Ezek 33:11).[141] God is therefore simply revealing that He takes no immediate pleasure in punishing the wicked. Yet in Proverbs we read that, "The LORD works out everything for his own ends—*even the wicked for a day of disaster*" (16:4, NIV). How is that these both can be true? On a three-will account, the answer would be that the Ezekiel passage falls under God's will of disposition, whereas the latter falls under God's sovereign, efficacious will. While

---

[138] Ibid., 195.

[139] Ibid., 196.

[140] Wayne Grudem, *Systematic Theology* (Grand Rapids: Zondervan, 1994) 684.

[141] Erickson, *Christian Theology*, 932.

it brings God no pleasure to punish the reprobate, He still intends to in order to fulfill a greater good which He has purposed in Himself.

A Logical Defense

We have seen, thus far, the manner in which Scripture supports monergistic regeneration and its corollary, irresistible grace. I now move to the task of attempting to demonstrate these doctrines using a combination of biblical axioms that bear on soteriology and a simple, syllogistic application of the rules of logic, especially, the law of non-contradiction and law of causality. Inasmuch as Pinnock stresses the need for a logical theology, this is intended to use logic—following the *sola Scriptura* premise—to demonstrate Scripture as favoring monergism and therefore compatibilistic freedom.

The *desire*[142] to receive Christ is either caused, or uncaused. If it is uncaused, then it is a self-created effect which is impossible. For, in order for something to create itself, it must exist prior to itself which violates the law of non-contradiction (since it would have to be and not be at the same time, in the same sense). Thus, the desire is caused by something. That something is either,

a. intrinsic (from inside the individual)—*intrinsic monergism*
b. a combination of intrinsic and extrinsic causes (from both inside and outside the individual)-*synergism*
c. extrinsic (from outside the individual)—*extrinsic monergism*

If the ultimate cause for the desire is intrinsic, then it is accomplished through one or more of the following constitutive human faculties:

a. body (somatic causation)
b. mind (cognitive causation)
c. spirit (pneumatic causation)

The desire cannot be attributed merely to the body. For, the actions of the body are governed by the mind and the body is without conscious involvement in the act of salvation. On the other hand, if the desire is ultimately caused by something in the mind, or cognitively, then it can be said that the mind that chooses Christly desire is vitally superior to that of the mind that rejects it. For, it is clearly better for the mind to choose Christ

[142] I am here considering the *desire* to receive Christ as the "efficient" cause of the decision to receive Christ. In the Aristotelian typology of causation, the efficient cause is distinguished from the material, formal, and final causes as that which functions as the instrument to bring about a change in something. See Aristotle, *Physics*, III.4.

than not to. A logical account, however, renders such a scenario absurd, by making salvation contingent upon one's inherent intellectual acumen. But Scripture abundantly affirms that salvation extends to the full range of human beings without respect to genetic content, congenital factors, or level of education. A worse problem, however, would be explaining how a choosing mind would ever elect to *desire* something. One does not, indeed cannot, choose, for example, to begin desiring liver as food if previously that desire were absent. Thus, isolating cognitive causation as the decisive factor in attaining desire for Christ is to suppose that one can first choose a desire for which previously none existed which is *prima facie* absurd.

From a biblical viewpoint, the third option, namely, that the desire is ultimately caused by something in the person's spirit, or pneumatically, is equally as unfruitful as the second option. For, in this case, the inherently possessed spirit of the one that attains the desire could be said to be superior, indeed more righteous, than the one that rejects Christ. Thus, we would be forced to declare that those persons who incline themselves toward salvation possess a spirit that is intrinsically more righteous than the spirit held by those who reject salvation. Intrinsic monergism must therefore be rejected.

The second option, synergism, may also be ruled out. For, we are concerned here with the fact of the desire, and thus, efficient causal agency as opposed to becoming lost in a panoply of prior conditions. Salvific desire, as efficient cause, must fall under the rubric of either intrinsic or extrinsic monergism. Synergism, then, only backs up a step the original issue of how one ultimately arrives at Christly desire. The synergist might argue that God, through prevenient grace, supplies the necessary conditions which form the backdrop for individual salvific desire, but that the final factor is left up to the individual. God's grace is a necessary but not sufficient condition for one's desire to receive salvation. God may graciously provide all manner of necessary conditions but the ultimate outcome hangs in the anthropocentric balance of human decision. But this puts us back at the same problems associated with cognitivism. The individual must exert cognitive force in willing desires that he or she does not already have if salvation is to be procured.

Thus, we are left with the final option: the desire and subsequent decision to receive salvation is accomplished through *extrinsic* monergism. God is the fully sufficient cause of salvation and its resultant regeneration. Thus, the decision to be saved is the result or fruit, not cause, of the regeneration that is wrought monergistically by God.

If this logic is correct, then regeneration is inescapably compatibilistic with regard to Divine sovereignty and human freedom and Pinnock's view of libertarian freedom must be abandoned. Again, this is an attempt to use the *sola Scriptura* principle which Pinnock himself follows. His own program is one which answers classical theology using biblical principles. But if Scripture favors a different account of how salvation is appropriated, then creative love theism must be jettisoned.

Chapter Summary

This chapter has identified and critiqued Pinnock's central premises upon which his theological program is built. I stated earlier that I not only agree with much of his rational methodology, but affirm the soundness of his theological conclusions inasmuch as his starting premises are valid. I have therefore concentrated on critiquing these premises and conclude that his openness proposal, while raising some important issues concerning Divine love and relationality, fails to build a strong enough case to become a sustainable theology within an Evangelical, *sola Scriptura* paradigm. I further argued, both biblically and philosophically, that monergistic regeneration is true and, by implication, compatibilistic human freedom.

In the next chapter, I build further upon this chapter in steadily moving toward an understanding of Divine-human relationality once Pinnock's libertarian supposition and corollary postulate of Divine nescience has been abandoned. I will expand my critique against libertarianism by marshalling biblical evidence which I believe clearly indicates both exhaustive divine foreknowledge and even the *omnicausality* of temporal events—all in a compatibilistic context for human freedom. I will also address related issues such as God's association to events within the flow of time, the problem of religious language (including the use of theological anthropomorphism), the philosophy of personhood, fatalism, and evil. I will also further expand upon my glory motif for the doctrine of God—a central component both in contesting openness theology and then in attempting to re-image Divine-human relationality on a Reformed platform.

5

Classicalism, Compatibilism, and Trinitarian Glory

IN AN April 2000 article of the *Journal of Pentecostal Theology*, Pinnock urged his readers to "resist the pressure from the paleo-Calvinist segment of Evangelicalism and persist in their witness to the relational dynamism of God."[1] A few years later, he addressed an audience at the University of Calgary and encouraged them not to be "dominated intellectually by paleo-Calvinists" and to "appreciate God's beauty more in relational and personal rather than abstract and deterministic terms"[2] adding that "Calvinists cannot stop the clock at 1619 AD and take their last stand at the Synod of Dordt as if the Reformed tradition had not gone on developing since then."[3]

Relational love, as we have seen, is at the center of Pinnock's disapproval of the classical Reformed view of the divine and human natures. He has concluded unequivocally that there cannot be a dynamic love relationship between God and humans if the actions of the latter are completely foreknown, much less, *foreordained* according to a pre-set divine plan. For Pinnock, the classical affirmation of exhaustive Divine foreknowledge is either hopelessly contradictory (as in Arminianism) or reduces to fatalism and robs human beings of significance since their thoughts and actions seemingly become the byproducts of the inalterable stamp of omnicausality (as in Calvinism).

I have agreed with Pinnock that the noncausal Arminian simple-foreknowledge position is inherently contradictory and that the frequent appeal of Arminians to *mystery* is an unsatisfactory attempt to circumvent

---

[1] Pinnock, "Divine Relationality: A Pentecostal Contribution to the Doctrine of God," *Journal of Pentecostal Theology*, 16 (November 16, 2000) 25.

[2] Pinnock, "Open Theism: "What is this? A new teaching? And with authority!" presented at the University of Calgary, February 3, 2003, 1; http://www.ucalgary.ca/ UofC/faculties/ HUM/RELS/chairs/cchair/crsrc/Pinnock.OpenTheism.pdf (April 12, 2003).

[3] Ibid., 3.

139

that fact. A thing can be noncontradictory, mysterious (even *incomprehensible*), and real. But a proper object of knowledge cannot be "mysteriously contradictory" or made up of "parallel lines that meet in eternity" and really exist. These are but euphemisms for the manifestly impossible. A contradiction, whether mysterious or not, is still a contradiction and therefore simply that which is impossible either modally or factually. Pinnock and I agree that that which is flatly contradictory cannot exist. We also agree that personal relationality is non-negotiably vital to the lifeblood of Christianity and that its explication on the Reformed side has been somewhat weak.

Pinnock's conclusion of *fatalism* attaching to the Reformed model, however, depends upon the presupposition of autonomous libertarian freedom as the only valid explanation for genuine freedom which I argued in the last chapter to be unsustainable. It is similarly improper to adjudge the Calvinistic view of freedom false when analyzing it strictly through the eyepiece of libertarianism, thus allowing only one definition of freedom. The Calvinistic model of freedom *rejects* libertarianism in favor of a compatibilistic *soft*-determinism and expressly denies fatalism.[4] One's criticism of Reformed anthropology cannot persist in assuming the libertarian position to be the only view available. To do so is simply to mix definitions. When Pinnock argues that Reformed models deny humans any "genuine" freedom,[5] in effect he is simply stating that any supposition other than his own is invalid. In so doing, contracausality is the only kind of freedom he is willing to consider as genuine while simply accusing different views of fatalism.

In rejecting Pinnock's view of freedom, I find we are presented with only two options concerning how and why the will inclines itself in one direction or the other: It is either *caused* by something or it is *uncaused*

---

[4] *Soft determinism* is really just another name for *compatibilism* so, in a sense, "compatibilistic soft-determinism" is a tautology. I use the terms together simply to emphasize the species of determinism that compatibilism enjoins. It cannot be denied that compatibilism and fatalism are both species of determinism, the latter often being referred to as "hard." The crucial difference, however, is that soft determinism places as much emphasis on *means* as it does *ends* and speaks of the relationship between the two as issuing from the purposive intentionality of God. Hard determinism, on the other hand, emphasizes ends which are produced of mechanistic necessity, *non*-purposively. I do believe this would indeed destroy human freedom. But on a soft-determinism model, "God ordains means as well as ends and employs our causal powers so that their voluntariness and spontaneity as well as our responsibility are not overridden." [Terrance Tiessen, *Providence and Prayer* (Downer's Grove, Ill.: InterVarsity, 2000) 237]. Pinnock does not distinguish between soft and hard determinism but seems to construe both of them as fatalism.

[5] Pinnock, *Most Moved Mover: A Theology of God's Openness* (Grand Rapids: Baker, 2001) 26.

phenomenon. If it is the latter, then we are confronted with what I have argued to be the intractable problem of explaining how or why it then acted at all. Further, we are awkwardly pressed to conceive of the inclinations of the will as random or arbitrary—uncaused phenomenon absent a plausible foundation. I therefore concluded that such a view does not so much *establish* a volitive human faculty as it does *destroy* it. On the other hand, if volition is caused by something, then we face the task of identifying that cause (or causes) and relating it to both the purposivity of God and to the meaningfulness of human existence. If we grant that human decisions are indeed meaningful, then such causality would not function as the defeater of freedom, but ironically as the establisher of it.[6]

In addition to the purely philosophical concerns, we have also seen that Pinnock's (and my own) commitment to *sola Scriptura* presents important exegetical considerations wherein one is obliged to heed a diverse range of biblical texts that appear to support the traditional understanding of God possessing exhaustive foreknowledge of the future—including volitive human actions. For, if the Bible provides strong evidence that God does indeed possess such foreknowledge, then we are faced with a second major reason to jettison Pinnock's openness view. Again, for Pinnock, this reduces merely to fatalism. I have argued, however, that he is excluding a viable third option for understanding relationality and a genuine reciprocity that bridges the ontological gap between humanity and divinity.

The purpose of this chapter is to build upon the last in steadily moving toward an understanding of Divine-human relationality (the focus of the next chapter) once Pinnock's libertarian supposition and corollary postulate of Divine nescience has been abandoned. This is a key component in rescuing the Reformed view from the accusation of fatalism. It is difficult to imagine how *any* theological model would find this *un*important and I am again appreciative of Dr. Pinnock's desire to rehash this perennial subject. If I am correct, however, in my contention that the coupling of love as the *definitive* essence of God along with human libertarianism is an untenable paradigm upon which to build relationality, then my own alternative must provide a ground for relationality which is nevertheless unimperiled by a glory teleology on the divine side and deterministic compatibilism on the human side.

---

[6] This was clearly the position of the Westminster Divines in declaring that the omnicausal providence of God meant "no violence offered to the will of the creatures, nor is the liberty or contingency of second causes taken away, but rather established." See *The Westminster Confession of Faith* (1646) III.1; http://www.creeds.net/Westminster/c05.htm. (April 20, 2003).

As to replacing Pinnock's creational motif of God's *love* with *glory*, I lay further groundwork here and demonstrate this motif to be equally critical in reconstructing relationality. For it changes our understanding of the very purpose of the universe and its creaturely inhabitants. Later, I will argue that my alternative—built upon these replacement suppositions—avoids both the pitfalls I have identified in Pinnock's openness model, but also that of wooden fatalism and that to offer only these two poles as available options is to posit a false dilemma. The third option I am proffering recognizes what I perceive to be compelling biblical evidence supporting exhaustive Divine foreknowledge and an omnicausal providence, yet uses these very axioms to *establish* Divine-human relationality, meaningfulness, and significance.

I will also deal with the two chief problems we are faced with when adopting a view of meticulous Divine providence. This includes the problem of evil (theodicy) and the foreboding issue of *reprobation*. The first of these I address in this chapter; the latter I will take up at the end of the next chapter, *after* my argument for a new model of Reformed relationality. The issue of reprobation cannot be ignored. Thus, I will attempt to establish both its Biblicity and logicality on the heels of this and the previous chapter's arguments and the manner in which this troubling doctrine fits with God's character and creational orientation.

Both of these are foreboding, but unavoidable, issues. On a "glory teleology," what implications arise concerning the nature of Divine love? During our correspondence, Pinnock enjoined me to "explain whether God loves out of his loving nature or on a whim. Does he just choose to love or is He love? You [must] explain how God justly blames sinners when they can do nothing but what God determines."[7] I will heed Pinnock's call and attempt to provide a satisfying answer to these important questions.

Evidence for Exhaustive Divine Foreknowledge and Compatibilism

This section expands my critique against libertarianism by marshalling additional biblical evidence indicating both exhaustive divine foreknowledge and that of the omnicausal model I am advocating which holds the totality of temporal events to be foreordained (and, indeed, therefore fixed). This consideration augments my arguments in the last chapter which bear more upon the predestinarian aspects of soteriology as distinguished from God's providential control over not only salvation but the very details of

---

[7] Pinnock, personal correspondence, October 7, 2004.

natural and human history itself. Predestination concerns salvation specifically whereas providence applies universally to *every* event within creation. Because later arguments require that we grant such foreknowledge and meticulous providence, it is important to make a biblical case for it. While I begin with some important texts concerning foreknowledge specifically as a constituent aspect of deity, I will consider more heavily the biblical evidence for meticulous providence which logically includes such foreknowledge. I believe an *exhaustive* study of strictly foreknowledge texts to be unnecessary as other works have set about the task of more comprehensively cataloguing them and a similar effort need not be duplicated here.[8] I also believe that the case is sufficiently demonstrated with the select examples I do address.[9]

Pinnock is fond of using Scriptural passages that seem to imply divine changeableness. Two such passages used by him which speak of divine "regret" will be addressed shortly. Conspicuously absent, however, is a treatment of key passages and texts that teach in what I believe to be unambiguous terms that foreknowledge is considered by the biblical writers to be a constituent part of God's very deity.

For example, in Isaiah 40–48, total foreknowledge of future events is presented as one the hallmarks of Divinity which the Hebrews took to contradistinguish Yahweh from the national idols or gods of surrounding nations. Bruce Ware, observes that, throughout Isaiah 40–48, "There are no fewer than nine separate occasions in the chapters whose point is essentially the same: Yahweh, the God of Israel, is known as the true living God in contrast to idols, whose pretense to deity is evident on the basis that the *true God knows and declares the future* (including future free human actions)

---

[8] See, for example, John Frame, *No Other God* (Phillipsburg, N. J.: Presbyterian & Reformed, 2001); Bruce Ware, *God's Lesser Glory: The Diminished God of Open Theism*, (Wheaton, Ill.: Crossway, 2000); Millard Erickson, *What Does God Know and When Does He Know It? The Current Controversy over Divine Foreknowledge* (Grand Rapids: Zondervan, 2003).

[9] It should also be observed that, from a *sola Scriptura* position (which Pinnock and I grant), there is no reason why a long list of canonical foreknowledge texts should be any more persuasive than a few good representative examples (or even *one* sufficiently clear text). Surely there is merit in reviewing foreknowledge texts for the purpose of collection and research, etc. But I find it rather peculiar and excessive that some opponents of open theism seem to think that merely listing numerous texts, which communicate the same basic principle, in any way improves the case made by a few good examples. This is made especially manifest by the manner in which Pinnock and other open theists tend to rely mainly on narrative biblical texts as opposed to didactic and tend to interpret the latter by the former, thereby reversing the standard exegetical practice of most exegetes (see chapter 3, pages 103–5).

before it occurs, *while those impostor rivals neither know nor declare any such thing*"[10] [emphasis original]. One such text is Isaiah 41:21-26:

> "Present your case," the LORD says. "Bring forward your strong arguments," the King of Jacob says. Let them bring forth and declare to us what is going to take place; As for the former events, declare what they were, that we may consider them and know their outcome. Or announce to us what is coming; Declare the things that are going to come afterward, that we may know that you are gods; Indeed, do good or evil, that we may anxiously look about us and fear together. Behold, you are of no account, and your work amounts to nothing; He who chooses you is an abomination. "I have aroused one from the north, and he has come; From the rising of the sun he will call on My name; And he will come upon rulers as upon mortar, even as the potter treads clay." Who has declared this from the beginning, that we might know? Or from former times, that we may say, "He is right!"? Surely there was no one who declared, surely there was no one who proclaimed, surely there was no one who heard your words.

John Wesley, well known to have opposed the Calvinism of his evangelistic counterpart George Whitefield, nevertheless comments rhetorically on Isaiah 41 saying "Which of [the] idols could foretell such things as these from the beginning of the world unto this day?"[11] He then contrasts this with Isaiah's portrayal of Yahweh who "represent[s] future things as if they were present."[12] Similarly, Ware quotes Stephen Charnock concerning this text who writes:

> [God] puts his Deity to stand or fall upon this account, and this should be the point which should decide the controversy whether he or the heathen idols were the true God. The dispute is managed by this medium: he that knows things to come is God; I know things to come, *ergo*, I am God: the idols know not things to come, therefore they are not gods.[13]

A parallel declaration is made in Isaiah 42:8-9 where the prophet says: "'I am the LORD, that is My name; I will not give My glory to another, nor My praise to graven images. Behold, the former things have come to

---

[10] Ware, *God's Lesser Glory*, 102.

[11] John Wesley, *Wesley's Notes on the Bible*, Isaiah 41:26-27 (Grand Rapids: Christian Classics Ethereal Library, 1999); http://ccel.org/ccel/wesley/notes.html (November 10, 2004).

[12] Ibid.

[13] Stephen Charnock, *Existence and Attributes of God* (Minneapolis: Klock and Klock, 1977) 203. Quoted in Ware, *God's Lesser Glory*, 104.

pass, now I declare new things; before they spring forth I proclaim them to you.'" John Calvin commented on this passage saying that, here, God, "recalls to remembrance the former predictions, by the fulfillment of which he shews that confidence ought to be placed in him for the future; for what we have known by actual experience ought to tend greatly to confirm our belief."[14] Kenneth Barker and John Kohlenberger write of this passage that "'the former things' refers to earlier prophecies given through Isaiah and already fulfilled, or, to the entire Israelite prophetic movement and its already fulfilled predictions. The point is that the God who has already proved his word true is able to make known new things."[15] As already mentioned, several other texts throughout Isaiah 40–48 make similar declarations of God's unique ability to know the future,[16] though 46:9-10 seems to sum up well: "Remember the former things long past, for I am God, and there is no other; I am God, and there is no one like Me, Declaring the end from the beginning, and from ancient times things which have not been done, saying, 'My purpose will be established, and I will accomplish all My good pleasure.'"

The point of these passages may be argued as twofold. First, it is to contrast the true deity of Yahweh against surrounding national idols. Second, it is to inspire confidence and trust in the Lord as both the foreteller, foreknower, and sovereign ruler over history. Raymond Dillard and Tremper Longman, for example, comment that:

> The major criterion used in the Old Testament for distinguishing the word of the true prophet from that of the false is the fulfillment of the prophetic utterances (Deut 18:21-22). The premise of this criterion is that the Lord who reveals his plans to his prophets (Amos 3:7) rules over the course of history to bring his purpose to fruition. This celebration of God's rule over history has reached its height in Isaiah 40–66 . . . Because he had spoken with power and authority before past events, God can be believed when he speaks about the future."[17]

---

[14] John Calvin, *Commentary on Isaiah*, vol. 3. Trans. William Pringle (Grand Rapids: Christian Classics Ethereal Library, 1999) http://www.ccel.org/c/calvin/calcom15/htm/xi.htm (October 12, 2004).

[15] Kenneth Barker and John Kohlenberger, *Zondervan NIV Bible Commentary* (Grand Rapids: Zondervan, 1994) 1118

[16] See, for example, Isaiah 43:8-12; 44:6-8; 45:5-7; 45:20-21; 46:8-11.

[17] Raymond Dillard and Tremper Longman, *Introduction to the Old Testament* (Grand Rapids: Zondervan, 1994) 280.

An important consideration when looking at these texts also concerns the manner in which the predictions involved not only Yahweh's actions, but also those of responsible human agents—both individually and corporately. Isaiah 45, for example, concerns the prophecy of the rebuilding of Jerusalem under the rulership of the Persian king, Cyrus. If the traditional early compositional date of Isaiah is granted (eighth century BC), we observe very specific predictions made concerning Cyrus' actions as well as those of the nations which will be destroyed by his hand. Cyrus and his armies will loot them following easily-won victories and, thus, become exceedingly powerful. Of interest here are the innumerable, presumably volitive, humans actions involved. Ware writes concerning Yahweh's future declarations of Cyrus that,

> . . . all this will occur despite the fact the Cyrus will not even know God (45:4b, 5b) and hence will not even be aware that God has named and anointed Cyrus . . . In the end, though, God will make clear to Cyrus and others that it is he (God) who has called Cyrus by name and has done all these things through him (45:1, 3b) . . . Clearly God predicts and then fulfills a multitude of future actions and events, all of them exactly as he so designs. But consider again here how much of what God predicts involves massive numbers of future free choices and actions of God's moral creatures.[18]

I believe Ware's point here to be essential. To consider it further, let us switch from Isaiah's portrayal of divine knowledge and sovereign rule over history to that of the Psalmist. Consider, for example, Psalm 139:1-7, 16-18a:

> O LORD, You have searched me and known me. You know when I sit down and when I rise up; You understand my thought from afar. You scrutinize my path and my lying down, and are intimately acquainted with all my ways. Even before there is a word on my tongue, behold, O LORD, You know it all. You have enclosed me behind and before, and laid Your hand upon me. Such knowledge is too wonderful for me; It is too high, I cannot attain to it. Where can I go from Your Spirit? Or where can I flee from Your presence? . . . Your eyes have seen my unformed substance; And in Your book were all written the days that were ordained for me, when as yet there was not one of them. How precious also are Your thoughts to me, O God! How vast is the sum of them! If I should count them, they would outnumber the sand.

---

[18] Ware, *God's Lesser Glory*, 112.

Classicalism, Compatibilism, and Trinitarian Glory

Psalm 139 is a classic *psalm of praise* of the declarative variety. The context is that of a prayer in which the psalmist asks that the Lord examine him as judge and that He vindicate his innocence. Verses 1-18 function as a sort of preamble to that prayer in which the Psalmist contrasts himself with "those who hate [God]" (verse 21), yet invites God to "search ... and know his heart" (verse 23). As Barker and Kohlenberger observe, "the psalmist testifies that the Lord is a righteous judge [and that] the Lord knows him through and through."[19] The psalmist basks in the unsearchable depths of God's wisdom giving five concrete examples of His intimate and detailed knowledge of both his person and his future. The Lord,

- Knows all of his thoughts (verse 2).
- Knows all of his ways (verse 3).
- Knows all his words *before* they occur (verse 4).
- Has "eyes" that saw his unformed "substance" (verse 16).
- Foreknows (and "*ordained*") all of his days (verse 16).

Though all five of these declarations are instructive, of particular interest here is the last: that God knows all the days ordained for him though, as yet, they had not yet come to pass. As I argued in chapter four, the Hebrew writers of the Old Testament tended to speak very matter-of-factly about such knowledge—in the absence of any attempt at a philosophical justification for the compatibility of such future knowledge with human significance or volition. Nevertheless, when we ponder this passage philosophically it is impossible not to be awestruck by the innumerable factors which must interplay with such knowledge. Not only has the Lord "seen" his very person (verse 16a), but he knows the very length of his days (verse 16b). We might couple this declaration with Paul's didactic teaching during the Mars Hill sermon that God, having "made from one man every nation of mankind to live on all the face of the earth" also "*determined their appointed times and the boundaries of their habitation*" (Acts 17:26) [emphasis added]. To know and to *determine* each person's appointed times, the boundaries of their habitation, and the precise length of their days strikes me as the logical equivalent of knowing every detail of their lives including the vast panoply of decisions they make during their entire life's course.

As an analogy, let us consider the life of one of my children. Was not their birth due, in part, to the joint *volitional* (and presumably free) decision on the part of my wife and I to marry and raise a family? In turn, was not also *our* existence contingent upon our own parents doing the same?

---

[19] Barker and Kohlenberger, *Bible Commentary*, 928.

But in order for the Divine mind to know, indeed to have "appointed" such times and "boundaries of habitation," would not our free decision to marry and raise children have to have been included in God's knowledge? Indeed the joint force of Psalm 139 and Acts 17 is such that our time, place, and duration are all foreordained and, logically and subsequently, foreknown.

Yet it is exceedingly more complex than only these few decisions and must extend even to the seemingly minute. There is a practically infinite number of other factors, some ostensively (or experientially) small and insignificant, that nevertheless *had to occur* if any one of my children were simply to exist. What if the day on which my wife and I met (in a coffee shop) had been rainy instead of sunny? Would we have gone out that day? What if there had been traffic, road construction, or an accident that made a day at the café impractical (or impossible)? Or suppose that a morning delivery to the café had been delayed such that no espresso (my favorite beverage) had been available leading to my decision to return home? The result, by logical extension, would be the non-existence of my child. Thus, an entire matrix of antecedent causal factors, both volitive and natural (or mundane), had to occur in order for my child to arrive at his or her "appointed" time.

Of course, Pinnock (or other open theists) could argue that, given all such contingencies, God could have creatively worked around them such that my child's existence would still have been secured despite various unforeseen circumstances. Indeed, Pinnock appears to argue this way.[20] For example, he might have "tried again" to influence my circumstances such that my future wife would be secured for me and that she and I could together bear the child that God had foreknown.

I find this implausible for two reasons. First, the biblical writers portray God as knowing not only the "unformed substance" of the person (which we might construe, in part, as that person's very biophysical composition), but his or her "appointed time" as well. This inevitably means that for God to know that Y occurs at t^2, X (the proximate cause of Y), must necessarily occur at t^1. Thus, it is impossible to separate the knowledge of *ends* from the very means that produce them.

Second, if God had not known the causal factors resulting in such a particular effect (my child's existence), then He must resort to other means to *causally ensure* that what he knows will happen will indeed occur (despite, on the openness model, what would have been His prior ignorance

---

[20] Pinnock says, "God may consider [circumstances, such as prayer] and include it in his plan." [Pinnock, personal interview; November 20, 2002]. In this sense, it is not that God's *plans* change, but that the *mode* of realizing them does.

of the contingencies that arose). In other words, God must unilaterally compel the antecedent causes. Such a unilateral incursion into space-time events would be required such that the time and place of my child's existence would definitely occur and thereby interlock with God's knowledge. For example, if traffic made going to the café impracticable, God might nevertheless override my natural volition such that I am *forced* to walk several miles (for reasons unknown to me?) through a construction zone to the café.[21] Similarly, once I get there, God would need to ensure that my future bride is present as well, so he must incur into her actions also to secure her part in the decision matrix.

Such a scenario, however, presents indomitable problems for the openness model. Pinnock and other open theists cannot possibly resort to such an explanation since this sort of *compelling* action must operate in spite of libertarian free will and must serve to override it in order for God to secure His purposes and foreknowledge. This is *precisely* what the model seeks to avoid, to wit, a Divine incursion into the self-determining free decisions of human beings to shape their own future (and additionally invite God's responses in reference to their decisions). Thus, when we consider the innumerable factors involved in the global matrix of natural and volitive causes that result in something as basic as one's very existence, it is not surprising that one theologian argues that Pinnock—along with other openness theologians—have simply "not thought through sufficiently the implications of their position."[22]

This argument is not to suggest that, were meticulous Divine providence *not* true, God would simply become flummoxed with reality and hamstrung to make temporal modifications befitting His goals. Rather, it observes that—on an open theistic model—in order for God to make His definite plans work, He would indeed at times need to "override" our wills which, to Pinnock and other open theists, means *forcing* us to act *against* them. This concomitantly means that any such forced choice will be a *disingenuous* choice unbefitting neither merit nor judgment. On a compatibilistic framework, however, we are never forced to do anything since our freedom itself is *established* by God's providence rather than militating against it. Similarly, the consequences of such established actions, whether

---

[21] I say *forced* because, on a noncompatibilistic model, this is precisely what Divine incursion into human volitive circumstances amounts to. The irony, is that it is *this* sort of understanding, unlike classical compatibilism, that reduces human beings to automatons when Divine incursion into human affairs occurs such that the Divine plans may be attained.

[22] Robert Strimple, "What Does God Know?" in *The Coming Evangelical Crisis,* ed. John Armstrong (Chicago: Moody, 1996) 143.

benedictory or maledictory, are a constituent part of that same establishment.

Given what I have been arguing are clear Scriptural expositions of God's knowledge and control juxtaposed alongside human freedom, Pinnock's reduction of humans as "puppets" and God as the "master who pulls all the strings"[23] (on the classical view) does not appear to be consistent with the thinking of the biblical writers. Indeed, the bible portrays the most central event of redemptive history, the passion and crucifixion of Christ, to be both foreknown and *foreordained* by God, yet holds each party involved to be complicit and accountable for their individual decisions. Peter, in his post-resurrection sermon at Jerusalem speaks in remarkably clear terms about the foreknowledge and predetermination of God which undergirded these important events:

> "Men of Israel, listen to these words: Jesus the Nazarene, a man attested to you by God with miracles and wonders and signs which God performed through Him in your midst, just as you yourselves know. This Man, delivered over by the predetermined plan and foreknowledge of God, you nailed to a cross by the hands of godless men and put Him to death. But God raised Him up again, putting an end to the agony of death, since it was impossible for Him to be held in its power." (Acts 2:22-24)

Here we see that the delivery of Jesus into the hands of his persecutors was according to "the predetermined plan and foreknowledge of God." Yet, only a few moments later, Peter refers to Jesus as the man, "whom *you* crucified" (Acts 2:26) [emphasis added]. He then labels them a "perverse generation" and calls upon them to "repent" for the egregious evil they have committed according to their own volitional capacity (Acts 2:38, 40). A similar compatibilism is made later in Acts 4:24-28 where, after referencing the wickedness of humanity in rising up against Christ, we read that ". . . truly in this city there were gathered together against Your holy servant Jesus, whom You anointed, both Herod and Pontius Pilate, along with the Gentiles and the peoples of Israel, to do whatever Your hand and Your purpose predestined to occur" (verses 27-28).

It is also interesting that Jesus, long before these events occurred, identified Judas as one of the principle architects of the evil that would befall him, calling him, "a devil" (John 6:70) even though he included Judas in the same verse as specifically one of the twelve disciples that He himself had

---

[23] Pinnock, "God Limits His Knowledge," in *Predestination and Free Will: Four Views of Divine Sovereignty and Human Freedom*, ed. David Basinger and Randall Basinger (Downer's Grove, Ill.: InterVarsity, 1986) 145.

chosen. The Fourth Gospel adds that, "Jesus had known *from the beginning* which of them did not believe and who would betray him" (John 6:64). John presents this foreknowledge as concrete but as forming no obstacle to the free decision of Judas to carry out his own desires or in being held accountable for them.[24]

The concurrence of God's sovereign knowledge and foreordination of these events, coupled nevertheless with the subsequent moral accountability assigned to the perpetrators, is an excellent example of the compatibilistic freedom I am advocating in my understanding of Divine-human relationality. The Genesis narrative concerning the life of Joseph is another good example (especially chapters 37–50). Here, Joseph's jealous brothers plot to kill him, but later determine to take advantage of a sudden opportunity to sell him into slavery. Later, when Joseph's brothers are morally restored to him, he forgives them for *their actions* saying, "You intended to harm me, but God intended it for good to accomplish what is now being done, the saving of many lives" (Gen 50:20). There is an apparent "layering" of intent here wherein two parties are involved in what occurs, but they each possess diametrically opposing *intentions* concerning the moral nature of their involvement. The very same thing is also seen in the book of Job where God permits Satan to afflict him. Though Satan's role is entirely self-serving and bereft any concern for the will of God, God's purpose is to vindicate His own name by "testing" Job. Later in the narrative, we learn more concerning God's purposeful intentions in unleashing Satan's fury upon him (see Job 1:6-12). Once again, the secondary cause, Satan, is held accountable for his actions even though it is *God* who granted the needed permission to afflict Job knowing full well what Satan intended to do to him. Satan's actions are never characterized as anything other than evil (Job 16:11) even though he operated strictly within God's own providence.

From the standpoint of reconciling evil with the justice of God, there is an operative *theodicy of intent* throughout the Bible in which remote and proximate causes are "layered" upon the foundation of agential moral accountability. Foreknowledge, bound up within the context of God's purposive causality, is a theme woven into the very fabric of the Scriptural portrait of deity itself. "The LORD is a God of knowledge" (1 Sam 2:3) and "works all things after the counsel of His will" (Eph 1:11). His servants "are chosen according to [His] foreknowledge" (1 Pet 1:2) and "His people" are

---

[24] An interesting parallel case involving Jesus' concrete knowledge of future (sinful) human decisions are Peter's three-fold denials of Him (Matt 26:34; cf. Mark 14:72; Luke 22:6; John 13:38). Here, Jesus specifically tells Peter—despite the latter's outspoken zeal for him—that he will choose to lie and deny his faith. In turn, Jesus promises to restore him in response.

those "whom He foreknew" (Rom 11:2). He is "high and exalted" dwelling "on a high and holy place" (Isa 57:15) and to Him, "a thousand years . . . are like yesterday when it passes by, or as a watch in the night" (Ps 90:4, cf. 2 Pet 3:8). Foreknowledge and sovereignty are properties of the Divinity of the Godhead and are that which, in part, separates God as Creator from creature. The biblical evidence is strong and, thus, it is little surprise, that there was a near univocity of agreement concerning this foreknowledge among the patristic, medieval, and Reformational-era theologians and that such agreement has been largely carried over today by most Christian theologians spanning the Catholic, Orthodox, and Protestant traditions. Divine foreknowledge appears to fall within the "Vincentian" guidelines discussed in chapter three.

God and Time

Having addressed the biblical evidence for omnicausal providence, an important corollary issue which bears significantly on the matter of relationality is God's association to events within the flow of time. How might we understand the manner in which God perceives space-time events and, in turn, how might we conceive of his actions within them? Traditionally, Christian theologians have held that God is free from the constraints of time and does not—even if thought of as temporally everlasting (sempiternal) as opposed to atemporal (timeless)—experience it in the same way humans do. Pinnock has abandoned this view, however, again in the interest of preserving his openness view of relationality. As he puts it, "God's relation is temporal and not totally different from ours. He too operates from within time."[25] The idea here is that God, along with His created humans, must experience each relational instance afresh, *as it occurs*. Events must be experienced in an *indexical* manner, rather than in a single Divine simultaneity. Again, Pinnock does not offer any concrete arguments in favor of Divine temporality and I am led to wonder whether he has thoroughly considered some of the logical and philosophical inferences that one faces in declaring God's experience of time to be "not totally different from ours" and once again I find what I believe to be insuperable difficulties.

Putting Pinnock's advocacy of Divine temporality in philosophical parlance, the relational events between God and humans must be *tensed*, that is, both God and humans must be able to have a thought such as, *right now I am experiencing X*, or, *a moment ago X occurred*. Temporal occurrences cannot be experienced as tensed only by humans while God remains

---

[25] Pinnock, *Most Moved Mover*, 32

metaphysically apart from temporal indexicality. God too must experience events *sequentially* in order for them to be genuine experiences. Otherwise, He cannot truly experience such things as surprise, regret, grief, joy, or delight as it relates to the actions of humans. In short, relationality depends upon God and humans *moving through time together* and mutually creating history moment by moment. Pinnock has affirmed as much saying, "As co-laborers with God, we are invited to bring the future into being together along with him."[26]

The philosophical literature concerning the nature of time is massive and the point here is not to recapitulate this complex and enduring debate. Indeed, I share the well-known Augustinian perplexity concerning time in that "I know well enough what it is, provided that nobody asks me."[27] But the question over the precise nature of time is very different from the question of whether or not time, as experienced by humans, also applies to the being of God. In this regard, some very engaging literature has issued in recent years defending both God as unqualifiedly atemporal[28] or temporal,[29] as well as mediating positions that posit some rather creative theories which the authors believe circumvent some of the problems that attach to the other views.[30]

Much of the debate over God's relationship to time begins with important prior theological commitments to a doctrine of God which places

---

[26] Pinnock, "An Interview With Clark Pinnock," in *Modern Reformation Magazine* (June 1998); http://www.modernreformation.org/mr98/novdec/mr9806freespace.html (November 16, 2003).

[27] Augustine, *Confessions*, XI.14.3, trans. R. F. Pine-Coffin (London: Penguin, 1961) 264.

[28] See especially, Paul Helm, *Eternal God: A Study of God Without Time* (Oxford: Oxford University Press, 1988); Eleonore Stump and Norman Kretzmann, "Eternity," *Journal of Philosophy*, 78 (1981) 429–58; and Brian Leftow, *Time and Eternity* (Ithaca, N. Y.: Cornell University Press, 1991).

[29] See especially, Nelson Pike, *God and Timelessness* (London: Routeledge, 1970); Nicholas Wolterstorff, "God Everlasting," *God and the Good*, ed. Clifton Orlebeke and Lewis Smedes (Grand Rapids: Eerdmans, 1975). Reprinted in Steven Cahn, editor, *Ten Essential Texts in the Philosophy of Religion* (Oxford: Oxford University Press, 2004) 57–66; and Nicholas Wolterstorff, "Unqualified Divine Temporality," in *God and Time*, ed. Gregory Ganssle and David M. Woodruff (Downer's Grove, Ill.: InterVarsity, 2001) 187–213.

[30] See, William Lane Craig, *Time and Eternity* (Wheaton, Ill.: Crossway, 2001). Craig defends the idea of "true temporality" in which "God is timeless without creation and temporal since creation," 241; and Alan Padgett, *God, Eternity and the Nature of Time* (1992, reprinted, Eugene, Ore.: Wipf & Stock, 2000); and Alan Padgett, "Eternity as Relative Timelessness," in *God and Time*, ed. Gregory Ganssle and David M. Woodruff (Downer's Grove, Ill.: InterVarsity, 2001) 92–110. Padgett defends what he calls "relative timelessness," the idea that "Our time, created time, exists within the pure duration of God's time, which is relatively timeless"; *God and Time*, 106.

a stronger emphasis on either transcendence or immanence. The move in one direction or another is further guided by the presuppositional stance one holds on the nature of human freedom. Those, like Pinnock, who stress God's immanent involvement, even dependence on the world, and couple this with libertarian freedom are obviously much more likely to posit Divine temporality. Those with a more transcendental leaning in their doctrine of God, coupled with compatibilistic human freedom, such as myself, are obviously more likely to adopt a view akin to atemporality. An atemporal view seems to mesh more naturally with the idea of exhaustive Divine foreknowledge in which God's knowledge of what I do one hour (or one *decade*) from now, is no less clear to him than that I presently type this sentence.

Nevertheless, Paul Helm has raised an issue which I believe to be a crucial component to the discussion over God's relationship to time, albeit one that is frequently ignored (including by Pinnock). This concerns the concomitant issue of God's relationship to *space*. Arguing against the temporalist idea that God's timeless eternity implies the impossible simultaneity of temporal events,[31] Helm points out that virtually the same exact argument can be made from spacelessness.[32] In other words, "if the timeless existence of God is incoherent then so is the spaceless existence of God."[33] Pinnock's flirtations with Divine corporeality notwithstanding, this means that there is an analogous relationship between the argument that a timeless God cannot interact with the *time*-bound world, and the argument that a spaceless God cannot interact with a *space*-bound world, since a non-spatial being supposedly could not be in any particular place(s) in space.

Of course, Pinnock might argue that this is simply another good reason to rethink Divine incorporeality. But this is hardly the case. Even if we granted God some kind of physicality (which I find not only *prima facie* absurd but deeply unbiblical),[34] this would simply back the question up a step when we inquire into the nature of God's agency in the world—especially his government of nature. If God is physical, does he then also govern the natural world in a physical manner? Why, then, do we not observe it since whatever is physical is therefore spatial and therefore empirically detectable? The notion is so manifestly bizarre and absurd that counterarguments seem unnecessary. Further, Pinnock offers precisely zero argumentation in favor

---

[31] Helm cites an argument from Richard Swinburne, *The Coherence of Theism* (Oxford: Oxford University Press; 1993) 220–21. See Helm, *Eternal God*, 45.

[32] Ibid., 46.

[33] Ibid.

[34] See discussion at page 185ff.

of his rumination over Divine corporeality beyond the statement that perhaps God's interaction "would be easier to envisage if he were in some way corporeal."[35] Yet even Pinnock believes in a kind of Divine sovereignty over creation (which he calls a "general sovereignty"[36]), by which God keeps the world in moment-to-moment existence. Hence, the issue does not magically dissolve for him. God's agency must be able to be in *all* created places at once in order that they simply *be*.

In this light, Millard Erickson asks, "is it possible that, just as with space, it is not *either* that God is timeless *or* that he is within time, but *both*?"[37] I believe it *is* possible, indeed *necessarily* possible. Erickson offers a further consideration which helps to elucidate this point. In an Einsteinian universe, time and space "are not simply analogous; they are inseparable."[38] Thus, the real question is not "What is God's relationship to time," but "What is God's relationship to *space-time*."[39] Further, it means that if we are ever to speak of God as "everywhere," then we must also speak of Him as "every*when*."[40] Time itself shifts along with space and gravity which, in short, means not only that time is intimately and inseparably intertwined with space, but that there is no such thing as an absolute, baseline metric time. Time and space are two sides of the same coin. Even the "rate" of time is relative to objects, gravity, inertia, speed, and other factors. Traveling at extremely high speeds and away from stronger gravitational forces, for example, will result in the passage of time being different for two or more entities (as has been proven in multiple experiments such as shooting rockets off Wallop Island, Virginia to a high altitude and noting differences in measured time with atomic clocks[41]). Thus, one not even need be God to be "beyond" time, at least as it is experienced by humans on earth. You simply need *speed*, albeit incredible speed. Surely Pinnock would at least not want to deny God speed.

All of this *necessarily* means, then, that if God is not limited by *these* factors, then He is not limited by time. Rather, He stands as their source, sustainer, and master. Thus, contra Pinnock, God's relationship to time

---

[35] Pinnock, *Most Moved Mover*, 33–34.

[36] Ibid., 53.

[37] Millard Erickson, *God the Father Almighty: A Contemporary Exploration of the Divine Attributes* (Grand Rapids: Baker, 1998) 136.

[38] Ibid.

[39] Ibid., 137.

[40] Ibid., 138.

[41] See Ibid., 138 where Erickson recounts this and several such experiments.

simply *cannot* be "not totally different from ours." It must be *radically* different.

But this also in no way implies that God cannot or does not remain *present in* time. In fact, it should strike us that these considerations only help establish the fact. A God unconstrained by the limits of space-time is able to unqualifiedly be present to everything and every*one*. John Frame comments that,

> God's temporal immanence does not contradict his lordship over time . . . These temporal categories are merely aspects of God's general transcendence and immanence as the Lord. The give-and-take between God and the creation requires, not a reduced, but an enhanced, view of his sovereignty. God is the Lord *in* time as well as the Lord *above* time.[42]

In sum, God's very Lordship and transcendence *over* time, is the very thing which enables Him to be in time, in relation with His creatures. As Erickson adds, "God both transcends time space-time and is immanent within it. He is atemporal/aspatial in his fundamental nature, or is ontologically atemporal/aspatial but actively or influentially present within the space-time universe."[43]

None of the above can be said, however, of Pinnock's creative-love theism which very much *depends* upon Divine temporality in the presentistic sense. On Pinnock's model, Divine simultaneity in space-time cannot be postulated of God's relationship to a genuinely free world, for it would render fixed "all things from eternity past"[44] which, in his calculus, precludes relationality and existential significance.

God, Time, and Personhood

Pinnock's *overall* concern, of course, is to rescue the personalism of God from the broader radical transcendence of classical theology which avows that God simply cannot move through time as humans do in virtue of his *sui generis, a se,* being. But, again, arguments are not offered by Pinnock and the assertion that personality must enjoin temporality is hardly obvious. For the coupling of conscious personality and atemporality (or any other kind of non-strictly-temporal relationship to time) to fail analytically,

---

[42] John Frame, *The Doctrine of God* (Philipsburg, New Jersey: Presbyterian & Reformed, 2002) 559.

[43] Ibid., 139.

[44] Pinnock, "From Augustine to Arminius: A Pilgrimage in Theology," in *The Grace of God and the Will of Man* (Minneapolis: Bethany, 1989) 25.

the objector must furnish a clear internal inconsistency. This has been tried by others, however, and has proven unsuccessful. J. R. Lucas, for example, argued against the coexistence of Divine atemporality and personality for years but ultimately conceded that, "My claim that time is a concomitant of consciousness, is of course only a claim, and I have been unable to argue for it, except by citing poetry . . . arguments would be better."[45] That Divine personhood and atemporality are mutually annihilating propositions would be analytically obvious only if the following premises were true: Personality exists; Personality can only exist within time; God is an atemporal being; Therefore, God is not personal. For Pinnock to make the first premise analytically true, he must marshal evidence for the second premise. This, however, I believe to be impossible for the following reasons.

Personhood (as with *free will* in the last chapter) must be defined and defended with arguments which Pinnock neglects to do. There have been many different definitions of personhood throughout the history of philosophy. The *Stanford Encyclopedia of Philosophy*, for example, lists at least three broad categories of ways in which philosophers have approached a definition of personality including the Psychological Approach, the Fissional Model, and the Somatic Approach.[46] The Encyclopedia concedes that it is exceedingly difficult to know which, if any, such approach should be granted higher or lower epistemic warrant.

In more recent philosophical discourse, the concept of personhood tends to be analyzed according to various mental predicates. Philosopher Daniel Dennett, for example, organizes personhood around three basic, mutually-interdependent characteristics including rationality, intentionality, and the ability to be perceived as rational and intentional.[47] Joel Feinberg offers conditions for personhood very similar to Dennett's enjoining consciousness, awareness, rationality, emotion, and the ability to plan.[48]

Perhaps the first thing we observe in these is the absence of any explicit temporal requirement. Concerning a *non*-temporal being, then, the question is whether such criteria could attach to a rational consciousness that is tenseless, changeless, and discursive (that is, encompassing all know-

---

[45] J. R. Lucas, *The Future: An Essay on God, Temporality, and Truth* (Oxford: Basil Blackwell, 1989) 213; cf. page 212. Quoted in William Lane Craig, "Divine Timelessness and Personhood," *International Journal for Philosophy of Religion*, 43.2 (April 1998) 112.

[46] Eric Olson, "Personal Identity" in *the Stanford Encyclopedia of Philosophy* (Stanford: Stanford University, 2004) http://plato.stanford.edu/entries/identity-personal.

[47] Daniel Dennett, *Brainstorms: Philosophical Essays on Mind and Psychology* (Cambridge, Mass.: Bradford, 1981) 267–85.

[48] Joel Feinberg, "Abortion," in *Matters of Life and Death*, ed. Tom Regan (New York: Random House, 1986) 262.

able truths at once). For example, can the being still be aware of rational propositions such as "no pink gnomes exist, whatever has shape has size, I exist (that is, self awareness), 2+2=4, duck-billed platypuses currently exist in Tasmania," and so on. The first and second are rational propositions, the third is properly basic to self-awareness, the fourth is a mathematical truth, and the fifth is factual knowledge concerning the temporal order. Let us then suppose that these truths are ones that have always been a part of this being, that is, they were never *acquired*. The result is that all of these truths are held simultaneously and eternally. Does a contradiction obtain? I think not. Consciousness and rationality have remained in tact and there is no demonstrable reason to deny intentionality. As William Lane Craig points out, "Short of a proof of the incoherence of all relational theories of time, we must grant that time would not be a concomitant of such a consciousness."[49] To wit, there is no reason to rule out, *a priori*, that such a consciousness could not function or qualify as properly personal. A being can hold to all manner of truths (including self-awareness), and therefore be rational and conscious, yet hold to these truths *tenselessly*. This violates no logical canon.

The properties of rationality and consciousness also provide a clue as to how Dennett's remaining *perceptual* criteria can be met (that is, ability to communicate and regard others as beings to which consciousness can be attributed) by a non-temporal being. Even in a timeless state, part of a timeless being's knowledge could still be that of other conscious persons. Whether those persons are themselves timeless or temporal is irrelevant. The knowledge itself would be timeless in nature as the other truths are and thus would be along the lines of "other atemporal (or temporal) persons exist" and so on. These are propositions that can be unacquired but real. The knowledge itself would be necessarily beginningless, endless, and errorless (it is difficult to conceive of "eternal error"), but nevertheless true knowledge. *Subscribing* to (not acquiring) alethic propositions is a hallmark of Dennett's criteria of consciousness, not error or tense. Similarly, interpersonal communication could take place in one or more ways. For example, temporal beings could be created in a tensed environment in which communication occurs simultaneously for the non-temporal being, but is experienced sequentially for the temporal being.

Of course, important differences in the manner in which timeless and time-bound persons would experience and manifest their personality must inevitably arise as already addressed in my discussion of presentistic simultaneity. For example, a timeless being would not have the attributes of

---

[49] Craig, "Divine Timelessness and Personhood," 112.

memory or anticipation. But these are not conditions of personality on either Dennett or Feinberg's definitions. This simply means, then, that when we think of personhood, we can begin with a broad genus (personality itself), but can further break the genus down into the species of *non-temporal personality* and *temporal personality*.

Implications emerge from both models, but the genus itself does not change—personality contains the basic rudiments in both species. Thus, the objection to timeless personality is unsuccessful and an appeal to presentism need not be invoked in order to rescue it. No definition of personhood has included the necessity of time or tense and Pinnock has not demonstrated why a non-temporal being or a being that relates somehow differently to time cannot enjoin the properties inherent in proper personhood. An atemporal, meta-temporal, or omni-temporal being can have consciousness, rationality, volitionality, and can be relational which function as the raw components. Only the manner in which these factors *exemplify* themselves are different. They do not disappear. The issue of God and time presents no defeater for genuine relationality, though it does assign *sui generis* prerogatives to a non-temporal being (such as errorlessness and unacquired knowledge)

The Problem of Divine Simultaneity

There is another vitally important issue that emerges here, however, that—not only has Pinnock apparently not considered—but is something I have not encountered in any critique of openness theology. Though presentism maintains that God experiences time and event-relationships indexically, does not the view still require that God experience *the collection of temporally concurrent events* as simultaneous? It is hard to imagine anyone arguing against the notion that finite human beings can only experience events singly as one event following after another. As we experience each event, we react to it cognitively, emotionally, physically, and so on. An event may produce in me, for example, joy or sadness. But I cannot be said to experience, and react to, multiple events at once. I may experience conflicting emotions as my thoughts transfer from one event to the next within a short timeframe, but I cannot be said to experience (or acknowledge) these thoughts or emotions simultaneously. I can only experience that which falls within my limited observational vantage point. This is a consequence of creaturely limitedness and an intrinsic inability to possess universal knowledge and experience in the context of finitude.

But even on a presentistic model, which nevertheless maintains God's total omniscience of all current and past events, must not the Divine mind experience *all of present reality* from an unlimited observational vantage point quite *unlike* humans? In other words, must not at least a certain level of Divine simultaneity occur even in presentism? Let us call this *presentistic simultaneity*. According to this view, which I believe to be an unavoidable consequence of Pinnock's openness model, God experiences a past, present, and future just like humans do and comes to know each event as it occurs. But, quite unlike humans, God experiences *every present event simultaneously*. Right now, God experiences the "new" knowledge that while I type this sentence, someone else is making a deposit at the Bank of Scotland; someone in Cape Town has gone fishing; someone in California is preparing to commit a crime; someone in China is converting to Christianity; while someone else in the West has just become an atheist, and on and on. Each individual instance must be multiplied several billion times over according to global population. But this appears to present unworkable and curious difficulties for Pinnock's contention that genuine Divine-human relationality can only take place in an indexical, non-simultaneous fashion.

Perhaps an example of the Divine/human contrast concerning experience is helpful here. Again, I'll refer to my children. As a father, I may be pleased with the actions of one of my children while displeased with the actions of another. But I cannot be said either to ruminate over or react to these actions simultaneously. My thoughts and actions toward each child are divided over time as I deal with each one in sequence. I may be angry with one child and punish him or her in one instance, while delighting in and rewarding the other child at another time. Whichever order these actions come in, however, they are divided over time and experienced sequentially. This is not to say that pleasure and displeasure, and the attending actions that spring forth from one or the other, cannot persist in humans in latent form. But they must be indexically recalled. For example, I turn my thoughts to one child and act accordingly at t^1, and my thoughts and actions to the other child at t^2, and so on. Human beings operate indexically.

But in God's case, this simply *cannot* be the case even on Pinnock's view. God's relation to temporal events cannot be said to be "not totally different from ours." This is a second reason why, as I said earlier, it must be *radically* different. There may be an *analogia entis* in the sense of human relational qualities (the dynamic relational faculty) which somewhat dimly reflect the Divine as human beings are created in that image. But one relational dynamic (the human) issues from a *limited* observational vantage point while the other (the Divine) issues from an *unlimited* observational vantage point. God is the only being operating according to an observational unlimitedness which therefore makes this quality decidedly *sui ge-*

neris. Humans deal with only one event or situation at a time, but God, of ontological necessity, must deal simultaneously with countless events as they occur at each temporal moment experienced by humans. While I experience regret over a particular situation at one point and joy over another at a different time, God must be conceived of as simultaneously *feeling* and *acting* upon experiences of regret, joy, and multitudinous other emotions all at once.

Anthropomorphism and the Nature of Religious Language

Classical theology has typically solved the preceding problem by construing God's "feelings" or emotions (as they are portrayed in Scripture) as *anthropopathic* and His actions as *anthropomorphic*. This has appeared an unavoidable necessity in order to accommodate language to the finite, creaturely vantage point. In this sense, passages such as Genesis 6:7 and 1 Samuel 15:11 which speak of divine "regret" or "repentance" do not communicate a particular attitude of God that He has experienced like humans do at a particular point in time, but rather reflects something of the general eternal character of God (that is, the *preceptive* or *dispositional* will) in relation to the created realm.[50] Thus, on a presentistic model, it is difficult—if not impossible—to imagine how God could pause, as humans do, to experience one particular emotion and to then react to it when we consider that it must be universal rather than singular (as with humans). Even presentism must grant that God transcends the boundaries of time in some way.

---

[50] A similar interpretation may be applied to the other "Divine repentance" texts Pinnock cites as covered in chapter three (that is, 2 Kings 20:1-6; Jonah 3:4; Jer 3:7; 26:3). To assume that such texts involved Divine ignorance of the future is to read too much into them. As John Piper observes:
> None of the passages of Scripture that is brought forth against the exhaustive definite foreknowledge of God teaches that God does not have such foreknowledge. Rather this denial is *inferred* from circumstances that *seem* to require it . . . reference is sometimes made to texts where God changes his mind from what he said he would do . . . is sorry for what he has done…seems surprised . . . and puts people to the test. In all these texts, the denial of God's exhaustive foreknowledge is an *inference* that *seems* necessary to some interpreters. However, in the history of the church right up to our own day, plausible explanations have been given to each of these texts which cohere with the wider, more explicit teaching of Scripture that God foreknows all that shall come to pass. [emphasis original]

(John Piper, "Grounds for Dismay: The Error and Injury of Open Theism," in *Beyond the Bounds*, ed. John Piper, et al. (Wheaton, Ill.: Crossway, 2003) 375.

Anthropomorphism and anthropopathism appear to be not only valid but *obligatory* ways of dealing with the Scriptural portrait of God's actions and emotions. God's passions are analogical, not univocal to the human experience. Pinnock, however, rejects the analogical use of language sensing that that it minimizes the literality of the Bible and its ability to veridically portray a genuine experience or emotion on God's part. To him, it means not taking Scripture or God's self-disclosure as *actual*. He writes, "What does it mean for God to grieve, to interact, to weep, to cry out, to respond to prayer?"[51] In response to this, he criticizes classicalism saying it is "wrong to [say] that biblical figures that convey such things are mere accommodations to finite understanding."[52] Further, "These are not naïvely anthropomorphic ideas, but the Bible's way of conceiving of God as living and active and genuinely responding to other free beings with whom he is dealing."[53]

But if *presentistic simultaneity* is a resistless corollary of the openness view, must not the classical understanding of God's passions and reactions as anthropopathic and anthropomorphic still be invoked with equal force? Either way, it appears manifestly impossible to take God's relationship to the flow of events in time and reduce it to as close a comparison with human experience as Pinnock does. God simply *cannot*, given His *sui generis* ontology, experience regret, joy, or other emotions; or respond to events in the world *just as* humans do. To say He does, not only risks further attenuating another aspect of Deity, but risks the possibility of dividing God into "parts" wherein one part feels and reacts one way, while another part feels and reacts another way such that God's emotions and activities are divided and sequential like humans.

Thus presentism does not appear to solve the *relational* problems that Pinnock hopes for. In fact, it complicates them. His criticism of anthropopathism and anthropomorphism as used by classicalists dissolves if presentistic simultaneity forces him to make the very same appeal to linguistic analogy as they do. Indeed, the writer of 1 Samuel, shortly after making the statement that God experienced "regret," nevertheless adds that God "is not a man that He should change His mind" (1 Sam 15:29). The differ-

---

[51] Pinnock, *Most Moved Mover,* 63.

[52] Ibid., 27. It is the same concern which leads Pinnock to think that God might also enjoin a physical body. Indeed, he seems to think that any *passibility* of God's part might be contingent upon physicality. He writes, "If he is with us in the world, if we are to take biblical metaphors seriously, is God in some way embodied . . . Perhaps God's agency would be easier to envisage if he were in some way corporeal," 33–34.

[53] Pinnock, "There Is Room For Us: A Reply To Bruce Ware," *Journal of the Evangelical Theological Society* (45.2; June 2002) 216.

ence in these passages is again the narrative versus the didactic as discussed in chapter three. The narrative portion speaks of God's "regret." But the didactic portion modifies this statement as a sort of internal commentary in which the author almost seems to go out of his way to modify his narrative by specifically teaching that God does not experience something new or do something novel from which we might then conclude that He committed a mistake, experienced grief or frustration, and then changed His plans based on the reception of new knowledge. Further, the reason given for this is that God *is not a man*. Thus, in order for the 1 Samuel 15:29 qualification to be valid, 1 Samuel 15:11 must be understood anthropopathically along with other biblical passages that speak of God's emotions and actions. Otherwise, the passages are simply contradictory in nature—a problem both Pinnock and myself wish to avoid in developing a cohesive *sola Scriptura* theology.

A vital corollary issue to the employment of anthropomorphism when approaching the biblical text, is the perennially-debated "religious language" factor in theological method. Though Pinnock and I share a firm commitment to the canons of logic in the deployment of a coherent theology, we differ radically concerning the manner in which human language finds a veridical referent in God. When Pinnock criticizes classicalism saying Divine revelation is not a "mere accommodation to finite understanding,"[54] the most obvious alternative is linguistic-epistemological univocity.

Yet even if Pinnock did not come right out and declare his rejection of classicalism's infinite-à-finite language accommodation, one can pick up this assumption implicitly in his writings. Univocity is implicit in statements such as his rhetorical objection: "What kind of *dialogue* is it where one party already knows what the other will say and do?"[55] [emphasis added]. And further, that "God's relation is temporal and *not totally different from ours*"[56] [emphasis added]. Simply put, Pinnock desires to bring God closer to humanity and uses a kind of univocal language to accomplish this end.

For Pinnock, words must apply to God in essentially the same manner as they do humans. Indeed, it is the same concern, coupled with an impatience with analogy, metaphor and anthropomorphism, which ultimately leads him to think that God might also enjoin a physical body. Thus, not only is God's own experience of time much like ours (that is, univocal), perhaps his *being* is also. He writes, "If he is with us in the world, if we

---

[54] Pinnock, *Most Moved Mover*, 27.
[55] Pinnock, "Systematic Theology," in *The Openness of God: A Biblical Challenge to the Traditional Understand of God* (Downer's Grove, Ill.: InterVarsity, 1994) 122.
[56] Pinnock, *Most Moved Mover*, 32

are to take biblical metaphors seriously, is God in some way embodied? . . . Perhaps God's agency would be easier to envisage if he were in some way corporeal."[57] This is a strange assertion. Pinnock's desire to "take biblical metaphors seriously" seems to be an example of not taking them to be metaphors at all, but as fairly precise denotative prescriptions for theological discourse. Yet the whole thrust of metaphors is that they are always exceeded by the reality to which they point. Taking metaphors seriously, then, is *not* to take them literally but to engage the imagination beyond them. Pinnock's treatment of metaphors, I am afraid, subsumes them into a broader program of ontic-epistemic univocity

This implicit univocity has not gone unnoticed by other Evangelicals. Douglas Kelly comments that Pinnock (and other open theists),

> . . . seem to work on the assumption of the univocal validity of language for both God and man. That is, a word must mean for God the exact same thing it does for a human. For instance, "before and after" impose on God's experience the same limitations they do on that of humankind. But one wonders how they could have neglected the church's pivotal teaching on the analogical usage of language (that is, that there are both similarities and differences when the same word is applied to created and uncreated being). A brief reading of a few sections of Saint Thomas Aquinas' *Summa Theologiae* . . . might have transformed their book. And long before Aquinas . . . Saint Hilary of Poitiers (fourth century) wisely remarked (in *De Trinitate* 4:14) that human words are subject to God, rather than God being subject to human words (in the sense of comprehensively defined and thus limited by them). The human mind "must not measure the divine nature by the limitations of [its] own." (*De Trinitate* 1:17)[58]

Kelly adds that this "impoverished grasp of the relationship of language to being" is connected with a failure "to think through the profound implications of the difference between created (finite) and uncreated (infinite) being." Simon Oliver observes that, "in order to bring God 'closer,' [Pinnock] adopts anthropomorphic language which ends in God obtaining a body."[59] In other words, Pinnock adopts anthropomorphism and literalizes it making it univocal *dei*morphism.

Other than his criticisms of classicalism's use of anthropomorphism and analogy, Pinnock offers no positive argumentation for his own use of

---

[57] Ibid., 33–34.

[58] Douglas F. Kelly, "Afraid of Infinitude," *Christianity Today* 39 (Jan. 9, 1995) 32.

[59] Simon Oliver, personal correspondence, March 1, 2005.

univocal predication. He rather implies that *not* granting univocity reduces to a relativization of the biblical text and of theology in general.

I believe the consequences of Pinnock's wholesale rejection of analogy and accommodation in theological discourse to be serious. Because the assumption of univocity fundamentally blurs the Creator-creature distinction, it has the ironic effect of actually *further* distancing God from genuine relations with the world. For, God becomes a univocally distanced object. This is precisely the opposite of what Pinnock seeks to accomplish in making God out to be "more human." Yet it is also the inevitable terminus unless there is an ontic-epistemic bridge to bring God and humans together. As I will show in a moment, analogical predication, in virtue of the archetypical-ectypal/Creator-creature distinction bridges this gap.

When Pinnock conjectures that "to take biblical metaphors seriously" we should consider whether God is in some way embodied, it is hard to imagine how such biblical metaphors therefore remain metaphors at all. If biblical metaphors such as God possessing eyes, arms, hands, and so on are construed to be indicative of Divine corporeality, then Pinnock has hardly read anything even remotely resembling what would normally classify as a metaphor. Rather, he has marshaled what he believes to be various sets of wooden-literal technical descriptions of God. Such an interpretation bespeaks the literalization of the figurative rather than the extraction of objective metaphorical referents. In fact, not only does Pinnock's literalization of anthropomorphism and metaphor often rob biblical texts of their substantive meaning, it actually *lessens* their import as figurative language. Functioning as symbols and sign-posts, metaphors and anthropomorphisms are always exceeded in reality by the objects to which they point. If God's "mighty hand" is able to "lift [us] up in due time" (1 Pet 5:6), significantly more is being communicated to the readers of Scripture than the idea that God can rescue us from clumsy fall down a well. The metaphor points to a much deeper reality, that is, that God can restore the inner being of humans from all peril. All metaphors and anthropomorphisms have this character. Pinnock would probably not deny such an understanding of this *particular* passage, but it must be noted that he has nevertheless left us with no way of knowing when metaphor and anthropomorphism should and should not be invoked and when they should be *de*-anthropomorphized and taken as literal description. Pinnock's conjecture over God's possible corporeality has not made the situation any better, but bespeaks what I perceive to be a penchant for blurring the hermeneutical lines.

Simon Oliver wonders to what extent Pinnock has thus embraced the very kind of fundamentalist hermeneutic he normally claims to eschew.

For, "once [he] starts on the trajectory of reading the Bible very literally and without recourse to analogy and metaphor (never mind allegory), he is bound at some point to realise that the God one thereby gleans from the Bible quite obviously changes his mind, reacts to human affairs, etc."[60] Herein, we find further evidence of Pinnock's own admission to placing a higher emphasis on the narrative over the didactic. What, for example, does Pinnock do with Christ's rather clear (that is, didactic) teaching that "God is spirit" (John 4:24); or the writer of First Samuel's qualifier that "[God] is not a man that He should change His mind" (1 Sam 15:29)? On what basis are narrative passages and *literalized* metaphor privileged over more clear, apparently didactic teachings and then reworked to become technically descriptive? The result is either an impossible hermeneutic-exegetical methodology that cherry-picks its own pet passages in service to one's own theological preferences, or else manifest contradictions in the various biblical descriptions of God. This is the weakness of Pinnock's position and the strength of the classical view in that anthropomorphisms and metaphors consistently stand as anthropomorphisms and metaphors, while the descriptive and didactic is always to be construed as analogical. In this manner, the biblical text—and the Christian theology we glean from it—can be harmonized. Further, the Creator-creature distinction is maintained. In this sense, *all* biblical language is analogical—a subject to which I will now give some further attention.

It is well known that Augustine and Aquinas, and later the Reformers (notably Calvin) adopted either a doctrine of analogy or accommodation. Regardless of whether one prefers analogy or accommodation, both positions agree that univocal predication in theology is inescapably problematic and wrongheaded. This agreement finds a common strain throughout nearly all subspecies of classicalism including Augustinianism, Scholasticism, and Reformed theology. As Michael Horton notes:

> With the ecclesiastical consensus, Reformed scholasticism accepted the view that talk about God was analogical, even in Scripture, where it is not only talk about God, but talk from God. In every analogy (warrior, king, father, good, angry, etc.) God is more unlike than like the human analogue. Does that leave us drowning in relativism? How can we know that God really is good if not even Scripture gives us access to God's inner being? The answer given by the Reformed has been that these analogies (hence, the "analogical"

---

[60] Ibid.

mode of God's self-revelation) are selected by God himself as sufficient approximations for weak creatures to understand for their salvation.[61]

The assumption of univocity between God and humanity begins to erase the Creator-creature distinction, in part, by implying an ontological autonomy that mutually ascribes an issuing of one-to-one epistemological correspondence. This ultimately reduces either to a pantheistic or panentheistic doctrine of God which, in turn, destroys genuine personal relations between the human and the divine. The reason for this is as follows: To blur the Creator-creature (or God-world) distinction is to conflate God with humanity; to conflate God with humanity leads to pantheism (or panentheism); pantheism and panentheism destroy God's distinct personhood; the destruction of God's distinct personhood destroys God's personal agency in the world; to destroy God's personal agency in the world is to destroy genuine relationality between the human and the divine; the theory of univocity blurs the Creator-creature distinction; therefore, univocity destroys genuine relationality between the human and the divine.

Even if one, such as Pinnock, advances univocal prediction while nevertheless seeking to maintain some level of distinction between God and humans, we would still be confronted with the difficult problem of gleaning knowledge of a God that is univocally and impassibly distanced from the created world. As Oliver explains:

> If God's being is univocal with ours, yet perfect and therefore infinitely greater, we could never traverse this "sea of sameness." It would not matter how far we traveled towards God, he would always be univocally at an infinite distance from us. It is precisely because of the ontological difference (the simplicity of *esse ipsum*) as maintained by Aquinas that God is proximate and not "outside" the world.[62]

Thus, it has long been recognized, since Aquinas, that analogical predication acts as an ontic-epistemic bridge between the finite and the infinite. This underscores one of Aquinas' most valuable insights—analogical predication of God by humans is rooted in metaphysics, not in an isolated discussion of human epistemology or language. Epistemology and its concomitant theory of religious language must always be intertwined with

---

[61] Michael Horton, "Our Debt To Heresy," *Modern Reformation*, 10.3 (May/June 2001) 33.

[62] Simon Oliver, personal correspondence, March 1, 2005.

a particular ontology, doctrine of God, and doctrine of creation. Aquinas expressed this distinction in the divine ontology as *ipsum esse*, existence itself, the self-grounded foundation of all being.[63] For this reason, Colin Brown observes that,

> Our language cannot be other than figurative and analogical. For God is no mere object in time and space. [God] breaks into our world: but . . . is above it. Nevertheless, Christian experience testifies to the fact that God reveals himself in a way that is comprehensible to men. Even though, in the nature of the case, divine truth has to be refracted and expressed in terms of human words and finite images, nevertheless it can be expressed in meaningful terms.[64]

Analogy bridges the gap between self-existent being and derived (or dependent) being. Otherwise, one will ceaselessly toggle between a doctrine of God that is either pantheistic/panentheistic or one that results in a univocally-*distanced* God. One must sacrifice either transcendence or immanence on the alter of univocity. In a classic text on the subject, Aquinas writes that,

> [The] names spoken of God are not synonymous . . . names signify the divine substance, although in an imperfect manner . . . [and] they have diverse meanings. For the idea signified by the name is the conception in the intellect of the thing signified by the name. But our intellect, since it knows God from creatures, in order to understand God, forms conceptions proportional to the perfections flowing from God to creatures, which perfections pre-exist in God unitedly and simply, whereas in creatures they are received and divided and multiplied.[65]

God's being is necessarily united—there are no predicates and subjects in God as there are in humans. In humans, our mind may be "wise" and our heart "good" as composite beings that possess attributes, that is, they are "attached" to our existence. But God is a tri-unity in which His "attributes" *are* His existence and thus are not things "added on" to Him. "For instance," Thomas says, "by the term 'wise' applied to man, we signify some perfection distinct from a man's essence, and distinct from his power and existence, and from all similar things; whereas when we apply it to God, we do not mean to signify anything distinct from His essence, or power,

---

[63] Thomas Aquinas, *Summa Theologica*, I.3.4. Trans. Fathers of the English Dominican Province (Grand Rapids: Christian Classics Ethereal Library, 1999) 21.

[64] Colin Brown, *Philosophy and the Christian Faith: A Historical Sketch from the Middle Ages to the Present Day* (Downer's Grove, Ill.: InterVarsity, 1980) 32.

[65] Aquinas, *Summa Theologica*, I.13.4, 84.

or existence."⁶⁶ Of course, it is true that, due to our creaturely limits, we cannot help but think of God as divided up into various attributes or parts. For Thomas, this merely underscores the limited, and therefore analogical or metaphorical, nature of human language about God.

Analogical Predication

Analogical predication derives from the metaphysical Creator-creature distinction in which God is not only *ipsum* esse, but *totaliter aliter* 67 while humans are contingent, dependent, derived, and *in re* ("in regard") to God. Thus, to posit univocity between that which is *necessary* and *eternal*, and that which is *dependent* and *finite*, is to create an insurmountable impasse. There would no longer be a relational or intelligible bridge between the two terms.

But exactly what, then, *is* analogical predication and how does it provide genuine knowledge of God and, at the same time, maintain the Creator-creature distinction? Hampus Lyttkens has written that, "The theological significance of analogy may be summarized by saying that some connection between God and the world is essential. We are then speaking of the analogy based on and implying a real likeness between God and creation."⁶⁸ Aquinas' famous dilemma is to be faced with either univocal or equivocal language about God, neither of which is acceptable. Univocity implies that we can make *exact* predications of God. Equivocity, on the other hand, suggests that our "God talk" is essentially meaningless, absent an objective, extramental referent. Thomas states the dilemma saying that,

> Univocal predication is impossible between God and creatures [because] every effect which is not an adequate result of the power of the efficient cause, receives the similitude of the agent not in its full degree, but in a measure that falls short, so that what is divided and multiplied in the effects resides in the agent simply . . . Neither, on

---

⁶⁶ Ibid., I.13.5; 85.

⁶⁷ Against some Evangelicals (for example, John Gerster, R. C. Sproul, and Arthur Lindsley in *Classical Apologetics* (Grand Rapids: Zondervan, 1984) 75), I believe it is perfectly appropriate, even healthy, to speak of God as "wholly other" provided this is understood ontologically, not relationally. Even the doctrine of analogy acknowledges similarity between God and humans to the extent that the latter are created in the *imago Dei*. This image is the very thing which enables Divine-human interchange through an act of grace. Therefore, "wholly other" is not to be confused with "utterly dissimilar" as some of the Neoorthodox seem to have done (see pages 95–96).

⁶⁸ Hampus Lyttkens, *The Analogy between God and the World: An Investigation of its Background and Interpretation of its Use by Thomas of Aquino* (Uppsala: Lundequistska bokhandeln, 1953) 477.

the other hand, are names applied to God and creatures in a purely equivocal sense . . . if that were so, it follows that from creatures nothing could be known or demonstrated about God at all."[69]

"Therefore," Thomas says, "it must be said that these names are said of God and creatures in an analogous sense."[70] Perhaps the easiest way to think of analogy is simply in terms of similarity and dissimilarity, that is, two analogates are partly the same and partly different. Analogates share a common "perfection," but exemplify that perfection differently depending on their ontology. True knowledge is communicated through analogy, but it is limited and incomplete.

The difficulty arises, however, of whether to interpret Thomas as advancing an analogy of *proportion*, or an analogy of *attribution*. At first, Thomas perhaps gives the impression of supporting the former by using the word *proportionem* during his discussion of the issue.[71] In the analogy of proportionality, a term is validly applied to the analogates, but in a manner proportional to their natures. For example, we describe Sparky as a "good dog," our spouse as a "good person," and the Lord as a "good God." In such cases, it is clear that a one-to-one correspondence is not implied in the manner in which Sparky and God exemplify goodness.

That much of our language in reference to God implies an analogy of proportionality is perhaps uncontroversial. For example, when considering God's power, we might be tempted to picture in our minds a mighty ocean or even a big, strong man (as in Michelangelo's depiction of Divine creation in the Sistine Chapel). Or, perhaps we might think of God's mind as being a "vast sum" of thoughts as even the Scripture does (Ps 139:17). All of this is fine up to a point. The limitation emerges in that the idea of proportionality does not necessarily imply a *relationship* between the analogates. In other words, the analogy of proportionality by itself is insufficient to realize Thomas' own goal of establishing a genuine relationship between the human and the divine because God, as *ipsum esse*, is wholly other.

Therefore, this brings to the fore the idea of the analogy of attribution, or, more specifically, the *intrinsic* analogy of attribution.[72] Thomas clarifies

---

[69] Aquinas, *Summa Theologica*, I.13.5., 85–86.

[70] Ibid., 86.

[71] Thomas Aquinas, [Latin Text] *Summa Theologica*, I.13.5. Made available by the George Mason University Department of Modern and Classical Languages (Fairfax, Vir.: George Mason University, 2005) http://www.gmu.edu/departments/fld/CLASSICS/aquinas.q1.13.html.

[72] To be contrasted with the *extrinsic* analogy of attribution in which only the principal

that, "... whatever is said of God and creatures, is said according to the *relation* of a creature to God *as its principle and cause*, wherein all perfections of things pre-exist excellently" [emphasis added]. This is to say that the relationship between the divine being and the human being is one of causal *participation*. For example, to predicate love of both God and humans is to understand this love in terms of the primacy of *God's* love. Or, whatever is genuinely good, is that which participates in the Divine goodness. Norman Geisler comments that,

> ... the analogy between creature and Creator based on causality is secured only because God is the principal, intrinsic, essential, efficient cause of the being and perfections of the world. In any other kind of causal relationship an analogical similarity would not necessarily follow. But in an analogy of being similarity must follow, for being communicates only being, and perfections or kinds of being do not arise from an imperfect being. Existence produces only after its kind, viz. other existences.[73]

Charles Hart also observes that, for Aquinas, such an analogy of intrinsic attribution, based on the Divine causality, becomes precisely that which *guarantees* a genuine relationship between created beings as *in re*, and God as *a se*.[74] This further enables intelligible, participatory predication of God by his creatures in that a causal nexus exists between the two, all the while maintaining a vital Creator-creature distinction.

Unlike the *extrinsic* analogy of attribution, this type of analogy can be properly predicated of both the principal analogate as well as the secondary analogates in which "the secondary analogate has it 'attributed' by virtue of participation in the primacy."[75] The nexus for analogy is built upon the secondary analogate deriving ontologically from the former, thereby endowing it with its perfections. Thus, humans "are" while God "is." This is to say that being itself is independent and *archetypal* in God while dependent and *ectypal* in humans. Being is properly predicated of humans to the extent that they receive their being from God in participation with His being just as there is always similarity and dissimilarity between effects and their causes. Juan Sanguineti offers several insightful observations on this front:

> *a)* Since one cannot give what one does not have, at least some perfections of the efficient cause will necessarily be reflected in its

---

analogate truly possesses the analogical perfection.

[73] Norman Geisler, *Philosophy of Religion* (Grand Rapids: Zondervan, 1974) 285.
[74] Charles Hart, *Thomistic Metaphysics* (Englewood Cliffs, N. J.: Prentice-Hall, 1959) 42.
[75] Simon Oliver, Personal Correspondence, December 28, 2005.

proper effects. The efficient cause is, therefore, also an exemplary cause of its proper effects. It follows that by studying the latter, we can, using the analogy of attribution, arrive at some knowledge of the former. It is in this way that we arrive at an analogical knowledge of the nature of God on the basis of the manifold perfections we find in creatures;

b) Consequently, analogy of attribution implies both similarity and dissimilarity. The analogical concept is predicated *per prius* of the cause, and *per posterius* of the effects. It is partly attributed to the effects inasmuch as they are similar to the cause; but it is partly not attributed to them since they are also unlike the cause. Hence, the universe is, at one and the same time, like God and unlike Him;

c) The foundation of the analogy of attribution is not an abstract idea but a real cause, the cause of the participated likenesses of the perfection in the secondary analogates. For example, if being is common to God and the world, it is not because the abstract notion of being is found in both of them, but because the being of the world points to the Being of God as its principle and cause. It would be an error to establish the foundation of this analogical community of being on the most abstract concept of being-in-general (*esse commune*), which is necessarily univocal;

d) The ontological priority of the principal analogate does not always mean gnoseological priority, for sometimes it is only through their effects that we acquire a knowledge of the causes. This is the case with our knowledge of God, the principal analogate of being. Though first in the ontological order, God comes after creatures in the noetical order since it is the latter that we first know and apply names to. In the order of knowledge, therefore, the meaning of our notions of being, goodness and truth applies primarily to creatures.[76]

Accommodationism

Importantly, the doctrine of analogy is also to be found in the Protestant Reformers—the difference being that the Reformers were generally not accustomed to philosophizing deeply about it. Their theory, much less complex than Thomas', is usually referred to as the *accommodation* theory or *accommodationism*. The concepts are quite similar and the manner in which analogy and accommodation are related is implicit in Donald Bloesch's statement that,

---

[76] Juan Sanguineti, *Logic* (Manila: Sinag-Tala, 1992) 68–69.

> ... the element [of] mystery in revelation ... was generally acknowledged by the church fathers and Reformers ... This means that our language about God can be, at the most, analogical, not univocal, since there can be no direct or exact correspondence between human, ideas and the veritable Word of God. It is also imperative for us to reaffirm the mystery of the *accommodation* of the Holy Spirit to the deficiencies and limitations of human language, an insight fully acknowledged by the great teachers of the church including Origen, Augustine, John Chrysostom, and Calvin[77] [emphasis added].

Accommodation refers "to the process by which God reduces or adjusts to human capacities what he wishes to reveal of the infinite mysteries of his being."[78] Calvin's well known description of the nature of revelatory language likens God's discourse with humanity to a kind of "baby talk": "God, in so speaking, lisps with us as nurses are wont to do with little children . . . Such modes of expression, therefore, do not so much express what kind of a being God is, as accommodate the knowledge of him to our feebleness."[79] For Calvin, created humans—in virtue of their bare creatureliness—simply *cannot* know God "as he is in himself" but only as he is "in *relation* to us."[80] This is to say that God discloses Himself to humanity in accord with his causal-relationality with them and condescends to the capacity of the human mind to give us a picture of who He is as our Creator. T. H. L. Parker notes that "From its very beginning, the *Institutio* teaches and practices a theology of revelation."[81] The question to be asked, according to Calvin, is not "What is God" (*quid sit Deus*), but "What is God like?" (*qualis sit Deus*) and what is appropriate to ask about His nature?[82] If God is truly like He is portrayed in Scripture, that is, "the God who cares actively for his creation and who therefore deserves man's *pietas* and *religio*, such a question as 'What is God?' betrays a complete lack of knowledge of God, apart from being unlawful curiosity about God's essence and majesty."[83]

God communicates with us analogically, which some fear but a mere euphemism for equivocity leading to agnosticism. Pinnock appears to share

---

[77] Donald G. Bloesch, "Crisis in Biblical Authority," *Theology Today* 35 (1979) 462.

[78] Edmund Dowey, *The Knowledge of God in Calvin's Theology*, 3rd ed. (Grand Rapids: Eerdmans, 1994) 3.

[79] John Calvin, *Institutes of the Christian Religion*, 1.13.1, trans. Henry Beveridge (Grand Rapids: Eerdmans, 1989) 110.

[80] Ibid, 1.10.2, 88.

[81] T. H. L. Parker, *Calvin* (London: Continuum, 2005) 14.

[82] Ibid., 16.

[83] Ibid.

this fear in his suggestion that analogy or accommodation is the inverse of taking the Bible "seriously."[84] But, for Calvin and the Reformers, the analogies employed are not just *any* analogies. They are divinely chosen and humans are *designed* as their proper recipients so that *true* knowledge is transferred.[85] B. A. Gerrish observes that, for Calvin, "God does not merely condescend to human frailty by revealing himself in the prophetic and apostolic word and by causing the Word to be written down in sacred books: he also makes his witness employ accommodated *expressions*"[86] [emphasis added]. These "expressions" are the very vehicles by which God imparts knowledge to us. Insisting upon univocal predication of God is not only to demand something of which we cannot have, but it is to diminish the inestimable value of the true disclosure God has condescended to deliver to us.

The use of anthropomorphism and metaphor in Scripture also played a big part in Calvin's understanding of accommodation. He criticized the "Anthropomorphites" who "dreamed of a corporeal God, because mouth, ears, eyes, hands, and feet, are often ascribed to him . . ."[87] To Calvin, the

---

[84] Pinnock, *Most Moved Mover*, 20.

[85] It is important to mention that Calvin's full-orbed doctrine of the knowledge of God places a central premium upon *loving* God. To truly *know* God is to *love* God. Theological knowledge is not merely propositional in nature or a matter of mere intellectual assent (*assensus*); it must also be experiential. Edward Dowey, rightly I believe, refers to Calvin's doctrine of knowledge as "existential knowledge." Edward Dowey, *The Knowledge of God in Calvin's Theology*, 3rd ed. (Grand Rapids: Eerdman's, 1994) 24.
Calvin himself writes that:

> . . . we cannot say that God is known where there is no religion or piety. I am not now referring to that species of knowledge by which men, in themselves lost and under curse, apprehend God as a Redeemer in Christ the Mediator. I speak only of that simple and primitive knowledge, to which the mere course of nature would have conducted us, had Adam stood upright. For although no man will now, in the present ruin of the human race, perceive God to be either a father, or the author of salvation, or propitious in any respect, until Christ interpose to make our peace; still it is one thing to perceive that God our Maker supports us by his power, rules us by his providence, fosters us by his goodness, and visits us with all kinds of blessings, and another thing to embrace the grace of reconciliation offered to us in Christ. [Calvin, *Institutes*, 1.2.1, 40.]

Pascal, with his quasi-Calvinist Jansenism, echoes this a century later saying, "The knowledge of God is very far from the love of Him" and that God will "only be perceived by those who seek Him with all their heart." Blaise Pascal, *Pensees*, 280, 194, trans. W. F. Trotter (Grand Rapids: Christian Classics Ethereal Library, 2002) 31, 46.

[86] B. A. Gerrish, *The Old Protestantism and the New: Essays of the Reformation Heritage* (Chicago: University of Chicago Press, 1982) 175.

[87] Calvin, *Institutes*, 1.13.1, 110.

folly of such a position is plain and the evidence of accommodation to our limited understanding clearly evident. The Scripture, for example, plainly teaches that God is a spirit (John 4:24) which by nature precludes such a literal rendering of anthropomorphism. Human beings, however, cannot possibly understand all that it means to be an eternal, self-existent, *personal* spirit. God, however, gives us a mode for *apprehending* His being even though we cannot fully *comprehend* it (*finitum non capax infinitum*).

Of course, what was apparently so obvious for Calvin is clearly not so obvious for Pinnock. Not only does Pinnock "give particular weight to [biblical] narrative," he charges others to "resist reducing important metaphors to mere anthropomorphic and accommodated language . . . We must take it all seriously, if not always literally."[88] Pinnock appears here to suggest that taking Scripture "seriously" equates with taking it literally (that is, univocally). His next step, as we have seen, is to consider God as fundamentally corporeal. Horton comments that this move on Pinnock's part "is a good example of how distinctions collapse in open theism."[89] In other words, accommodated or analogical language permits a multifaceted understanding of God's own self-disclosure in which we understand that disclosure to be constituted of sign-posts along the way to the person of God, but ones which never exhaust His being or provide a total understanding. Scripture, in this manner, can be unified in contrast to a methodological univocity which inevitably drives the theologian toward "pet passages" which are given a higher or even controlling standard over other equally relevant passages that are either downplayed or wholly ignored. Thus, an analogical approach "listen[s] to the symphony of biblical analogies, knowing that none of the analogies by itself can be reduced to the whole (univocal) score."[90] Accommodation affirms that we have a word from God, but reminds us that "to understand it [we] must pay full attention to the human words in which it is said."[91]

Application to Human History and Theodicy

The preceding discussions of foreknowledge, omnicausalism, time, and religious language, were included as further reasons in favor of the classical conception of Divine metaphysics and the weaknesses of Pinnock's newer model. This should bolster the case for a view of Divine providence

---

[88] Pinnock, *Most Moved Mover*, 20.
[89] Horton, *Beyond the Bounds*, 220.
[90] Ibid., 212.
[91] Jack Rogers, "A Response [to Avery Dulles]" in *Theology Today*, 38 (1981) 348.

in which God's involvement is not simply general and "laissez faire," but meticulous. God ordains, and therefore foreknows, the events of history and "observes" world events from the standpoint of a metaphysical simultaneity. Further, God does not *react* to situations *based on newly derived information*, nor does He become flummoxed by his indexically prior actions. God declares in Isaiah, "I form the light and create darkness, I bring prosperity and create disaster; I, the LORD, do all these things" (Isa 45:7). Indeed, "The counsel of the LORD stands forever, the plans of His heart from generation to generation" (Ps 33:11). Further, "Many plans are in a man's heart, but the counsel of the LORD will stand" (Prov 19:21) and though "The mind of man plans his way . . . the LORD directs his steps" (Prov 16:9). Indeed, "The LORD has made everything for its own purpose, even the wicked for the day of evil" (Prov 16:4).

Pinnock cannot conceive of this as anything other than a descent into a wooden fatalism.[92] Surely, though, fatalism is not advocated by the biblical writers and if my deduction of a no-risk view of providence is biblically accurate, then clearly the relational dynamic between God and humans was not construed by them to hinge upon Divine nescience or the absence of God's presence in human volition. In fact, an ironic factor that begins to emerge when comparing a "no-risk" view of providence with Pinnock's "risky" view is that Pinnock's concern for Divine immanence actually begins to look almost quasi-deistic in comparison.[93] In order to explain evil, for example, Pinnock appeals to God's "hands-off" approach in allowing humanity to freely do whatever might result from the free exercise of their wills. He writes, "Evil was not what God willed, though he did make it possible by giving freedom for the sake of love . . . The openness model accepts that certain evils ought not to be."[94] Further, "God is not in control of the powers of evil at this time in history, so they do not always play into the hands of God."[95] Pinnock cites such things as child burning[96] and the Holocaust[97] as examples.

Is this not, though, by resistless inference a decidedly *non*-immanentistic understanding of God's agency, exactly that which Pinnock wishes to avoid? Could God not have personally intervened, "for the sake of love,"

---

[92] Pinnock, *The Grace of God and the Will of Man*, 27.

[93] Robert Reymond charges Pinnock with this very deduction in his *New Systematic Theology* (Nashville: Thomas Nelson, 1998) 350.

[94] Pinnock, *Most Moved Mover*, 132–33.

[95] Ibid., 133.

[96] Ibid.

[97] Pinnock, *The Grace of God and the Will of Man*, 21.

and simply halted the Nazi atrocities once they began to occur? Not only would God here be construed to be non-immanent, but He would be truly *distant* from the horrors of Auschwitz, Dachau, etc. and the Nazi program in general. On a view of meticulous providence, however, coupled with a theodicy of intent, God was indeed sovereignly present over the events of Auschwitz to the extent that He is involved in every detail that happened. But this involvement was not for sadistic purposes in which evil was allowed to occur for the sake of evil itself. Rather, it was intended for a good purpose located in God himself that can only be viewed *sub specie aeternitatis* ("under the aspect eternity"). There is a Divine purposivity involved in historical circumstances the details of which are simply unavailable to humans as they remain situated on this side of the ontological boundary between the human and Divine. But if, as Paul says, "God causes *all things* to work together for good to those who love God" (Rom 8:28), then this is not cause for despair but part of the hope bestowed by the gospel. As Dietrich Bonhoeffer wrote from his Nazi prison cell, "I believe that God will bring good out of evil, even the greatest evil."[98] God's purpose in ordaining evils are a part of the inscrutable wisdom of his eternal purpose and plan for creation as it "groans and suffers the pains of childbirth" in redemptive anticipation (Rom 8:22).

From a purely biblical point of view, I find it manifestly impossible to read Scripture and not conclude that suffering and evil are a fundamental part of both God's will and plan. For many, this is a positively repugnant assertion. Pinnock, of course, vehemently recoils at such a notion alleging it turns God into a sadist or an "oriental despot."[99] But the challenge remains, I believe, to examine the portrait of God's agency in the Scriptures and persist in a theodicy which divorces the *purposes* of God from human suffering, blaming it instead only on Satan or the consequences of improperly exercised free will.

Though God is not pictured in the Bible as the "author" of sin, suffering, and evil *for the sake of those things in themselves*, it most certainly does teach that there is a purpose for these things behind which God stands as ultimate causal agent according to His eternal plan both for *His glory* and for the good of those who trust in Him. Peter writes to his fellow believers saying, "after you have suffered a little while, [God] will restore you and make you strong, firm and steadfast" (1 Pet 5:10). He also says that "those who suffer *according to God's will* should commit themselves to their faith-

---

[98] Dietrich Bonhoeffer, quoted in Uwe Siemon-Netto, "Justified and Sinner," *Issues Etc. Journal* (2004) 16.

[99] Pinnock, *The Grace of God and the Will of Man*, x.

ful Creator and continue to do good" (1 Pet 4:19; emphasis added). He further exhorts believers to "rejoice, though now for a little while you may have to suffer various trials, so that the genuineness of your faith, more precious than gold which though perishable is tested by fire, may redound to praise and glory and honor at the revelation of Jesus Christ. (1 Pet 1:6-7). He also says that the suffering example of Christ is a model for us in this life: ". . . Christ suffered for you, leaving you an example, that you should follow in his steps" (1 Pet 2:21).

The biblical view of evil appears such that it is ordained by God with a view toward His glory manifested in His just or merciful response to it. His justice responds to evil in punitive retribution while His mercy responds in forgiving grace. Nevertheless, God's exaction of justice and mercy both serve to magnify His own eternal glory. Evil itself is not a good thing. But when viewed *sub specie aeternitatis*, it is most assuredly a thing willed by God as a temporal phenomenon wrested in servitude to Him. Indeed, the very existence of evil itself should serve as further evidence that the universe was not principally designed with human happiness in mind but rather for the manifestation of the glorious perfections of God. This is not to say that human felicity is *at odds* with Divine glory. Quite to the contrary, it is the very awaited promise of the "elect." But it can hardly be said to be *the* means. Indeed, if human felicity is argued as the central means for the magnification of God's glory, one might question whether the program is garnering much success.

What makes us recoil from the idea that God actually ordains or wills that we suffer is a misunderstanding of precisely what it means when the Bible teaches that it is nevertheless within the sole province of the Divine will. It does not mean that God wills that anyone should suffer for the sake of suffering itself so that God watches them "squirm in agony while taking delight in it."[100] Rather, it is indicated as being for the fruit yielded by that suffering through the furnace of affliction and through Divine justice that, theologically, the glory of God is manifested, and anthropologically, the human soul is molded for eternity. God, in the inestimable wisdom extolled by Isaiah and other prophets, orchestrates all temporal events in order to bring about a good purpose—centered in His own eternal glory. Though all analogies are necessarily crude, perhaps another may help. If my purpose in bringing my children to the dentist were simply to make them feel the pain of the dentist's drill, my intent would be evil. But if my intent in subjecting my children to the pain of the drill is with the end in mind of

---

[100] Pinnock, "The Conditional View," in *Four Views on Hell*, ed. William Crocket (Grand Rapids: Zondervan, 1996) 140.

"redeeming" their teeth, then the action is a "righteous" one and the pain of the drill itself must be viewed under the aspect of its intended teleology.

The Bible seems to teach very much the same type of thing as standing behind God's temporarily willing suffering and evil in the world. Evil is transient to His overall plan. Indeed, the biblical promise is that a day is coming when perfect justice and mercy will reign and, in the end, "There will be no more death or mourning or crying or pain" (Rev 21:4). God Himself promises that He will wipe away every tear from our eyes (Rev 21:4). The present order of things will become the old order and a new day will dawn. This, after all, is central to biblical eschatology. In this sense, evil itself must be viewed eschatologically. As Wolfhart Pannenberg has argued as a component of his eschatologically-oriented systematics, salvation is processive and a fuller revelation of God's nature and purpose will come to light only within the eschatological completion of the divine plan for the world.[101]

When it is also acknowledged that Divine providence operates not only within ends, but within the very means to those ends, His agency in visiting evil or suffering upon someone can be better understood, especially as it concerns relationality. One of the deepest paradoxes of suffering is the manner in which experiencing it can manifold one's love and devotion for God. Many of Christianity's great hymn writer's were those who suffered terribly but learned through their afflictions how to better devote themselves to God.[102]

The very message of the New Testament is such that, in the victory of the cross, Jesus gained victory over sin and evil and—as His kingdom reigns *already*—He has paved the way for, what remains for us, an eschatological dualism in which the *not yet* aspect (eternal felicity with God) is still future. Jesus therefore promised His disciples that, "In this world you will have trouble. But take heart, I have overcome the world" (John 16:33). Paul affirms this saying,

> Death has been swallowed up in victory. Where, O death, is your victory? Where, O death, is your sting? The sting of death is sin,

---

[101] Wolfhart Pannenberg, *Systematic Theology*, vol. 3, trans. Geoffrey Bromiley (Grand Rapids: Eerdmans, 1998) 527–55. I agree with Pannenberg's view of progressive revelation but not with truth as being primarily eschatological in nature.

[102] Eighteenth century hymnist, William Cowper, for example, suffered from continual bouts of acute depression and even attempted suicide on several occasions. Yet he only further exulted in God's sovereignty and goodness despite his affliction and it is to him that we owe the phrase, "God works in mysterious ways." Another such hymnist was Georg Neumark who wrote many hymns in the midst of his suffering which praised God.

and the power of sin is the law. But thanks be to God! He gives us the victory through our Lord Jesus Christ. (1 Cor 15:54b-56).

He adds that "I consider our present sufferings are not worth comparing with the glory that will be revealed in us" (Rom 8:18) and that "Our light and momentary troubles are achieving for us an eternal glory that far outweighs them all" (2 Cor 4:17).

Contra Pinnock, God does appear to be in complete control of the evil that occurs in our world and is decidedly *present* in it. But His purpose for it is altogether good. Pinnock cannot envision how God could allow such terrible evils if historical events were all a part of a settled plan. It is instructive to observe, however, that the evils which Pinnock usually cites in defense of his openness model (as an objection to omnicausality) are almost always those that involved human libertarian agency.[103] No examples are given from natural evils such as earthquakes, floods, congenital defects, and so forth. Again, could God not have intervened in the birth of a mentally retarded child such that the malady were removed enwomb? Even Pinnock cannot circumvent the inescapable conclusion that it must have in some sense been God's "will" to allow a child to be born afflicted. If God, on Pinnock's view, still possesses total knowledge of the past and present, then did he not see the condition forming in the prenatal state? Why, then, did he not intervene? Pinnock's system declares God not to be in control of such evils. But if this is so, is God not further consigned to the very non-immanent hyper-transcendence he wishes to avoid? In addition, such a view raises serious questions about Isaiah's contention that God's sovereign control of history should be a cause for our further faith and trust in him, not an indictment of the Divine character in orchestrating the details of history (Isa 41:21-27; 42:8-9).

On the compatibilistic model of theodical intent I am advocating, the answer to God's actually willing that the child be born afflicted with mental retardation would again be not for the sake of the malady itself (which would indeed, I believe, establish the Divine sadism Pinnock accuses Calvinism of), but for a greater good which God intends to being out of the otherwise terrible circumstance. This does not magically transform the disease itself into something that is good rather than evil. On its own, the disease is an evil thing. The good is the *intent* attached to the ultimate Divine purposivity. In this manner, the theist does not cease to contradistinguish between good and evil. What he or she recognizes, however, is that

---

[103] For example, Pinnock, *Most Moved Mover*, 133; and *The Grace of God and the Will of Man*, 21.

both good and evil occurrences are temporally secondary in nature, having a remote cause which springs forth from an inscrutably good intention.

It was apparently quite important to Paul in his letter to the Roman church to labor the point that understanding God's good purpose in willing evil should not lead us to blur the distinction between the two. Regarding sinful unbelief, Paul makes the rhetorical statement that ". . . if our unrighteousness demonstrates the righteousness of God, what shall we say?" (Rom 3:5). Paul does not doubt that human unrighteousness does indeed do this very thing by providing an opportunity for God to demonstrate His justice is response to it. But he then adds the question "why not say (as we are slanderously reported and as some claim that we say), let us do evil that good may come?" (Rom 3:8a). Paul responds to this by denying such a practice and states that those who contend as much are justly condemned for their *own* intentionality (Rom 3:8b). This again suggests a theodicy of intent coupled with a creational glory teleology. God will make his own righteousness known by punishing the sinful unrighteousness of humans. But for a creature to take upon himself the prerogative of committing evil in order to glorify God is a falsehood and those who would do as such in reality sin for they are acting against the preceptive will of God which admonishes them to obey God's commands and leave the "sorting of things out" to God alone. In effect, the individual would be assuming the mantel of God in attempting to complete His own purposes for Him, instead of acting in accord with the subordinate role given him by God. As argued in the last chapter, humans are held accountable for following God's preceptive will *only*, in marked contradistinction to the decretive or dispositional wills.

Fatalism Versus Glory Teleology

We still may ask, however, whether the preceding arguments merely reduce us to puppets as Pinnock contends. Is this really fatalism cloaked behind the curtain of purpose? I believe the answer to this begins in a further consideration of the "glory teleology" I proposed earlier and that an understanding of God's foreordination of all events, including good and evil (and the eternal destinies of individuals) must begin here and work its way downward. This view not only rejects Pinnock's "logic of love"[104] methodology which he uses to explain both theodicy and personal eschatology, but that it admits of a frightful severity in God which makes Him, and Him alone, the central concern of the universe and which puts him at the center of every natural event. This, in part, is where I sense a reluctance on the part

---

[104] Pinnock, *Most Moved Mover*, 131.

of some Reformed theologians in their ostensive interest to preserve the Divine benevolence. I will argue, however, that this "extreme" understanding of theocentricity is itself also a "good." Indeed, it is that which provides the basis for a Reformed reconstruction of relational reciprocity between creature and Creator.

It has been said that the most basic, vital philosophical question concerns why there is anything at all. Why is there something rather than nothing? For the theist, the question has a ready answer: God is the reason why something exists instead of just pure nothingness. Further, the fact that something exists *contingently* means that something else exists *necessarily*. That is, something has always existed that has the intrinsic power of being wrapped up entirely within itself. God is *a se*, He is self-existent and has always been. He has no beginning and no end. Were this not true, then there would be nothing now. For, *ex nihilo nihil fit*, out of nothing, nothing comes. If there has ever been a time when God was not, there would be nothing now, including God. Or, there would be an infinite regress of causes and effects extending back into eternity's past which is *prima facie* absurd. For an infinite regress of causation is no more able to cause itself than a *single* phenomenon.

Thus, God exists and explains the phenomenon of the material universe. But for the theist, the questioning certainly does not find its terminus there. For he or she, there is no question more awe-inspiring than *why* the eternal God created. Alternative theories such as Pinnock's "logic of love" are many. Perhaps God created in order to produce joy; or He created to show His love and to be loved; He created to generate the possibility of mutual relationships; He created to generate communities of fellowship; He created in order to redeem, and various others.

But if my view of meticulous providence is correct, then none of these theories are adequate. For they would then merely feed upon one part of the architectonic of the Divine plan and confuse it for the whole. It is a sort of synecdochical fallacy, much like someone calling the moon nothing but an object of orbitation while forgetting its illumination. But more, such theories fail to properly account for doctrines crucial to a full-orbed *sola Scriptura* understanding of God's nature and His activity in creation. The doctrine of Hell, for example, is a particularly pernicious and troublesome doctrine for those who treat of God's creative activity as suggested above and as Pinnock does. Hell becomes the "enemy" of God instead of His own creation. Even in Pinnock's version of conditionalism, it is God that does the eschatological annihilating which itself could hardly be called a "good" on it's own. Conditionalism is also a minority position and has a difficult time addressing those biblical passages which appear to speak very clearly about a living Hell which consists of never-ending duration.[105]

I would further argue that any non-glory teleology for creation also runs the risk of making God out to be "needy" as though He needed love relationships or communities beyond that inherent within His own triune nature which is itself eternally *relational*. How could such a conclusion be avoided on Pinnock's view that God created the world for the sake of love in which the outcome is *hoped* for but innately unknown? God often becomes a very disappointed person in Pinnock's model, while at other times He becomes *happier*. It might also suggest a Divine expansionism of some sort in which openness theology is pushed further toward processianism.

Critics of my own view, of course, will recognize that the accusation of neediness on the part of God might also be made, however, with equal force in regard to a glory teleology. In other words, we might ask whether God Himself was somehow in need, or in short supply, of His own eternal glory that He found it necessary to increase it through creation. I do not believe, however, that the glory motif suffers from this implication as Pinnock's love model does.

Creation as Inter-Triune

The key to understanding the preceding is a recognition of the act of creation as entirely inter-Triune. It is *by* the Trinity and *for* the Trinity that creation was instantiated and now presently sustained. Paul, for example, writes that "all things have been created through Him and for Him" (Col 1:16b). It is a constituent part of the perichoretic tri-unity of the Godhead in which the temporal order is an active and manifest gift from the Son to the Father through the Holy Spirit and in which the three are mutually glorified. In the incarnation, the Father pours himself into the Son, and the Son—doing whatsoever the Father does (John 5:17)—returns this gift to the Father. Creation is a thoroughly reciprocal creative activity within the being of God. It is *activity* rather than *necessity* issuing from lack. John Piper writes:

> . . . when God says that He created us for His glory, it cannot mean that He created us so that He would become more glorious, that His beauty and perfection would be somehow increased by

---

[105] Arguments against conditionalism are beyond the scope of this work. To mention one of them, however, Jesus appears to weaves a parallelism in Matthew 25:46 between the eternality of salvation in heaven, and the eternality of reprobation in Hell saying that the reprobate, "will go away to eternal punishment, but the righteous to eternal life." See also, Matt 10:15; 11:21-24; 16:27; Luke 12:47-48; John 15:22; Heb 10:29; Rev 20:11-15; 22:12.

us. It is unthinkable that God should become more perfectly God by making something that is not God. It is a staggering but necessary thought that God has always existed, that He never came into being, and that everything which exists which is not God is from His fullness and can never add anything to Him which did not come from Him. That is what it means to be God . . . This means that when God says, He made us for His glory, He does not mean He made us so that He could become more glorious in Himself. Instead [this] means that He created us to display His glory, that is, glory might be known and praised.[106]

The creation is an *expression* of God's glory rather than a means to enhance it. The Bible pictures God as creating for His glory, according to His own sovereign predilection and good pleasure (Rev 4:11; Phil 3:13b) and that God "rejoice[s] in his works" (Ps 104:31).

When this is contrasted with a "risky" view of providence in which God creates merely the *possibility* of love relationships (His primary creative orientation), yet is frustrated when they fail, it is God who awaits in anticipation to behold the end result of His creative work and, inexorably, His own felicity hangs in the precarious balance of what *humans* decide. Pinnock must concede that the Divine "gamble" of creation could have resulted in precisely *no one* choosing to love God, or perhaps very few. Indeed, one must wonder how God, on the openness view, must "feel" about the success of His project so far. How much has the world historically loved Him? How have they typically chosen to exercise their supposed powers of autonomy? Following on the heels of the twentieth century, by all accounts the bloodiest in human history, the answer does not seem to be a particular encouraging one.

Creation, then, though ontologically separate from God, is nevertheless an inter-Triune activity. It is a part of the wondrous and enigmatic circuminsession of the Triune Godhead in which unending glory is manifested in every meticulous Divine action. Christ's sacrifice on the Cross and subsequent resurrection—performed in time-space—is itself an *incarnation* of the glory shared in the Godhead and its diffusive expression for one another. The Son is the "radiance of God's glory" (Heb 1:3) and "the Image of the invisible God" (Col 1:15), but performs His loving-glorifying service unto the Father. Human beings are relationally *brought into* this purchasing gift and are presented to the Father inter-Trinitarily. They are adopted into it and made a part of the eternal Triune activity, though they are also

---

[106] John Piper, "God Created Us For His Glory," [sermon] (Minneapolis: Bethlehem Baptist Church, 1980) 2.

to be distinguished from it. Believers are not a constituent element of the Tri-unity of God in a sort of crass pan[en]theism, but rather are brought *in* to it and share in God's glory, *by glorifying Him*. Creation in this sense is *by* God, *in* God, *for* God.

Neglecting to adequately reflect upon the mutually-interrelated Trinity in eternal subsistent relations as the basis upon which to predicate genuine Divine-human relationality, I believe, has been the seedling of Pinnock's assertion that God, sans an autonomously-free creation, is in some kind of "majestic solitude" that renders him a "solitary monad."[107] Pinnock calls upon God's "gracious interactivity" with humans as the locus of his glory instead of locating it in the Trinity itself. This is to hinge too much on humans and to make God's own felicity dependent upon them. Consequently, it is also to ascribe something autonomously glorious to humans which they can render in turn to God—something God had not had before. But what else is *in* humans that God lovingly adores other than Himself? This assertion will be unpacked further in the next chapter as I attempt to reconstruct Divine-human relationality within a meticulously-providential, compatibilistic framework. But we must further lay some groundwork in understanding the Tri-unity of God as subsistent relations and how this relates to the creative purpose.

My intention here is not recapitulate the lengthy and complex historical development of the doctrine of the Trinity as embodied in the early ecumenical creeds[108] (especially the Nicene and Constantinopolitan). Rather, I take the orthodoxy and accuracy of these creeds as the base upon which I explore the mystery of the Triune perichoresis as subsistent relations.[109]

Augustine, echoing the early creeds, wrote that ". . . the Father, and the Son, and the Holy Spirit is one God, the Creator and Ruler of the whole creature; and that the Father is not the Son, nor the Holy Spirit either the Father or the Son, but a trinity of persons mutually interrelated, and a unity of an equal essence."[110] The Bishop of Hippo expands on this mutual interrelatedness of the Trinity in an enormously helpful passage from *De Trinitate*:

> . . . if the Father, in that He is called the Father, were so called in relation to Himself, not to the Son; and the Son, in that He is called

---

[107] Pinnock, *Most Moved* Mover, 5–6.

[108] For this, I recommend Reymond, *New Systematic Theology*, 317–41.

[109] See the Nicene Creed: http://www.reformed.org/documents/nicene.html; the Constantinopolitan Creed: http://www.reformed.org/documents/2_council_of_constan.html.

[110] Augustine, *De Trinitate*, IX.1, trans. Arthur Haddan (Grand Rapids: Christian Classical Ethereal Library, 2005) 170.

> the Son, were so called in relation to Himself, not to the Father; then both the one would be called Father, and the other Son, according to substance. But because the Father is not called the Father except in that He has a Son, and the Son is not called Son except in that He has a Father, these things are not said according to substance; because each of them is not so called in relation to Himself, but the terms are used reciprocally and in relation each to the other; nor yet according to accident, because both the being called the Father, and the being called the Son, is eternal and unchangeable to them. Wherefore, although to be the Father and to be the Son is different, yet their substance is not different; because they are so called, not according to substance, but according to relation, which relation, however, is not accident, because it is not changeable.[111]

Augustine calls attention here to the fact that the Trinity, while unchangeable, is never *inert*. Indeed, even sans creation, it would be manifestly impossible for God ever to be a "solitary monad." Rather, the Triune God exists in an eternal relational reciprocality in which the Tri-unity of God is fully *in act*. This is quite unlike human relationships which always manifest themselves in continual potentiality, which can indeed lead to *solitude*. This ongoing potentiality necessarily means that human beings never exist in a purely relational state which, in turn, means that they can never give themselves completely over to one another. But as Thomas Weinandy explains, this is not true of God:

> The persons of the Trinity are eternally constituted in their own singular identity only in relation to one another, and thus they subsist as who they are only within their mutual relationships. In their relationships to one another each person of the Trinity subsistently defines, and is equally subsistently defined by, the other persons. Thus the persons of the Trinity are subsistent relations. These mutual subsistent relationships, which constitute and define the identity of the persons of the Trinity, are founded upon origin and action.[112]

Given the inter-Triune subsistency, we note, then, that the Persons of the Trinity "are fully, completely, and absolutely relational."[113] Indeed, to refer to God as *the Trinity*, is to refer to God as *the Relationship*. Calvin notes that the recognition of the mutual subsistence of the three persons

---

[111] Ibid., V.5. 121.

[112] Thomas Weinandy, *Does God Suffer?* (Notre Dame, Ind.: University of Notre Dame Press, 2000) 116.

[113] Ibid., 118.

is the only manner in which to maintain both the unity and tri-versity of God:

> When we profess to believe in one God, by the name God is understood the one simple essence, comprehending three persons or hypostases; and, accordingly, whenever the name of God is used indefinitely, the Son and Spirit, not less than the Father, is meant. But when the Son is joined with the Father, relation comes into view, and so we distinguish between the Persons . . . In this way the unity of essence is retained, and respect is had to the order, which, however derogates in no respect from the divinity of the Son and Spirit.[114]

We only speak of Father, Son, and Holy Spirit in terms of relationship and, thus, every time we enjoin God as "Father," bespeak his native relationality. Weinandy notes that because the persons of the Trinity are eternally subsistent relations,

> . . . they are relations in act and only relations in act. As designating subsistent relations or relations fully in act, the terms "Father," "Son," and "Holy Spirit" are therefore *verbs*, for they refer to, define, and name, solely and exclusively, the interrelated acts by which all three persons are who they are. The Father is not "someone" who possesses fatherhood. The term "Father" designates that the Father is completely and solely "fatherhood in act" . . . the Son is sonship itself for he is begotten by the Father in the Spirit and so gives himself in the same Spirit to the Father as Son.[115]

We must now carry this back over into the creational orientation of the Trinity. That the instantiation and processive nature of creation is entirely inter-Triune for the circuminsessionary pleasure and glory of the Godhead is made uniquely manifest in Jesus' High Priestly Prayer recorded in the Fourth Gospel. The information revealed in this prayer concerning the Divine purpose for creation is deeply rich and I will draw upon its themes throughout the remainder of this chapter and the next.

> Jesus spoke these things; and lifting up His eyes to heaven, He said, "Father, the hour has come; glorify Your Son, that the Son may glorify You, even as You gave Him authority over all flesh, that to all whom You have given Him, He may give eternal life.

---

[114] Calvin, *Institutes*, I.13.20, 127.
[115] Weinandy, *Does God Suffer*, 118.

"This is eternal life, that they may know You, the only true God, and Jesus Christ whom You have sent.

"I glorified You on the earth, having accomplished the work which You have given Me to do. Now, Father, glorify Me together with Yourself, with the glory which I had with You before the world was.

"I have manifested Your name to the men whom You gave Me out of the world; they were Yours and You gave them to Me, and they have kept Your word.

"Now they have come to know that everything You have given Me is from You; for the words which You gave Me I have given to them; and they received them and truly understood that I came forth from You, and they believed that You sent Me.

"I ask on their behalf; I do not ask on behalf of the world, but of those whom You have given Me; for they are Yours; and all things that are Mine are Yours, and Yours are Mine; and I have been glorified in them.

"I am no longer in the world; and yet they themselves are in the world, and I come to You. Holy Father, keep them in Your name, the name which You have given Me, that they may be one even as We are one . . .

"The glory which You have given Me I have given to them, that they may be one, just as We are one; I in them and You in Me, that they may be perfected in unity, so that the world may know that You sent Me, and loved them, even as You have loved Me.

"Father, I desire that they also, whom You have given Me, be with Me where I am, so that they may see My glory which You have given Me, for You loved Me before the foundation of the world.

"O righteous Father, although the world has not known You, yet I have known You; and these have known that You sent Me; and I have made Your name known to them, and will make it known, so that the love with which You loved Me may be in them, and I in them." (John 17:1-11;22-26)

No passage of Scripture better condenses and explicates both the glory-teleology and the nature of Divine-human relationality I am advocating as a replacement to Pinnock's. This prayer of Jesus sheds light on both the thoroughly perichoretic nature of the glory-oriented purpose and activity in both creation and redemption, as well as the reciprocal, unitive-relational component between Father and Son which is *brought over* into humanity through the adoptive work of subsuming the "elect" *in to* this unitive relationality. This theme will be discussed in greater detail shortly as I move from the theocentric aspects of creation into the anthropological benefits that issue from it. For the moment, however, this inter-Triune glory-centered creational orientation must be dealt with more fully.

The Theocentricity of a Glory Teleology

That God's primary reason for creating is for the purpose of His own glory may strike us as unspeakably self-centered. I reply, in short, that this assessment is fundamentally correct in at least one important aspect—creational orientation. A better term, however, which might help to avoid the pejorative attachments of *self-centered*, is *self-focused*. In this respect, I will in fact argue that God is *calculatedly* self-focused.

The Scriptures present God as one who not merely invites, but literally *demands* worship of Himself (Ps 83:18; 86:10; Neh 9:6). He is a "jealous God" (Ex 20:5) who does "not yield [His] glory to another" (Isa 48:11). Scriptural anthropology locates any revulsion we might have toward this self-focusedness of God squarely on humanity, rather than in some faulty hubris on the part of the Deity. The self-focusedness of God confronts us with the miserable, joyless situation in which we find ourselves—that we are repelled by the notion rather than finding delight and repose in it and perceiving further cause for praise. If God is *self*-focused, humans are to be *God*-focused. Such God-focusedness is the highest calling and greatest pleasure of humanity. This is at the heart of Augustine's opening words of the *Confessions* when he says:

> Man is one of your creatures, Lord, and his instinct is to praise you. [But] He bears about him the mark of death, the sign of his own sin, to remind him that you thwart the proud. But still, since he is a part of your creation, he wishes to praise you. The thought of you stirs him so deeply that he cannot be content unless he praises you, because you made us for yourself and our hearts find no peace until they rest in you.[116]

The desire to praise and glorify God and an innate sense of His presence (*sensus Divinitatis*) is a natural part of human existence because humans are created to be finite mirrors who reflect God's infinite glory. Yet because fallen humanity bears what Augustine calls the "mark of death," we are transiently dislodged from the ultimate purpose to which we are created. We have become spiritually inoculated against the glory teleology of the universe. Thus, God's own self-focus repels us when it should rather

---

[116] Augustine, *Confessions*, I.1, 21.

fill us with inestimable delight. We construe it as an acute case of megalomaniacal narcissism when Scriptural anthropology indicates that we should *desire* to adoringly receive the centrality of God's glory as a treasure of the highest sublimity.

It is interesting that John Calvin opens the *Institutes* very similarly to Augustine's opening of the *Confessions*—with a register of human misery as we attempt to fill the spiritual vacuum that repairs only when the creature begins to align him or herself, by Divine grace, with God's own creational *teleos*. This human design was not lost in the primordial Fall. Rather, humans are now torn in two directions. On one hand, the deepest desire of our hearts is to know, love, and glorify God. On the other, an inherent blindness to the proper object of our affections plagues us. Thus men and women turn inward, focusing on the self for *self*-fulfillment when, in fact, their very nature only lends itself to *God*-fulfillment. Thus, we can say, "The man who knocks on the door of a brothel is looking for God."[117] The inevitable misery that issues from this distortion is therefore used of God heuristically to point humans away from themselves and toward their Creator. Thus Calvin writes:

> . . . no man can survey himself without forthwith turning his thoughts towards the God in whom he lives and moves . . . Here, again, the infinitude of good which resides in God becomes more apparent from our poverty. In particular, the miserable ruin into which the revolt of the first man has plunged us, compels us to turn our eyes upwards; not only that while hungry and famishing we may thence ask what we want, but being aroused by fear may learn humility. For as there exists in man something like a world of misery, and ever since we were stript of the divine attire our naked shame discloses an immense series of disgraceful properties every man, being stung by the consciousness of his own unhappiness, in this way necessarily obtains at least some knowledge of God. Thus, our feeling of ignorance, vanity, want, weakness, in short, depravity and corruption, reminds us, that in the Lord, and none but He, dwell the true light of wisdom, solid virtue, exuberant goodness. We are accordingly urged by our own evil things to consider the good things of God; and, indeed, we cannot aspire to Him in earnest until we have begun to be displeased with ourselves. For what man is not disposed to rest in himself? Who, in fact, does not thus rest, so long as he is unknown to himself; that is, so long as he is contented with his own endowments, and unconscious or

---

[117] This quote is reported to come from G. K. Chesterton, but its origin is disputed. This version is quoted in Brent Curtis and John Eldredge, *The Sacred Romance* (Nashville: Thomas Nelson, 1997) 136.

unmindful of his misery? Every person, therefore, on coming to the knowledge of himself, is not only urged to seek God, but is also led as by the hand to find him.[118]

We learn something of our true condition and, at the same time, something of the radiance of God's unique glory, in part, by the inevitable sorrow we encounter in a context of existential estrangement. The sting of this estrangement points us away from ourselves and toward the theocentricity of glory.

Self-centeredness is a social evil. But the Bible does not portray the self-focusedness of the Triune God as an evil at all. Why? First we must ask what constitutes the depreciatory nature of *creaturely* self-centeredness. The answer to this, in a word, is *creatureliness* itself. The prerogative of self-focusedness is one reserved for the deserving. Creatures cannot justifiably claim this prerogative for themselves because they are in the inextricable position of an undeserving state. For a finite human being to demand worship of him or herself would make that person a narcissistic sociopath of the first order meriting scorn at least, if not confinement befitting a lunatic. We would worry deeply over the person claiming that all human eyes should focus solely in their direction. Finitude does not possess the requisite of infinite glory which makes debtors of friends and enemies alike, and places an *injonction de payer* on the willing and unwilling. The Bible pictures God as the only being thoroughly warranted in His self-centeredness, grounded in His own infinite worth (2 Sam 22:4; Ps 18:3; Rev 4:11; 15:4). Not only does God exult in His own glory, but He calls upon his creation to follow suit. God is to be *self*-focused, while we are to be *God*-focused. This is a matter not so much of morality as one of logic. The grounding logic of impious self-focusedness is a creature's unworthiness, but the logic of justified self-centeredness is the Creator's infinite worth. We need a thoroughly metaphysical theology, as I will seek to demonstrate further, if we are to begin effectively sustaining a relational anthropology oriented in communion with a self-focused God.

Of course there are dangers in ascribing such self-focusedness to God. J. Scott Horrell, for example, argues against the notion saying, "We discover that the three-personed God of Scripture is profoundly and infinitely self-giving. The God of Love in calling for glory is not necessarily selfish at all. His glory is a shared glory, each delighting in the other."[119] The

---

[118] Calvin, *Institutes*, I.1.1, 37–38.

[119] J. Scott Horrell, "The Self-Giving Triune God, The Imago Dei and the Nature of the Local Church: An Ontology of Mission." Paper delivered at the Evangelical Theological Society Annual Convention (Santa Clara, Cal., 1997) 5.

potential pitfall of subscribing to the self-focusedness of God is to negate the equally important *self-giving* nature of the Godhead of which Horrell speaks. Worse, it runs the risk of accusing God of the worst sort of narcissistic pathos. To be sure, I do not dispute for a moment that the relational Trinity is *inherently self-givingly* reciprocal, nor that God delights in freely sharing His love with humans as He brings them into adoptive communion with Himself. Further, the mystery of the gospel itself is God the Son incarnationally condescending to humanity and freely giving of Himself in an unspeakable act of loving grace. In so doing, the Lord has provided humanity with the paradigmatic model of *selfless* giving.

The two poles may seem contradictory, but they are not. The selfless giving of the Son, in relation with the Father and Spirit, changes nothing of the creational self-focusedness of the Trinity. What Horrell and others overlook, I believe, is that by calling humans to be focused only on Himself, God is self-givingly inviting them into the very spiritual nexus which will fill their deepest, God-given desires. God's self-focusedness is our great benefit. The incarnation and resurrection have paved the way to make this *our* gift. But we must not forget that the incarnation and resurrection were also intended to bring glory to the Trinity in virtue of the Redeemer. Christ's paradigmatic standard of selfless giving *itself* calls glory to the Godhead. Jesus says, "If I glorify Myself, My glory is nothing; it is My Father who glorifies Me" (John 8:54). He also prays, "Father, the hour has come; glorify Your Son, that the Son may glorify You" (John 17:1). The act of Redemption is a reciprocity of Trinity-glorifying movements.

The gospels present us with a paradox concerning God's glory wherein we learn that for us to exult in it, as God Himself does, is to produce in us a spiritual joy of matchless pleasure. It is a joy that confounds the world and often causes it to recoil with contempt as it searches for an alternative remedy to its discovered mire of estrangement. The fullness of this joy comes to those who concern themselves not with the *self* but with what they should joyously render unto their Creator. Jesus portrays death to oneself as the gateway to paradise (John 12:20-33).

Chapter Summary

This chapter began by providing arguments in favor of exhaustive Divine foreknowledge, coupled with a compatibilistic understanding of human freedom. A subsequent discussion of the relationship between God and time argued that God simply cannot be related to time in the same manner as humans (as Pinnock contends). Just as God transcends space, so too must he transcend time. In speaking of God's nature, and how to conceive of it within finite understanding, I argued for both analogical predication and Reformed accommodationism. This does not suggest that our speech about God is flatly incorrect, but that it is incomplete. We may apprehend truths about God, but we cannot fully comprehend God.

An application of the issues of foreknowledge, compatibilism, time, and religious language was made to our understanding of history, with special emphasis on the problem of evil. I argued that God ordains, and therefore foreknows, the events of history and "observes" world events from the standpoint of a metaphysical simultaneity. Further, examples of God's reacting to events within the flow of time are to be understood as anthropomorphic in nature, not an indication of the temporal limitedness or nescient disposition of God.

Lastly, I argued for a creational glory teleology and fundamentally God-centered universe. To be God-centered is to enter into the highest calling and greatest delight of humanity. Each of these elements have laid the groundwork for what the next chapter brings together as the final step in reconstructing Divine-human relationality.

6

Toward a Reformed Reconstruction of Divine-Human Relationality

THE LAST two chapters laid the groundwork for what I now bring together as the final step in reconstructing Divine-human relationality upon the substructure of compatibilism, meticulous Divine sovereignty, and a Trinitarian glory motif which I have maintained is a more coherent and orthodox system than that proposed by open theism. I have already stated my sympathy with Pinnock's desire to preserve a theology that remains deeply relational. I have further argued, however, that such relationality is untenable on Pinnock's openness view due to its unsustainable reliance on both libertarian human freedom and a purely "logic of love" creational orientation.

In order to understand the anthropological context in which I offer a Reformed reconstruction of Divine-human relationality, I first offer here a brief word about the nature of the human soul. My purpose is twofold. First, to provide a workable understanding of human constitution such that it can be better seen how we are to conceive of our relational dynamism with the Trinity. Secondly, to proactively avoid a descent into pantheism by maintaining the distinct created personhood of individuals as they are made *one* with God. This *oneness* is the relational model I will argue for following this section in which I center on the *Christus in nobis* principle and elements of theōsis.

The Human Soul

Discourse concerning theological anthropology often becomes a deeply complex exercise in which proponents attempt to marshal evidence for a dualistic substance ontology, a quasi-monistic relational ontology, or some other form of understanding. Indeed, numerous recent theological works have attempted to approach Divine-human relationality along these lines as a sort of post-Kantian project in which theological anthropology is directed away from substance ontology toward a more versatile, less category-based relational ontology.¹ Such was also the concern of the existentialists like Kierkegaard who contested "the dualistic legacy of Plato and the popular conception of the soul or self as substance, comparable to the body. The self is essentially intangible and must be understood in terms of possibilities, dread, and decisions."²

My own sense of such discussions is that they tend to become too mired in attempting to disprove one or another position and that, in the process, lose sight of the possibility of a more dialectical approach in which human ontology may be thought of as *both* substantial *and* relational in which the two are designed to function in existential tandem. Indeed, human nature may be such that a substance ontology is not opposed whatsoever to relational ontology, but rather that the former is the very equipment designed to facilitate the relational paradigm. It thus becomes the very God-glorifying machinery for which it was designed.

Pure substantialism or relationalism concerning the soul, then, are extremes to be avoided. Descartes, for example, so embraced substance dualism that it led him to separate any function of the physical brain from truly *thinking*. Minds think, but lack spatial magnitude; physical bodies have spatial magnitude, but do not think. To solve the problem, Descartes forwarded the pineal gland as the interfacial mechanism between the non-physical mind and the physical brain and even considered it the seat of the soul.³ The view is quite obviously wrong,⁴ but that it ever gained currency bespeaks the degree to which an over-indulged philosophy of substance dualism can force us into intellectual chambers. Even apart from the contemporary scientific insights which explode the view, on its own it is self-referentially absurd, begging the question: How does a *physical* gland mediate between the physical and the non-physical? Would the gland itself not need a mediator of its own? An infinite regress ensues.

---

[1] See, for example, F. Leron Shults, *Reforming Theological Anthropology: After the Philosophical Turn to Relationality* (Grand Rapids: Eerdmans, 2003) and Nancey Murphy, *Bodies and Souls, or Spirited Bodies?* (Cambridge: Cambridge University Press, 2006).

[2] Walter Kaufmann, *Existentialism From Dostoevsky to Sartre* (Hecho En Brattleboro, Ver.: New American Library, 1975) 17.

[3] Descartes, "Passions of the Soul," *Descartes, Selected Philosophical Writings*, trans. John Cottingham et al. (Cambridge: Cambridge University Press, 1988) 231. For a helpful analysis of Descartes' view of the nature and function of the pineal gland and it's consequence regarding substance dualism, see Gert-Jan Lokhorst, "Descartes and the Pineal Gland," in *The Stanford Encyclopedia of Philosophy* (Stanford: Stanford University, 2005) http://plato.stanford.edu/entries/pineal-gland.

[4] See Lokhorst, "Descartes and the Pineal Gland," 3.1–3.2.

Well known, also, is the manner in which substance dualism heavily dominated the anthropological trajectory of the Medieval scholastics. The contradistinction between form and substance, for example, is an Aristotelian brew of which Aquinas drank deeply in identifying the functions of body, soul, and intellect. The body is added to an "intellectual soul" to provide it with "an organ of equable temperament."[5] Aquinas adds to this a dizzying discussion of the various categories, functions, and powers of the soul. There are five genera of powers of the soul. Of these, three are called souls themselves including the rational, the sensitive, and the vegetative. Four of these genera Thomas calls "modes of living" and include the sensitive, intellectual, appetitive, and locomotive.[6] He attempts to further breakdown the manner in which each soul and mode is exemplified and interconnected. The discussion certainly is not *"un*biblical" *per se*, but it is mercilessly taxing and, when finished, leaves one with an image of human beings divided up among jelly jars variously labeled "Substance X," "Substance Y," etc. Augustine also, unfortunately, had an overly-dualistic conception of the body and soul which tended to derogate the value of the former.[7]

Thinkers like Spinoza, on the other hand, so identified with anthropological monism that it led him to a broader *metaphysical* monism wherein "God" became synonymous with *nature* and the Creator-creature distinction was terminally muffed. Indeed, "Every substance is necessarily infinite."[8] In Spinozian monism, "only God is substance—full stop."[9] Numerous modern attempts have resulted in one thinker after another plunging themselves into either an overly dichotomic or hyper-physicalist view. These extreme views, in turn, have a tendency to give rise to the need for abandoning one or more Vincentian dogmas bearing on theological anthropology such as the *imago Dei*, the Fall, and inherited sin.

On the matter of the soul, I take the general position of the Reformers. Unlike the Medieval scholastics, the Reformers tended to avoid these sorts of discussions because of the seemingly interminable rabbit trails they cre-

---

[5] Thomas Aquinas, *Summa Theologica*, 1.76.5, trans. Fathers of the English Dominican Province (Grand Rapids: Christian Classics Ethereal Library, 1999) 502.

[6] Ibid, 1.78.1, 518–19.

[7] For a thorough discussion of Augustine's body-soul dichotomy, see Roland Teske, "Augustine's theory of soul," in *The Cambridge Companion to Augustine* (Cambridge: Cambridge University Press, 2001) 116–22.

[8] Benedict de Spinoza, *Ethics*, Part I, Proposition 8. Trans. R. H. M. Elwes (Murfreesboro, Tenn.: MTSU Philosophy WebWorks Hypertext Edition, 1997) http://www.mtsu.edu/~rbombard/RB/Spinoza/ethica1.html (November 10, 2004).

[9] D. W. Hamlyn, *History of Western Philosophy* (London: Penguin, 1987) 157.

ate, preferring instead to simply grant the biblical terms of *spirit* and *body* and to recognize a *distinction*, yet without a *separation*. Luther, of course, detested overly-philosophical discussions concerning theology and showed little reluctance in hurling invective at those whom he felt placed too heavy an emphasis on reason. Terms like "pagan beasts," "rascals," "stinking philosophers," and "billy goats" were common fare for Luther when describing those who he thought over-philosophized.[10] Calvin sometimes referred to philosophers with such terms as "stupidity" or "madness."[11]

Though I do not share the extent of Luther and Calvin's disdain for philosophy, I do resonate with their wish to avoid over-philosophizing the precise nature of theological anthropology. Barring the invective, I agree with the Reformers that in so doing, the various mind-body philosophies have been unceasingly discordant and that, "for the edification of [the church] a simple definition will be sufficient."[12] Of necessity, this must include some rudimentary understanding of both the nature of the soul and the manner in which it can be "indwelt" by the spirit of God. Here, I advance Calvin's view which he sums up thusly:

> . . . the soul is incorporeal...not properly enclosed by space . . . [though it] occupies the body as a kind of habitation, not only animating all its parts, and rendering the organs fit and useful for their actions, but also holding the first place in regulating the conduct. This it does not merely in regard to the offices of a terrestrial life, but also in regard to the service of God . . . [T]he principal action of the soul is to aspire [to unity with God].[13]

Calvin speaks plainly about a material and immaterial self, nevertheless conjoined, unified, and inseparable (save the supernatural power of God to do the latter, for example, at death in which the immaterial soul is translated to an immaterial existence[14]). As Calvin does not make an attempt at philosophically dissecting the body-soul problem, so too do I remain agnostic on the matter. I categorically reject neither anthropological monism nor dualism, but rather wish to acknowledge that both bespeak an aspect of the truth concerning a *di*unity in the ontology of man. The New Testament appears to speak plainly about the constituent nature of

---

[10] John Gerster, et al, *Classical Apologetics* (Grand Rapids: Zondervan, 1984) 196.

[11] John Calvin, *The Institutes of the Christian Religion*, 1.5.11, trans. Henry Beveridge, (Grand Rapids: Eerdmans, 1989) 59.

[12] Ibid., 1.15.6, 167.

[13] Ibid.

[14] A crude analogy might be radio signals still existing absent a mechanical body (that is, a transistor) in which to operate or become "animated."

humanity as a unity of both *soma* (body) or *sarx* (flesh) and *psuche* (soul) or *pneuma* (spirit). Paul, for example, tells the church at Philippi that "if I am to live on in the flesh [*sarx*], this will mean fruitful labor for me; and I do not know which to choose. But I am hard-pressed from both directions, having the desire to depart and be with Christ, for that is very much better; yet to remain on in the flesh [*sarx*] is more necessary for your sake" (Phil 1:22-24). Jesus appears to imply the di-unity of the body-soul make-up of humanity when he taught his disciples to "not fear those who kill the body [*soma*] but are unable to kill the soul [*psuche*]; but rather fear Him who is able to destroy both soul [*psuche*] and body [*soma*] in hell" (Matt 10:28). In another place he says "That which is born of the flesh is flesh [*sarx*], and that which is born of the Spirit is spirit [*pneuma*]" (John 3:6). In looking at the biblical evidence, I agree with John Cooper who writes that,

> The problem is not with the body-soul distinction per se but with understanding it in terms of a dualistic Greek matter-spirit worldview or a dualistic medieval nature-supernature worldview . . . there is no tension between affirming that God created us as integrated physical-mental-spiritual bearers of his image on earth and at the same time holding that God keeps persons in existence between bodily death and future resurrection . . . A biblical Reformed view both insists on a kingdom-focused vision of the Christian life and an adequate body-soul distinction.[15]

On a creational glory motif, I take human ontology to be naturally subservient to this goal as body and soul *united* are intended to serve as living vessels of God's glory.

The *Christus in Nobis* Principle

Following the constitution just outlined, I believe the key to understanding the genuineness of Divine-human relationality to be situated in a deeper understanding of the *Christus in nobis* principle commended most notably by the Reformers, but expanded upon in the concept of *theōsis* notable in Antiochene patristical theology. This latter concept has been largely ignored by classical Western systematicians, especially those of the Evangelical persuasion (though not always unjustifiably so, as I will address shortly, being partly theological caution but also partly historical confusion). Consideration of the *Christus in nobis* principle, coupled with

---

[15] John Cooper, "The Importance of Reformed Anthropology for Ethics," *Theological Forum* 21.1 (1993) 12.

elements of theotic soteriology forms the central component of my alternative model of relationality to Pinnock's open theism.

My argument centers around the *Christus in nobis* principle being operatively "top down," stemming from God's own self-glorifying purpose. It is this very purpose which secondarily establishes genuine relational love between the human and Divine. Relational love in Pinnock's model is located *anthropologically* as humans do or do not autonomously appropriate it. Yet Pinnock himself has offered no explanation concerning why a particular human agent uses his or her libertarian freedom to move in one direction or the other, nor *where* human love for God comes from. It is simply declared to be the result of their own uncaused free will.

A curious irony emerges in this scheme when we consider that its stated intention is to rescue relational dynamism. For, when relational love is located anthropologically, God's love itself becomes metaphysically immobile and "aloof" *until it is drawn upon by the human agent*. That is, God's love does not "move" unless it is first *moved on*, or, invited to do so. It does not incur into our world unless it is first given requisite permission by the recipient. God, then, becomes like a stationary "love bank" from which human beings make autonomous withdrawals as they are so moved by the vacillations of their will. Thus, it is not that "we love because he first loved us" (1 John 4:19), but that we marshal love in ourselves *first* in order that God might love us in proportion to our own autonomous initiative. God does not inspirit His own love into human hearts monergistically such that love for Him is the natural and inevitable fruit (as argued in chapter four). Rather, God *responds* to human agents as *they* seek and love Him. God takes His salvific cues from humans.

Building upon my previous arguments for monergistic regeneration, my replacement model for relational dynamism takes the *Christus in nobis* principle and reverses this order through an outworking of meticulous and purposive providence that serves God's own self-glorifying orientation. It grounds the love of God in humans *theologically*. Human love for God is established *in God* such that its reality is produced in humans precisely *because* it is God's own self-love *given and returned* as the faithful are brought into adoptive communion with the Trinity. As Thomas Schreiner and Ardel Caneday put it, "Our love is a response to and the effect of [God's] love for us."[16]

The principle is rather simple: one must *desire* love in order to act upon it. The biblical portrait of humans is such that the choices they make

---

[16] Thomas Schreiner and Ardel Caneday, *The Race Set Before: A Biblical Theology of Perseverance and Assurance* (Downer's Grove, Ill.: InterVarsity, 2001) 330.

must *of necessity* issue from the desires of their heart, or, their *nature*. As such, the will itself is "the mind choosing according to its desires," not a detached faculty that turns itself wherever it desires in the absence of prior inclination. Pinnock's model separates the *choice* of love, from the *desire* of love. For, if a human agent chooses to love God, is this not merely an expression of the love already present in that person which stimulated them into action? And, if so, from whence did that love issue? If all that *love* is, *God* is (1 John 4:16)[17], then genuine love must issue from the creative Architect of love itself. It must, in turn, be given in order to be acted upon. Love is not "created" by humans, but by God.

Christus in nobis ("Christ in us") speaks to the mystical union (*unio mystica*) in which the faithful are translated following a unilateral pneumatological regeneration. *Christus in nobis* and *unio mystica* are closely allied terms. I will use both where appropriate, though—for purposes of this work—I prefer the former term in that it appears to me to better communicate the operative principle at work in which the latter is established. At times, I will use them almost synonymously, but I nevertheless deliberately choose one term over the other in order to bring out a nuanced difference between the "mechanism" and the "fruit." Union with Christ is the basis for genuine relationality; *Christus in nobis* is the theologically-centered, unilateral principle which produces that reality in accord with meticulous providence.

Wayne Grudem describes the doctrine of union with Christ as, "a phrase used to summarize several different relationships between believers and Christ, through which Christians receive every benefit of salvation. These relationships include the fact that we are in Christ, He is in us, we are like Christ, and we are with Christ."[18] A. H. Strong observes that the doctrine encompasses both regeneration and conversion which in turn encompass "repentance, faith, justification, and sanctification"[19] (To this I add *glorification* which I deal with in my consideration of theōsis). *Christus in nobis* applies to every step—beginning, middle, and end—of the *ordo salutis*.

The reality of genuine union with Christ was hardly a tangential idea to the New Testament writers. Nor is it something mentioned in only a handful of scattered biblical texts. Indeed, it is *thematic* in no less a fashion than the doctrine of justification, perhaps even more so. Numerous

---

[17] See discussion on pages 122–27.
[18] Wayne Grudem, *Systematic Theology* (Grand Rapids: Zondervan, 1994) 840.
[19] Augustus Strong, *Systematic Theology* (Valley Forge, Pa.: Judson, 1907) 793.

passages bear on this important subject—several of which I will address in a moment. Strangely absent, however, is an explicit treatment of the mystical union (much less theōsis) within the broader corpus of doctrinal arrangement and integration in most of the popular post-Reformational *Evangelical* systematic theologies. Of the roughly forty-eight major theologians since the Reformation who specifically composed a systematic theology (or that which closely resembles one), only nine of them include an explicit treatment of the mystical union.[20]

I see two possible reasons for this. First, it is another example of Evangelicalism and Western theology in general concentrating more heavily on the forensic and objective (contra subjective) aspects of systematization. A second possible reason is what I perceive to be a general reluctance on the part of Evangelicals to address anything deemed to be too "mystical" or anagogic and, therefore, that which tends not to lend itself as well to systematization as the more *legal* aspects of theology do. For many Evangelical systematicians, the words *mystical* or *mysticism* do not carry with them positive connotations. They seem to smack of a faith in which emotions and doctrinal relativism rule over the synthesization of propositional content. (The situation is arguably worse concerning the deification theology I consider later).

Nevertheless, the absence of such explicit treatments is particularly bizarre considering the words of one well-known Reformed theologian who speaks of the mystical union as actually being "the *central* truth of the whole doctrine of salvation not only in its application but also in its once-for-all accomplishment in the finished work of Christ"[21] [emphasis added]. He adds that, "the whole process of salvation has its origin in one phase of union with Christ and salvation has in view the realization of other phases of union with Christ. . . . Union with Christ is the central truth of the whole doctrine of salvation."[22]

The *Christus in nobis* teaching is certainly deeply mysterious and exceedingly difficult to systematize. Indeed, Calvin wrote that, "this mystery of the secret union of Christ with believers is incomprehensible by nature."[23]

---

[20] These figures are based, in part, on Wayne Grudem's cataloguing of systematic theologies in Appendix 4 of his *Systematic Theology*, 1224–30. The nine exceptions include theologians Louis Berkhof, Robert L. Dabney, Millard Erickson, Wayne Grudem, Edward Arthur Litton, Edgar Young Mullins, Robert Reymond, Augustus H. Strong, and Henry Clarence Thiessen.

[21] John Murray, *Redemption Accomplished and Applied* (Grand Rapids: Eerdmans, 1984) 161.

[22] Ibid., 161, 170.

[23] John Calvin, *Institutes of the Christian Religion*, 4.17.1, trans. Henry Beveridge (Grand

Given the already problematic nature of philosophical anthropology, the ease with which it can be misunderstood and therefore misconstructed is a present danger even at its most basic levels. Yet the Reformational forbears of modern Evangelicalism, notably Luther and Calvin, placed a tremendous premium upon the importance of recognizing Christ's personal activity in the mystical union. Luther, for example, so emphasized the vitality of this union that he spoke of those adopted into God's family as being . . .

> . . . so intimately with Christ, that He and you become *as it were one person*. As such you may boldly say: "I am now one with Christ. Therefore Christ's righteousness, victory, and life are mine." On the other hand, Christ may say: "I am that big sinner. His sins and his death are mine, because he is joined to me, and I to him."[24] [emphasis added]

Calvin, perhaps even more so than Luther, placed *central* emphasis on the believer's union and *oneness* with Christ. I find it both strange and unfortunate that this emphasis of Calvin's seems to so often go unnoticed even by those who thoroughly espouse his theology.[25] Abraham Kuyper remarked that "although Calvin may have been the most rigid among the reformers, yet not one of them has presented this, *unio mystica*, this spiritual union with Christ, so incessantly, so tenderly, and with such holy fire as he."[26] Calvin writes that "to that union of the head and members, the residence of Christ in our hearts, in fine, the mystical union, *we assign the highest rank*, Christ when he becomes ours making us partners with him in the gifts with which he was endued. Hence we do not view him as at a distance and without us, but as we have put him on, and been ingrafted into his body, he deigns *to make us one with himself*, and, therefore, we glory in having a fellowship of righteousness with him."[27] [emphasis added]. Calvin further draws upon this oneness language saying, "Christ does not so much come to us as become encumbered with our nature to make us one with

---

Rapids: Eerdmans, 1989) 557.

[24] Martin Luther, *Commentary on St. Paul's Epistle to the Galatians* (Grand Rapids: Zondervan, 1939) 77

[25] For example, no less a Calvinist than B. B. Warefield, in his essay "The Theology of John Calvin," while correctly stating that "the doctrine of predestination is not the formative principle of Calvinism" but only "its logical implication" stemming from "God in His majesty," he nevertheless makes no mention of Calvin's stress upon our mystical union with God. [B. B. Warefield, "The Theology of John Calvin"; http://www.the-highway.com/theocal_Warfield.html (December 21, 2005).

[26] Abraham Kuyper, *The Work of the Holy Spirit*, trans. Henri De Vries (Grand Rapids: Eerdmans, 1946) 325.

[27] Calvin, *Institutes*, 3.11.10, 46.

him."[28] He elaborates on this by drawing a distinction between the unitive and legal aspects of Christ's indwelling:

> The phrase *in ipso* (in him) I have preferred to retain, rather than render it *per ipsum* (by him) because it has in my opinion more expressiveness and force. For we are enriched in Christ, inasmuch as we are members of his body, and are engrafted into him: nay more, being made one with him, he makes us share with him in every thing that he has received from the Father.[29]

As Evangelicals and their predecessors have attempted to systematize biblical doctrine since the sixteenth century, the *Christus in nobis* principle has generally been eclipsed theologically by the more justificatory principle of *Christus pro nobis* ("Christ *for* us"). *Christus pro nobis* speaks to doctrines more specifically concerned with satisfaction, atonement, and justification. These are obviously vital concerns to Reformational and post-Reformational theology, yet in explicating them, the resultant *unitive* aspect of soteriology has not received nearly as much attention as it deserves. Mention is made here and there (often in sermons), but substantial scholarly treatments are noticeably lacking. This deficiency may, in part, be why Pinnock and other self-styled immanentists have felt the need to recourse into a totally different construction of the Divine complexion in their efforts to save relationality—not realizing that a fuller-orbed understanding of the mystical union (as well as elements of the theōsis paradigm) may be viable solutions (which also retain the benefits of remaining in fidelity with the broader Vincentian understanding of the incommunicable Divine attributes including exhaustive foreknowledge). Instead, Pinnock recasts nearly the entire doctrine of God in order to rescue that which doubtfully needs rescuing.

Of course, the manner in which the mystical union is understood will be markedly different depending upon each theologian's particular integrating motif for theological discourse. That which forms his or her apical feature for doing theology (for example, love, glory, community, etc.) "trickles down" into every other aspect of their theological program. It shapes the contours of the theologian's primary doctrine of God, the doctrine of creation, and conception of theological anthropology and bears crucially upon libertarian or non-libertarian suppositions. Pinnock's theological agenda is dominated by *love* as the focal point for doing theology and this has in-

---

[28] John Calvin, *Commentaries*, trans. and ed. Joseph Haroutunian (Philadelphia: Westminster, 1958) 598.

[29] John Calvin, *Commentary on Corinthians*, vol. 1, trans. John Pringle (Grand Rapids: Christian Classics Ethereal Library, 1999) http://www.ccel.org/c/calvin/comment3/comm_vol39/htm/viii.ii.htm (October 10, 2004).

formed his understanding of God's nature, the purpose for creation, and of the general faculties of humanity.

I have already argued that love is an inadequate starting point and have replaced it with *glory* as the optimal integrating motif for systematic discourse. Concomitantly, I have argued for glory as the most basic characteristic of God and, consequently, as the fundamental creational teleology of the universe. Part of God's glory includes meticulous sovereignty which then issues in a non-libertarian view of theological anthropology. Naturally, then, the remaining discussion concerning the mystical union is borne of these suppositions.

Key passages in this discussion (along with John 17 as quoted earlier) include those wherein a refrain is seen of believers being "in" Christ, and Christ "in" believers. We are "in Christ" (*en Christō*), "in Him" (*en autos*) (alternatively "in him," that is, Christ in the believer), "into Christ" (*eis Christon*), "in the Lord" (*en kyriō*), and "in Me" (*en emoi*). For example, 2 Corinthians 5:17: ". . . if anyone is in Christ [*en Christō*], he is a new creature; the old things passed away; behold, new things have come." Jesus declares, "Whoever eats my flesh and drinks my blood remains in me [*en emoi*], and I in him [*en autos*]" (John 6:56). In Ephesians, Paul says: "Blessed be the God and Father of our Lord Jesus Christ, who has blessed us with every spiritual blessing in the heavenly places in Christ, just as He chose us in Him [*en autos*] before the foundation of the world, that we would be holy and blameless before Him" (Eph 1:3-4). And also, ". . . we are His workmanship, created in Christ Jesus [*en Christos Iesous*] for good works, which God prepared beforehand so that we would walk in them" (2:10). Paul says to the Colossians that ". . . the mystery which has been hidden from the past ages and generations, but has now been manifested to His saints, to whom God willed to make known what is the riches of the glory of this mystery among the Gentiles, which is Christ in you [*Christos en umin*], the hope of glory." The very mystery (greek: *musterion*; literal: "secret") which has been revealed is the *Christus in nobis* principle itself. Paul says to the Galatians that, "I have been crucified with Christ; and it is no longer I who live, but Christ lives in me" (Gal 2:20a). In other places, Paul refers to Christ and the church as the head and body (Eph 1:22-23; 4:12-16; 5:23-32). This "in" language has enormous implications for the manner in which the believer carries out God's work. Paul says "continue to work out your salvation with fear and trembling, *for it is God who works in you* to will and to act according to his good purpose" (Phil 2:12a-13) [emphasis added].

Jesus uses parables to describe the mystical union such as a vine and branches: "'Abide in Me, and I in you. As the branch cannot bear fruit of itself unless it abides in the vine, so neither can you unless you abide in Me. I am the vine, you are the branches; he who abides in Me and I in him, he bears much fruit, for apart from Me you can do nothing'" (John 15:4-5). Jesus also speaks of dwelling within the believer: "If anyone loves Me, he will keep My word; and My Father will love him, and We will come to him and make Our abode with him" (John 14:23).

The *Christus in nobis* principle is as difficult to grasp as it is important. So deeply mysterious is it, that a conscious limit to the parameters of analogy and apophaticism often seem warranted. What is it *really* to be made *one* with God? Kuyper observed that the mystical union in which Christ indwells us:

> . . . has a nature peculiar to itself; it may be compared to other unions, but it can never be fully explained by them. Wonderful is the bond between body and soul; more wonderful still the sacramental bond of holy Baptism and the Lord's Supper; equally wonderful the vital union between mother and child in her blood, like that of the vine and its growing branches; wonderful the bond of wedlock; and much more wonderful the union with the Holy Spirit, established by His indwelling. But the union with Immanuel is distinct from all these . . . It is a union invisible and intangible; the ear fails to perceive it, and it eludes all investigation; yet it is very real union and communion, by which the life of the Lord Jesus directly affects and controls us. As the unborn babe lives on the mother-blood, which has its heart-beat outside of him, so we also live on the Christ-life, which has its heart-beat not in our soul, but outside of us, in heaven above, in Christ Jesus.[30]

Kuyper's comparisons are quite useful. Especially poignant, I find, is the metaphor of mother and child. When a child, a baby for example, is left to itself crying, it is unconnected and, in a sense, *inauthentic* to use a Heideggerian term.[31] It is not as though the baby has either ceased to exist, nor that it lacks distinct personhood. Rather, it is ungrounded in estrangement. Its world is one of unrelated aloneness. Yet, when the mother arrives, and the baby beholds her face, the child's world is transformed. The child is enveloped in the world of the mother and is "authenticated" in the sense of being grounded and relationally contextualized as the child "subsists" in its life source or sustainer. Similarly, our unitive bond with Christ trans-

---

[30] Kuyper, *The Work of the Holy Spirit*, 337.
[31] Martin Heidegger, *Being and Time* (New York: Harper & Row, 1962) 232.

forms our world of disconnected aloneness into one in which *the Lord is our world*. This unspeakable bond is incomplete in this life, though progressively increased through sanctification (and *theotic* in nature as I will soon arguer). As such, God's elect are caught between two worlds: the world of man which is ultimately one marked by unceasing estrangement, and the world of the Lord which is our true home.

Metaphors and analogies abound in descriptions of the *union mystica*. The Puritan Thomas Watson referred to the mystical union as "a marital union between Christ and believers" and suggested that its composition was twofold.[32] First, it forms a natural union which all human beings share, believer and unbeliever alike. This natural union is presented due to Christ having taken on human nature whereas the same was not done of the angelic realm (Heb 2:16). For Watson, however, this union was merely incidental and bore no significance upon being *relationally* united with Christ.

The second, however, was what Watson called the "sacred union."[33] By this, Watson believed, we are mystically united to Christ. He admits that "It is hard to describe the manner of it…It is hard to show how the soul is united to the body, and how Christ is united to the soul. But though this union is spiritual, it is real."[34] Oddly, Watson adds the statement that this "union with Christ is not personal."[35] Watson was apparently concerned that if we spoke of Christ as being personally united with us, it would be tantamount to Christ's essence being transfused into the person of a believer such that all the person does becomes meritorious.[36] Watson preferred, then, to think of the mystical union in more objective terms. First, the union is *federal*. Second, it is *effectual*. It is federal in the sense that believers are federally represented by Christ. It is effectual in the sense that Christ becomes *conjugally* united to the faithful. In this sense, believer's become "one" with Him.

I find much of what Watson says concerning the union to be helpful. The conjugal metaphor is certainly Scriptural (for example, Matt 9:15; Luke 5:35; John 3:29; Rev 21:2) and does say something of the *positional* nature of the union. I fear, however, that Watson's treatment of the mystical union reduces to merely objective elements (indeed *forensic*) instead of including both the objective and subjective. Watson calls the union spiritual,

---

[32] Thomas Watson, "Mystical Union between Christ and the Saints," in *The Godly Man's Picture* (Edinburgh: Banner of Truth, 1987) 35.

[33] Ibid.

[34] Ibid.

[35] Ibid., 2.

[36] Ibid.

but denies that it is personal. When considering the union, it is difficult to see what the operative difference is between the spiritual and the personal or what Watson's statement accomplishes. Is Christ's spirit *non*-personal? Even on the purely conjugal understanding, why cannot the union still be thought of as a personal one? Indeed a *deeply* personal one? Watson may be trying to avoid pantheism with this statement, by which the person of Christ and person of the human become so amalgamated as to be nearly annihilated. As I will argue later, though, this need not be the case.

Watson is also not clear about what problem is presented by the idea of meritorious works being performed by the Christian as they issue from the mystical union. If, for example, those very works were actually *given* to them by God (Eph 2:10) and it is God that works in them to do them (Phil 2:12-13), then they are the fruit, not cause, of the unitive work of the Trinity made manifest in the life of the believer. Further, such meritorious works could be conceived of as being rewarded in which the reward (and its basis) were both given as gifts of grace from God. I believe Watson to be a brilliant expositor of the Christian faith, but these issues underscore the manner in which wrestling with an understanding of the mystical union has been difficult in the forensics-dominated Western theological climate.

Augustus Strong may have moved toward a better balance of the objective and subjective elements of the union with Christ. Strong writes, "As the Holy Spirit is the principle of union between the Father and the Son, so he is the principle of union between God and man. Only through the Holy Spirit does Christ secure for himself those who will love him as distinct and free personalities."[37] He further underscores the subjective aspects in tandem with the concept of "mutual interpenetration":

> The Scriptures declare that, through the operation of God, there is constituted a union of the soul with Christ different in kind from God's natural and providential concursus with all spirits, as well as from all unions of mere association or sympathy, moral likeness, or moral influence, a union of life, in which the human spirit, while then most truly possessing its own individuality and personal distinctness, is interpenetrated and energized by the Spirit of Christ, is made inscrutably but indissolubly one with him, and so becomes a member and partaker of that regenerated, believing, and justified humanity of which he is the head.[38]

---

[37] Strong, *Systematic Theology*, 793.

[38] Ibid., 794.

For Strong, to be a Christian at all is to literally *indwell* with Christ. It is more than "mere juxtaposition or external influence."[39] Christ's work is not performed as an *external* agent, but as one conjoined *within* the very nature of the redeemed. Loving God and obeying His commands is *granted* by the Spirit of God Himself inclining and motivating the secondary agent to do so.

Louis Berkhof recognized two equal and opposite dangers when considering the subjective union. One is to understand the union as "a union of essence, in which the personality of the one is simply merged into that of the other, so that Christ and the believer do not remain distinct persons."[40] The other is to . . .

> . . . represent the mystical union as a mere moral union, or a union of love and sympathy, like that existing between a teacher and his pupils or between a friend and friend. Such a union does not involve and interpenetration of the life of Christ and that of believers. It would involve no more than a loving adherence to Christ, friendly service freely rendered to him, and ready acceptance of the message of the Kingdom of God.[41]

This latter error is built on the philosophy of libertarianism and, as I have argued, is the unavoidable deduction of it. The love of God on Pinnock's view is chosen autonomously and voluntaristically according to the vicissitudes of the will. But as I have argued, this love has no *theologically* grounded explanation, but in fact becomes anthropocentric and quasi-deistic.

If, however, Pinnock's human libertarianism/Divine nescience model runs the risk of deism, perhaps my own runs the opposite risk of pantheism due to a putative blurring of the axiomatic (that is, orthodox) God-world distinction. To some, this may seem a logical inference to the extent that God is "in" all events—especially here as it concerns the mystical union operative through *Christus in nobis*. But herein lies the crucial link between Divine-human relationality and a workable model of providence. I have maintained that Divine omnicausalism *grounds* human significance as opposed to destroying it. I have also labored to show that Pinnock's model is unsustainable both logically and biblically and that we must therefore locate relationality in view of meticulous, compatibilistic providence.

---

[39] Ibid., 800.
[40] Louis Berkhof, *Systematic Theology*, (Grand Rapids: Eerdmans, 1996) 451
[41] Ibid.

Deism and pantheism are the equal and opposite errors that can result from an unorthodox doctrine of providence. Berkhof was wary to consider the dangers of both. First, regarding deism, he writes that,

> . . . God's concern with the world is not universal, special, and perpetual, but only of a general nature. At the time of creation He imparted to all His creatures certain inalienable properties, placed them under invariable laws, and left them to work out their destiny by their own inherent powers. Meanwhile He merely exercises a general oversight, not of the specific agents that appear on the scene, but of the general laws which He has established.[42]

The degree to which this description of deistic providence mirrors that of Pinnock's openness theology is striking. We recall Pinnock writing that, "God does not will to rule the world alone but wants to bring the creature into his decisions . . . God does not choose to rule the world without our input. It also suggests that the future has not been exhaustively settled."[43] Rather, "God . . . grants humans significant freedom to cooperate with or work against God's will for their lives" and "works with human decisions, adapting his own plans to fit the changing situation."[44] On this model, it is humans, not God, that first determine the steps of the future and God who responds or reacts to whatever is decided by them. Here again, I find God's immanence in human affairs dwindling, not increasing as God "waits to see" how the drama of human history will play out and whether or not His will for it will be accomplished. Further, it is humans creating their own love for God from somewhere within, not the love of God being wrought *en Christō*.

But what of the pantheistic implication of the *Christus in nobis* principle being engendered theologically according to meticulous Divine sovereignty? Berkhof is again helpful and provides a guard against misconceiving the mystical union within a faulty treatment of providence:

> Pantheism does not recognize the distinction between God and the world. It either idealistically absorbs the world in God, or materialistically absorbs God in the world. In either case it leaves no room for creation and also eliminates providence in the proper sense of the word. It is true that pantheists speak of providence, but their so-called providence is simply identical with the course of nature, and this is nothing but the self-revelation of God, a self-revelation that leaves no room for the operation of second causes in any sense

---

[42] Ibid., 167.
[43] Pinnock, *Most Moved Mover* (Grand Rapids: Baker, 2001) 42.
[44] Pinnock, et al, *The Openness of God* (Downer's Grove, Ill.: InterVarsity, 1994) Preface.

of the word. From this point of view the supernatural is impossible, or, rather, the natural and the supernatural are identical, the consciousness of free personal self-determination in man is a delusion, moral responsibility is a figment of the imagination, and prayer and religious worship are superstition.[45]

Berkof's allusion to "second causes" is important in avoiding what could otherwise descend into a Calvinistic pantheism. The Westminster Divines apparently recognized the importance of making a distinction between both the idea that *God does everything as sole and immediate cause*, and the idea that, *God causes some things, nature or man the other*. The famous formulation produced at their hands was that God's sovereign ordination of temporal events neither does "violence . . . to the will of the creatures, nor is the liberty or contingency of second causes taken away, but rather established."[46] In classic pantheism, however, God is All, and All is God leaving no room for a distinction between either world and God, nor between primary and secondary causation. On a classical or Reformed model, however, it is a mistake to think of God as working in the world apart from secondary causes.

God's actions neither fill a gap in human action, nor do they rob the creature of its own causal agency such that the functions of human proximate causation are in any way rendered disingenuous. Rather, the causal agency of creaturely acts in the world are the result of living in the uncreated power of God as pure act. Thus, the mystery of God's providence in the acts of finite agents is the presence of His uncaused power superintending creaturely agency. God acts wholly through His creation—its ends and its means—and, as such, is wholly present in each event, just as each proximate agent is wholly present in the specific act and established in it thereby. A *single* effect results from primary and secondary causation, not separate accounts, while as yet, the two stand in different relationships to the effect. One, the human, operates in finite causal succession; the other in infinite, non-indexical self-existence.

In functioning as the primary cause operative through secondary causes in nature, God so empowers humans to be causes themselves, such that they are *genuine* causes. It is in this manner that the Westminster Divines conceived human causal agency not to be vanquished but rather established, and it is similarly this which crucially distinguishes meticulous Divine sovereignty from a crass pantheism in which causal distinctions

---

[45] Berkhof, *Systematic Theology*, 168.
[46] Westminster Confession of Faith (1646) III.1; http://www.creeds.net/reformed/Westminster/c05.htm (April 20, 2003).

are not made. God is thus everywhere present and active, working within the world to carry out the Divine purpose within a system that subsumes creaturely efficacy. Instead of pitting Divine and human cause against one another as separate forces (that is, in which human autonomy is espoused), this model espouses a decidedly *both/and* scenario that "guarantees the integrity of the created causal nexus while affirming the gracious and intentional immanence of the transcendent God active within worldly purposiveness."[47] This is a distinction made both by Aquinas in the Scholastic tradition,[48] and by Jonathan Edwards in the Reformed.[49]

In applying these considerations to the phenomenon of the *unio mystica*, we can conclude that believers do indeed *invite* Christ into union with them as distinct individuals and, as such, proximate causes through an act of the will. But this act of the will is superintended by the providence and

---

[47] Elizabeth Johnson, "Does God Play Dice? Divine Providence and Chance," *Theological Studies* 56 (1996) 13. It should be noted that, while I agree with Johnson's language in this passage, I do not share her conclusions in the broader essay.

[48] Aquinas writes: "Though a natural thing produces its own effect, it is not superfluous for God to produce it, because the natural thing does not produce it except in the power of God. Nor is it superfluous, while God can of Himself produce all natural effects, for them to be produced by other causes: this is not from the insufficiency of God's power, but from the immensity of His goodness, whereby He has wished to communicate His likeness to creatures, not only in point of their being, but likewise in point of their being causes of other things . . . When the same effect is attributed to a natural cause and to the divine power, it is not as though the effect were produced partly by God and partly by the natural agent: but the whole effect is produced by both, though in different ways, as the same effect is attributed wholly to the instrument, and wholly also to the principal agent." [Thomas Aquinas, *Summa Contra Gentiles*, III.70.R2, 3, trans. Joseph Rickaby (London: Burns and Oates, 1905). Jacques Maritain Center at the University of Notre Dame: http://www.nd.edu/Departments/Maritain/etext/gc.htm (December 29, 2005).] And also, rather simply, ". . . the providence of God produces effects through the operation of secondary causes." [Thomas Aquinas, *Summa Theologica*, I,q23,a5. Trans. Fathers of the English Dominican Province (Grand Rapids: Christian Classics Ethereal Library, 1999) 176].

[49] Edwards distinguishes between "true" cause and "vulgar" cause. He writes of the latter that it is ". . . that, after or upon the existence of which, or the existence of it after such a manner, the existence of another thing follows." [Jonathan Edwards, "The Mind," 26, *The Works of Jonathan Edwards* 1 (Grand Rapids: Christian Classical Ethereal Library, 2003) 416.]. True cause, however, is to thought of as self-existent and not subject to *succession*: ". . . when we speak of cause and effect, antecedent and consequent, fundamental and dependent, determining and determined, in the first Being, who is self-existent, independent, of perfect and absolute simplicity and immutability, and the first cause of all things: doubtless there must be less propriety in such representations, than when we speak of derived dependent beings, who are compounded, and liable to perpetual mutation and succession." [Jonathan Edwards, *Freedom of the Will*, IV.VII.4 (Grand Rapids: Christian Classical Ethereal Library, 2000) 145. True cause is to be thought of as *sufficient* cause, which only God can render (See ibid., II.IV.2, 31)].

purposes of God as First Cause in which He *inclines* the whole person. The human agent is not the sufficient cause of the *unio mystica* in either an initial or ongoing sense, but exhibits cause as the fruit of God's first working the miracle of regeneration in them and continuously in their sanctification. In accord with the arguments made earlier,[50] this cannot be said to be a violation of the human will. Rather, the will itself—as created by God—is liberated and given a new direction. The desires of the will itself are supplanted. The will which formerly raged against the unitive presence of God's in one's life is eliminated.

Thus, my alternative to Pinnock's model results in a genuine relationality on an omnicausal footing that issues *not* from autonomous human choice, nor from a pantheistic blurring of the Creator-creature distinction and the ordering of causes. Rather, it brings together God's own creational glory teleology with a doctrine of providence that translates the believer *into Christ* such that the perichoretic Trinity delights in Himself and His own glory, *in us*. Blaise Pascal rightly said that,

> The God of Christians is not a God who is simply the author of mathematical truths, or of the order of the elements . . . He is not merely a God who exercises His providence over the life and fortunes of men, [in order] to bestow on those who worship Him a long and happy life. . . . the God of Abraham, the God of Isaac, the God of Jacob, the God of Christians, is a God . . . who fills the soul and heart of *those whom He possesses*, a God who makes them conscious of their inward wretchedness, and His infinite mercy, who *unites Himself to their inmost soul*, who fills it with humility and joy, with confidence and love, who *renders them incapable of any other end than Himself*.[51] [emphasis added]

There *is no love* that humans can render unto God other than *God's own love* relationally given to them. Relationality is reciprocally given, returned, and received as believers are brought *into* the very being of God Himself as creatures who mutually benefit from enjoying their own subjective experience of this union; a union that nevertheless begins, obtains, and subsists in God's own being. This model avoids what I have argued are the "laissez faire," deistic implications of Pinnock's model on the one hand, while avoiding pantheism on the other. It makes the creational initiative a Divine "glory activity" rather than a necessity, and grounds the vitality of existence *theologically* rather than anthropologically. Indeed, the unitive

---

[50] See section 4.3 on pages 137–46.

[51] Blaise Pascal, *Pensees*, 556 (Grand Rapids: Christian Classics Ethereal Library, 2002) 90.

benefits poured over to us through Christ, *are* a principle means through which God is glorified. Oswald Chambers wrote that becoming spiritually awakened "exhibits . . . the very life of God Himself. The individual person is [brought] into a personal oneness with God, and God's stride and His power alone are exhibited."[52]

It might be said further that this model avoids fatalism by locating *purposivity* in God, rather than according to some mechanistic necessity. God calls His elect, according to unmerited favor, in order to bring them into Himself that they may glorify and enjoy Him forever. That love *for* the Divine, is *itself* Divine in origin leads the recipient into the praise of the glorious perfections of the Deity. Human beings are not created that, perchance, they might love God out of their own volition but that God's own love might be manifested in them as an expression of His glory and self-giving nature.

Theotic Relationality

To the foregoing discussion of *Christus in nobis* and the *unio mystica*, I now add a consideration of the theōsis concept commonly associated with the East.[53] My use of the term theōsis is almost synonymous with the mystical union, the difference being one of emphasis. It is my hope that elements of theōsis may further elucidate the *Christus in nobis* principle as one in which Christians truly become *divinized*. Theōsis relates to *Christus in nobis* in speaking of *operation*. It is God's very Being shared *with* and *in* His elect that effects the oneness that is salvation itself.

There are, of course, manifold risks in appropriating a theotic component into the broader framework of the relational model I have been presenting. Chief among these risks is the possibility for ambiguity and misunderstanding, especially that which results in a gross overstatement of the doctrine. My intention is to unpack an understanding of theōsis that provides the substructure for Divine-human relationality, but which nevertheless remains in fidelity with Reformed theology and in which the

---

[52] Oswald Chambers, "Getting Into God's Stride," October 12, *My Utmost For His Highest* (Uhrichsville, Ohio: Barbour, 1935, 1993).

[53] Interestingly, Pinnock at one point began considering *theōsis* for incorporation into his system in the context of his pneumatology and its relationship to our union with God; see, *Flame of Love: A Theology of the Holy Spirit* (Downers Grove, Ill.: InterVarsity, 1996) 150–51. This consideration seems to have been left undeveloped, however, as Pinnock subsequently began to concentrate more heavily on the development of his openness project. Of course, I will later argue in this chapter that theotic soteriology works *best* in a *Reformed* context. Nevertheless, I am interested to see if Pinnock will return in the future to his consideration of theōsis and how it might affect his current view of Divine-human relationality.

Creator-creature distinction is thoroughly upheld. No doubt, *any* Christian formulation of the doctrine of theōsis must set an impassable limit on its elucidation which guards against the idea of created humanity ever being construed to become, ontologically, God or *a* god.

Thus, my advocation of the doctrine is one in which God's elect do literally share or become "partakers" in the Divine, but in which their creaturely status and individual personality is not distorted or erased. On the contrary, the theotic aspect of *Christus in nobis/unio mystica* does not involve erasure of the human person, but *actualization*. Our entire person—mind, body, soul—are designed to be in communion with the Trinity, to be totally embraced by God, and enveloped by the glory of the Lord.

It is further the case that the cause of the "glory" that God's elect will exude in the eschaton is always theologically centered and, in this sense, not an autonomously generated phenomenon but a *finite* reflection and enjoyment of *Infinite* glory. A Reformed doctrine of theōsis must be consistent with the monergistic soteriology articulated in chapter four. This distinguishes a uniquely Reformed theōsis from others in which the engagement of *autonomous praxis* and *assent* is often thought to be necessary in order to appropriate or attain theōsis as a kind of reward for holy behavior. A Reformed understanding must ground theōsis and its fruits in the unilateral operation of God in the believer in both ends and means. As such, theōsis is certainly in a sense "acquired" through praxis, but never autonomously. It is rather the processive product of God working in, through, and for the believer to His own eternal glory.

As I have already alluded, *theōsis* (literally "deification") and the cognate *theōpoiesis* ("being made God") are terms that tend to mean very different things to varying ecclesiastical bodies. In Roman Catholic theology, theōsis has not typically been thought of as either primarily eschatological nor as a universal phenomenon applicable to *all* Christians. Rather, it is entirely a *hic et nunc* phenomenon capable of realization among a select few people of saintly stature. Further, unlike some other versions of theōsis, it is not thought of as a state of sinless perfection or completed sanctification. Rather it is "a more perfect knowledge of God possible in this life, beyond the attainments of reason even enlightened by faith, through which the soul contemplates directly the mysteries of Divine light. The contemplation in the present life is possible only to a few privileged souls, through a very special grace of God: it is the *theōsis mystike enosis*."[54] Theōsis, in much

---

[54] George Sauvage, "Mysticism," in *The Catholic Encyclopedia*, ed. K. Knight, 2002; http://www.newadvent.org/cathen/10663b.htm (October 12, 2004).

of Western Catholicism, is a rarely attained temporal enlightenment and is more experiential than ontological.

Theōsis has also been used within the Wesleyan Methodist tradition (especially in the Pietist Movement) to describe the possibility of *realized sanctification* in the course of this life. Wesley himself referred to realized sanctification as "the highest state of grace" or as being "perfected in love" and that those who claim to have "attained" it in this life should be "exhort[ed] . . . to pray fervently, that God would show them all that is in their hearts"[55] to be sure that the attainment is true. Roman, Reformed, and Lutheran bodies have uniformly rejected the Wesleyan interpretation. Indeed, some four centuries earlier at the Council of Vienne (1311) the Roman general council declared to be heretical the notion that "a person in this present life can acquire a degree of perfection which renders him utterly impeccable and unable to make further progress in grace."[56] The Westminster Divines opposed the idea of realized sanctification saying "sanctification is throughout, in the whole man; yet imperfect in this life, there abiding still some remnants of corruption in every part; whence arises a continual and irreconcilable war, the flesh lusting against the Spirit, and the Spirit against the flesh."[57] Lutherans stressed the forensic concept of *simul iustus et peccator* ("at the same time just and sinner") and taught that the struggle with sin is never fully conquered in this life but that we must *continually,* "engage in callings which are commanded, render obedience, avoid evil lusts, and the like."[58]

What, then, does it mean to be or to become "divinized" or "deified" if not that humans become gods? Some of the most interesting theotic writings from the Patristical Age issue from St. Athanasius. Athanasius penned some of the strongest theotic language of the early church, yet it was also he who furiously defended a *homoousios* Christology in which Christ is "of one substance" with God the Father as opposed to the "of similar substance" (*homioousios*) as held by Arius and his followers. While Arius believed that

---

[55] John Wesley, "A Plain Account of Christian Perfection," in *The Works of John Wesley*, vol. 11; ed. Thomas Jackson (Grand Rapids: Christian Classics Ethereal Library, 1999) http://www.ccel.org/w/wesley/perfection/perfection.html (November 8, 2004).

[56] Council of Vienne (1311), 28.1, *Decrees of the Ecumenical Councils*, ed. Norman P. Tanner (Washington, D. C: Georgetown University Press, 1990) http://www.ewtn.com/library/councils/vienne.htm (November 12, 2004).

[57] Westminster Confession of Faith (1646) 13.2, http://www.creeds.net/Westminster/c13.htm (November 14, 2004).

[58] The Augsburg Confession (1530), 20.11, *Vanderbilt University Divinity Library* (Nashville: Vanderbilt University, 2004) http://divinity.library.vanderbilt.edu/div/academics/courses/johnson/augsburg.html (December 5, 2004).

Christ was a *created* being of the highest order, Athanasius defended a Christology in which Christ is uniquely and fully Divine. Interestingly, it is this very Christology upon which Athanasius built his understanding of theōsis. Beginning Christologically, Athanasius argued that in order for humans to be ushered into a divine state, God first needed to descend to earth, take on the nature of a man, represent humanity as a man, become glorified, and thus pass this glory onto all of humanity as they become partakers in Divinity. Athanasius writes:

> [Jesus] is thus become the Deliverer of all flesh and of all creation. And if God sent His Son brought forth from a woman, the fact causes us no shame but contrariwise glory and great grace. For He has become Man, that He might deify us in Himself, and He has been born of a woman, and begotten of a Virgin, in order to transfer to Himself our erring generation, and that we may become henceforth a holy race, and "partakers of the Divine Nature," as blessed Peter wrote.[59]

Athanasius' soteriology was inextricably bound up with his Christology. God's intention from the beginning of the world was to make his church and those men and women in it genuine partakers of the Divine. Christ's assuming human flesh was the practical means to realize this objective. In his well known *On the Incarnation*, Athanasius writes that "The Word Incarnate, as is the case with the Invisible God, is known to us by His works," and "by them we recognise His deifying mission."[60] He continues saying,

> ... if a man should wish to see God, Who is invisible by nature and not seen at all, he may know and apprehend Him from His works...[and] let him marvel that by so ordinary a means things divine have been manifested to us, and that by death immortality has reached to all, and that by the Word becoming man, the universal Providence has been known ... For He was made man that we might be made God.[61]

---

[59] Athanasius, Letter 60, to Adelphius (para. 4) Nicene and Post-Nicene Fathers, Series II, vol. IV. Trans. Philip Schaff and Henry Wace (Grand Rapids: Christian Classics Ethereal Library, 1999) http://www.ccel.org/fathers2/NPNF2-04/Npnf2-04-114.htm#P10078_3609272 (October 10, 2004).

[60] Athanasius, *On the Incarnation of the Word*, 54, Nicene and Post-Nicene Fathers, Series II, vol. IV. Trans. Philip Schaff and Henry Wace (Grand Rapids: Christian Classics Ethereal Library, 1999) http://www.ccel.org/fathers2/NPNF2-04/Npnf2-04-16.htm#P1830_678055 (October 10, 2004).

[61] Ibid.

Vladimir Lossky, perhaps the most preeminent theotic theologian of the twentieth century, calls these writings of Athanasius and those similar among the Cappodocians, to be nothing less than "the very essence of Christianity."[62] God descends to the nadir of existence—fallen humanity, marked by death—so that a pathway of ascent can be made for humans to the Divine. Lossky calls this the "descent (*katabasis*) of the divine person of Christ mak[ing] human persons capable of ascent (*anabasis*) in the Holy Spirit."[63]

It is baffling to me that such a central concept has been so ill-pursued in Western theology—especially within Reformed theology. For, this is a soteriology that is entirely God-centered, focused on the unilateral purpose and plan of God becoming realized among His creation. Indeed, I maintain that it is a soteriology *best* explained through the monergistic initiative that is axiomatic to Reformed thought. It focuses on what God is doing, as opposed to the autonomous powers of humanity. Further, it grounds the *unio mystica* and, in turn, genuine love and relationality between the human and the Divine by emphasizing true love having always a Divine rather than human etiology. Humans do not choose to love God unless God's love is first put in them.

Two Scriptural texts are crucial to the study of theōsis: Genesis 1:26 and 2 Peter 1:4. The first of these illustrates the creational uniqueness of humanity. God declares, "Let Us make man in Our image, according to Our likeness" (26a). Robert Rakestraw observes that "the Greek Fathers taught that, in the fall, humanity lost the likeness but retained the image." Rakestraw quotes Gerald Bray:

> The Christian life is best conceived as the restoration of the lost likeness to those who have been redeemed in Christ. This is a work of the Holy Spirit, who communicates to us the energies of God himself, so that we may become partakers of the divine nature (2 Peter 1:4). The energies of God radiate from his essence and share its nature; but it must be understood that the deified person retains his personal identity and is not absorbed into the essence of God, which remains for ever [sic] hidden from his eyes.[64]

---

[62] Vladimir Lossky, *In the Image and Likeness of God* (New York: St. Vladimir's Seminary Press, 1974) 97.

[63] Ibid.

[64] Gerald Bray, "Deification," in *New Dictionary of Theology* (Downers Grove, Ill.: Inter-Varsity, 1988) 189. Quoted in Robert Rakestraw, "Becoming Like God: An Evangelical Doctrine of Theōsis," *The Journal of the Evangelical Theology Society* 40 (1997) 257.

The issue at hand is not whether it is the image or likeness that is restored (or whether these are a kind of hendiadys in which they have essentially the same referent) but with "the Christian's reintegration into the life of God."[65]

The second epistle of Peter breaths new life into this reintegration, locating its realization in the advent of Christ. Peter writes, ". . . seeing that His divine power has granted to us everything pertaining to life and godliness, through the true knowledge of Him who called us by His own glory and excellence. For by these He has granted to us His precious and magnificent promises, so that by them you may become partakers of the divine nature, having escaped the corruption that is in the world by lust" (1:3-4). Here Peter tells the church that, on the basis of Christ's own commitment and work, believers become genuine participants in the life of God. This new life is engendered *en Christō*; and translates the redeemed from both physical and spiritual death unto new life. John 17 and the "in Christ" biblical texts which I covered under my discussion of the mystical union are also key in theotic theology.

The Byzantine monk, Gregory Palamas (1335), called theōsis "God [setting] before us all His riches and truly beneficial gifts to share . . . 'The person who has been deified by grace will be in every respect as God is, except for His very essence.'"[66] That Palamas and the Greek Fathers made a careful distinction between theōsis as participation in the Divine "energies" as opposed to God's essence is widely known among students of Eastern Orthodoxy and should serve to placate the fears of the theological West that theotic soteriology somehow implies either pantheism or man as attaining to substantial Godhood. George Mantzaridis, commenting on Palamas, writes,

> Man's deification is not realized through participation in God's essence, but through communion in His divine energy. Man may share in God's glory and brightness, but the divine essence remains inaccessible and nonparticipable. Thus, the deified man is made god in all things, but he neither is identified with the divine essence nor shares it.[67]

---

[65] Robert Rakestraw, "Becoming Like God: An Evangelical Doctrine of Theōsis," *The Journal of the Evangelical Theology Society* 40 (1997) 257.

[66] Gregory Palamas, "Homily Eight," *The Homilies of Saint Gregory Palamas*, vol. 1 (South Canaan, Pa.: Saint Tikhon's Seminary Press, 2002) 90–91. In the second part, Palamas quotes Maximus the Confessor, *Letters to Thalassius*, XXII.

[67] George Mantzaridis, *The Deification of Man* (Crestwood, NewYork: St. Vladimir Press, 1984) 122.

The distinction made by the Eastern theologians between God's energies and essence, knowability and unknowability, is remarkably similar to points raised by the Scholastics and Reformers in which created humanity cannot know God *as he is in himself*, nor can they share in His essence.[68] St. Basil writes that "The operations [of deification] are various, and the essence simple, but we say that we know our God from His operations, but do not undertake to approach near to His essence. His operations come down to us, but His essence remains beyond our reach."[69]

Deification, our nexus of union with Christ, occurs through participation in God's energies (which are nevertheless *truly* God), but not through sharing in God's essence. This is vitally important both in understanding the theotic dynamic and in preserving an Orthodox biblical theology. Timothy Ware (Bishop Kallistos of Diokleia) notes that,

> This distinction between God's essence (*ousia*) and His energies goes back to the Cappadocian Fathers . . . however remote from us in His essence, yet in His energies God has revealed Himself to men. These energies are not something that exists apart from God, not a gift which God confers upon men: they are God Himself in His action and revelation to the world. God exists complete and entire in each of His divine energies . . . It is through these energies that God enters into a direct and immediate relationship with mankind. In relation to man, the divine energy is in fact nothing else than the grace of God; grace is not just a 'gift' of God, not just an object which God bestows on men, but a direct manifestation of the living God Himself, a personal confrontation between creature and Creator . . . When we say that the saints have been transformed . . . by the grace of God, what we mean is that they have a direct experience of God Himself. They Know God—that is to say, God in His energies, not in His essence.[70]

This deification through God's energies is, first and last, a work of God's grace. Palamas (in part defending Hesychasm[71]), wrote that "union with God" is accomplished only through the "deifying grace of the Spirit."[72] Further,

---

[68] See discussion on pages 184ff.

[69] Basil, "Letter CCXXXIV," *Basil: Letters and Select Works*, translated, ed. Philip Schaff (Grand Rapids: Christian Classics Ethereal Library, 2003) 525.

[70] Timothy Ware, *The Orthodox Church* (London: Penguin, 1963, 1964) 77–78

[71] The Hesychasts were a sect of monks in the Greek church, especially at Mount Athos, who practiced stillness and contemplative prayer according to certain fashions such as withdrawal, isolation, solitude, repetition of the Jesus Prayer, and general ascesis.

[72] Gregory Palamas, "The Declaration of the Holy Mountain," *The Philokalia*, trans. and

> ... if deification is accomplished according to a capacity inherent in human nature and if it is encompassed within the bounds of nature, then of necessity the person deified is by nature God. Whoever thinks like this should not attempt, therefore, to foist his own delusion upon those who stand on secure ground and to impose a defiled creed upon those whose faith is undefiled; rather he should lay aside his presumption and learn from persons of experience or from their disciples that the grace of deification is entirely unconditional, and there is no faculty whatever in nature capable of achieving it since, if there were, this grace would longer be grace but merely the manifestation of the operation of a natural capacity.[73]

Theōsis through God's energies is by grace. This theōtic grace speaks to God's intentions and work in making genuine relations possible between Himself and created humanity. This very thing is itself the mystery of the Christian faith. Paul writes that it is God's purpose to "reconcile all things to Himself, having made peace through the blood of His cross" and that Christ "has now reconciled you in His fleshly body through death, in order to present you before Him holy and blameless and beyond reproach" (Col 1:20, 22). Paul calls this the "mystery which has been hidden from the past ages and generations, but has now been manifested to His saints" (Col 1:26).

Theōsis, in part, may be thought of as a summary term for the subjective, relational nature of salvation. This emphasis on the subjective aspects of salvation is precisely where Pinnock and I perceive a deficiency in Reformed thought. Whereas justification and satisfaction refer to the forensic *appeasement* of God such that created humans might be positionally "clean" in God's eyes, theōsis encompasses the subjective aspects of the *ordo salutis*—regeneration, sanctification, and glorification—and explains each of them as the sole work of God. Each of these I construe as subspecies of theōsis such that we might even rename them, respectively: *inaugural theōsis, progressive theōsis,* and *consummative theōsis*.

Rakestraw refers to the anthropological reception of this gift as "Christification"[74] preferring this to deific terminology. Another theologian uses the term "Trinification."[75] These terms may be helpful in Western circles to avoid possible misunderstandings of *deification*. But the principle is essentially the same. Relationality is possible as humans are brought

---

ed. G. E. H. Palmer et al. (London: Faber and Faber, 1995) 420.

[73] Ibid.

[74] Rakestraw, "Becoming Like God," 265.

[75] James Beilby, Lecture on the Doctrine of God, Bethel Theological Seminary (October 9, 2000).

progressively into the relational being of God by His grace or energies. Whatever humans render unto God that is pleasing to Him, is that which was sovereignly given. This work is theologically centered in God's own purpose but is graciously extended to His church for its mutual fulfillment, that they may become "one" with Him, and that the glory of God may shine forth in all that God does.

This model of relationality also precludes the necessity of recourse to the radical step of Divine nescience. It grounds vital relationality in God Himself and establishes it in humans according to the purposes of the Divine will. Exhaustive Divine foreknowledge presents no obstacle to the view as the theotic relationality and *Christus in nobis* principle at once grounds genuine relationality but simultaneously unfolds according to the movement and sovereign predilection of the Triune God. As with creation, it is a Triune activity, never "adding" to the Divine nature, but expressing the eternal perfections. The view similarly avoids fatalism because it is always the glorious purposes of God at work accomplishing His ends through means that concurrently infuse humanity with its creational significance. This is quite opposed to the purposeless machinations of the "Fates" which fundamentally lack *telos*. Basil writes:

> Through His aid hearts are lifted up, the weak are held by the hand, and they who are advancing are brought to perfection. Shining upon those that are cleansed from every spot, He makes them spiritual by fellowship with Himself. Just as when a sunbeam falls on bright and transparent bodies, they themselves become brilliant too, and shed forth a fresh brightness from themselves, so souls wherein the Spirit dwells, illuminated by the Spirit, themselves become spiritual . . .[76]

The Means of Theotic Relationality

The preceding, of course, raises the question of how the benefits of inaugural, progressive, and consummative theōsis communicated to us. Consummative theōsis (or *glorification*) is an eschatological realization—an eternity of perfected fellowship and communion between recipient and Trinity. But inaugural and progressive theōsis (or *regeneration* and *sanctification*) relate to experiences in the present life of the believer. How, then, are they normatively mediated such that we enjoy the unitive fruits of God's grace? What are the God-ordained means of grace whereby the sanctifying

---

[76] Basil, *On the Spirit* in *Basil: Letters and Select Works,* trans. and ed. Philip Schaff (Grand Rapids: Christian Classics Ethereal Library, 2003) 125.

influences of the Spirit are communicated to humans? I advance three primary means: the *Word*, *Sacrament*, and *prayer*.

The Word

The Word, quite simply, is Christ Himself—condescending to humankind in the *words* of the gospel message, *as they are believed by the Spirit*. Christ the Word, is to be found in Scripture, which, Calvin wrote, is "effectually impressed on the heart by the Spirit; if it exhibits Christ, it is the word of life converting the soul, and making wise the simple."[77] God calls us by His Word, Jesus Christ, the *Logos* known through the power of the Spirit operating in the simplicity and mundaneness of the gospel preached. By the hearing of the word, the theotic blessings of God pour over to those in whom the Spirit inwardly inclines. This is true of both inaugural and progressive theōsis; in the former instance as God works through His word to inlodge faith, in the latter as He sustains those in whom He instills it.

The Sacraments

In the sacraments, the same is true but with a different mode of operation. The sacraments, baptism and the Lord's Supper, add to the theotic blessings of God a *physical* expression of the Word and an imbuing of empowering, unitive grace. None of this is to add a crass, magical component to the sacraments in which God has blindly bound Himself to them such that the sacraments themselves, *ex opere operato*, communicate the theotic blessings of the Spirit. Rather, Calvin—echoing Augustine[78]—stressed that "the efficacy of the word is produced in the sacrament, not because it is [performed], but because it is believed."[79] Indeed, St. Paul speaks of the Lord's Supper heaping condemnation upon the recipient who takes of it in a "unworthy" manner (1 Cor 11:27-29), especially one in which the body of the crucified Lord is left unrecognized (1 Cor 11:29).

To the regenerate communicant, however, the sacraments are a principal means through which God "signs and seals" *Himself*—His promises, His salvation, and our theotic communion with Him. The sacraments are not a constituent part of inaugural theōsis, but of progressive only through

---

[77] Calvin, *Institutes*, I.9.3, vol. 1, 86.

[78] Augustine says, ". . . this is what belongs to the virtue of the sacrament, not to the visible sacrament; he that eateth within, not without; who eateth in his heart, not who presses with his teeth." Augustine, *Homilies on the Gospel of John*, Tractate XXVI.12 (Grand Rapids: Christian Classics Ethereal Library, 2005) 218. See longer discussion at pages 217–19.

[79] Calvin, *Institutes*, IV.14.7, vol. 2, 495.

the life of the believer. They are a spiritual picture and a spiritual food, intended for those already regenerated through the Spirit by His Word.

Calvin spoke of the sacraments as a symbol: "an external sign, by which the Lord seals on our consciences his promises of good-will toward us, in order to sustain the weakness of our faith, and we in our turn testify our piety towards him, both before himself, and before angels as well as men."[80] The sacraments visibly signify and seal the reality of *Christus in nobis*. B. A. Gerrish, commenting on Calvin's sacramentology, summarized things saying "The very nature of the symbolism suggests to Calvin that the Supper is a matter of nourishing, sustaining, and increasing a communion with Christ to which the word and Baptism have initiated the children of God."[81] As such, the sacraments are a spiritual food, operating in a progressive theōsis, binding us more and more to Christ, until such union is made perfect in heaven (consummative theōsis).

Some in ecclesiastical history, wishing to emphasize more strongly the spiritual and noncorporeal over the earthly and mundane (notably the Anabaptists, Remonstrants, Zwinglians, Socinians, and others),[82] have divested the sacraments (with particular attention to the Lord's Supper) of being actual means carrying with them objective Divine grace as a physical seal, preferring instead to consider them merely commemorative or celebratory in nature. It is interesting here to observe the quasi-Platonic undertones of the view which is reluctant to connect the outworking of the Spirit of God to anything physical. Yet, while commemoration and celebration are rightfully attached to the significance of the Eucharist (*promise* and *declaration* to Baptism), it has largely been recognized by the Reformed—without recourse to what they deem an extremity of superstition in Roman sacramentology—that the sacraments are far more than mere external rites reminding the faithful of Christ's ministry. Rather, they are real spiritual sustenance brining with them real spiritual presence. Gerrish observes that, for Calvin, the Lord's Supper is in fact the occasion for a double act of unitive self giving: Christ giving Himself to the church and the church reciprocally giving itself to God. "It is this double self-giving," Gerrish writes, "that makes the Supper both embody and represent the perpetual exchange of grace and gratitude that shapes Calvin's entire theology. The sacred banquet prepared by the Father's goodness is the actual giving, not merely the re-

---

[80] Ibid., IV.14.1, vol. 2, 492.

[81] B. A. Gerrish, *Grace and Gratitude: The Eucharistic Theology of John Calvin* (Minneapolis: Fortress, 1993) 134.

[82] See Charles Hodge, *Systematic Theology*, III.XX.2. (Grand Rapids: Christian Classics Ethereal Library, 2005) 353–54; Berkhof, *Systematic Theology*, 607–08.

membering, of a gift of grace, and precisely as such it demands and evokes the answering gratitude of God's children.[83]

With Calvin, though in the theotic language I have used, the sacraments are a means of progressive theōsis in which they "[do] not so much confirm his word as *establish* us in the faith of it."[84] Moreover, in so ordaining the sacraments as a means of grace, ". . . our merciful Lord, with boundless condescension, so accommodates himself to our capacity, that seeing how from our animal nature we are always creeping on the ground, and cleaving to the flesh, having no thought of what is spiritual, and not even forming an idea of it, he declines not by means of these earthly elements to lead us to himself, and even in the flesh to exhibit a mirror of spiritual blessings."[85]

Contemporary pretensions may find themselves resistant to the notion that God has bound himself to something so "animal," deeming it a crude throwback to antiquated, religious primitivism. Some may thus fear the doctrine as minimizing the Deity and tying Him to something less powerful and or even less "spiritual." Yet this fear should be abated and swiftly replaced with gratitude and thanksgiving when we recognize in the sacraments a tangible expression of the Deity having not neglected that we are sensuous beings. As such, both the body and soul are included among those means which God uses to manifest and sustain us in the abundance of His theotic blessings—the communication of Himself *to us*, holistically, *as we are*. God does not discard the corporeal nature of His children in His means of communion with them. Calvin quotes Chrysostom saying, "Were we incorporeal, he would give us these things in a naked and incorporeal form. Now because our souls are implanted in bodies, he delivers spiritual things under things visible. Not that the qualities which are set before us in the sacraments are inherent in the nature of the things, but God gives them this signification."[86] The sacraments, then, are a principal means of theotic grace.

Prayer

Augustine referred to prayer as "a turning of the heart" and a "purification of the inner eye."[87] As a means of grace, it "purifies our heart, and makes

---

[83] B. A. Gerrish, *Grace and Gratitude: The Eucharistic Theology of John Calvin* (Minneapolis: Fortress, 1993) 156.

[84] Calvin, *Institutes*, IV.14.3, vol. 2, 492.

[85] Ibid., 493.

[86] Ibid.

[87] Augustine, *On the Lord's Sermon on the Mount*, II.3.14 (Grand Rapids: Christian Classics

it more capacious for receiving the divine gifts, which are poured into us spiritually."[88] Calvin considered prayer to "draw as from an inexhaustible fountain."[89] To neglect availing ourselves of this inestimable privilege "were just as if one told of a treasure were to allow it to remain buried in the ground."[90]

Prayer might literally be considered "converse of the soul with God."[91] Yet, as with the inlodging of the Word in our hearts, and the efficacy of the Sacraments as the Spirit indwells the disposition of the communicant, genuine prayer begins with the instigation of the Spirit unitively sanctifying the soul, urging it toward communion with God. Paul speaks of true prayer as prayer *en Pneuma* ("in the Spirit"; Eph 6:18). Calvin acknowledged the work of the Spirit in prayer saying that to "pray aright is a special gift."[92] As the Spirit literally *gives* us prayer, and inasmuch as that prayer fills our souls with the theotic blessings of God, it too is a powerful means of grace.

In this manner, prayer is an awesome expression of the unitive nature of progressive theōsis in which we uniquely experience Jesus' promise to the believer that He, the Father, and the Spirit "will come to him and make Our abode with him" (John 14:23). Prayer also brings out "all gracious affections: reverence, love, gratitude, submission, faith, joy, and devotion."[93] Moreover, "When the soul thus draws near to God, God draws near to it, manifests his glory, sheds abroad his love, and imparts that peace which passes all understanding."[94] Prayer, as with salvation itself, brings our focus upon the praises of God's glory which reciprocally fills our spirit.

The Normativity of These Means

Calvin, couched in a polemic against Pelagianism, wrote that "God works in his elect in two ways: inwardly, by his Spirit; outwardly, by his Word. By his Spirit illuminating their minds, and training their hearts to the practice of righteousness, he makes them new creatures, while, by his Word, he stimulates them to long and seek for this renovation."[95] These "two ways" may seem to contradict Calvin's later identification of Word *and Sacrament*

Ethereal Library, 2000) 65.

[88] Ibid.

[89] Calvin, *Institutes*, III.XX, vol. 2, 146.

[90] Ibid.

[91] Hodge, *Systematic Theology*, III.XX.2.

[92] Calvin, Institutes, III.20.5, vol. 2, 150.

[93] Hodge, *Systematic Theology*, III.20.20, 507.

[94] Ibid.

[95] Calvin, *Institutes.*, II.5.5, vol. 1, 277.

as the normative means of grace (and identification of the true church),[96] but they do not. Calvin consistently maintained, as I have, that regenerative grace (as well as preservation in faith) are the unmerited gifts of God bestowed upon the "elect" through a unilateral operation of the Spirit.[97] This salvation, in turn, follows normatively through the *hearing* of the Word. Yet further, the sacraments themselves "[*consist*] of the *word* and the external sign."[98] Thus, salvation comes by faith in Christ, *through* God's grace, normatively mediated through Word and sustained by prayer, Word, and Sacrament according to the power of the Holy Spirit. Further, it is through Christ's Holy church that the Spirit brings the Word and Sacraments to those whom God the Father calls. Naturally, then, Scripture considers the temporal mission of the church to be both the proclamation of the Word and the administration of the Sacraments (Matt 28:19; Luke 22:19). In this manner, the benefits of theōsis are normatively communicated to the believer throughout the interadvental epoch.

It is important to stress the *normativity* of this operation. The Reformed in general (myself included) have often acknowledged the possibility that God can, and perhaps does, work in a special operation of grace upon those lacking access to the visible church and its ministry of Word and Sacrament. An "arch-Calvinist" no less than Loraine Boettner, for example, confessed, "We do not deny that God can save some even of the adult heathen people if He chooses to do so, for His Spirit works when and where and how He pleases, with means or without means . . . Certainly God's ordinary method is to gather His elect from the evangelized portion of mankind, although we must admit the possibility that by an extraordinary method some few of His elect may be gathered from the unevangelized portion."[99] But such operation is not normative, nor is it admonished in Scripture as the commonplace means through which the Lord condescends to spiritually feed those whom He gathers and calls His own. In this sense, God has "bound" Himself to Word and Sacrament, not such that He is held captive to them, but insofar as the Lord has seen fit to offer Himself to His church in mediate form of ordinary, altogether *human* means.

Neither is this to deny, nor derogate, the general providence of God in directing human affairs, freely bestowing His grace according to His own

---

[96] Ibid., IV.1.9, 289 (Calvin treats of prayer in a separate place. See III.XX, 145–201).

[97] Calvin writes that "the Lord both begins and perfects the good work in us, so that it is due to." Ibid., II.3.9, 260 (cf. I.13.14; II.5.2; III.1.4; III.11.23).

[98] Ibid., IV.14.4, 493 (emphasis added).

[99] Loraine Boettner, *The Reformed Doctrine of Predestination* (Grand Rapids: Christian Classics Ethereal Library, 2004) 67.

sovereign predilection, and enjoining communion with the created order through limitless means. Similarly, the gathering of the church in general as the *coetus fidelium* (that is, apart from only its administration of the sacraments) is also a vital means of communion with the Lord. Participation and fellowship in the church is indeed a mediative ministry of the Word as the Spirit indwells the movement. But should we seek the prominent means, spoken of in Scripture, and identified generically in the course of Reformed theological reflection, we come back to the normativity of Word, Sacrament, and prayer. And first among these, unifying and directing the others, is the Word.

The Problem of Reprobation

The notion of theotic relationality through Word, Sacrament, and prayer, most certainly is a magnificent thing for the *redeemed* to partake of according to God's own providential grace. But what of those who are excluded from this experience? What of the so-called "reprobate"? If the divine purpose in creation is oriented toward Trinitarian glory, in what manner does *reprobation* serve this goal? Further, if God is the very standard of love itself, how is this love not weakened or even annihilated by the prospect of sovereignly determining to consign some people to Hell?

I personally find this to be the most difficult issue in a *sola Scriptura* theology. I agree with Wayne Grudem when he writes that:

> In many ways the doctrine of reprobation is the most difficult of all the teachings of Scripture for us to think about and to accept, because it deals with such horrible and eternal consequences for human beings made in the image of God. The love that God gives us for our fellow human beings and the love that he commands us to have toward our neighbor cause us to recoil against this doctrine, and it is right that we feel such dread in contemplating it. It is something that we would not want to believe, and would not believe, unless Scripture clearly taught it.[100]

John Calvin is often revisionally broad brushed as though he boldly declared his famous *decretum horribile*[101] with delight. Reprobation is the "dreadful" side of Calvin's doctrine of election in which God, before the foundation of the world, destined some for eternal damnation according to the immutable counsel of His own will.[102] There is, of course, no doubt

---

[100] Grudem, *Systematic Theology*, 685.

[101] Calvin, *Institutes*, 3.23.7, 232

[102] Reformed theologians have traditionally distinguished between *reprobation* and *pret-*

that Calvin maintained the doctrine. But that he took any pleasure in it is demonstrably false to anyone who has read his fuller treatment. Calvin firmly believed that the human mind could only go so far in understanding the very Christian doctrines that the Bible nevertheless exhorts us to accept. Concerning the *decretum horribile*, he accepted it as biblical, but in terms of fully comprehending it in juxtaposition with God's goodness, he conceded that "Here the most loquacious tongues must be dumb."[103] Some may suppose that Calvin was directing this comment at others. I believe rather, he was at least equally directing it at himself. Calvin was always concerned about being overly garrulous and speculative in theology and I see this comment as more of a self-deprecatory concession than an external reprimand.

With Calvin and the (pre-Barthian)[104] Reformed tradition, I take the biblical evidence for a reprobation decree to be compelling. Logically, this evidence is "negatively" compelling once the evidence for the monergistic regeneration of the "elect" is granted as I set forth in chapter four. In this sense, I think Berkhof rightly observes that: The doctrine of reprobation naturally follows from the logic of the situation. The decree of election inevitably implies the decree of reprobation. If the all-wise God, possessed of infinite knowledge, has eternally purposed to save some, then He *ipso facto* also purposed not to save others. If He has elected or chosen some, then He has by that very fact also rejected others.[105]

If election is an unavoidable reality both historically and theologically, then the inverse of *non-election* must also be true. *Theological* election was discussed in chapter four. *Historically* speaking, though, the concept of election permeates the Scriptures. God elects Abraham from Ur of the Chaldees (Neh 9:7), He elects Isaac over Ishmael (Gen 25:23); Jacob over Esau (Rom 9:6-13); in sum, the nation of Israel over all the other nations of

erition. While the former pertains to eternal efficaciousness of the fact, the latter refers to the operative manner in which it is carried out, namely, by God "passing over" or "moving past" (Lat. *praeter*) the non-elect. This is a helpful distinction but is not crucial to our discussion.

[103] Calvin, *Institutes*, 3.23.7, 232.

[104] The scope of this work does not allow for a treatment of Karl Barth's contribution to the development of the Reformed doctrines of election and reprobation. Let it suffice here, however, to say that, while I find Barth's desire to re-cast election *Christologically* to be an important contribution [see especially, Karl Barth, *Church Dogmatics*, vol. 2, Part 2 (Edinburgh: T. & T. Clark, 1957) 145–48], it should be clear from my argumentation to this point that I am not convinced that we can avoid the Scriptural implications for an eternal decree applicable to *humans*. Additionally, I do not find convincing arguments that suggest Calvin overlooked the locus of Christ in his own development of the eternal decree; see especially, Calvin, *Institutes*, 3.24.5, 244.

[105] Berkhof, *Systematic Theology*, 117–18.

the earth (Deut 7:6)[106] to be the cupbearers and broadcasters of His promises. Quite obviously, this elective action is conversely *not* to elect others.

But the doctrine is also "positively" compelling when considering several key biblical texts. Jude, for example, speaks of "certain persons [who] have crept in unnoticed, *those who were long beforehand marked out for this condemnation*, ungodly persons who turn the grace of our God into licentiousness and deny our only Master and Lord, Jesus Christ" (verse 4; emphasis added). The words "beforehand marked" come from the Greek *prographō* meaning "to write beforehand" to have been "already written" or previously "written in the past."[107] As David Wallace observes, "The occasion of [Jude's] letter was the intrusion of ungodly persons into the fellowship of the church."[108] Jude does not view this occurrence, however, as mere chance. Rather, the influence of such persons he construes as a part of God's eternal plan "written" before it happened. Another similar passage is found in second Peter:

> But there were also false prophets among the people, just as there will be false teachers among you. They will secretly introduce destructive heresies, even denying the sovereign Lord who bought them–bringing swift destruction on themselves. Many will follow their shameful ways and will bring the way of truth into disrepute. In their greed these teachers will exploit you with stories they have made up. Their condemnation has long been hanging over them, and their destruction has not been sleeping. (verses 1-3)

It might be argued that this "condemnation" is merely general, applying to whoever *might* deny God and repudiate the gospel. I believe this is a difficult approach to take, however, since few would argue that the New Testament pictures *all* people as being in this same situation which is, after all, precisely why we need the gospel. But for Jude and Peter, the referents are already proclaimed to be condemned. They are not portrayed as sinners who might receive the true gospel, repent, and be saved, but as those "marked out" for the condemnation that "has long been hanging over them." The nature of this language seems specifically targeted at distinguishing such people from those still bearing the hope of redemption.

---

[106] John Frame, *The Doctrine of God*, (Philipsburg, N. J.: Presbyterian & Reformed, 2002) 318. Frame includes a helpful, fuller survey of historical election from pages 317–25.

[107] Edward Goodrick and John Kohlenberger, *Zondervan NIV Exhaustive Concordance*, (Grand Rapids: Zondervan, 1999) 1586.

[108] David Wallace, "Jude," in *The Wycliffe Bible Commentary* (Chicago: Moody, 1962) 1488.

Of course, the *central* passage concerning reprobation is Romans 9. It is important to point out though that, as John Frame observes, this passage "deals with both historical and eternal reprobation, and that fact has confused some readers . . . we must acknowledge at the outset that the primary issue that Paul faces here is that of Israel's salvation."[109] I agree with Frame that this passage must deal with election in the native context of Paul's concern for his fellow Jews. Nevertheless, because the passage also deals with the nature of salvation itself (as outlined in chapter four), I believe this consideration in no way diminishes the theological force of the reprobation doctrine, but further establishes it. Paul taught that salvation was "first for the Jew, then for the Gentile" (Rom 1:16). The question that painfully confronted him, however, was why his fellow Jews were rejecting Christ. He even expresses his own wish that he be "cut off from Christ for the sake of [his] brothers . . . the people of Israel" (verses 3-4). One might wonder whether God's word had simply failed to accomplish its purpose. Paul's conclusion is that it has not failed (verse 6a) but that the key to understanding the situation finds its locus in the sovereign choice of God. God's word *is* powerful and it *is* doing its job. The reason that many of Paul's brethren are rejecting it is because "not all who are descended from Israel are Israel" (verse 6b), and so that "God's purpose in election might stand: not by works but by him who calls" (verses 11b-12a). Paul's illustration is God's choosing Jacob over Esau "*before* the twins were born or had done anything good or bad" (verse 11a). Frame comments saying:

> Paul is not distinguishing here between historical and eternal election. Rather, he is focusing on the principles that these two forms of election have in common. In both cases, election is by grace, apart from works (verse 12). In all these cases, election is in accordance with God's purpose (verse 11) and calling (verse 12). Esau is reprobate (whether historically or eternally) before he is born (verse 11), hated by God (verse 13). It is impossible to avoid the conclusion that Paul is making the same point about the eternal election of unbelieving Israelites: they reject Christ because God has not called them. They are reprobate by the sovereign decision of God.[110]

If this understanding is not correct, then it is difficult to understand why Paul would bring up the Jacob-Esau issue at all, if not to answer the original question he raises concerning the disbelief of his fellow Jews and to make an application to their own situation. Similarly, the subsequent question Paul raises in verse 14 concerning whether there is injustice in God for do-

---

[109] Frame, *The Doctrine of God*, 332.
[110] Ibid., 333.

ing this does not seem to make any sense unless it springs from a concern over Divine election as opposed to autonomous free choice.

The next portion of Romans 9 (verses 15-21) was also dealt with in chapter four in which Paul quotes the words of the Lord in Exodus saying, "I will have mercy on whom I have mercy, and I will have compassion on whom I have compassion" (verse 15). To those who might object to this, Paul simply reminds them of their creatureliness and lack of prerogative in calling God's justice into question. Just as God "questioned" Job, Paul says "who are you, O man, who answers back to God? The thing molded will not say to the molder, 'Why did you make me like this?'"

But the key portion here in understanding the manner in which reprobation might square with the creational glory orientation of God is found in verses 22-24. Paul does not merely end the discussion with a rhetorical rebuke, but in fact "want[s] to present a deeper answer . . . to the question of Israel's unbelief."[111] Here, Paul "theologizes" for us and falls back on God's own ultimate purpose in manifesting His own glory:

> What if God, although willing to demonstrate His wrath and to make His power known, endured with much patience vessels of wrath prepared for destruction? And He did so to make known the riches of His glory upon vessels of mercy, which He prepared beforehand for glory, even us, whom He also called, not from among Jews only, but also from among Gentiles.

No doubt, this is a "hard saying" of Scripture. Though Paul does do some theologizing for us, verses 14-24 essentially place everything within the sole, inscrutable wisdom of God and seems to put a muzzle over the objector's right to challenge God in doing whatsoever He pleases. Grudem comments that Paul is teaching that "somehow, in God's wisdom, the fact of reprobation and the eternal condemnation of some will show God's justice and also result in his glory."[112] Exacting punitive judgment on "the vessels of wrath prepared for destruction" is used by God to illustrate the inverse parallel of mercy upon the "vessels of mercy which He prepared beforehand for glory." This means that somehow, in the theotic eschaton, God's church made "one" with Him, will find further cause to praise God's glory *in light* of His sovereign choice to save some but not others.

Pinnock writes that this position must "explain whether God loves out of his loving nature or on a whim. Does he just choose to love or is He love? [It must] explain how God justly blames sinners when they can do

---

[111] Ibid.

[112] Grudem, *Systematic Theology*, 686.

nothing but what God determines."[113] But is this not essentially the same objection that Paul addresses here? Paul responds to his interlocutor that God does whatsoever He will with His own creation and if He chooses to destine some to mercy and glory and others to destruction for their sin, that is His right. To *this* issue, Paul does not so much provide an answer concerning the basis upon which God justly blames sinners that were destined for condemnation as much as he simply declares that "God is God" and is under no obligation at all to do what humans would have him do.

Gordon Clark makes the point that God's "right" to do as he pleases is an *ontological* one. God is not accountable to a standard of justice beyond Himself as humans are. He is accountable to no other. God does not have precepts that he was given to follow as humans have. He has "rights" over His own creation because of who and what He is—the *sui generis, a se*, God. The English Puritan John Owen observed that the God who created all things *ex nihilo* cannot be judged according to human standards, for "Whatever God doth, and towards whomsoever, be they many or few, a whole nation, or city, or one single person, be they high or low, rich or poor, good or bad, all are the works of his hands, and he may deal with them as seems good unto him."[114] Clark writes:

> Is it just then for God to punish a man for deeds that God himself "determined before to be done"? Was God just in punishing Judas, Herod, Pontius Pilate, and the others? The Scriptures answer in the affirmative and explain why. Not only is God the creator of the physical universe, not only is he the governor and judge of men, he is also the moral legislator. It is his will that establishes the distinction between right and wrong, between justice and injustice; it is his will that sets the norms of righteous conduct . . . But for some peculiar reason people hesitate in applying this same principle of sovereignty in the sphere of ordinary ethics. Instead of recognizing God as sovereign in morals, they want to subject him to some independent, superior, ethical law.[115]

Clark's point might be taken to merely lead us back to the other side of Plato's famous *Euthyphro* problem, in which we might ask if God's justice, love, or other attributes are then merely the byproducts of an arbitrary fiat.[116] But this need not be the case. Instead, when Scripture teaches us that

---

[113] Pinnock, personal correspondence, October 7, 2004.

[114] John Owen, "Exposition of Psalm 130," in *The Works of John Owen*, vol. 6, ed. William Goold (Edinburgh: Banner of Truth Trust, 1991) 627.

[115] Gordon Clark, *Religion, Reason, and Revelation* (Nutley, N. J.: Craig, 1978) 231–32.

[116] The Euthyphro problem concerns Socrates' discussion with a young man by that name.

all that *love* is, *God* is, we can understand His love as genuinely operating in those to whom He chooses to give it. Or when it says that God is just, this too reflects something of His eternal character. But in trying to gain a comprehensive understanding of the manner in which the Divine attributes coalesce in God's own self-glorifying prerogative to issue justice to one and mercy to another, we enter a room with no exit. This is not because none exists or that a demonstrable contradiction is present, but simply because it is beyond our capacity to know. The Deuteronomic author writes that, "The secret things belong to the LORD our God, but the things revealed belong to us and to our sons forever . . ." (Deut 29:29). The basis upon which the Divine choice is made of one and not another is a matter upon which the Bible is utterly silent. There is no reason, however, to take this silence as evidence of there being no basis at all. Quite the contrary, there must be a basis which is entirely consistent with God's eternal nature and self-glorifying orientation.

Nevertheless, if such a doctrine of reprobation does not shock us, then we are not adequately contemplating it. Calvin contemplated it and thought it *dreadful*. It is unspeakably frightening to imagine anyone being consigned to a destiny apart from the theotic pleasures of God. Perhaps even more difficult to imagine is rendering eternal praise to the *Consigner*. If it truly is the purpose of God to predetermine the reprobation of some humans with an eye toward His own glory, then perhaps it is simply the case that, until those whom God redeems enter into that promised state of consummative theōsis, they will not be able to deal fully with this doctrine morally or intellectually. They must instead grant it on faith and trust in God's perfect goodness, justice, and wisdom.

There is also a sense, however, in which the Bible teaches us *not* to be comfortable with the doctrine. As argued in chapter four, the *decretive* will of God is inscrutable and impervious to the vacilatory prerogative of humans. Further, human beings bear no Scripturally-revealed responsibility for the sovereign decrees of God. They are, however, responsible for heeding the Divine *preceptive* will. They are commanded by God to love their neighbor as themselves (Luke 10:27) and to never pass anything even remotely resembling eternal judgment on them (Luke 6:37), *nor even to*

The discussion evolves into the question over the proper grounding of piety and morals. Euthyphro declares that, "what all the gods love is pious and holy, and the opposite which they all hate, impious." Socrates, however, points out a dilemma in return by retorting, "is the pious or holy beloved by the gods because it is holy, or holy because it is beloved of the gods?" Plato, *Euthyphro*. Dialogue 105, 108; trans. Benjamin Jowett (Cambridge, Mass.: Massachusetts Institute if Technology, The Internet Classics Archive, 2005) http://classics.mit.edu/Plato/euthyfro.html (January 5, 2005).

desire it. Paul teaches that God alone has the sovereign prerogative of reprobation and punishment, but, as for humans, he tells them to ". . . be at peace with all men. Never take your own revenge, beloved, but leave room for the wrath of God, for it is written, 'vengeance is mine, I will repay,' says the Lord" (Rom 12:18-19). Christian believers have their "marching orders." They are to show the love of Christ to others and not overly concern themselves with God's decretive plan for each human life.

The Bible further portrays God as not taking any kind of sadistic-like delight in the destruction of the wicked. In chapter four, I set forth the case for understanding this as God's "will of disposition." The Lord says in Ezekiel 33:11, "I take no pleasure in the death of the wicked, but rather that they turn from their ways and live . . ." (Ezek 33:11; cf. Ezek 18:23; 1 Tim 2:3-4; 2 Pet 3:9). Yet in Proverbs 16:4 we read that, "The LORD works out everything for his own ends—even the wicked for a day of disaster" (NIV). Now, if both of these passages are taken to be indicative of the decretive will of God, irreconcilable contradiction is result. As Calvin observes, "the [Ezekiel] passage is violently wrested, if the will of God, which the prophet mentions, is opposed to his eternal counsel."[117] Indeed, if the former passage is taken to be decretive, then of resistless necessity we must conclude that no one ever *will* perish which naturally leads to universalism and thus proves too much for Pinnock, other open theists, and Arminians in general. If, however, we understand the Ezekiel passage as an example of God's revealed will of disposition, then here we learn something of the eternal character of God in which *saving* sinners manifests a singular kind of delight which *punishing* sinners does not. This is not to suggest that the "passions" of God are indexically divided over time,[118] but to understand the Scriptures as communicating, through the condescension of Divine self-disclosure, the infinite love of God in His works of redemption.

Chapter Summary

By way of conclusion, this chapter—built upon the foundation laid in the previous two—has done three things: 1) It has expanded on the argument for monergistic regeneration by proffering an understanding of Divine-human relationality which obtains *in light of* meticulous providence through the *Christus in Nobis* principle (and the *unio mystica*) and theōsis. 2) It dealt with Pinnock's chief objections from evil and reprobation and the manner in which these juxtapose with God's eternal character. 3) It advanced Word,

---

[117] Calvin, *Institutes*, III.24.15, 254.

[118] See my discussion of Divine simultaneity on page 169ff.

Sacrament, and prayer as the normative means through which the benefits of theōsis are communicated.

The chapter can be summarized as an attempt to avoid the fatalism that Pinnock believes attaches to a Reformed view of providence and, in so doing, to concentrate more heavily on Divine-human relationality from a shared concern that it has been given insufficient attention in modern Reformed theology. It reorients theology away from human autonomy toward what Paul Helm calls "a general reliance upon God, based on the fact that [Christians], in common with all humanity, live in a world that God has made and upholds, and which he has not abandoned or become indifferent to,"[119] but in which He is working everything toward His own inscrutable purpose. This purposivity is intrinsically inimical to fatalism, for—unlike the latter in which blind, mechanistic forces rule—the purpose of God is that which guides history and is precisely that which establishes human significance and suffuses it with ultimate meaning.

---

[119] Paul Helm, *The Providence of God* (Downer's Grove, Ill.: InterVarsity, 1993) 222.

7

Summary and Conclusion

THIS BOOK began by noting the controversy over open theism taking place within the Evangelical Theological Society. The original charges brought against Clark Pinnock in 2002 (which resulted in a referral to the Executive Committee) were finally voted upon by the entire Society on the evening of November 19, 2003 at the ETS Annual Meeting in Atlanta, Georgia. With a vote of two hundred and twelve votes in favor of expulsion and four hundred and thirty-two votes against, the charges were ultimately *not* sustained.[1] Interestingly, both before the vote and on the morning after, Pinnock openly admitted making a mistake in reference to the "unfulfilled prophecies" footnote in his latest book, *Most Moved Mover*. This crucial footnote caused perhaps the most consternation among his critics and was one of the major issues cited in Roger Nicole's official charges against him. Pinnock referred to the footnote as "a careless expression"[2] and actually offered to revise it in later editions of the book. During the year-long examination period by the Executive Committee in which Pinnock had an opportunity to address his colleagues *in camera*, his agreement to revise the footnote apparently satisfied both the committee and Nicole. The committee returned a recommendation back to the Society against expulsion with a nine to zero vote. Just before the vote, Pinnock addressed the Society saying, in part:

> The committee did its duty by me. Its members were zealous in pursuit of the truth of the charges. But they did not rush to judgment and they showed me grace and treated me fairly. I have no complaints. Indeed, I am the richer for it. Concerning the charges,

---

[1] As noted in chapter 1, charges were also brought against Dr. John Sanders of Huntington College. The proposal to expel him received three hundred and eighty-eight votes in favor and two hundred thirty-one votes against, thus narrowly missing the required two-thirds majority needed for expulsion.

[2] Specifically, the expression was, "We may not want to admit it but prophecies often go unfulfilled . . ." Pinnock, *Most Moved Mover: A Theology of God's Openness* (Grand Rapids: Baker, 2001) 51, note 66.

the committee had valid concerns. Not around every point that was raised but around a particular section in *Most Moved Mover*. They observed a degree of ambiguity there and pressed for clarity. This was perfectly appropriate. They also insisted on some modifications which I could supply. In the end, they were satisfied and I was relieved.[3]

While this present work has made it clear that I do not favor Pinnock's theology, I am personally glad that the ETS has seen fit to retain him as a member. I believe the charges brought against him were a circuitous path on the part of his critics; a diversion away from dealing with his proposal *theologically*—and from *within* the Society. I would rather see Pinnock and his fellow colleagues within the ETS discuss his proposal and offer arguments, collegially, in defense of their respective positions. Barring an *explicit* denial of the ETS's twin doctrinal requirements, scholars within the Society should attempt to persuade one another, not resort to quasi-judicial mechanisms in an attempt to silence an opponent.

Additionally, and perhaps more importantly, the ETS is not an ecclesiastical body but a scholarly society. A *church* might follow the Vincentian Rule and gauge Pinnock's theology to be properly and historically aberrant or even heretical. Indeed, if exhaustive divine foreknowledge does indeed fall within Vincentian guidelines, it is perhaps difficult to see how historically-minded *Evangelical* churches could *not* reach this conclusion. In terms of historic orthodoxy, sundry theological proposals have been deemed to be heterodox. Yet, many of these very same positions could be held to within the limited doctrinal context of biblical inerrancy and Trinitarianism. One could hold, for example, to a Nestorian christology but still affirm the twin creedal axioms of the ETS. Or, it would be possible to maintain an entirely Roman Catholic view of justification—the denial of which (in light of *sola fide*) was the material cause of the entire program of Reformational theology which Evangelicalism so passionately embraces. Countless other examples could be cited. But church and academia are separate spheres, and the latter cannot act as a litmus test for ecclesiastical orthodoxy. Churches themselves must decide whether Pinnock's views are consistent with their theological commitments.[4] But as long as Dr. Pinnock has, in good faith,

---

[3] Pinnock, Remarks By Pinnock at the ETS Special Business Meeting, Atlanta, Georgia, Wednesday, November 19, 2003; http://www.etsjets.org/members/challenge/2003-vote-pinnock.html (December 31, 2004).

[4] Indeed, the Southern Baptist Convention (SBC) did this very thing in response to open theism. In 2000, the SBC carried a resolution to revise their "Baptist Faith and Message" to include the statement that "God is all powerful and all knowing; and His perfect knowledge extends to all things, past, present, and future, including the future decisions of His free

signed the Society's limited doctrinal statement and has not publicly denied its positions, he should be free to theologize amongst his peers without fear of judicial reprisal.

The purpose of this book has been to critically examine the arguments and theological implications of Pinnock's openness theology. Using the Bible as the fundamental theological resource for a new theology within the Evangelical fold, Pinnock raises a host of issues for both the doctrine of God and theological anthropology. Chief among these are the notions that classical formulations of God's exhaustive foreknowledge of future events ultimately destroys genuine, Divine-human relationality, calls God's character into question, and reduces to fatalism.

After tracking through Pinnock's life and career with a theological biography, I examined (in chapter three) and later critiqued (in chapters four and five) his arguments in favor of the openness view summarized in three central theses: 1) That classical theology has been negatively affected by the metaphysics of Hellenism, 2) That love is God's primary attribute; even more His fundamental *essence*, and 3) That human beings posses autonomous libertarian freewill which forms the basis of both human responsibility and Divine-human relationality. I concluded that, while I believe Pinnock's reasoning from these premises to openness theology to be consistent (and formally valid), there are significant reasons to deny, or at least significantly temper, the premises themselves.

In brief, I argued that premise 1 is both ambiguous, ill-defined, and commits a type of genetic fallacy. I further argued that the reasons Pinnock offers in favor of the premise can be leveled with equal force against his *own* position. Thus, the premise is an insufficient basis upon which to deploy a critique of classical theology. Various commonalities with ancient Hellenistic thought neither support nor destroy either classical or openness models.

In response to the second premise, I argued that Pinnock has not sufficiently demonstrated why *love* should be privileged as the central attribute of God. As a replacement, I argued in favor of *Trinitarian glory* as the fundamental aspect of Deity and provided arguments to that effect. I further argued that the concept of glory ultimately furnishes a better integrating motif within which Christian theological systematization is equipped to deal with other concerns including the doctrine of God, theological anthropology, soteriology, and eschatology.

---

creatures." [*Southern Baptist Confession*, "The Baptist Faith and Message"; http://www.sbc.net/bfm/bfm2000.asp#ii (January 5, 2005)].

I argued against Pinnock's third premise by citing both biblical examples which appear to countermand it, as well as theological and philosophical reasons why libertarian, contra-causal freedom is both logically incoherent and ultimately incapable of sustaining what it purports to uphold, namely, responsibility and relationality. In its place, I argued for both compatibilistic freedom (or the liberty of spontaneity) as well as monergistic regeneration citing, again, both scriptural and theo-philosophical arguments in their favor.

Lastly, this book sought to reconstruct Divine-human relationality in a Reformed theological context while avoiding both a reduction into fatalism and a denial of exhaustive Divine foreknowledge. This reconstructed model built upon my replacement theses of Pinnock's and brought into them a consideration of the *Christus in nobis* principle coupled with theotic soteriology. My advocacy of the latter doctrine is one in which God's elect literally share or become "partakers" in the Divinity of the Godhead, but in which their creaturely status and personality is not erased. My argument centered around theōsis being the integrating concept for the subjective aspects of the *ordo salutis* in which the *Christus in nobis* principle is operatively "top down," stemming from God's own Trinitarian glory and resultant self-glorifying purpose. It is this very purpose, I have argued, which—far from destroying it—actually establishes genuine relational love between the human and Divine

Building upon my replacement theses, this model of relational dynamism takes the *Christus in nobis* principle and reverses Pinnock's order (in which relationality tends toward anthropocentrism) through an outworking of purposive, meticulous providence that serves God's own creational orientation. It grounds the love of God in humans *theologically*. Human love for God is established *in God* such that its reality is produced in humans precisely *because* it is God's own self-love reciprocally shared as the faithful are brought into adoptive communion with the Trinity. I further argued against the extremes of both pantheism and a situation in which the Creator-creature distinction is blurred—consequences which have sometimes followed on the heels of theotic soteriology.

Along the way, I have repeatedly stated my shared commitment with Dr. Pinnock to unearth the issue of Divine-human relationality which seems to have received too little attention within post-Reformational, Evangelical theology—especially within Reformed models. I have been thoroughly challenged throughout the process and, with John Frame, affirm that, "Open theism has provided a valuable service to us traditional theologians, for it has forced us to think harder about some important issues: God's love, his sovereign rule, human freedom, God's relationship to time and change, his suffering, and his knowledge."⁵ I am especially grateful to Dr. Pinnock who has given liberally of his time to me in both several personal meetings, as well as in a continued written correspondence through which he provided feedback on this work and has encouraged me to deal with the very difficult issues that inevitably attach to my own theology.

I am hopeful that this contribution—to an enduring theological issue—will provide at least one small brick in the foundation of a renewed emphasis on systematic theologies that attempt to better understand the mysterious, though rich, relationship between God and humans within a context that remains consistent with the legacy of Reformed theology—a theology in which God ultimately delights in Himself, *in us*.

---

⁵ John Frame, *No Other God: A Response to Open Theism* (Phillipsburg, N. J.: Presbyterian & Reformed, 2001) 211.

Bibliography

Anselm. *Proslogium*. Translated by Sidney N. Deane. Grand Rapids: Christian Classical Ethereal Library, 2000.

Aquinas, Thomas. *Shorter Summa*. Translated by Cyril Vollert. Manchester, N. H.: Sophia, 1993.

―――. *Summa Contra Gentiles*. Translated by Joseph Rickaby. London: Burns and Oates, 1905. Online. Jacques Maritain Center at the University of Notre Dame: http://www.nd.edu/Departments/Maritain/etext/gc.htm (April 2, 2003).

―――. *Summa Theologica*. Translated by Fathers of the English Dominican Province. Grand Rapids: Christian Classics Ethereal Library, 1999.

Aristotle. *Metaphysics*. Translated by W. D. Ross. Cambridge, Mass.: Massachusetts Institute if Technology, The Internet Classics Archive, 2005. Online. http://classics.mit.edu/Aristotle/metaphysics.12.xii. html (April 8, 2005).

―――. *On Interpretation*. Translated by E. M. Edghill. Cambridge, Mass.: The Internet Classics Archive, Massachusetts Institute of Technology, 2005. Online. http://classics.mit.edu/Aristotle/ interpretation.1.1.html (June 22, 2006).

Arminius, Jacobus. *The Works of Jacobus Arminius*. Vol. I. Grand Rapids: Christian Classics Ethereal Library, 2002.

Athanasius. "Letter 60, to Adelphius," in *Nicene and Post-Nicene Fathers*, Series II, vol. IV. Translated by Philip Schaff and Henry Wace. Grand Rapids: Christian Classics Ethereal Library, 1999. Online. http://www.ccel.org/fathers2/NPNF-04/Npnf2-04-114.htm#P10078_3609272 (October 10, 2004).

―――. "On the Incarnation of the Word," in *Nicene and Post-Nicene Fathers*, Series II, vol. IV. Translated by Philip Schaff and Henry Wace. Grand Rapids: Christian Classics Ethereal Library, 1999. Online. http://www.ccel.org/fathers2/NPNF-04/Npnf2-04-16.htm#P1830_678055 (October 10, 2004).

Augsburg Confession, The (1530). The Vanderbilt University Divinity Library. Nashville: Vanderbilt University, 2004). Online. http://divinity.library.vanderbilt.edu/div/academics/courses/ johnson/augsburg.html (December 5, 2004).

Augustine, "The Enchiridion." In *The Fathers of the Church*. Translated by J. F. Shaw. Online. http://www.newadvent.org/fathers/1302.htm (April 13, 2004).

―――. *Confessions*. Translated by R. F. Pine-Coffin. London: Penguin, 1961.

―――. *The City of God*. Translated by Marcus Dods. Grand Rapids: Christian Classics Ethereal Library, 2001.

―――. *De Trinitate*. Translated by Arthur W. Haddan. Grand Rapids: Christian Classical Ethereal Library, 2005.

―――. *Homilies on the Gospel of John*. Grand Rapids: Christian Classics Ethereal Library, 2005.

―――. *On Christian Doctrine*. Translated by J. F. Shaw. Grand Rapids: Christian Classics Ethereal Library, 2001.

―――. *On Free Choice of the Will*. Translated by Thomas Williams. Indianapolis: Hackett, 1993.

Bibliography

———. *On the Lord's Sermon on the Mount*. Grand Rapids: Christian Classics Ethereal Library, 2000.

———. "A Treatise On Grace and Free Will." *St. Augustin: Anti-Pelagian Writings*. Edited by Phillip Schaff. Grand Rapids: Christian Classics Ethereal Library, 2005.

———. "Treatise on the Predestination of the Saints." *Saint Augustin's Anti-Pelagian Works*. Translated by Peter Holmes and Robert Wallis. Revised by B. B. Warfield. Grand Rapids: Christian Classical Ethereal Library, 2005.

Baptist General Conference. "How Do We Decide 'Orthodoxy.'" Online. http://www.bgcworld.org/4know/clark.htm (April 10, 2003).

Barker, Kenneth, and Kohlenberger, John. *Zondervan NIV Bible Commentary*. Grand Rapids: Zondervan, 1994.

Barth, Karl. *Church Dogmatics*. Translated by G. W. Bromiley. Edinburgh: T. & T. Clark, 1957.

Basil. "Letter CCXXXIV." In *Basil: Letters and Select Works*. Translated and edited by Philip Schaff. Grand Rapids: Christian Classics Ethereal Library, 2003.

———. *On the Spirit* in *Basil: Letters and Select Works*. Translated and edited by Philip Schaff. Grand Rapids: Christian Classics Ethereal Library, 2003.

Beilby, James. Lecture on the Doctrine of God. Bethel Theological Seminary, October 9, 2000.

Berkhof, Louis. *Systematic Theology*. Grand Rapids: Eerdmans, 1996.

Bilezikian, Gilbert. *The Openness of God: A Biblical Challenge to the Traditional Understanding of God*. Downer's Grove, Ill.: InterVarsity, 1994. Back cover.

Bloesch, Donald. "Crisis in Biblical Authority." *Theology Today* 35 (1979).

Boethius, *The Consolation of Philosophy*. Translated by W. V. Cooper and J. M. Dent. Edited by Israel Golancz. London: Temple Classics, 1902.

Boettner, Loraine. "Evangelical." In *Wycliffe Dictionary of Theology*. Edited by Everett Harrison et al. Peabody, Mass.: Hendrickson, 1960.

———. *The Reformed Doctrine of Predestination*. Grand Rapids: Christian Classics Ethereal Library, 2004.

Bonhoeffer, Dietrich. Quoted in Uwe Siemon-Netto, "Justified and Sinner." *Issues Etc. Journal* 3.3 (2004).

Boyd, Greg. *God of the Possible*. Grand Rapids: Baker, 2000.

———. *God of the Possible: A Biblical Introduction to the Open View of God*. Grand Rapids: Baker, 2000.

———., et al. "What is Open Theism?" Online. http://www.opentheism.org (June 5, 2002).

———. *Letters from a Skeptic* Colorado Springs, Col.: Chariot Victor, 1994.

———. *Trinity and Process: A Critical Evaluation and Reconstruction of Hartshorne's Di-Polar Theism Towards a Trinitarian Metaphysics*. New York: Lang, 1992.

Brand, Chad Owen, "Orthodoxy and Open Theism and Their Connections to Western Philosophical Traditions." In *Beyond the Bounds*. Edited by John Piper, et al. Wheaton, Ill.: Crossway, 2003.

Bray, Gerald. "Deification." In *New Dictionary of Theology*. Downers Grove, Ill.: InterVarsity, 1988.

———. *The Doctrine of God*. Downer's Grove, Ill.: InterVarsity, 1993.

Brow, Robert. "Clark H. Pinnock (1937-)." Online. http://www.brow.on.ca/Articles/Pinnock.html (August 19, 2003).

Brown, Colin. *Philosophy and the Christian Faith: A Historical Sketch from the Middle Ages to the Present Day*. Downer's Grove, Ill.: InterVarsity, 1980.

Bibliography

Brunner, Emil. *The Christian Doctrine of God.* Cambridge: James Clarke, 2002.
Bultmann, Rudolph. *Theology of the New Testament.* London: Scribner, 1951.
Callen, Barry L. *Clark H. Pinnock: Journey Toward Renewal.* Nappanee, Ind.: Evangel, 2000.
Calvin, John. *Commentaries.* Translated by Joseph Haroutunian. Philadelphia: Westminster, 1958.
———. *Commentary on Corinthians*, vol. 1. Translated by John Pringle. Grand Rapids: Christian Classics Ethereal Library, 1999. Online. http://www.ccel.org/c/calvin/comment3/comm_vol39/ htm/viii.ii.htm (October 10, 2004).
———. *Commentary on Isaiah*, vol. 3. Translated by William Pringle. Grand Rapids: Christian Classics Ethereal Library, 1999. Online. http://www.ccel. org/c/calvin/calcom15/htm/xi.htm (October 12, 2004).
———. *Institutes of the Christian Religion.* Translated by Henry Beveridge. Grand Rapids: Eerdmans, 1989.
Carnell, E. J., *The Case for Orthodox Theology.* Philadelphia: Westminster, 1959.
Carson, D. A. *The Difficult Doctrine of the Love of God.* Wheaton, Ill.: Crossway, 2000.
Chambers, Oswald. "Getting Into God's Stride." [October 12] In *My Utmost For His Highest.* Uhrichsville, Ohio: Barbour, 1935, 1993.
Charnock, Stephen. *Existence and Attributes of God* (1797). Minneapolis: Klock and Klock, 1977.
Chicago Statement On Biblical Inerrancy, The (1978). "Summary Statement." Online. http://www.iclnet.org/pub/resources/text/history/chicago.stm.Tex.t (April 2, 2003).
Childs, Brevard S. *Biblical Theology in Crisis.* Philadelphia: Westminster, 1970.
Clark, Gordon. *Religion, Reason, and Revelation.* Nutley, N. J.: Craig, 1978.
Clark, Mary. "De Trinitate." In *The Cambridge Companion to Augustine.* Edited by Eleonore Stump and Norman Kretzmann. Cambridge: Cambridge University Press, 2001.
Constantinopolitan Creed. Online, 2005 http://www.reformed.org/ documents/2_council_of_constan.html.
Cooper, John. "The Importance of Reformed Anthropology for Ethics." *Theological Forum*, 21.1 (1993.
Copleston, Frederick. *A History of Philosophy.* vol. I. Paramus, N. J.: Newman, 1950.
Council of Vienne (1311) in *Decrees of the Ecumenical Councils.* Edited by Norman P. Tanner. Washington, DC: Georgetown University Press, 1990. Online. http://www.ewtn.com/library/councils/vienne.htm (November 12, 2004).
Craig, William Lane. "Divine Timelessness and Personhood." In *The International Journal for Philosophy of Religion*, vol. 43, Iss. 2. (April 1998).
———. "The Middle-Knowledge View." In *Divine Foreknowledge: Four Views.* Edited by James Beilby and Paul Eddy. Downers Grove, Ill.: InterVarsity, 2001.
———. *The Only Wise God.* Eugene, Ore.: Wipf & Stock Publishers, 2000.
———. *Time and Eternity.* Wheaton, Ill.: Crossway, 2001.
Cranfield, C. E. B. *The Epistle to the Romans.* International Critical Commentary. Edinburgh: T. & T. Clark, 1979.
Curtis, Brent and Eldredge, John. *The Sacred Romance.* Nashville: Thomas Nelson, 1997.
Dembski, William. "Transcendence." In *The New Dictionary of Christian Apologetics.* Downers Grove, Ill.: InterVarsity, forthcoming. Online. http://www.designinference.com/documents/2003.10.Transcendence_NDOCApol.pdf (March 10, 2004).
Dennett, Daniel C. *Brainstorms: Philosophical Essays on Mind and Psychology.* Cambridge, Mass.: Bradford Books, 1981.

Bibliography

Descartes, Rene. "Passions of the Soul." In *Descartes, Selected Philosophical Writings*. Translated by John Cottingham, Robert Stoothoff, and Dugald Murdoch. Cambridge: Cambridge University Press, 1988.

Dillard, Raymond and Longman, Tremper. *Introduction to the Old Testament*. Grand Rapids: Zondervan, 1994.

Dowey, Edmund. *The Knowledge of God in Calvin's Theology*, 3rd ed. Grand Rapids: Eerdmans, 1994.

Dutra, Bruce. "A New Criticism of Molina's Theory of Middle Knowledge" Presented at the Midsouth Philosophy Conference. Memphis, Tex.: The University of Memphis, February 21, 2003.

Edwards, Jonathan. *The Freedom of the Will*. Grand Rapids: Christian Classics Ethereal Library, 2000.

———. "The Mind." *The Works of Jonathan Edwards*. Vol. 1. Grand Rapids: Christian Classical Ethereal Library, 2003.

Elwell, Walter, editor. *Evangelical Dictionary of Theology*. Grand Rapids: Baker, 1996.

Erickson, Millard. *Christian Theology*. Grand Rapids: Baker, 1998.

———. *God the Father Almighty: A Contemporary Exploration of the Divine Attributes*. Grand Rapids: Baker, 1998.

———. *The Evangelical Heart and Mind*. Grand Rapids: Baker, 1993.

———. *What Does God Know and When Does He Know It? The Current Controversy over Divine Foreknowledge*. Grand Rapids: Zondervan, 2003.

Evangelical Theological Society. "Charges Against Dr. Pinnock By Roger Nicole" presented on November 21, 2002 at the fifty-fourth ETS conference.

———. "Doctrinal Basis." Online. http://www.etsjets.org (April 21, 2003).

———. "Purpose Statement." Online. http://www.etsjets. org (April 20, 2003).

Feinberg, Joel. "Abortion." In *Matters of Life and Death*. Edited by Tom Regan. New York: Random House, 1986.

Feinberg, John. *No One Like Him: The Doctrine of God*. Wheaton, Ill.: Crossway, 2001.

Frame, John. *No Other God*. Phillipsburg, N. J.: Presbyterian & Reformed, 2001.

———. *The Doctrine of God*. Phillipsburg, N. J.: Presbyterian & Reformed, 2002.

Frei, Hans. *The Eclipse of Biblical Narrative*. New Haven: Yale University Press, 1974.

Fretheim, Terence. *The Suffering of God: An Old Testament Perspective*. Minneapolis: Fortress, 1984.

Fry, C.G. "Monergism" in *The Evangelical Dictionary of Theology*. Grand Rapids: Baker Books, 1984.

Gavrilyuk, Paul. *The Suffering of the Impassible God: The Dialectics of Patristic Thought*. Oxford: Oxford University Press, 2004.

Geisler, Norman. *Baker Encyclopedia of Christian Apologetics*. Grand Rapids: Baker, 1999.

———. *Philosophy of Religion*. Grand Rapids: Zondervan, 1974.

Gerrish, B. A. *Grace and Gratitude: The Eucharistic Theology of John Calvin*. Minneapolis: Fortress, 1993.

———. *The Old Protestantism and the New: Essays of the Reformation Heritage*. Chicago: University of Chicago Press, 1982.

Gerstner, John. "A Primer of Free Will." In *Primitive Theology*. Morgan, Penn.: Soli Deo Gloria Publications, 1996.

Gilson, Etienne. *The Christian Philosophy of St. Thomas Aquinas*. Notre Dame, Ind.: University of Notre Dame Press, 1956, 2002.

Goetz, Ronald. "The Karl Barth Centennial: An Appreciative Critique." *The Christian Century* (May 7, 1986). Reprinted: *Religion Online*: http://www.religion-online.org/showarticle.asp?title=1037 (April 15, 2003).

Goodrick, Edward and John Kohlenberger. *Zondervan NIV Exhaustive Concordance*. Grand Rapids: Zondervan, 1999.

Gonzalez, Justin. *Manna: Christian Theology from a Hispanic Perspective*. Nashville: Abingdon, 1990.

Gorski, Eric. "Theological Society Debates 'Open Theism' Teaching." *The Baptist Standard* (December 3, 2001). Online. http://www.baptiststandard.com/2001/12_3/pages/open_theism.html (April 15, 2003).

Grenz, Stanley. Editorial review of Barry L. Callen, *Clark H. Pinnock: Journey Toward Renewal: An Intellectual Biography*. Nappanee, Ind.: Evangel, 2000.

——— and Olson, Roger. *Twentieth Century Theology: God & the World in a Transitional Age*. Downers Grove, Ill.: InterVarsity, 1992.

Grudem, Wayne. *Systematic Theology*. Grand Rapids: Zondervan, 1994.

Haar, Murray Joseph. "Book Review: The Suffering of God: An Old Testament Perspective." *Theology Today* 42 (1985.

Habermas, Gary and Moreland, J. P.. *Beyond Death: Exploring the Evidence for Immortality*. Wheaton, Ill.: Crossway, 1998.

Hamlyn, D. W. *History of Western Philosophy*. London: Penguin, 1987.

Hanegraaff, Hank. *The Counterfeit Revival*. Nashville: Word, 2001.

Hart, Charles. *Thomistic Metaphysics*. Englewood Cliffs, N. J.: Prentice-Hall, 1959.

Hartshorne, Charles. "The Dipolar Conception of Deity." *Review of Metaphysics* 21 (December 1967).

———. *The Divine Relativity: A Social Conception of God*. New Haven: Yale University Press, 1948.

Hasker, William. "A Philosophical Perspective." In *The Openness of God: A Biblical Challenge to the Traditional Understanding of God*. Downers Grove, Ill.: InterVarsity, 1994.

Hayes, John and Carl Holladay. *Biblical Exegesis*. Rev. ed. Atlanta: John Knox, 1987.

Hegel, G. W. F. *The Phenomenology of Mind*. Translated by J. B. Baillie. New York: Harper Torchbooks, 1967.

Heidegger, Martin. *Being and Time*. New York: Harper & Row, 1962.

Helm, Paul. *Eternal God: A Study of God Without Time*. Oxford: Oxford University Press, 1988.

———. *The Providence of God*. Downers Grove, Ill.: InterVarsity, 1993.

Heschel, Abraham, J. *The Prophets*. New York: Harper & Row, 1955.

Hodge, Charles. *Systematic Theology*. Grand Rapids: Christian Classics Ethereal Library, 2005.

Horrell, J. Scott. "The Self-Giving Triune God, The Imago Dei and the Nature of the Local Church: An Ontology of Mission." Paper delivered, Evangelical Theological Society Annual Convention. Santa Clara, Cal., 1997.

Michael Horton, "Hellenistic or Hebrew? Open Theism and Reformed Theological Method." In *Beyond the Bounds*. Edited by John Piper, et al. Wheaton, Ill.: Crossway, 2003.

———. "Our Debt To Heresy." *Modern Reformation* 10.3 (May/June 2001).

Howe, Alan. "The Evangelical Megashift & the Theology of Clark Pinnock." *The Christian Research Network*. Online. http://web.ukonline.co.uk/crn/page15.html (August 10, 2003).

Bibliography

Hunt, David. "The Simple-Foreknowledge View." In *Divine Foreknowledge: Four Views*. Edited by James Beilby and Paul Eddy. Downers Grove, Ill.: InterVarsity, 2001.

Hunter, Milton R. *The Gospel through the Ages*. Salt Lake City: Deseret, 1946.

Jerome. *Against the Pelagians*, in *The Principal Works of St. Jerome*. Translated by W. H. Fremantle. Grand Rapids: Christian Classics Ethereal Library, 1999.

Johnson, Elizabeth, "Does God Play Dice? Divine Providence and Chance." *Theological Studies* 56 (1996).

Jordan, Mark. "The Alleged Aristotelianism of St. Thomas Aquinas." *The Etienne Gilson Series* 15. Toronto, Canada: Pontifical Institute of Mediaeval Studies, 1990.

———. "Theology and Philosophy." In *The Cambridge Companion to Aquinas*. Cambridge: Cambridge University Press, 1993.

Justin Martyr. "Dialogue with Trypho." In *The Apostolic Fathers with Justin Martyr and Irenaeus*. Edited by Philip Schaff. Grand Rapids: Christian Classics Ethereal Library, 2002.

———. "Second Apology." In *The Apostolic Fathers with Justin Martyr and Irenaeus*. Edited by Philip Schaff. Grand Rapids: Christian Classics Ethereal Library, 2002.

Kant, Immanuel. *Critique of Pure Reason*. Translated by Norman Kemp Smith. New York: Macmillan, 1929.

Kaufmann, Walter. *Existentialism From Dostoevsky to Sartre*. Hecho En Brattleboro, Ver.: New American Library, 1975.

Kelly, Douglas F. "Afraid of Infinitude." *Christianity Today* 39 (Jan. 9, 1995).

Kierkegaard, Søren. *Concluding Unscientific Postscript*. Translated by David Swenson, et al. in Robert Bretall (editor), *A Kierkegaard Anthology*. Princeton, N. J.: Princeton University Press, 1946.

Knight, Henry H. Editorial review of Barry L. Callen, *Clark H. Pinnock: Journey Toward Renewal: An Intellectual Biography*. Nappanee, Ind.: Evangel, 2000. Back cover.

Koop, Doug. "Evangelical Theological Society Moves Against Open Theists." *Christianity Today* (November 22, 2002). Online. http://www.christianitytoday.com/ct/2002/145/54.0.html (April 21, 2003).

———. "Open Theists Called To Account." *Christian Week* 16.19 (2002). Online. http://www.christianweek.org/stories/vol16/no19/story1.html (August 8, 2003).

Kuyper, Abraham. *The Work of the Holy Spirit*. Translated by Henri De Vries. Grand Rapids: Eerdmans, 1946.

Lang, Helen. "The Structure and Subject of Metaphysics." *Phronesis* 38 (1993).

Lee, Brian J. "Lewis's Reflections of Hell." *Modern Reformation* 11.3 (May/June, 2002).

Leftow, Brian. *Time and Eternity*. Ithaca, N. Y.: Cornell University Press, 1991.

Lewis, C. S. *Mere Christianity*. New York: MacMillan, 1960.

Lewis, G. R. "Impassibility of God." In *The Evangelical Dictionary of Theology*. Grand Rapids: Baker, 1984.

Lindsell, Harold. *The Bible in the Balance*. Grand Rapids: Zondervan, 1979.

Lloyd-Jones, Martyn. *What is an Evangelical?* Edinburgh: Banner of Truth, 1992.

Lokhorst, Gert-Jan. "Descartes and the Pineal Gland." In *The Stanford Encyclopedia of Philosophy*. Stanford: Stanford University, 2005. Online. http://plato.stanford.edu/entries/pineal-gland.

Lombard, Peter. *The Sentences*. Vol. 1. Translated by Opera Omnia S. Bonaventurae. Online. *Franciscan Archive*: http://www.franciscan-archive.org/lombardus/opera/ls1-06.html (April 11, 2003).

Lossky, Vladimir. *In the Image and Likeness of God*. New York: St. Vladimir's Seminary Press, 1974.

Bibliography

Lucas, J. R. *The Future: An Essay on God, Temporality, and Truth*. Oxford: Blackwell, 1989.
Luther, Martin. *Commentary on St. Paul's Epistle to the Galatians*. Grand Rapids: Zondervan, 1939.
———. *On the Bondage of the Will*. Translated by Henry Cole. Online. http://www.truecovenanter.com/truelutheran/luther_bow.html#cpref (April 10, 2003).
Lutheran Book of Concord, The. Translated, edited by Theodore G. Tappert, et al. Philadelphia: Fortress, 1959.
Lyttkens, Hampus. *The Analogy between God and the World: An Investigation of its Background and Interpretation of its Use by Thomas of Aquino*. Uppsala: Lundequistska, 1953.
MacDonald, Nathan. "From Augustine to Arminius, and Beyond." In *Reconstructing Theology: A Critical Assessment of the Theology of Clark Pinnock*. Edited by Tony Gray and Christopher Sinkinson. Carlisle, Cumbria, UK: Paternoster, 2000.
McGrath, Alister. *Christian Theology*. Oxford: Blackwell, 2001.
Mendelson, Michael. "Saint Augustine." In *The Stanford Encyclopedia of Philosophy*. Stanford: Stanford University, 2005. Online. http://plato.stanford.edu/entries/augustine.
Moltmann, Jurgen. *The Spirit of Life: A Universal Affirmation*. Minneapolis: Fortress, 1992.
Moore, Russell D. "Evangelical Theological Society Rejects 'Open Theism,' Affirms God's Foreknowledge." *Southern Baptist Theological Seminary News* (November 20, 2001). Online. http://www.bpnews.net/bpnews.asp?ID=12210 (December 15, 2002).
Mounce, Robert. "Romans." In *The New American Commentary*. Nashville: Broadman and Holman, 1995.
Murray, John. *Redemption Accomplished and Applied*. Grand Rapids: Eerdmans, 1984.
Nash, Ronald. *The Word of God and the Mind of Man*. Grand Rapids: Zondervan, 1982.
———. "Open Theism: An Interview with Dr. Ronald Nash." Online. http://www.christkirk.org/stannespub/nash.shtml. June 22, 2006.
Neff, David. "Foreknowledge Debate Clouded by 'Political Agenda.'" *Christianity Today* (November 19, 2001). Online. http://www.christianitytoday.com/ct/2001/147/13.0.html (April 20, 2003).
Nicene Creed. Online, 2005. http://www.reformed.org/ documents/nicene.html.
Nicole, Roger. "Dr. Pinnock and Inerrancy: A Document Charging That Dr. Pinnock in his 'Most Moved Mover' Has Violated the ETS Doctrinal Basis." *Evangelical Theological Society*. Online. http://www.etsjets.org/members/challenge/Nicole-v-Pinnock.PDF (April 12, 2003).
Knox, John. "Letters to His Brethren and the Lords Professing the Truth in Scotland 1557." In *Selected Writings of John Knox*. Dallas: Presbyterian Heritage, 1995. Online. http://www.swrb.com/newslett/actualNLs/ltrbreth.htm (April 26, 2003).
North, Stafford. "Church and Culture." *Oklahoma Christian University Faculty Websites*. Online. http://www.oc.edu/faculty/ stafford.north/culture.html (August 5, 2003).
Oliver, Simon. *Philosophy, God and Motion*. Oxford: Routledge, 2005.
———. Written Correspondence. March 1, 2005.
———. Written Correspondence. December 28, 2005.
Olson, Eric T. "Personal Identity." In *Stanford Encyclopedia of Philosophy*. Stanford: Stanford University, 2005. Online. http://plato.stanford.edu/entries/ identity-personal (November 12, 2004).
Owen, John. "Exposition of Psalm 130." In *The Works of John Owen*. Vol. 6. Edited by William Goold. Edinburgh: Banner of Truth Trust, 1991.
Owens, Joseph. "Aristotle and Aquinas." In *The Cambridge Companion to Aquinas*. Cambridge: Cambridge University Press, 1993.

Bibliography

Packer, J. I. "Forward." Pinnock, *Biblical Revelation—The Foundation of Christian Theology.* Chicago: Moody, 1971.

———. *Evangelism and the Sovereignty of God.* Leicester: InterVarsity, 1961.

Padgett, Alan. *God, Eternity and the Nature of Time.* 1992. Reprinted Eugene, Ore.: Wipf & Stock, 2000.

———. "Eternity as Relative Timelessness." In *God and Time.* Gregory Ganssle (Editor). Downer's Grove, Ill.: InterVarsity, 2001.

Palamas, Gregory. "The Declaration of the Holy Mountain." In *The Philokalia,* translated and edited by G. E. H. Palmer, et al. London: Faber and Faber, 1995.

———. "Homily Eight." In *The Homilies of Saint Gregory Palamas.* Vol. 1. South Canaan, Pa.: Saint Tikhon's Seminary Press, 2002.

Pannenberg, Wolfhart. *Systematic Theology,* vol. 3. Translated by Geoffrey W. Bromiley. Grand Rapids: Eerdmans, 1998.

———. "A Trinitarian Synthesis" (Book Review of Robert W. Jenson's, Systematic Theology). *First Things* 103 (May 2000) 49–53.

———. "What is Truth?" *Basic Questions in Theology.* Vol. 2. Translated by George Kehm. Philadelphia: Fortress, 1970.

Parker, T. H. L. *Calvin.* London: Continuum, 2005.

Pascal, Blaise. *Pensees.* Grand Rapids: Christian Classics Ethereal Library, 2002.

Pike, Nelson. *God and Timelessness.* London: Routeledge, 1970.

Pink, Arthur W. *The Sovereignty Of God.* Grand Rapids: Baker, 1984.

Pinnock, Clark. "A Pilgrim on the Way." *Christianity Today* (February 9, 1998) Vol. 42.2. Online. http://www.ctlibrary.com/ct/1998/february9/8t2043.html (November 16, 2003).

———. "An Inclusivistic View." *Four Views on Salvation in a Pluralistic World.* Edited by Dennis Okholm and Timothy Phillips. Grand Rapids: Zondervan House, 1996.

———. "An Interview With Clark Pinnock." *Modern Reformation Magazine* (June 1998). Online. htttp://www.modernreformation.org/mr98/novdec/mr9806freespace.html (November 16, 2003).

———. "Between Classical and Process Theism." In *Process Theology.* Edited by Ronald Nash. Grand Rapids: Baker, 1987.

———. "Divine Relationality: A Pentecostal Contribution to the Doctrine of God." *Journal of Pentecostal Theology* 16 (November 16, 2000) 3–26.

———. "Fire, Then Nothing." *Christianity Today* (March 20, 1987).

———. "From Augustine to Arminius: A Pilgrimage in Theology." *The Grace of God and the Will of Man: A Case for Arminianism.* Grand Rapids: Zondervan: 1989.

———. "God Limits His Knowledge." *Predestination and Free Will: Four Views of Divine Sovereignty and Human Freedom.* Edited by David Basinger and Randall Basinger. Downers Grove, Ill.: InterVarsity, 1986.

———. "God's Sovereignty In Today's World." *Theology Today* 53 (1996) 15–21.

———. "How I Use the Bible in Doing Theology." In *Religion Online.* Online. http://www.religion-online.org/cgi-bin/relsearchd.dll/showarticle?item_id=9 (June 10, 2003).

———. "How My Mind Has Changed." In Barry L. Callen, *Clark Pinnock: Journey Toward Renewal.* Nappanee, Ind.: Evangel, 2000.

———. "I Was A Teenager Fundamentalist." *The Wittenburg Door* 70 (December 1982—January 1983).

———. "Introduction." *The Grace of God and the Will of Man: A Case for Arminianism.* Grand Rapids: Zondervan, 1989.

Bibliography

———. "Open Theism: "What is this? A new teaching? And with authority!" Presented at the University of Calgary, February 3, 2003. Online. http://www.ucalgary.ca/UofC/faculties/HUM/RELS/chairs/cchair/crsrc/Pinnock. OpenTheism.pdf (April 12, 2003).

———. "Reconstructing Evangelical Theology: Is the Open View of God a Good Idea?" Presented at the Evangelical Theological Society. Colorado Springs, Col.: November 14–16, 2001.

———. "Religious Pluralism: A Turn to the Holy Spirit." *McMaster Journal of Theology and Ministry* (November 2002). Online. http://www.mcmaster.ca/mjtm/5-4.htm (July 8, 2003).

———. Remarks By Clark Pinnock at the ETS Special Business Meeting, Atlanta, Georgia, Wednesday, November 19, 2003. Online. http://www.etsjets.org/members/challenge/2003-vote-pinnock.html (December 31, 2004).

———. "Systematic Theology." In *The Openness of God: A Biblical Challenge to the Traditional Understand of God*. Downer's Grove, Ill.: InterVarsity, 1994.

———. "The Conditional View." In *Four Views on Hell*. Edited by William Crocket. Grand Rapids: Zondervan, 1996.

———. "The Destruction of the Finally Impenitent." *Criswell Theological Review*. Iss. 4, (Spring 1990).

———. "There Is Room For Us: A Reply To Bruce Ware." *Journal of the Evangelical Theological Society* 45.2 (June 2002).

———. *A Defense of Biblical Infallibility*. Philadelphia: P&R Publishing, 1967.

———. *A Wideness in God's Mercy: The Finality of Jesus Christ in a World of Religions*. Grand Rapids: Zondervan, 1992.

———. *Biblical Revelation—The Foundation of Christian Theology*. Chicago: Moody Publishers, 1971.

———. Et al, editor *Searching for an Adequate God: A Dialogue Between Process and Free Will Theists*. Grand Rapids: Eerdmans, 2000.

———. *Flame of Love: A Theology of the Holy Spirit*. Downers Grove, Ill.: InterVarsity, 1996.

———. *Grace Unlimited*. Minneapolis: Bethany, 1975.

———. *Most Moved Mover*, Grand Rapids: Baker, 2001.

———. Personal correspondence, August 3, 2004.

———. Personal correspondence, October 7, 2004.

———. *Set Forth Your Case: An Examination of Christianity's Credentials*. Chicago: Moody, 1968.

———. *The Scripture Principle*. San Francisco: Harper & Row, 1984.

———. *Tracking the Maze: Finding our Way Through Modern Theology from an Evangelical Perspective*. San Francisco: Harper & Row, 1990.

———. Interview in *Ship of Fools Theology*. Online. http://ship-of-fools.com/Shop/Theology/2001_11/PinnockInterview.html. August 4, 2003.

———. Personal Interview. Evangelical Theological Society. Toronto, Canada, November 20, 2002.

———. Personal interview. Evangelical Theological Society. Atlanta, Georgia, November 19, 2003.

——— and Delwin Brown. *Theological Crossfire: An Evangelical/Liberal Dialogue*. Grand Rapids: Zondervan, 1990.

——— and Robert Brow. *Unbounded Love: A Good News Theology for the Twenty-First Century*. Downer's Grove, Ill.: InterVarsity, 1994.

Bibliography

Piper, John. "Grounds for Dismay: The Error and Injury of Open Theism." In *Beyond the Bounds*. Edited by John Piper et al. Wheaton, Ill.: Crossway, 2003.

———. *God Created Us For His Glory* (Sermon). Minneapolis: Bethlehem Baptist Church, 1980.

Plato. *Euthyphro*. Translated by Benjamin Jowett. Cambridge, Mass.: Massachusetts Institute if Technology, The Internet Classics Archive, 2005. Online. http://classics.mit.edu/Plato/euthyfro.html. January 5, 2005.

———. *Meno*. Translated by Benjamin Jowett. Cambridge, Mass.: The Internet Classics Archive, Massachusetts Institute of Technology, 2005. Online. http://classics.mit.edu/Plato/meno.html. April 12, 2005.

———. *Statesman*. Translated by Benjamin Jowett. Cambridge, Mass.: The Internet Classics Archive, Massachusetts Institute of Technology, 2005. Online. http://classics.mit.edu/Plato/stateman.html. April 12, 2005.

———. *Timaeus*. Translated by Benjamin Jowett. Cambridge, Mass.: Massachusetts Institute of Technology, The Internet Classics Archive, 2005. Online. http://classics.mit.edu/Plato/timaeus.html. April 8, 2005.

Plotinus. *Enneads*. Translated by Stephen Mackenna and B. S. Page. Philadelphia, Pa.: University of Pennsylvania, 2005. Online. http://ccat.sas.upenn.edu/jod/texts/plotinus. April 12, 2005.

Popkin, Richard and Stroll, Avrum. *Philosophy Made Simple*. Oxford: Made Simple, 1993.

Rakestraw, Robert. "Becoming Like God: An Evangelical Doctrine of Theōsis." *Journal of the Evangelical Theology Society* 40.2 (1997).

Reymond, Robert L. *A New Systematic Theology of the Christian Faith*. Nashville: Word, 1998.

Rice, Richard. "Biblical Support for a New Perspective." In *The Openness of God: A Biblical Challenge to the Traditional Understand of God*. Downer's Grove, Ill.: InterVarsity, 1994.

———. "Divine Foreknowledge and Free-will Theism." In *The Grace of God and the Will of Man: A Case for Arminianism*. Edited by Clark Pinnock. Grand Rapids: Zondervan, 1989.

Riddle, Jeff. "Book Review: Most Moved Mover: A Theology of God's Openness, by Clark Pinnock." *Jefferson Park Baptist Church*. Online. http://www.jpbc.org/writings/br-most_moved_mover.html (October 15, 2003).

Ritschl, Albrecht. *The Christian Doctrine of Justification and Reconciliation*. Translated by H. R. Mackintosh and A. B. Macaulay. Edinburgh: T. & T. Clark, 1900.

Rogers, Jack. "A Response [to Avery Dulles]." *Theology Today* 38.3 (1981).

Rossi, Philip. "Kant's Philosophy of Religion." In *The Stanford Encyclopedia of Philosophy*. Stanford: Stanford University, 2005. Online. http://plato.stanford.edu/entries/kant-religion/

Roy, Steven. "How Much Does God Foreknow? An Evangelical Assessment of the Doctrine of the Extent of the Foreknowledge of God in Light of the Teaching of Open Theism." Doctoral Dissertation: Deerfield, Ill.: Trinity Evangelical Divinity School, 2001.

Ryan, Maxwell. "Clark Pinnock's Uneasy Journey." *Christianweek* 14.5 (May 30, 2000). Online. http://www.christianweek.org/stories/vol14/no05/story4.htm (July 15, 2003).

Sanders, John. *The God Who Risks: A Theology of Providence*. Downers Grove, Ill.: InterVarsity, 1998.

Sanguineti, Juan Jose. *Logic*. Manila: Sinag-Tala, 1992.

Sauvage, George. "Mysticism." In *The Catholic Encyclopedia*. Edited by K. Knight. 2002. Online. http://www.newadvent.org/cathen/ 10663b.htm (October 12, 2004).
Schaeffer, Francis. "Escape From Reason." In *Trilogy*. Wheaton, Ill.: Crossway, 1990.
Schleiermacher, Friedrich. "On Religion: Speeches to its Cultured Despisers." In *A History of Christianity*, Edited by Clyde Manschreck. Grand Rapids: Baker, 1981.
Schriener, Thomas. "Does Romans 9 Teach Individual Election Unto Salvation?" In *The Grace of God, The Bondage of the Will*. Edited by Thomas Schreiner and Bruce Ware. Grand Rapids: Baker, 1995.
Schreiner, Thomas and Caneday, Ardel. *The Race Set Before: A Biblical Theology of Perseverance and Assurance*. Downer's Grove, Ill.: InterVarsity, 2001.
Shults, F. Leron. *Reforming Theological Anthropology: After the Philosophical Turn to Relationality*. Grand Rapids: Eerdmans, 2003.
Stump, Eleonore and Kretzmann, Norman. "Eternity." *Journal of Philosophy* 78 (1981).
Southern Baptist Confession. "The Baptist Faith and Message." Online. http://www.sbc.net/bfm/bfm2000.asp#ii. (January 5, 2005).
Spinoza, Benedict de. *Ethics*. Translated by R. H. M. Elwes. Murfreesboro, Tenn.: MTSU Philosophy WebWorks Hypertext Edition, 1997. Online. http://www.mtsu.edu/~rbombard/RB/Spinoza/ethica1.html (November 10, 2004).
Sproul, R. C. *Chosen By God*. Wheaton, Ill.: Tyndale, 1986.
———. *Now That's a Good Question*. Carol Stream, Ill.: Tyndale, 1996.
Sproul, R. C., John Gerster and Arthur Lindsley. *Classical Apologetics*. Grand Rapids: Zondervan, 1984.
Strimple, Robert. "What Does God Know?" In *The Coming Evangelical Crisis*. Edited by John Armstrong. Chicago: Moody, 1996.
Strong, Augustus H., *Systematic Theology*. Valley Forge, Pa.: Judson, 1907.
Tangelder, Johan D. "The Teaching of Clark Pinnock." *The Banner of Truth*. Online. http://www.banneroftruth.co.ukarticles/2001/11/ teaching.htm (August 10, 2003).
Tertullian. *Against Marcion*. Translated by Peter Holmes. Grand Rapids: Christian Classics Ethereal Library, 1999. Online. http://www.ccel.org/fathers2/ANF-03/anf03-29.htm#P4271_1391977 (April 10, 2003).
———. *The Prescription Against Heretics* in Ante-Nicene Fathers, Vol. III. Translated and edited by Alexander Roberts and James Donaldson. Grand Rapids: Christian Classics Ethereal Library, 1999. Online. http://www.ccel.org/fathers2/ANF-03/anf03-24.htm#P3125_1133921.
Teske, Roland. "Augustine's theory of soul." In *The Cambridge Companion to Augustine*. Edited by Eleonore Stump and Norman Kretzmann. Cambridge: Cambridge University Press, 2001.
Tiessen, Terrance. *Providence and Prayer*. Downers Grove, Ill.: InterVarsity, 2000.
Tillich, Paul. *The Eternal Now*. New York: Scribner, 1963.
Turretin, Francis. *Institutes of Elenctic Theology* (1688–90). Edited by James T. Dennison. Phillipsburg, N. J.: P&R Publishing, 1992.
Vincent of Lerins, "A Commonitory for the Antiquity and Universality of the Catholic Faith Against the Profane Novelties of all Heresies." *The Fathers of the Church*. Translated by C. A. Heurtley. Online. http://www.newadvent.org/fathers/3506. htm (December 8, 2004).
Wallace, David. "Jude." In *The Wycliffe Bible Commentary*. Chicago: Moody, 1962.
Ware, Bruce. *God's Lesser Glory: The Diminished God of Open Theism*. Wheaton, Ill.: Crossway, 2000.
Ware, Timothy. *The Orthodox Church*. London: Penguin, 1963, 1964.

Warfield, Benjamin. *The Inspiration and Authority of the Bible*. Phillipsburg, N. J.: Presbyterian and Reformed, 1948.

———. "The Theology of John Calvin." Online. http://www.the-highway.com/theocal_Warfield.html (December 21, 2005).

Watson, Thomas. "Mystical Union between Christ and the Saints." In *The Godly Man's Picture*. Edinburgh: Banner of Truth, 1987.

Weinandy, Thomas. *Does God Suffer?* Notre Dame, Ind.: University of Notre Dame Press, 2000.

Wesley, John. "A Plain Account of Christian Perfection." In *The Works of John Wesley*, Vol. 11, Edited by Thomas Jackson. Grand Rapids: Christian Classics Ethereal Library, 1999. Online. http://www.ccel.org/w/wesley/perfection/perfection.html (November 8, 2004).

———. *Wesley's Notes on the Bible*. Grand Rapids: Christian Classics Ethereal Library, 1999. Online. http://ccel.org/ccel/wesley/notes.html. (November 10, 2004).

Westminster Confession of Faith, The (1646). Online. http://www.creeds.net/ Westminster/c05.htm (April 20, 2003).

Wolterstorff, Nicholas. "God Everlasting." In *God and the Good*, Edited by Clifton Orlebeke and Lewis Smedes. Grand Rapids: Eerdmans, 1975. Reprinted in Steven Cahn (editor), *Ten Essential Texts in the Philosophy of Religion*. Oxford: Oxford University Press, 2004.

———. "Unqualified Divine Temporality." *God and Time*. Edited by Gregory Ganssle. Downers Grove, Ill.: InterVarsity, 2001.

Yong, Amos. *Time and Eternity, Divine Foreknowledge and Creaturely Freedom: Historical and Contemporary Issues*. St. Paul, Minn.: Bethel Theological Seminary, 2002.

Zacharias, Ravi. *An Absence of Meaning, An Empty Heart*. Norcross, Ga.: Ravi Zacharias International Ministries, 2003. Online. http://www.gospelcom.net/rzim/ publications/slicetran.php?sliceid=8 (November 5, 2003).

Zanchius, Jerome. *Absolute Predestination*, Chapter 1, Position 3. Online. http://www.straitgate.com/books/zanchius/zanchius.htm (April 1, 2003).

www.ingramcontent.com/pod-product-compliance
Lightning Source LLC
Chambersburg PA
CBHW062008220426
43662CB00010B/1275